With These Hands

Daniel Rothenberg

With These Hands

The Hidden World of Migrant Farmworkers Today

UNIVERSITY OF CALIFORNIA PRESS
Berkeley · Los Angeles · London

University of California Press
Berkeley and Los Angeles, California

University of California Press, Ltd.
London, England

Library of Congress Cataloging-in-Publication Data

Rothenberg, Daniel.
    With these hands : the hidden world of migrant farmworkers today /
Daniel Rothenberg.
        p.   cm.
    Originally published: New York : Harcourt Brace & Co, c1998.
With new preface by the author.
    Includes index.
    ISBN 0-520-22734-4 (alk. paper)
    1. Migrant agricultural laborers—United States.   2. Migrant
agricultural laborers—United States—Interviews.   3. Migrant
agricultural laborers—Legal status, laws, etc.—United States.
I. Title.

HD1525.R67   2000
331.5'44'0973—dc21

                                                    00-028711

Text set in Bodoni and Tiffany
Designed by Camilla Filancia

Printed in the United States of America

08   07   06   05
9 8 7 6 5 4 3 2

To my brother, David.

Contents

Foreword

THERE WAS A time, back in the middle of the 1960s, when many who worried about the fate in America of migrant agricultural workers had good reason for optimism. Indeed, they would not have believed that thirty years later a book such as this would be published, because they believed that the conditions described in this book would soon enough be a thing of the past. Those were the days of the activist 1960s and early 1970s, of Cesar Chavez and Robert Kennedy, of civil rights workers who not only fought segregation in places like Mississippi or Alabama so that African Americans might, in a democracy, avail themselves of the vote, or send their children to the schools attended by other youngsters, but also took on other kinds of social and economic injustice. Not least of these was how extremely hard-working harvesters manage in a country that has not given them the kind of protection most other individuals can take for granted, whether they be members of a labor union or not.

I remember, for instance, a meeting of SNCC (the Student Nonviolent Coordinating Committee, perhaps the most daringly assertive branch of the Civil Rights Movement) in which the plight of migrant farmworkers was discussed. One of the SNCC members had just begun to learn how it goes for those migrants: who recruits them and transports them across the nation's various states; where they live; what they're paid for what they do—the story, in sum, this book tells. He was troubled indeed by what he had been discovering, to the point that he wanted to organize a special effort on behalf of the thousands of families caught in an obviously hard-pressed, vulnerable, and transient life. But his comrades in a tough political struggle saw no chance that they could assume the burden of yet another one, at least for awhile. Besides, there was a subcommittee of the United

States Senate on "migratory labor" devoted to the issue (Harrison Williams of New Jersey was its chairman and later Walter Mondale would have the same position). Moreover, migrants had been the subject of fairly visible public attention in contrast to the relative invisibility of the South's ordinary African American people, who lived so significantly in rural areas or small towns, and whose segregated and impoverished life was simply taken for granted, a given of a region's long-standing history. "We've got enough to do here," he concluded, "without figuring out how to organize migrants so they can get better wages and live better."

In a few years Cesar Chavez was doing just that and again the nation paid close attention. Peter Matthiessen wrote a fine profile of Chavez for the *New Yorker* and later a book. Robert Kennedy sought out Chavez and embraced him as an important moral leader and labor organizer. Under Senator Mondale, the Senate subcommittee made strenuous efforts to find out exactly the way migrants lived, their various problems, and the medical and educational handicaps with which they had to contend.

But the migrant agricultural workers who then seemed on their way at least to some political and economic and social progress a quarter of a century ago are, arguably, worse off now. The Senate no longer has its subcommittee continually on the lookout for wrongdoing in those "camps" where thousands of men, women, and children live under the most primitive of conditions. Cesar Chavez is dead, and before he left us his struggle as a labor organizer had faltered. Every once in a while a reporter takes an interest in migrants, writes a story about them—alas, to no great effect. We have no national political figures like Robert Kennedy, who went out of his way to visit migrant communities to learn of the fate of those who lived in them. The terrible circumstances that a generation or two of writers and photographers and filmmakers and national legislators investigated, described, decried, and struggled to improve through increased public awareness and lawsuits and legislation still persist and are to be found in the East, in the center of our country, and out West—a melancholy state of affairs, indeed.

I was surprised, then, to encounter this book's manuscript—evidence that an idealistic young American was willing to spend months and months with migrant workers, earn their confidence, learn of their difficulties, engage them in such a way that they told him about themselves, their kin, their work, their experiences as they picked various crops, and their relationships with the "crew leaders" who recruit them and make sure they get from farm to farm, sometimes from state to state. Nor are these workers the only ones whom Daniel Rothenberg has come to know. He has immersed himself, really, in a whole way of life, and so he has conversed with those crew leaders and with those who hire them, the landowners and farmers whose crops are, of course, what we consumers can take for granted in our abundantly stocked supermarkets.

The result is an extraordinary documentary study of American migratory farmworkers at the very end of this twentieth century— one life after another brought before us to read, to contemplate. These are the individuals who enable us to fill our bellies quite regularly and at quite reasonable cost, yet these are also the fellow citizens of ours who in certain respects live outside the pale, as it were: they have scant if any access to medical care; they are paid far less than other workers and yet labor as hard as any; their children usually get poorer educations or simply miss schooling altogether; and sometimes they virtually become peons—as several cases in our federal courts have shown all too clearly and sadly.

Not that some migrants, despite the constant hardships in their way, don't become most impressively strong, thoughtful, and wise human beings. Here is the mystery, yet again, of suffering—out of it can emerge an ironic stoicism, a gentleness and a patience and a decency that are astonishing, even unnerving to behold: amidst so many burdens, there is such evident dignity. Still, many migrants are crushed in body, mind, and soul by the traveling life they live—and to be fair, many of them, unsurprisingly, come to that life already hurt and ailing in various ways. In this regard, I have heard certain growers or crew leaders justify the menial circumstances of those who pick crops, sunup to sundown, as one grower in Florida did when he told me in 1968, "They're the bottom of the barrel, so you can't feel too sorry for them because this is the only work they know how to do." He most certainly didn't fall prey to any such temptation of pity but he most assuredly was not ready to count those workers out: they harvested all his crops quite regularly and well, so that he could sit in great comfort as he spoke so harshly of people responsible, in a way, for all he had, and was proud to have.

In contrast, I will never forget a discussion I had with a girl whose parents worked on that grower's land. The girl was ten years old and had already started her own career as a picker of beans. I had asked her to draw various pictures of herself, her parents, friends, brothers, and sisters, and too, the man she called the "bossman," the abovementioned grower whom I'd had to meet and persuade to let me do my interviews on his property. She drew him, with respect and care, standing at the edge of a stretch of farm land whose crops were clearly ready for harvest. He was, however, looking up toward the sky, his head noticeably tilted back—seemingly indifferent to all the nearby black earth with its luxuriant cover of "beans." I asked the child what had caught the bossman's notice, and she told me "the Lord." I was surprised, perplexed: I wondered out loud why that had happened and was told this: "He wants to make sure God is on his side. The minister says Jesus was on the side of the poor, so that could mean trouble for him [the grower], and he's trying to avoid that, getting himself on the wrong side of the Lord, because that can mean big, big trouble."

I asked whether the Lord was listening to the bossman's prayers, or whether He would, someday. "I don't know," the girl replied. Then, as an afterthought, she added, "I hope He does—it'll be bad for him if God doesn't."

Afterwards, I couldn't help thinking of Zora Neale Hurston's *Their Eyes Were Watching God*, although there it was the migrants who kept in mind the Creator, even as they lived the same life of jeopardy as this girl I had gotten to know did. In a sense, I eventually figured out, the child had found some mercy for the bossman, some cause to worry about his moral and spiritual condition, so she had put him "out there," *his* eyes "watching God," his mind seeking moral reassurance.

So it can go among the most impoverished of us, as this book wants us to know: unconscionable poverty and pain, even the denial of citizenship, for all practical purposes, but at times also an all-the-more impressive thoughtfulness, at times even a grim eloquence, that won't be denied. What follows, then, is not only a social document but a moral one—a careful, thorough, wide-ranging chronicle of what happens from day to day among the weakest of us, no matter their huge importance to our daily (eating) lives. One can only hope and pray that now, as never before, a rich and powerful America will pay heed, that it will attend Daniel Rothenberg's fair-minded, compellingly instructive narrative—the many voices he brings us—and will pay him the compliment he most wants: an aroused interest in the fate of those whose circumstances he so accurately and devotedly renders in the pages that follow.

ROBERT COLES
March 1998

Preface to the Paperback Edition

WHEN I FIRST encountered the world of migrant farmworkers, about ten years ago, I was moved by the fact that the fresh fruits and vegetables we consume each day are only available through the difficult hand labor of a million and a half individuals who are overwhelmingly poor and rarely recognized for their important contributions to American society. I wrote *With These Hands* as a way of responding to this situation, a means of drawing attention to the ways in which all Americans are intimately bound to the lives and labor of our nation's farmworkers.

This new paperback edition of *With These Hands* contains some changes from the original text, including updated statistics and a bibliographical essay ("Sources") for those interested in using the book for research purposes. Since the original book was completed, our country has experienced a period of sustained economic growth. Unfortunately, farmworkers have not benefited from the nation's good fortune. The real value of their wages continues to decline and the workforce is increasingly dominated by the most vulnerable of American laborers, recent immigrants who lack legal papers.

It is the premise of *With These Hands* that the living and working conditions of our nation's farmworkers are best approached on moral terms. The basic statistics regarding agricultural labor reveal an ethical challenge that raises questions about our professed belief that honest labor should be justly rewarded.

Sadly, this is nothing new. From the 1930s to the present, the struggles of farm laborers have continually been evoked as a powerful element of America's attempt to reckon with its moral identity. Whether recounted poignantly by John Steinbeck, Carey McWilliams,

Edward R. Murrow or Robert Coles, farmworkers' status represents a central ethical claim within twentieth-century America. It is similarly significant that the country's Latino population entered the national political stage through the farmworker rights movement of the 1960s and 1970s. To this day, Latino politics remains bound, at both a symbolic and grassroots level, to the struggles of farm laborers.

Often, when people first learn about farmworkers, they want to know what can be done to improve their situation and, more specifically, what can they do as individuals to make a difference in the lives of migrants and their families. While *With These Hands* is not a work on farm labor policy, the book presents a general argument that the continued poverty of America's farmworkers is a product of the farm labor system. While individuals can make significant contributions to particular farmworkers and their families, and while there exist many valuable private and governmental programs, serious structural reform presents the only means of improving the overall status of our nation's farm laborers.

Nevertheless, there is great power in simply recognizing farmworkers and thinking seriously about the impact of their labor upon our lives. Almost every farmworker I have ever spoken with has expressed both an understanding of their marginalized status and a desire to be treated with the respect owed to anyone who plays a necessary and productive role in society.

In the end, farmwork is an employment category and farm laborers are a collection of men, women and children who engage in a particular type of work within a specific industry. Farmworkers' poverty does not relate to any essential element of the workers themselves—their skills, abilities, social positioning, attitudes, or nationality—but is instead an expression of the inequities of the farm labor system. The troubling situation of migrant farmworkers today is neither an accident nor an inevitable state of affairs and there is no inherent reason why these conditions must continue into the twenty-first century.

Political debates regarding farm labor issues are enormously divisive, often in ways that mask the commonalties and potential cooperation that might be found between agricultural employers and the workers they depend upon. Real world politics is typically crass and vicious, a realm of negotiations and power plays where those with influence virtually always triumph over those with less money and fewer connections. There is no question that the agricultural industry significantly outweighs farmworkers and their advocates in terms of political influence. This situation is unlikely to change and it is for this reason that the farmworkers' strongest demands are, ultimately, of an ethical nature.

If those with political influence were to see farm laborers as people like themselves, could they accept the current status of America's migrants, here in our country, where we ostensibly believe that those who work hard should be able to provide for themselves and their families? If farmworkers were viewed as similar to those with greater social power, what freedoms, rights, safe working conditions, decent wages, or adequate health care would the larger society feel comfortable denying them? How we understand our relation to the people who harvest our crops has everything to do with imagining that there is, in fact, a different and more equitable future for our nation's farmworkers.

Preface

Our supermarkets are filled with glistening produce—crisp green lettuce, glowing red tomatoes, juicy pink melons. Like so many consumer products, fruits and vegetables appear before us as if by magic, ready to be selected, purchased, and brought home to eat. While we know these products come from somewhere—that they are grown, harvested, and shipped to the stores where we buy them— few people realize that virtually every vegetable and piece of fruit we eat was handpicked by a farmworker, a member of our nation's poorest and most disadvantaged class of laborers.

Each year over 2 million seasonal farmworkers, in nearly every region of the country, provide the manual labor necessary to grow and harvest the fruits and vegetables we consume. Of this group, 900,000 are migrants, workers who travel from one place to another following the harvest. Farmworkers earn an average of $7,500 per year and commonly suffer abuses that would be inconceivable in other industries. They are threatened, cheated out of their wages, housed and transported in dangerous conditions, and in the most extreme cases held in debt peonage. Farmworkers have always been recruited from among the most vulnerable members of American society—recent immigrants, the homeless, the rural poor—and have consistently been denied the legal protections provided to other workers. The poverty and marginalization of migrant farmworkers calls into question America's vision of itself as an egalitarian nation that offers a fair deal to anyone willing to work hard for a living.

Several years after graduating college, I took a job as a paralegal with a federally funded Legal Services program in Florida that defended farmworkers' rights. My job required that I travel throughout the state, from one rural community to another, talking with workers and their families about their legal rights and about the free services our office provided. I visited thousands of farmworkers in the labor camps and dilapidated apartments where they lived—crumbling shacks hidden in the forest, rusting trailers on dirt roads, rows of concrete-block barracks. I struck up conversations with migrants in Laundromats, parking lots, flea markets, and convenience stores. I would introduce myself, pass out literature and business cards, and present a short review of farmworkers' rights—minimum-wage protections, child labor regulations, housing standards, and questions related to immigration. In the event the workers were interested in pursuing legal claims, our office would file complaints with state and federal agencies and often develop workers' claims into lawsuits against their employers.

When I first arrived in Florida, all I knew about farmworkers was that they had difficult jobs and earned low wages—things I'd learned in passing from books and journalistic exposés. As I began working closely with farmworkers I was both shocked and fascinated by what I found; I was surprised at the severity of their situation and drawn to their stories by my growing understanding of how our nation's farm labor system reveals painful contradictions within American society. The worst conditions were appalling—entire crews paid in wine and drugs, isolated labor camps with collapsing roofs and dirt floors, employers who controlled workers with threats and violence. The more typical cases were less dramatic, yet equally disturbing—workers earning below minimum wage, lacking the most basic of workplace protections, drifting from one temporary job to another—an entire class of unprotected and unrecognized laborers deeply aware of their powerlessness and vulnerability. Daily, I encountered men and women who played a central role in a billion-dollar industry, yet found themselves struggling to survive on the margins of American society. Few workers I encountered knew much, if anything, about their legal rights, and I doubt I ever met a farmworker who could not recount at least one striking story of abuse. Workers' employers—contractors and growers—threatened me, vandalized my car, and had me jailed.

What I found most surprising was that the subterranean world of farmworkers existed side by side with the America I had grown up in—shopping centers, fast-food restaurants, multiscreen movie theaters, convenience stores. I visited frightened, underpaid workers housed in shacks a stone's throw from golf courses, malls, and pris-

tine retirement communities, complete with artificial lakes and foun-
tains. Some of the worst labor camps were located near major highways or set beside condominiums, gas stations, and grocery stores. I
was struck by farm laborers' social invisibility, by the fact that their
struggles and poverty went largely unrecognized even where workers'
lives were neither isolated nor hidden from view. Ultimately, it wasn't
only farmworkers' poverty that shocked me, but my growing understanding that migrants' difficult lives were a product of our country's
farm labor system. I saw firsthand how the uncertainty, fear, and
desperation of America's farmworkers grew out of a long history of
governmental and societal neglect, that their struggles were in no way
accidental.

After talking with workers about their rights, our conversations
often touched on other issues, and we sometimes continued talking
long into the night. Workers told me about growing up in the fields,
wandering across the country in a collection of old school buses and
rusting cars; they spoke of their loneliness and dislocation, having
left families back home in Mexico, Haiti, or Guatemala; they described midnight border crossings, smugglers' promises and lies, purchasing false papers, and the challenge of trying to understand
American society from the margins. While visiting migrants, I was always an outsider, a strange presence, a distraction, and often a
source of entertainment. Workers asked me about my own life, and
immigrants plied me with questions about American culture. In many
cases, I was the first Anglo that Latino migrants had ever spoken
with, even those who had spent years in the United States.

The more time I spent with workers, the more impressed I was with
their eloquence and dignity. The farmworkers I met often had extraordinary lives—immigrants who had left their homes to support their
families back home, arriving with no money and no idea what they
would find; political refugees fleeing torture and burned villages in
Central America; African Americans whose lives were marked by chill-
ing stories of discrimination and abuse; "fruit tramps" who had long
since abandoned the idea of a stable home. In general, workers were
eager to talk about their lives. They wanted someone to listen to them,
to hear their voices, record their stories, and provide them, both individually and as a group, with some form of public recognition.

I decided to document the world of farmworkers by writing a
book. I left my job as an advocate and began collecting workers' stories. Soon after I began interviewing workers, I realized that accurately describing the farm labor system required that I also speak

with the workers' employers—contractors and growers. While working as an advocate, the adversarial nature of my job made it difficult, if not impossible, to have meaningful discussions with workers' employers. Freed from the confines of advocacy, I was able to talk openly with growers and contractors. I discovered, not surprisingly, that their lives were equally complex and fascinating, and that listening to their voices was necessary for understanding the larger farm labor system. While some growers and contractors were apprehensive about being interviewed, most were eager to talk, often expressing anger at their negative public image, frustrated at having been repeatedly misunderstood and misrepresented by the media.

Gradually, I expanded my interviews to include still more voices, with the goal of showing how understanding our nation's farm labor system requires a consideration of a broad array of issues: immigration policy, the role of legislation in both protecting the disempowered and enabling social marginalization, the importance of unions, the relationship between moneyed interests and government policy, and the profound impact of racism on American society. *With These Hands* includes the voices of political lobbyists, government investigators, union organizers, *coyotes* who smuggle workers across the border, physicians and teachers who serve farmworkers, migrant children, workers' families in Mexico, and others.

To research this book, I traveled throughout the United States and Mexico with the assistance of several small grants, limited savings, and the goodwill and kindness of old friends and others I met along the way. I conducted hundreds of interviews in labor camps, farm offices, homeless shelters, living rooms, yards, and fields. Each interview that made the initial cut was transcribed, translated when necessary, edited, and reedited many times. The oral portraits presented here are the product of a process of creative editing. The interview questions have been deleted, some grammatical inconsistencies have been cleaned up, and sections of the original interview have been rearranged at times. I have worked hard to retain the integrity and individuality of each voice. With the exception of public figures, everybody interviewed for this book had the opportunity to request that their names not be mentioned. Consequently, many of the names presented are pseudonyms and some of the defining characteristics and descriptions have been changed to protect the identities of those interviewed. The photographs in the book illustrate the kind of life migrant farmworkers lead, not the specific individuals, none of whom are pictured, interviewed in the book. Though the people represented in these photographs are not those named in the text, these photographs accurately portray various elements of the world of migrant farmworkers.

Viewed from a distance, through the cold lens of social statistics, or glimpsed in a field from a passing car, farmworkers may appear unitary—a cluster of bodies bent over working, a social group defined by their poverty and struggles. Still, there is enormous diversity among the farmworker population. The more one listens to workers, to their personal stories, their tales of struggle, travel, romance, or adventure, the more complex and compelling their world becomes. *With These Hands* is not simply an attempt to show that farmworkers lead difficult lives or deserve more than what they receive. That, quite honestly, is easy to do. It is the premise of this book that any group of laborers who works hard and fulfills such an obviously important role in our society should earn enough to provide for themselves and their families. Farmworkers should not be the epitome of our nation's working poor.

Simply naming an injustice often fails to touch upon the real issue at hand, which is always the people themselves. Exposés typically present pressing social problems as clearly defined conflicts between right and wrong. The rhetoric of shock and revelation that dominates our society's engagement with social problems—its seduction, noise, and commotion—encourages people to seek simple visions of a complex world. This process does a certain violence to the inherent richness of people's lives—whether laborers, contractors, growers, government investigators, or others—flattening their world for easy labeling, masking the real beauty, horror, suffering, and joy that defines our world.

The voices of ordinary people are precious and convey a unique authority. *With These Hands* provides the people interviewed with an opportunity to be heard, setting their distinct voices in conversation with each other. To the degree that farmworkers are ever considered in our society—in periodic exposés or government reports—they are typically portrayed as a unitary mass, as powerless, weak, often hopeless victims. While farmworkers are clearly at the bottom of the employment ladder, their lives are not defined solely by their labor. All too often the lives of poor people are presented as something otherworldly, strange, distant, and impossible to understand. Farmworkers are no different from most people. They fall in love, raise families, and deal with the mundane intricacies of their lives, as we all do. These issues are part of their story and in many ways tell the real tale of social injustice. The tragedy of our nation's farmworkers lies not in their difference from other Americans but rather in their great and overwhelming similarity.

As the gap between rich and poor continues to widen in our country, the comfortable lives of the more fortunate are increasingly distanced from the daily struggles of those less fortunate. People with higher-wage jobs, university degrees, and steady incomes often have little or no direct contact with those who move in different, less-empowered social worlds. The more fortunate live in separate communities, send their children to special schools, and know little to nothing about the low-wage workers their high standard of living depends upon. This lack of contact and understanding is heightened by the shifting structure of our nation's economy, which is marked by a growing separation between consumers and producers, especially where production involves physical work or hand labor. In general, production is becoming increasingly invisible in American society as there is a growing distance, both geographic and social, dividing consumers from producers. Recognizing farmworkers' existence, seeing how closely their lives are linked to the lives of all Americans helps shed light on our ties to other social worlds, similarly hidden.

When we shop for produce, our actions mirror that of the migrant. When we reach into a bin to choose an apple, orange, or plum, our hands stretch out in much the same way as a farmworker's hands—harvesting our nation's fruits and vegetables, piece by piece. While the produce may have been mechanically sorted and packed, supercooled, chemically treated, waxed, and shipped hundreds, if not thousands, of miles, often the last hand to touch the fruits and vegetables we buy was that of a migrant farmworker. Through the simple act of purchasing an orange or a head of lettuce, we are connected with a hidden world of laborers, a web of interconnected lives, with hands on both ends. This book uses people's voices to help bridge the gap between these hands.

1. Farmworkers
I Earned That Name

Each year, over 1.3 million migrant farmworkers and their families labor in America's fields and orchards. They stoop among long rows of vegetables, filling buckets with produce under the stark heat of the summer sun and the bitter cold of late autumn. They climb ladders in orchards, piling fruit into sacks slung across their shoulders. They prune vines, tie plants, remove weeds, sort, pack, spray, clean, and irrigate. They travel across the nation, drifting from one field to another, crossing state lines and international borders. Farmworkers labor in every region of the country, wherever there are fields to be planted, tended, or harvested—in isolated rural communities, within the shadows of great cities, scattered among suburban tracts.

Few Americans know much about the world of farmworkers— their struggles, their travels, the key role they play in our lives. Farmworkers provide the hand labor necessary to produce and harvest the fruits and vegetables we eat, and in this sense, they are bound to every consumer in a direct, almost visceral manner. Every orange, peach, tomato, or watermelon we purchase was handpicked by a farmworker. Every pepper, apple, head of lettuce, or bunch of grapes—pulled from the earth, plucked from a bush, or picked from a tree—was harvested by a farm laborer, a member of the poorest and most disadvantaged class of American workers.

Each year, migrant farmworkers fan out across the nation, traveling the country in a collection of old cars, buses, vans, and trucks. They pass through thousands of communities, finding temporary homes in labor camps, trailers, or cheap motels, sometimes sleeping by the side of the road, under bridges, or in the fields and orchards where they work. Every year, the $40 billion fruit-and-vegetable industry spurs the mass movement of workers and their families. They arrive where they're needed, guided to the fields by intermediaries and informal networks, by necessity and, at times, desperation.

James "Shorty" Spencer Jr. ♦ *Angier, North Carolina*

It's Sunday afternoon at the height of the tobacco season. The sky is clear and the sun, though low in the sky, still shines brightly. The air is beginning to cool and there is a lazy, relaxed mood to the labor camp. Workers lounge around, talking, sitting under trees, watching television, sleeping, and drinking.

James "Shorty" Spencer has been up since the early morning. Instead of resting, he went to a nearby pond, returning to the camp with a bucketful of small, silvery fish. Spencer has just finished cleaning and scaling the fish, covering the finger-sized filets with aluminum foil. A dog passes by, snapping up the insides of the fish from the ground by Shorty's chair. There are flies everywhere.

Spencer is a small, dark, wiry man. He has a thin goatee and wears an oversize baseball cap. He gestures wildly while he talks, making picking motions with his hands, pausing dramatically, and grinning. Spencer ran away from home when he was ten years old. Since then, he has spent his whole life working in the fields, spending the winter months in Florida and traveling up the East Coast from early spring through late fall. Spencer moves from one crew to another, living almost exclusively in labor camps. He is now forty-one. Spencer has no mailing address and no set home.

I am a real migrant worker. I earned that name. I been knocked down with the bruise. I been kicked down with the bumps. I fell a lot. I rolled. Yes, I stumbled. I got my little nose scarred up. I got knocked in the head.

But, I didn't steal, see. For a workingman, the money you earn is good money. Just going out and pulling a gun sounds good. You sure can get a Cadillac in one walk. "Let's hit this store." *Boom, bam!* But, it ain't no good. Once you learn that pulling a gun ain't good, there's nothing for you to do but to get your hands in order. Fast hands—quick on pulling leaves, quick on picking oranges, quick on cutting cabbages, quick on picking bell peppers, fast on peaches, superfast when it comes to the potatoes. Just make those hands real slow when it come to stealing. Let your hands be quick on getting it right. Don't let them be quick on getting it wrong. That's all you got to pray to God for. He'll hear you.

You see, I got all the right licks and all the right moves because I am a real migrant worker. Around here, when I'm stripping tobacco, they call me the Bear. I stick my hand in the bush, and *whap,* I got all these leaves. Say you got twenty-seven stalks of tobacco on this bush. Twenty-seven stalks. A little bitty hand like this here won't get it all, will it? Can't hold it. Ain't no way. Well, I go down about eight here—*ktch, ktch*—eight here—*ktch, ktch*—eight here—*ktch, ktch*—get the three out the top; I got twenty-seven. With the move I show, you get all of 'em in one wipe. I got all these leaves in my hand and I am proud to step back from the stalk— because I am a real migrant worker.

Suppose I wasn't no migrant worker? I'd be tired. I'd be bushed out. I'd be blowing out my breath. With the move I showed you—when you hit it rushin'—your arms be full of tobacco. See what I'm saying?

I bet you not an exercise person you know could sand lug all day. Sand lugging is when you get the four leaves off the bottom of the tobacco plant. You don't touch no more leaves, just the four off the bottom. If you can do that there for eight or ten hours, then you's a good one.

Potatoes? If you can run to that truck every fifteen minutes with about seventy-five pounds of potatoes, then you's a good one. Cutting cabbages? If you can pick that cabbage up and sling it at that truck while the wagon's moving, I tell you, you's a good one. Orange picker? You reach out there and snatch your orange, grab the limb and shake it down to the ground, and fill that bag up in fifteen minutes, you's a good one. That's when you could name yourself a real migrant worker.

Now, Bo Jackson can't deal with no migrant worker. Could Bo Jackson crop tobacco in a-hundred-and-five-degree weather? Carl Lewis can't deal with no migrant worker. Tony Atlas? I look at that man. I sit down and analyze him. He got all the muscles in the world, but with all the muscles he got, he can't deal with no watermelon thrower. There's no way. I mean it ain't for him. Arnold Schwarzenegger? I'd like to see him run from six o'clock in the morning till seven o'clock at night with a bucket of potatoes on his back. He can't do it. There's no way. Now, he could probably pick me up with one hand, couldn't he? But he couldn't tote that many buckets of potatoes 'cause he ain't no migrant worker.

See, Jesus Christ work in mysterious ways and once he plant that seed in your head, then you is you. You got that thing. You can't be nobody else. That's why this name, migrant worker, stands tall.

Man, I've been in the migrant stream for thirty years. I done did it all, all kinds of work. I look straight at migrant work. It don't make no difference what situation we in. Sometimes, the sun is too hot—ooh, God is shootin' that heater down on there, ain't he? Well, the heat might beat you about twelve noon, but then Jack Frost might come out there and hit you in the head with a bat at five. Now, Jack Frost don't play. I've picked potatoes when it's been so cold that I was scared my hand was gonna come off.

You've got to judge yourself. Do you need a pair of shoes this week? Better get you about four or five buckets of potatoes. Do you need something to keep Jack Frost from really knocking you down? Better give me ten, eleven more buckets. It's just a mind game that God's got on this earth. I'm telling you the truth. If you don't believe in God, if you don't believe in Jesus, the season ain't friendly. Every night I go in there and lay down on my bed, I pray to God, "Don't let me forget to tell you thanks and tell my father to please remember me." I never forget them words.

If a man want to be a man, he better hurry up and make up his mind. If he wants to live as a migrant, he's got a bucket to carry. And in that bucket, he has his own soul. The bucket that he's totin' holds his soul and it's bad when Jesus Christ look at you and tell you to get out of his line. Good friend I hope you been to all the people in your life—you know that your mama like you, your daddy like you, your sister adore you, your granddaddy wouldn't give you nothin' but a helpin' hand—still, you got to have a honest heart.

You see, I'd rather be on one of these camps than in the city. In the city, you got to seem all cool, calm, and slick. The city is a sink machine, a big machine that just carries you straight down there to the bottom, nonstop. Sink you straight up under that ground. The city—that unendurable monster—don't care nothin' about my heart, your heart, or our neighbor's heart. Now, on a labor camp, you can find peace within you. I'm a honest man. I want a honest day's work.

I've seen a great lot of change in all these years. Now, the boss men will put up with a lot of stuff that boss men in those years would never put up with. You know, back in the time when I first started comin' on the season, people were killing people. Killin' 'em. Beating 'em up, knockin' their eyes out, stompin' down on 'em like a fly. Ooh, Lord, I been on camps where you couldn't even try to go to town. They hit you, kick you, stick dogs on you, scare you. I've seen some bad incidents and bad accidents, and stuff like that is really bad, let me tell you. It's pitiful, man, really pitiful. It creates a pressure on everything. Man, there's a lot of dead that people don't know nothin' about. If you go down and dig deep around these camps, you'll see you some souls still screaming for justice.

Man, I'm telling you the God's heaven truth. I have seen the time it didn't matter if your tongue was hanging out of your mouth, you better not go and get no water. You better not even play like you want some water, 'cause one of them henchmen gonna smack you—"Ain't nobody tell you to come over here and get no water, nigger." They kick you, beat you, knock your eyes out of your head.

Now, it's no problem. Now, I can get some water. Now, if I get tired and don't feel like I want to work no more, I go in. Now, you can talk to them and they talk to you with kindness. Now, if anything happen to you, all you gotta do is run to the labor board. Labor board is pleasing to a migrant worker. It helps you. Labor board helps to keep your working mentality. Is it better now? Super better.

You can tell a bad crewleader from a gem very quickly. A bad crewleader don't have time for you. A bad crewleader insults you. He'll lash out with dumbness. Some of them scare me with their idea of greediness. I wouldn't want to be no crewleader. It's dangerous. The crewleader has to think for all the people, see. He can't have one mind, he got to have all the minds. A migrant worker is nine thousand times freer than a crewleader.

Me? I'm working just to keep living in life. I know that. That's what migrant work is really about. I ain't got to worry about no hotel or motel. I know people that won't even stay in the missions. They'd rather sleep out in a field, or in a cock house, because they don't like orders—"You do this. You do that. Pick up that shirt. Go there and eat." They just don't like it. They too independent.

I like moving around. I like traveling. I plan to keep doing this till the day I die. Right now, I have fun. Oh, man, there ain't nothin' to it. But, when a migrant worker get old—forty, forty-five, maybe fifty years old— he have to hope that God give him that little extra burst, you know? There gonna be a day come when I ain't going to be able to really go get it, you know? That's why I pray. I pray to Jesus Christ every night that I'll just keep on livin' and stay in that migrant stream.

A migrant worker ain't got no staying place. He'll move on. You know, if I found a sack of money, I still be trying to go to work today. I'd be doing something, not just standin' still. It just ain't me to sit around. Still, I can't buy my own house. I ain't got no car. I ain't got no wife. I ain't got no children. Wherever I go at, I go for that moment, then it's gone. Just like with the sea.

Last night, I met a girl. If I had been a stable man with my own house and land, I could have took her and she would have never escaped my eyesight as long as God lived. But knowing I ain't able to do those things, I got to show my love at that moment, by passing with my heart and letting go. I might see this little girl again before I go, but if I don't, it's not going to hurt me that bad, because it passes, like with the sea.

You know, everything come and go like that.

I hate to see the tobacco go.
I hate to see the potato go.
I love the moonlight.

There are currently over 1.8 million seasonal farmworkers in the United States, laborers whose employment shifts with the changing demands of planting, tending, and harvesting our nation's crops. These workers have over 3 million dependents, most of whom are children, bringing the nation's total population of seasonal farmworkers and their families to over 4.8 million. Migrant farmworkers are those seasonal farm laborers who travel from one place to another to earn a living in agriculture. There are 900,000 migrant farmworkers in the United States, who are accompanied by 300,000 children and 150,000 adult dependents, bringing the country's total population of migrant farmworkers and their families to over 1.3 million.

Migrant farmworkers have special needs related to their continual movement, dislocation, and status as outsiders in the communities where they work. When arriving in a new community, migrant workers must find temporary housing, either in labor camps provided by their employers or in short-term rental housing. If they don't have their own vehicles, migrants need to find ways of getting from one place to another, from their temporary homes to the fields, to stores, from one harvest to another. Since migrant farmworkers have limited resources and few contacts in the communities they pass through, they rely upon intermediaries and informal networks in order to survive. In this way, migrant workers are socially invisible; they play a crucial role in the local economies where they labor, yet their struggles are generally hidden from view.

Seasonal farmworkers are the poorest laborers in the United States, earning an average of $7,500 each year. Farmworkers who migrate are poorer than settled seasonal laborers, with over half of all migrants earning less than $5,000 per year. The most vulnerable migrant workers, such as those laboring for farm labor contractors in eastern states, earn average annual wages as low as $3,500. Although migrant families commonly pool the wages of several workers, over two-third of our nation's migrant households and 80 percent of migrant children live below the poverty line.

Farmworkers' life expectancies are lower than that of most Americans and infant mortality among farmworker children is double the national average. Physicians treating farmworkers generally compare their health to that of residents of the developing world. Farm-

workers suffer from chronic infections, advanced untreated diseases, and numerous problems resulting from limited access to medical care. Farmwork is the second most dangerous job in the nation. Workplace accidents, many of which involve children, are common, and farm labor has the nation's highest incidence of workplace fatalities and disabling injuries.

Most farmworkers are men, although many women also labor in the fields. The average age of farmworkers is 31, with over half under 29. Nearly 90,000 farmworkers are between the ages of 14 and 17. Farmworker families often work together, with children laboring beside their parents and eventually becoming key contributors to the family's survival. Forty percent of migrant children work in the fields. Farmworker families often have difficulty balancing the economic demands of farm labor with the children's education. In general, farmworker children do poorly in school. Fifty percent of migrant children fall below national scholastic averages as early as the first grade and the majority never graduate high school.

Seasonal farm labor draws workers from a variety of backgrounds and ethnic groups. Currently, two out of every ten seasonal farmworkers were born in the United States, a diverse mix of Latinos, African Americans, whites, and Native Americans. The remaining 80 percent of the nation's farmworkers are immigrants, over 90 percent of whom are from Mexico. Other immigrants come from Central America, particularly Guatemala or El Salvador, or Caribbean nations such as Haiti or Jamaica. A small percentage of farmworkers are from Asian countries such as the Philippines, Laos, and Vietnam.

Farmworkers born in the United States generally hold more stable, higher-wage positions, while the less-appealing jobs are filled with recent immigrants, who are virtually all minorities. These immigrants generally have low levels of formal education and often speak little to no English. Nationally, about half of all farmworkers are undocumented. The percentage of farm laborers who lack working papers has been steadily increasing over the last decade.

Over the last thirty years, immigrant farmworkers have steadily displaced domestic laborers, even in regions such as the southeast that have long been dominated by African American crews. Our nation's farm laborers are increasingly young, male, Mexican-born immigrants.

Salvador Moreno ♦ *Clinton, North Carolina*
Salvador Moreno and Miguel Valenzuela sit inside a wooden cabin at a labor camp where they've lived for the last several months. It is

early evening and the sky is dark blue, still too early to see the stars. The camp is quiet except for the steady whine of insects and the soft sounds of norteño music from a neighboring cabin. Moreno and Valenzuela have just finished packing, loading duffel bags of clothes and plastic garbage bags filled with gifts into a used car Moreno bought with money he earned picking cucumbers. Although there are still several seeks left in the season, Moreno and Valenzuela plan to drive south in a few hours, returning home to Mexico.

Moreno has a wide face, a mustache, and dark circles under his eyes. He is slightly overweight and clenches his teeth when he smiles. Valenzuela is rail thin, with a long ponytail and stooped shoulders. He remains silent, listening, staring out through the open door at the cucumber fields on the other side of the road.

I arrived in the United States with dreams, illusions. These dreams came from others, friends in my hometown who returned from the United States with cars and trucks, telling stories about how good things are here—how in America you have lots of fun, travel, and earn plenty of money.

I first came here when I was fifteen. I was in school, but I wanted a better life. I thought, "I'm going to the United States, too. I'm going to go have myself a good time and return home with a nice truck."

When you're in Mexico, you can't imagine what a sacrifice it is to come here. You suffer crossing the border. You suffer looking for work. You suffer while working, because the bosses mistreat you and you don't understand why. You suffer trying to make something of yourself. When you first arrive, there are so many things you don't understand. You're alone. You can't speak English. You have no papers, no transportation, and no one to help you. You arrive with no idea of what it takes to succeed. There's nothing in your head but the desire to come to the United States to work.

There's no security in farmwork. Most jobs are temporary and often you can only find work during the harvest. When the harvest ends, the work stops. As the harvest is ending, you start wondering, "Now, what will I do? How will I find another job? Where should I go?" There are always people telling you about some town where another harvest is about to start. Sometimes there's someone who knows about a job in another state and they'll invite you to travel with them. Still, if you go, you never know what you'll be doing or what it will really be like. It makes you wonder, "Will there really be work there? Or, will I spend a month with no job and nowhere to live?" Many times you're afraid it might be worse, so you just stay where you are.

The suffering makes a deep impression on you. You really think about life. You remember your friends who told you that the United States was like paradise. You wonder why they never spoke about the pain. Many Mexicans living here start drinking to feel better, so as not to think so much.

For me, what's most difficult is being away from my family. I think about my family all the time, so far away. I wonder how they are. Are they satisfied? Content? Happy? Are they sad because I'm not there with them? I think about how we live back home, with the whole family together—all fifteen of us. Then I think about my life in the United States, wandering around, on the other side of the border, alone. Whenever I receive a letter from home, I'm happy. They tell me they're fine and that I shouldn't worry, and then I feel better. I travel easier knowing my family is well. Sometimes, I think about the letters I write home to my mother and father, telling them everything's fine, even when I have no job and no money. Then I wonder if they tell me that they're well just so I won't worry.

Some people have good fortune and others bad. Not everyone is lucky. The truth is, I can't complain. I've achieved what I wanted. This is the third time I've come north. The first time, it was my dream to save money to buy a truck to take back to my town. I did it. The second time, it was my dream to earn enough money to build myself a house. I did that, too. This time, it's my dream to save money so I can get married.

This season went well, and now I'm leaving, going back to Mexico to see my family. When you go home, you return a bit like a hero. You feel more of a man. When you return, you're one of those people who've been to *el norte.* You know what it's all about. You've lived through it. I'm the oldest in my family and my brothers still haven't come north. I have one brother who's fourteen. He's seen me return home in my truck. He's seen me build my house and bring him presents. Now he writes me letters saying that next time he wants to come north with me. I give my brother advice, telling him it's better to stay in Mexico and study. I don't want him to suffer like me.

Still, it's difficult to tell someone back home the truth, to explain what life is really like here, and why they should stay in school. Until you see the United States, you feel anxious. It's satisfying to know what things are like here. I imagine this is how my brother feels. I've been through it. I've felt the desire to come north. Still, if I could do it all over again, I think it would have been better to keep studying, to choose a profession instead of coming here to suffer in the fields.

Will I return to the United States? Maybe, maybe not. I'm not sure. Perhaps the happiness of seeing my family again will touch me so that I'll never be able to leave them again. Or, maybe I could still study, become a teacher or something. It's probably too late for me since I've started living the life of one who travels north. Maybe when I get married I'll find out that it's too hard to find a good job in Mexico. I might need money and not know what to do. Then, I might start thinking, "Well, I can always go back to the United States."

Seasonal farmworkers labor in virtually every region of the country. California, Florida, and Texas employ the largest number of seasonal farmworkers, followed by North Carolina, Washington, Michigan, New York, Oregon, Arizona, and Georgia. Migrant farmworkers generally work in southern states during the winter months and travel north from the spring through the early fall.

Farmworkers' travels are often described as involving three migrant streams—western, central, and eastern. Each of the streams begins in one of three base states—California, Texas, or Florida—where workers spend the winter. Migrants in the eastern stream leave Florida in late spring and follow the fruit and vegetable harvest through Georgia, the Carolinas, Maryland, New Jersey, and New York, continuing as far northeast as Maine and as far west as Michigan. In the central stream, migrants travel north out of Texas to different sites throughout the Midwest and West, working in Arizona, Colorado, Iowa, Illinois, Indiana, Minnesota, Wisconsin, and Michigan. Migrants in the western stream spend the winter months in southern and central California and then travel up through northern California, Oregon, and Washington State. Although the three-stream approach is widely used to describe farmworkers' travels, migratory patterns are rarely as smooth or directed as the term *stream* would imply and often involve circuitous twists and backtracking.

Because of the temporary nature of most jobs, farmworkers are almost always on the lookout for better opportunities. Rumors about different job possibilities circulate constantly through farmworker communities. Workers pass information back and forth and commonly ask their employers to hire family members and friends. Recent immigrants generally rely on social networks to help them find work, and some crews are composed entirely of extended families or immigrants from the same small cluster of Mexican towns. Currently, about 70 percent of the nation's farmworker population finds employment through personal contacts.

Intermediaries, known as farm labor contractors, crewleaders, or *contratistas*, are one of the primary ways growers find crews of workers. By using an intermediary, growers can efficiently ensure that enough workers will arrive at the fields when they're needed. Contractors also allow growers to avoid the responsibilities of managing temporary laborers. Many of the worst abuses of farmworkers' rights are committed by farm labor contractors, who are known to steal workers' wages, underreport hours and production, place crews in substandard housing, and use threats and even severe physical violence to control their workers.

Harvesting employs more farmworkers than any other task, with 60 percent of migrants working in hand harvesting fruits and vegetables. While machine harvesting is now available for some crops that once employed tens of thousands of American farmworkers—such as cotton, potatoes, and tomatoes used for processing—most fresh produce must still be harvested by hand. Fruits and vegetables are fragile and easily damaged, as are the trees, vines, and plants they grow on. Farmworkers are far more skilled than machines at deciding which fruits and vegetables are ready to be picked and are much less likely to damage either the produce or the plants.

In addition to harvesting, farmworkers also prepare the fields, plant, weed, irrigate, and apply pesticides. Following the harvest, farmworkers wash, grade, sort, weigh, and load fruits and vegetables both in the fields and in packinghouses. Farmworkers are also involved in various postharvest activities, from clearing fields to pruning trees and vines.

Seasonal farmworkers are profoundly, if paradoxically, modern. While the labor provided by farmworkers is traditional in nature—hoeing; weeding; pruning; and, above all, hand harvesting—the pressing need for large numbers of temporary laborers is a function of the industrialization of agricultural production. Before fruit and vegetable farms became large-scale commercial enterprises, seasonal labor was generally provided by family members or residents of rural communities. Farms were relatively small, and produce grown in one place could not easily be transported and sold across large distances. Throughout the twentieth century, mechanization and improved farming techniques, coupled with advances in refrigeration, storage, and modern transportation networks, have allowed farmers to produce ever-larger quantities of produce that can be safely shipped over extraordinary distances. Now, fruits and vegetables travel thousands of miles from where they are grown to where they are consumed, crossing oceans, continents, and international borders in refrigerated containers on trains, trucks, ships, and airplanes.

The industrialization and technological sophistication of modern agriculture has produced an increased need for temporary, itinerant laborers to provide the most traditional forms of hand labor. At the same time, the steady supply of low-wage laborers has provided employers with little incentive for increased mechanization. As agricultural production becomes increasingly technological, with laser-leveled fields, genetically engineered seeds, and computer-controlled irrigation, and as farms begin to look more like other large corporations, the difference between seasonal laborers and their employers becomes ever more striking.

Gino Mancini ♦ *Guatemala City, Guatemala*

Gino Mancini was born in Sacramento, California. Growing up, he had no contact with farmworkers although he remembers seeing groups of skid-row workers waiting to be taken to the fields. Mancini graduated high school, entered college, dropped out, joined the Air Force, and went to Vietnam. He returned to the United States disillusioned with American society. By accident, he drifted into farm labor.

For decades now, Mancini has been a self-professed "fruit tramp," spending the summer and fall months picking apples and pears in Washington and Oregon. Mancini earns around $3,000 per year picking fruit. In the early 1980s, he bought a small house in Guatemala. When the season ends, he travels to Guatemala where he can stretch his earnings until the following spring, when he returns north.

When I went to Vietnam, I didn't really think about the war. Joining the military was just what was expected of you. I wasn't for or against the war. I didn't really know anything about it. I just figured that if we were in a war, there must be a good reason. I was just a stupid American kid.

Then I came back home on leave and there were people yelling and screaming at me. All my friends were freaks. My brother had long hair and beads. When I first saw him, I ripped the beads off his neck. Then Robert Kennedy got shot and Kent State happened. By that time, I was against the war and completely agreeing with my brother. I saw what the war was about. I knew it was stupid. I demonstrated against the war wearing my uniform.

At that time everything seemed wrong—the war, racism, materialism, middle-class society with everybody wanting a car, a garage, and a boat. I didn't want any of that. I didn't want anything to do with regular nine-to-five society. Then, me and my brother decided to hitchhike our way across the country. That trip completely changed my life. When we were in Washington State at a rock concert, some friends said we could make money picking apples. That's what started it. I went with a bunch of hippie friends to pick apples. We worked with some Mexicans and a lot of old-timer fruit tramps, Okies and Arkies.

That's how I got into picking fruit.

Once I started picking, I thought, "Hey, I can work in the summer and travel in the winter." So, then I just started going back every year. I made money and I traveled. For the first ten years, I didn't leave the country. I was making my money in Washington, and then I'd go to North Carolina and Florida and maybe get some odd job. For three years, I went to Key West. One time, I went to Hawaii.

Then a friend told me about Guatemala. So one year I came down and had a great time. For a couple of years when the war was really heavy I stayed away. That's when I went to Australia to pick apples. I came back down to Guatemala in 1984, and I've come back every year since then. I come down for four or five months, sometimes more, depending on my financial situation. I usually stay in Guatemala as long as I can. Right now, all I own is my house in Guatemala which I bought for thirteen hundred dollars, my backpack, and a couple of things in a guy's van. I don't own a TV, radio, or car—none of that.

My first year at picking I had two friends who would go to work at one job, pick two bins, just enough to buy a bottle of wine, and then they'd quit. The next day, they'd go to the next orchard and get another job. Back then, you could move around and do what you wanted, work as little or as much as you felt like working, depending on your ambition. Now, if you don't work all day for the farmer, then *boom,* you're gone, and you might not get another job. Washington used to be a workers' paradise. You could walk off one job and go to the next orchard and get another job. It used to be loose. It was lots of fun. After work, there were parties, good times, and women. Now, there are lots of workers and most of them are from Mexico so they're willing to work cheap. Now, there ain't no women. There ain't no nothin'. I just go there to work, nothin' else.

The big conglomerates are buying up all the small orchards and the family farmers are going out of business. The family farmers were really into farming. For them, it wasn't just the money; they loved growing fruit. Most of their sons and daughters went to college and didn't want to run the orchard. They'd get into banking or things like that, so when they inherited the orchard, they'd either sell it or turn it over to be run by someone else. I used to work for several orchard owners who really cared about you. They'd bring doughnuts out to the fields and do nice things for you. They used to know your name.

Years ago, I worked for a grower named Bob. He was the best. He loved his orchard. One day we were pickin' pears and it was pourin' rain. Everybody was quittin'. Bob walked up to me and said, "If you stay out here and pick another bin, I'll pick it with you." This was the owner talking. This guy went to Harvard. He was a millionaire. So, me and him sat in a tree, pickin' fruit in the pourin'-ass rain, and he's talkin' about all of these fruit-tramp friends of his. If he was alive, I could call him right now from here in Guatemala and say, "Hey, Bob, I'm broke. I wanna come to work." He'd mail me a plane ticket. He was the greatest.

You don't see that anymore. Now, most of the orchards are run by big companies. To them, you're just a machine to get fruit off the tree. I never meet the owners anymore. They're not involved. A lot of 'em aren't even in Washington. These days, you just deal with whoever is hired to run the orchard.

When Bob died, his son took over the orchard and fired all of us. He turned it completely Mexican. If you're an American, most of the big orchards won't even discuss hiring you. At the big orchards, a white picker just can't get a job. I'd say I'm part of the last generation of white fruit pickers. I'm forty-nine and most of the white pickers I know are at least forty. I doubt very seriously if any of the kids of the people I know want to pick fruit. My theory is that the growers prefer to hire Mexicans because of how poorly they treat the workers. I think they feel guilty giving an American substandard housing and paying us low wages. If a worker comes from across the border, they feel like they're helpin' him out, doin' him a favor, bringin' him up from poverty.

If somebody asks me what I do for a living, I say, "I'm a fruit tramp." To me, fruit tramp is not an insult. I'm proud of what I do. I pick fruit. I migrate. Once, I cut out an article that listed two hundred and fifty jobs, from the most prestigious to the least prestigious. The last job, number two hundred and fifty, was migrant worker. Bottom of the list. It actually made me feel good. I chose this lifestyle and I like it. Look at what a lot of other people do—advertising and shit like that. What does that do for the world? At least I'm helping to feed somebody. I mean, it might not be much, but I'm not destroying anything. A lot of stuff I see just seems mindless to me. Just think of the jobs people have—"I'm a public relations officer"; "I'm a consultant"—What do they really do? Mostly nothing.

I do physical labor. It's honest. I'm not especially proud, but I work hard. I make an honest living. I don't know what farmwork is about to everybody else, but to me it's good hard work. You know, we're all different. Everybody's an individual. For the Hispanics, farmwork is all about makin' money. They're all tryin' to get into this society. Not me. I'm tryin' to get out.

Migrant work is a good lifestyle. You're out in the sunshine all day. Usually nobody's screwing with you. Nobody's looking over your shoulder. Nobody's standin' there watchin' you pick. You're out there by yourself all day with the trees and the sunshine. Where I pick, there are mountains and lakes. It's beautiful. When you're doing piecework, you take a break whenever you want. I bring out some beer and drink. You're screamin' across the trees to the workers in the other rows. You're bullshittin'. The Mexicans are singin'. It's cool.

For the last two years I've been thinkin' of getting out of farmwork and doin' something else. It's gettin' harder, man. I wanna get out of it, but what am I gonna do? For me, picking fruit is the only way I know to make money. Every time I think about goin' to work every day nine to five, goin' back each night to a house, and living in a little town somewhere in the States and always bein' bored, it seems better to put in some hard work during the summer, and then come down to Guatemala. I couldn't handle a year-round job with maybe three weeks' vacation a year. I like to move around, to live day to day. That's the way I've always lived. That's the only way I know. To me, farmwork is about freedom.

Few Americans work as hard as farm laborers and yet earn so little. Farmworkers are paid either an hourly wage or a piecework rate. Most nonharvest work is paid by the hour and most harvest work is paid by the piece, with workers earning a set amount of money for every box, bin, bucket, flat, or tub they fill. When earning hourly wages, farmworkers are generally paid at, or slightly above, the minimum wage. From 1991 through most of 1996, the minimum wage remained constant at $4.25 per hour. In October 1996, the minimum wage increased to $4.75 per hour, and in September 1997, it increased again to its current rate of $5.15 per hour. In terms of real purchasing power, the minimum wage has declined steadily since the 1970s, contributing to the growing numbers of working poor in the United States.

Piece rates vary significantly depending on the crop and region. Although employers must guarantee that workers paid piece rates earn at least the minimum hourly wage, many do not. At the same time, fast workers harvesting certain crops often earn significantly more than the minimum wage. In general, piece rates have stayed

constant or risen only slightly over the last fifteen to twenty years. Workers harvesting these crops often labor extremely hard to earn relatively low wages. Piece rates exert significant pressure on slower pickers, particularly older workers, who have great difficulty competing with the steady influx of young immigrants.

Migrant farmworkers have two distinct strategies for earning a living through low-wage, seasonal employment. One strategy is to follow the crops, traveling from one harvest to another. About 300,000 farmworkers follow the harvest in this fashion, the majority of whom are men traveling without their families. These workers are the most transient of migrants, traveling hundreds or even thousands of miles, crisscrossing the nation in search of work. Another strategy involves leaving a stable home base to work at a single site and then returning home at the end of each season. About 600,000 migrants live this way. These workers either labor for a single employer or for several employers clustered around the communities where they take up temporary residence. By migrating to a single site, workers and their families are spared the costs, inconvenience, and uncertainty of constant movement.

Gilberto Perez ♦ *Calexico, California*

Gilberto Perez lives in Mexicali, Mexico. Each morning, he crosses the border to Calexico, California, to work in the fields of the Imperial Valley. Like hundreds of others, Perez approaches farm labor contractors—known as mayordomos *or* contratistas—*who provide busloads of workers to area farms. Often, workers pay unauthorized drivers—*riteros—*to carry them to the fields. Perez can move freely back and forth across the border because he has a* mica, *a work-authorization card. Legally, Perez could live in the United States. However, he prefers to stay in Mexico where his low wages can more easily support his wife and four children.*

Perez has a round face with a thin, graying beard. He wears a well-ironed white shirt and a broad-brimmed cowboy hat, also white. Despite his easy manner, Perez is both tired and frustrated. It is midmorning and he won't be working today.

Every day, I get up at around one in the morning. While I wash, my wife makes me tortillas and coffee, and cooks tacos or burritos for me to take to work. Then I walk a few blocks from my house and grab a taxi which takes me to the border. It's early. It's cold and dark. The taxi costs a dollar each way.

Then I walk across the border to Calexico.

You have to cross over by two in the morning so that one of the *mayordomos* will put you on his list. You get on the bus and wait there until the sun rises at around five. Then, they start up the bus and you go out to the fields to work. You leave home at one-thirty in the morning and get to the fields by six, so it's about four and a half hours from your house to work. Some people work as far away as San Clemente, which is three hours by bus each way to and from Calexico—six hours each day. You try to sleep a bit on the bus.

If you don't get there early, you might not work that day. If the *mayordomo* says he needs thirty people and you get there late, he may have already filled his crew. A lot of times, there are too many people, and you have to go back home. Sometimes you can find a stable job with a company. Then you can sleep until three in the morning—calm, satisfied, knowing that you'll have work. When it rains, the *mayordomo* might say, "We'll have to wait to see if the rain stops." Then you might wait four or five more hours to go to work.

The real bosses, the *rancheros,* don't even talk with us. We only get to speak with the *mayordomos.* The *mayordomos* want you to work fast so the *rancheros* are happy. It doesn't matter to the *mayordomo* if your foot hurts or your back aches. All they care is that you work, and work fast. They get mad at you if you take a break or use the bathroom. Sometimes you spend ten hours bending over, crawling around on your knees. Hoeing is hard. Weeding is hard. They make you work fast and you leave the field exhausted, your back tired, your hands aching. The bosses look at us as machines, things that are always supposed to be working. A machine works and works, but a person can't keep at it if he's tired or in pain.

People are afraid of the *mayordomos.* If you have an argument with the contractor, he'll fire you. That's it. Then, there's no more work for you. People are afraid to complain. If you get the workers together to talk with the boss about something, to resolve some problem, they'll throw you out. Then that *mayordomo* will tell the other *mayordomos* about you and no one will hire you. Sometimes the *mayordomos* make you buy beer, soda, or food from them. If you don't buy anything, the next day when you come looking for work, they'll say, "Sorry, I've got a full crew."

There are often food trucks in the field. If you earn minimum wage, you can't afford the luxury of buying food, which costs five or six dollars a day. It's better if your wife makes your lunch. If you spent six dollars a day, every day, that would be forty-two dollars a week. After work, you come back tired and a friend might say, "Hey, Gilberto, let's go drink a beer." A beer costs another dollar fifty. So, you have to tell your friend that you'll drink a beer with him another day.

There are times when it rains while you're out in the fields and you have to stop working. Then you don't earn anything. California law says that when a *mayordomo* takes a crew out to the fields and they only work an hour or two because of rain, then the *mayordomo* owes the workers for a half day, four hours' labor. That's the law, but they never pay.

At the end of the day, you go back to Calexico. Then you cross back into Mexico and take a taxi home. By that time, it's night. You bathe, eat, sleep for a few hours, and then wake up again at one the next morning.

From when you arrive in Calexico at two to when you return from work is anywhere from eleven to fifteen hours, depending how far away the fields are. Still, they only pay you for the eight hours you work in the fields. If you work eight hours at four fifty an hour, that's thirty-six dollars. After taxes, the government leaves you with about thirty-two dollars. Very few companies have their own buses. So to get to work you often have to pay a *ritero* three dollars to and from work. You pay three dollars to the *ritero,* and two dollars to the taxi driver, which leaves you with about twenty-eight dollars for eight hours' work.

If I work in San Clemente, I leave my house at one in the morning and don't make it back to home until nine at night. Then it's twenty hours for the same twenty-eight dollars. If you ate lunch off of a food truck for five dollars and drank a beer for a dollar fifty, after taxes and transportation, you'd take home twenty-one dollars and fifty cents. Then, there's the chance that the *ritero*'s van will have a blowout and flip over, or something will break, and you'll be stuck out there in the hills.

Every morning I'm afraid that I won't find work and that I'll have to return home without having earned a thing. I can feel the fear among the other workers, too. There are so many of us, so much competition. That's what allows the *contratistas* to pay so little. This is a big valley. There's a lot of lettuce here and four fifty an hour is very little. If the people thought about it, they might get together and say, "OK, today no one will go to work. We want another dollar an hour, and if you don't pay us that, you'll lose all your lettuce because we'll refuse to cut it."

Seasonal farmworkers' real wages have fallen over 10 percent in the 1990s, despite increases in the minimum wage and a growth economy. The economic stress of falling wages on workers' lives has been heightened by a marked decrease in the number of employers who provide workers with housing, transportation, and other assistance either free of charge or at subsidized rates.

Increased immigration is the key reason that farmworkers' wages have fallen so steadily. In most regions of the country, there is a significant oversupply of farm laborers. In some cases, there are as many as three workers for every position. The competition brought on by an oversupply of immigrant workers, both those with legal papers and those without, has produced a steady decrease in real wages and has driven domestic workers out of farm labor. Virtually all workers currently entering the farm labor workforce are immigrants, often the most vulnerable of recent arrivals. For many workers, farm labor is a stepping-stone to better jobs or a short-term means of saving some money to build a house or invest in a project back home. Farmwork is characterized by high turnover rates; one out of every ten farm laborers leaves agriculture each year.

The decline in real farm wages has made it difficult for workers to raise families in the United States on their earnings. Consequently, American agriculture is growing increasingly dependent on transnational migrants, workers who labor in our nation's fields and then return each year to their home countries. Currently, a third of all seasonal farmworkers—almost all of whom are Mexican men—return to their countries of origin at the end of the season. There are now thousands of Mexican communities that are completely dependent on the wages of migrant farmworkers laboring in our nation's fields.

As immigrants represent an ever-larger percentage of our country's farm laborers, the distinction between seasonal and migrant farmworkers is becoming less significant. Immigrant workers, particularly men traveling without their families, generally retain strong ties to their home countries and weak ties to the communities where they work. Many workers drift in and out of the migrant stream, settling in a particular community only to start migrating again a year, or two later. Given the fluid nature of seasonal farmwork, workers and their families are always looking for new ways to improve their wages and increase job stability. Many transnational migrants, particularly those with legal papers, choose to settle in farmworker communities in the United States, creating a stable home base from which to travel to jobs in other regions of the country. As these immigrant workers establish more ordered lives, they often bring their families across the border, shifting their status from migrant workers to settled farm laborers.

Antonio and Estela Solares ♦ *San Joaquin Valley, California*
Antonio and Estela Solares grew up in a small city in Michoacán, Mexico. They married when he was nineteen and she was sixteen. After living together for several years in Mexico, Antonio traveled north to California, borrowing money from his brother to pay a

coyote to smuggle him across the border. He worked one season and then returned to Mexico, where he found a job picking avocados for export to the United States, earning the equivalent of six dollars per day. A year passed and Antonio decided to return to California, this time taking his family with him. That was five years ago.

Antonio and Estela now live with their three children in a small apartment in a state-subsidized housing complex. We sit at the kitchen table as their children play in the living room under the glow of a television tuned to a Spanish-language station. The apartment is neat and well cared for. The walls are covered with decorations—plastic flowers, a heart-shaped clock, porcelain butterflies, a picture of Jesus surrounded by a golden halo. Although neither Antonio nor Estela have working papers, they are now comfortably settled into life in the San Joaquin Valley, spending most of the year in California and traveling north each season to Oregon. Antonio works in the fields with Estela's extended family, including her seventy-year-old father. Antonio rents a small piece of land outside of town where he raises and trains fighting cocks.

ESTELA When we first arrived, we started looking for work. We ended up in Stockton, picking cherries.

ANTONIO We spent three weeks there, sleeping under the trees, out in the open air. We spread blankets and sheets on the ground and cooked over a fire.

ESTELA Then we went to Oregon.

ANTONIO My in-laws had cars and they took us with them. At the *rancho* where we worked, there were over a hundred people. Like in Stockton, we all slept outside. In the afternoon it would get cold. There were no showers and no hot water. To bathe we had to fill up a bucket with water and go out into the orchard. Many people brought children.

When we saw this, we thought about going back home. When you're in Mexico, you imagine that the United States is a beautiful country, like what you see in the movies—a place filled with opportunities. Then when you arrive, you discover that the reality is quite different.

ESTELA I thought that people here didn't work. I thought they dressed well, had lots of conveniences; and didn't have to do very much. I thought the people here were elegant, fashionable, all fixed up. Life in Mexico is hard, but when you get here and find yourself sleeping in an orchard, it starts you thinking. In Mexico, even poor people have houses. We didn't come to the United States expecting to be sleeping out in the open air or working in the fields.

ANTONIO In Oregon, there were days when we earned forty dollars and other days we made only twenty-five. Then some people invited us to work in the cannery at night.

ESTELA We'd get up at five in the morning and go out to the fields. We'd work until around one in the afternoon, rest a bit, wash up, eat, and then go to the cannery at around five, where we'd work until about one in the morning. We hardly had time to sleep.

ANTONIO There were times when we worked almost twenty-four hours a day. Some nights we'd leave the cannery at six in the morning, and instead of going home to rest, we'd go back to the fields to pick cherries. Some days we'd sleep only two or three hours. Other days, when the cannery closed early, we'd go home and sleep a few hours.

When we arrived in Oregon, we thought we could live well and save up a bit of money by working eight hours a day. The truth is, if you want to save money, you need to work fourteen to sixteen hours a day.

ESTELA We got used to it. The harvest season is short and we dreamed of earning money. If you know what it's really like here, then you know that in the United States workers suffer. If you want to make money, you have to struggle. You've got to work hard to earn fifty dollars.

ANTONIO After Oregon, we returned to California where we worked thinning nectarines, peaches, and plums. We put all our money together and rented an apartment here. Then, we bought a little truck from my wife's cousin. I kept working. During the season, wherever you go there are jobs. I was making pretty good money, so we sold the old truck and bought a better one.

We're not afraid to be here without papers. It's easy to find work because I have a false *mica.* Wherever you go, there are people who sell fake papers. Mine cost sixty dollars. You go out and buy the photos and bring them along with your information and they make you a fake *mica.* There are thousands and thousands of people like us. The bosses don't care if you've got a real *mica.* Everyone knows that.

ESTELA Sometimes when we go out, we'll see Immigration. Then, we feel afraid. It reminds us of how tough life is here. We know it isn't as easy as it used to be to cross the border. Sometimes there are people who spend two weeks in Tijuana trying to cross. They just keep struggling.

ANTONIO People always make it across the border. Even if the *gringos* say they don't want any more Mexicans, they can't stop people from coming here.

ESTELA It would be difficult to return to Mexico and have to start all over again. Little by little, we're trying to get ahead. The nicest thing would be to have a stable place to live and not to have to travel around. I hope that our children won't have to migrate or work in the fields, suffering through hunger and cold. I hope our children will have a better life.

ANTONIO We don't want our children to work the way that we've had to work, to suffer what we've suffered. We want our children to have toys and new shoes, and to study as much as they can. We want them to learn to speak English so that they can find good jobs. We don't want our children carrying a picking sack to the orange groves.

A year later, the Solareses' apartment is empty. The plot of land where Antonio raised fighting cocks is vacant, the cages disassembled and the ground bare. No one seems to know where the family has gone. Their neighbors say that the family left when work got slow.

Farmworkers' poverty does not result from their low wages alone, but from the combination of low wages and temporary, seasonal employment. While their hourly wages vary considerably and are often in excess of the minimum wage, the lives of farmworkers are marked by fluctuating periods of unemployment and underemployment. Currently, farmworkers are employed for less than half the year, as the average annual employment has declined from 26 weeks in the early 1990s to 24 weeks by the end of the decade. The number of weeks farmworkers are employed does not take into consideration the time they spend searching for work, working part time early or late in the season, or being unemployed as a result of weather or market conditions. In addition, there is a general oversupply of workers. Every nationwide study has concluded that there are more farmworkers than available positions although exact figures vary by region and season.

Since the United States employs 70 percent more farmworkers in September than in January, many farmworkers spend a considerable amount of time and resources searching for work or stuck between jobs. Half of all farmworkers are employed in jobs that last seven weeks or less. The length of time that a specific job lasts varies considerably, depending on the crop and the region. Some jobs, such as work in the mushroom industry, provide employment almost year-round. Other jobs, such as harvesting raisin grapes, require tens of thousands of workers for a season lasting only several weeks. Citrus harvesting in Florida and California continues for as long as eight months, while the apple season in the northern states rarely lasts more than four months.

In agriculture, the workers—the most vulnerable participants in the system—are forced to bear the burden of virtually all of the costs associated with farmwork's temporary, seasonal nature. When farm-workers find jobs far from home, they cover their own travel expenses, including transportation, lodging, and food. Once workers arrive at a particular job site, they often have to wait days or even weeks for work to begin, and again they are responsible for all the related costs. Even after a job begins, full-time employment is often not available immediately. The inherent unpredictability of agriculture—the freezes, droughts, heat waves, crop diseases, and market-price fluctuations—only heightens the general uncertainty of farm labor. Farmworkers are almost never given extra compensation to cover the constant displacement and downtime that marks their lives.

Jobs involving seasonality and migration do not necessarily force employees into poverty. Many seasonal workers—from schoolteachers to construction workers in northern states—earn a steady living. Similarly, many workers whose jobs involve travel—flight attendants, truck drivers, consultants—earn wages that keep them and their families well above the poverty line. Typically, seasonal or travel-based industries pay workers enough money to cover periods of unemployment or underemployment, and provide adequate benefits to compensate workers for the expense, dislocation, and stress of constant travel. At the very least, these industries ensure that their workers earn a living wage.

The nation's agricultural industry has always relied on the existence of a large number of poor workers who have few job options. Workers accept low wages and take on the burdens of uncertain seasonal labor for the simple reason that there is little else available to them. Not surprisingly, only the most marginalized workers—recent immigrants, undocumented workers, the dispossessed—accept these conditions. The powerlessness of farmworkers breeds dependence, which serves to marginalize and isolate them further. Their alienation from general society encourages and enables the informal, unregulated character of the farm labor system as farmworkers commonly experience abuses not found in other industries.

Algimiro Morales ♦ *Oceanside, California*
We are standing in a dirt parking lot at the bottom of a hill. Above, a thin trail winds its way between a collection of small houses built by immigrant farmworkers out of scavenged materials. Below the shanty-town, there are lush green fields planted with thick, ordered rows of vegetables where the residents of the community work. All of the workers here are Mixtec Indians, one of several groups of indigenous

Mexicans who began crossing the border in the 1970s. There are now over 40,000 Mixtecs in California, many of whom work in agriculture. Half of Mixtec farmworkers report earning less than the minimum wage, and a quarter have been cheated out of their wages at least once. As many as 14,000 Mixtecs live in San Diego County, many of whom build makeshift camps in uninhabited canyons near the fields where they work.

Algimiro Morales first arrived in the United States in 1979. When he was an undocumented worker, he lived on the same hill where this shantytown now stands and worked in the same fields. He eventually legalized his status, sent for his family, and found a better job in a local factory. Morales is the founder of the Comité Civico Popular Mixteco ("Mixtec Popular Civic Committee"), one of a number of Mixtec community organizations that have sprung up throughout California.

To arrive at the shantytown, you exit the highway and travel along a road lined with shopping centers and convenience stores. On both sides of the street there are newly constructed developments, large houses with walls of windows. Beside a retirement community with a golf course, there is a dirt road, hidden by a thick cluster of trees. The Mixtec shantytown is down the road, past signs that read, "No Trespassing."

When I used to live here on this hill, life was much more difficult. Back then, very few people had papers. We couldn't live out in the open because Immigration was always looking for us. There were raids all the time. Whenever Immigration came, people would be running everywhere. They'd catch some of us and others would get away. Usually after a raid, we'd sit around and laugh about what happened. Once Immigration caught me and about twenty others. They took us all to Tijuana. Two days later we crossed back over the border.

To avoid Immigration, we used to live in little rooms, like caves, that we built underground. The rooms were about six by six feet—just big enough to sleep in—and had wood roofs that we covered with dirt. There were caves all over this hill. The *ranchero* built a communal kitchen, a big house with empty oil drums which he cut in half. We cooked together, making fires in the oil drums and storing our food in boxes we'd built. Our underground rooms were always set away from the kitchen so that when Immigration arrived at the building they wouldn't find the places where we slept.

Since then, the community has changed a great deal. Now, there are no more Immigration raids because many people have papers. Instead of caves, the people build aboveground houses made out of wood, cardboard, sheets of plastic, and parts of old cars. There's no electricity or running water. The televisions here run on car batteries and water is carried in from the fields, which are quite far away. There's a spigot down below where people go to bathe. The community is growing. More and more people are coming. All the children here go to school. They walk about a mile to the edge of the road where the bus stops to pick them up.

Each community elects a committee and a president to provide basic rules of conduct and make sure the place is kept clean. The president is generally an older man because, among the Mixtec, older people are always the most highly respected. In this community, there's a rule that single men must live on one side and families on the other. The single men drink and make noise, so to avoid problems, they're required to live apart from the families. This community is named Kelly, in honor of the man who owns the land. Kelly allows people to live here. Other landowners call the police, who send in bulldozers to destroy the houses. This community is illegal, but Kelly is a kind man. It costs six hundred dollars a month to rent an apartment in this area. In the fields, you earn twenty to thirty dollars a day, and in Kelly, there's no rent.

As a migrant, you find yourself living in a different, uncomfortable world. Because of this, you suffer. In the community where you were born and where you own land you're somebody. There you live day to day among your people. You have an opportunity to control your life, to work to become a good citizen, to be respected. Then a time comes when you have to leave your town, which these days is very common. When you leave home, you're often mistreated. This is difficult, especially if you're used to being treated with respect. There's so much rejection and hostility. People look at you as if you are beneath them. They see you as nothing, and then you begin to feel that, outside of your community, perhaps you really are worthless. You might be respected at home, but in the outside world, you are nothing, nobody.

The first Mixtec immigrants to a place return to their communities and tell others to come. Little by little, a Mixtec community grows. Now, we have Mixtec communities all over California. As Mixtecs, we've learned to defend ourselves. Our communities are very unified. There's now a large network of Mixtecs. They can help you find your relatives or cross the border. When you go back to your town, people give you letters. You might arrive in America carrying a suitcase full of letters and it's the same when you return home. It's like our own post office. When you arrive here, or when you go back home, people always ask you about their families.

We stay in direct contact with our communities. In fact, we're more concerned with our communities back home than with what's happening here. Wherever there are several Mixtec families from a particular town, they meet, talk, and agree on the best way to serve their community. We call this *tequio*. *Tequio* is voluntary work that a person provides as community service. Usually a *tequio* is physical work, like fixing the streets or building a church. Local leaders figure out how many men they need and then each person donates one or two days of work, giving the community his *tequio*. It's an obligation. Since we're living in the United States, we send money based on the value of a day's work to our communities as *tequio*.

For Mixtecs, the suffering of a place like this is nothing strange. The poverty in our land is extreme, and while here we may be poor, at least we can survive. Still, it's difficult here and sometimes dangerous. Americans look down on the poor. They reject us. They blame us for the problems that overwhelm their country. They allow themselves to be influenced by people of bad faith. There are also men who come here to steal, and last year, a group of skinheads began shooting at the houses. The people who live here are cautious. They've formed a community defense group to protect themselves from outsiders.

The worst part of all this is that we can't respond. Our words mean nothing to the Americans. They don't listen to us and we have no way of showing them that they're wrong, that the problems in this country come from inside their own society. We haven't come here to take things away from the Americans. We've come here to contribute. We don't live on public assistance. Our people come here to work. The truth is, we don't really want to be in the United States. It's necessity which brings my people here to live through these dangers, face social rejection, and watch as their families are torn apart as fathers leave their families at home and children grow up alone. This is not the way things should be.

I would like Americans to understand that living like this, in houses we've built on a hillside, is not the same as being ignorant. There is a great deal of wisdom in our communities. There are rules in our culture that are often superior to those in Anglo-Saxon society. We look at the family differently. Children respect their parents. Mixtecs revere their elders.

The young people here are Mixtec. Perhaps this will change after a generation or two, but for now they identify with our people. They go to Mixtec dances and tell Mixtec tales. I'm still not used to the idea that we're leaving our communities in Mexico. Perhaps the most important thing is not that we're leaving, but that we're maintaining our unity, our identity.

A year after this interview was conducted, Kelly and another neighboring Mixtec shantytown were torn down by local authorities, who gave residents a set time to relocate and helped a number of families find rental housing. A few months later, all that was left of Kelly were pressed-dirt floors, postholes, burned mattresses, old bottles, and torn bits of clothing. Many of the Mixtecs who lived there drifted off to build new makeshift homes in other more hidden canyons.

2. Farmworkers
What Sort of Future Awaits Us?

THE AMERICAN agricultural industry has always relied on marginalized workers. Fruit and vegetable farms have employed successive waves of recent immigrants from China, Japan, the Philippines, Mexico, Europe, the Caribbean, and Central America as well as poor domestic laborers such as African Americans in the rural South, poor white workers from Appalachia, dust bowl refugees, and alcoholics recruited off skid row. The history of farmworkers in the United States is the story of repeated government action aimed at providing powerful agricultural interests with a steady supply of low-wage labor by a variety of means, from denying farmworkers basic labor protections to allowing growers to hire foreign guest workers on special temporary contracts.

The first seasonal farmworkers in the United States appeared in California in the mid-nineteenth century when the state's agricultural industry was dominated by large grain farms. These workers were generally Native Americans or poor whites who had migrated west in search of new opportunities. Chinese immigrants, originally brought to the United States to build railroads and work in mines, began laboring in the fields in the 1860s, playing a key role in the rapid expansion of California's fruit-and-vegetable industry. By 1880, over 75 percent of all California farmworkers were Chinese, most of whom labored in segregated work crews supervised by Chinese foremen. Anti-Chinese sentiment led to the passage of a series of laws culminating in the 1882 Chinese Exclusion Act, which suspended the immigration of Chinese workers for ten years, a restriction that was later extended indefinitely. Anti-Chinese protests increased during the 1880s, marked by riots and crowd violence, and by the 1890s, most Chinese laborers left rural communities to live in segregated urban neighborhoods.

In the late 1890s, California growers began recruiting Japanese immigrants to work in the fields. At first, growers praised the Japanese for their obedience, docile nature, and willingness to work long hours for low wages. Japanese immigration steadily increased, and by 1910, the majority of workers in the California fruit-and-vegetable industry were Japanese. As Japanese immigrants grew accustomed to life in the United States, they initiated harvest strikes and slowdowns whose success helped them become the highest-paid farmworkers in the region. Japanese workers also began to rent land, sharecrop, and pool their savings to buy small farms, which successfully competed with the larger operations where they had previously worked.

The success of Japanese farms spurred California's growers to press for state legislative action, leading to the passage of the Alien Lands Act of 1913, which prevented noncitizens from purchasing or owning land in California. When Japanese immigrants continued farming through rental and other agreements, the legislature revised the law in 1920 to prevent noncitizen immigrants from leasing land, buying stock in land companies, or acting as guardians for land held by their children. On the national level, Japanese immigration to the United States was reduced in 1907 by an agreement between the two nations and formally terminated by the Immigration Act of 1924.

In the early twentieth century, growing numbers of Mexicans migrated to the United States to work on railroads, in mines, and in agriculture. These workers were pushed north by the Mexican government's radical dismantling of traditional communal landownership, which forced 5 million rural Mexicans—over 97 percent of the *campesino* population—off their land. By the 1910 Revolution, Mexican labor migration was well established with nearly 20,000 workers crossing into the United States each year. Mexican migration increased steadily during the First World War, spurred by the labor needs of the war economy, special U.S. government programs to encourage workers to cross the border, and the violence and uncertainty of the revolutionary era. Mexican migration continued to increase in the 1920s when the United States passed the first national-origins restrictions designed to limit immigration from southern and eastern Europe. Immigrants from the Western Hemisphere were excluded from these restrictions, largely as a way of allowing the continued migration of Mexican workers to farms in the southwest.

By the 1920s, about 50,000 Mexicans were entering the country each year, and Mexican laborers represented half of all California's farmworkers. By the 1930s, there were over 350,000 Mexicans working in the United States. In the early twentieth century, western growers also began recruiting Filipino workers, generally from the Hawaiian Islands where they worked on large sugar plantations. By 1930, over 50,000 Filipinos were employed in the United States, mostly in agriculture. Growers deliberately recruited workers from different ethnic groups and created an oversupply of labor in order to reduce the threat of strikes and union organizing.

In contrast to California and the southwestern states, commercial agriculture in the pre–Civil War South was dominated by plantations that relied on slave labor. When slavery was made illegal, plantations generally remained in the hands of large landowners. From the 1870s through the 1920s, southern agriculture relied on sharecroppers and tenant farmers, dependent laborers who lived on, but did not own, the land they worked. Although many sharecroppers dreamed of saving enough money to become independent farmers, their situation was so tenuous and their earnings so low that they were rarely successful. In fact, many sharecroppers were unable to cover the debts they incurred with their employers prior to each year's harvest.

Migrant farmworkers in the East appeared as early as the 1890s, providing labor to the many truck farms that had sprung up near expanding urban areas. These crews were composed of African Americans from the South and European immigrants, such as Italians living near Philadelphia and Poles out of Baltimore. At the time, the U.S. government was directing recent European immigrants to farm labor with the idea that farmwork would provide the first step toward life as an independent farmer. By the 1920s, there were enough truck farms along the East Coast that migrant workers could piece together a living by traveling from one harvest to another.

In Florida and some other areas in the South, commercial agriculture more closely resembled the big farms of the West. In the 1920s, large sections of the Everglades were drained, opening up thousands of acres of fertile muck soil and creating an important winter vegetable industry. From the late 1920s on, poor whites and African Americans were lured south to work on large vegetable and sugarcane farms and live in labor camps, company towns, and rapidly expanding farmworker communities. Farmworkers' neighborhoods, often lacking paved roads or indoor plumbing, were typically set apart from the homes of growers and permanent residents and were often placed outside the city limits. Workers were generally paid a set rate per day, and labor unrest was held in check by local police. By the 1930s, agriculture was big business in Florida, and by 1940, Florida had over 100 farms larger than 10,000 acres and between 40,000 and 60,000 farmworkers.

In the early twentieth century, the majority of midwestern farms were small and run by families who provided most of the necessary hand labor. Some farms also relied on limited numbers of seasonal farmworkers, most of whom were recent European immigrants. Many of these farmworkers went on to run their own farms or abandoned farm labor for manufacturing jobs in cities. Migrant farmworkers first appeared in the Midwest in the 1930s, as farms grew in size and increased production. The first migrants were poor whites and crews of African American laborers from the rural South. Over the years, Mexican Americans and their families, often traveling north out of Texas, provided most of the seasonal labor for fruit and vegetable farms in the region.

In the 1930s, the introduction of new farm technology in the South, particularly inexpensive tractors, greatly reduced the number of workers needed to prepare the soil, plant, and tend the crops. These changes led growers to force many sharecroppers and tenant farmers off their land. Many former sharecroppers left agriculture and moved to the cities, while others began working as wage laborers. Since growers still needed large numbers of workers for the harvest, the dismantling of the sharecropping and tenant-farming system led to the development of a migrant labor system throughout the Southeast. Those workers with vehicles traveled independently from farm to farm, while the majority of laborers were dependent on farm labor contractors, who often exercised considerable control over migrant crews.

In the 1930s, over 300,000 workers and their families migrated to California from Missouri, Arkansas, Oklahoma, and Texas. The massive migration of dust bowl refugees to the West coupled with the large population of Mexican workers created an enormous labor surplus. Responding to high unemployment and growing anti-immigrant sentiment, the U.S. government began denying visas to Mexicans and instituted a series of raids and mass deportations. Between 1930 and 1933, the government forcibly repatriated 300,000 to 400,000 Mexicans, many of whom were legally entitled to stay in the United States.

The 1930s represented a particularly important time for farm labor organizing. There was a marked increase in the size and militancy of

farm labor unions, particularly in California, where workers engaged in hundreds of slowdowns and strikes. Growers often responded to demands for improved wages and better living conditions by hiring armed thugs, leading to numerous violent incidents. The plight of California's farmworkers, who by that time were mostly white dust bowl migrants, received national attention through the publication of John Steinbeck's highly popular *Grapes of Wrath* and various exposés, such as Carey McWilliams's *Factories in the Fields*.

The 1930s also saw the passage of a series of basic federal labor protections under Franklin Roosevelt's New Deal, including the federal minimum wage, overtime provisions, Social Security, unemployment compensation, child labor protections, and the legal framework for union organizing. Farmworkers were specifically excluded from all of these fundamental protections, thereby institutionalizing their status as second-class workers. While farmworkers' wages were almost 70 percent of industrial workers' wages in the early twentieth century, by 1940, farmworkers earned only a quarter of what factory workers earned.

When the United States entered the Second World War, western growers became concerned about the possibility of farm labor shortages. Large numbers of Mexican immigrants had been deported or pressured to return home, and poor white workers were finding better jobs in the war economy or were entering the armed forces. Worried about the possibility of competing with industry for workers, growers petitioned the federal government to set up a system allowing Mexican laborers to be brought into the United States to work in agriculture. The government created a guest worker system in 1942, which later became known as the bracero program. Although it had originally been approved as a special wartime measure, the bracero program continued, expanding considerably in the 1950s. The program was finally terminated in 1964 after vigorous opposition from labor unions, religious organizations, and community groups. Over twenty-two years, the bracero program admitted between 4 million and 5 million Mexican workers into the United States.

Norberto Herrera ◆ *Penjamillo, Michocán*
Norberto Herrera is sixty years old. When he was still a small boy in Mexico, his father was killed and he was forced to drop out of school and work to support his mother and five brothers and sisters. At nine, he herded cows and worked the fields. At fourteen, he labored as a sharecropper, planting corn for a local landowner. Her-

rera's family was too poor to buy shoes. In the mid-1950s, Herrera went to the United States through the bracero program. He signed up for six contracts as a bracero and then spent years traveling north independently to work as a farm laborer. Eventually, he returned to the small city where he was born.

We sit in the shade of an open courtyard in Herrera's spacious house. There is a car in the garage, and another on the street. The house is filled with modern appliances. Herrera has a wide, boyish face, with graying curls and a thin mustache. He is a gracious man, relaxed, content, and proud.

We all saw how the braceros came back with good clothes for their families and nice shoes. They said that they suffered a lot in the United States, but I saw how much better they lived. I wanted to do the same. I thought to myself, "God willing, I'm going to go to the United States too."

I was twenty when I first went north as a bracero. If you wanted to go work in the United States, you had to get on the official list. Many people signed up, so I couldn't get on the list. Still, there were lawyers who could fix things for you if you bribed them. A group of us found a lawyer who worked with another lawyer at the recruitment center. We each paid the lawyer five hundred pesos. He put us on the official list from the state of Sinaloa and wrote up some papers that said we were sugarcane cutters. If those two lawyers helped a thousand workers get on the list, they'd split half a million pesos.

In those days, we earned six or seven pesos for a day's work, so five hundred pesos was a fortune to us. Still, we knew that if we made it to the United States we could pay off the debt in a month. Each of us borrowed around fifteen hundred pesos from a moneylender. We used a third of the money to pay the lawyer, another part to pay for transportation to the recruitment center and food while traveling, and left the rest of the money with our families. We paid three percent interest per month.

Back then, there were lots of tricks. We'd all heard stories of people who were cheated by lawyers. There was one lawyer who came to town and convinced a hundred men to sign up in a single night. Each man paid a thousand pesos. He left town and no one ever saw him again. We were afraid the same thing would happen to us. If the lawyer cheated us, how would we ever pay back our debt? We expected the worst.

The recruitment center was in the state of Sonora. Each day, thousands of men arrived at the center. The buses showed up all day long and there were crowds of people—whites, blacks, Indians. There were men who looked rich, with money and new clothes, and others who arrived barefoot, wearing rags. Most of the men came with only a pair of pants, a shirt, and a jacket, nothing else. At the recruitment center, we found out that we were on the list. There were about a hundred of us from town, waiting. We spent eight days there, sleeping on the ground.

Finally, they told us to form a line. They brought out the list and a group of Americans who spoke Spanish asked us questions: "What's your name?" "Where do you work?" "Where do you live?" Then, they looked at the papers to see if you were telling them the truth. After the questions, you went to the eye exam. There, they put you a certain distance from some letters and asked you to read them, first with one eye and then with the other. Since I didn't know how to read, I told them what I saw by making gestures. Then, you got an X ray to see if your lungs were all right. Then, they took blood samples. There were some men who had hardly eaten, so when they took out their blood, they fainted. Finally, they passed you on to sign some papers. Although I couldn't read the document, I knew I was signing a contract. There was only one out of our group who didn't pass. They took him out because he had a spot on his lungs. We took out a collection to pay for his bus fare home.

They put us on a train. It was my first trip on a train. It moved very fast and only stopped for fuel and water. They put us in cars with no seats and no windows, like what they use to transport cattle. We wondered what was going to happen to us. What would it be like to go to a different country? Where were we going to sleep? Who would feed us? What were we going to do there?

They took us to Mexicali on the Mexican side of the border and then put us on buses to Calexico, California, on the other side of the border. The first thing I saw when I entered the United States was the gate dividing the two countries. On one side was the Mexican flag, and on the other, the American flag. All the braceros were waiting in Calexico. There were so many people, and every minute, more workers kept arriving. They loaded thirty-five of us in an old bus and took us to a labor camp for braceros. They gave each person a bed, a blanket, and some food. We were used to being poor and living badly. The camp was more or less the same.

They treated us like animals. The *mayordomos* insulted us. If you did something wrong, they'd yell, "What are you? an idiot? a fool?" There was a lot of discrimination. They kept the American workers and the Mexican braceros in separate crews. The Americans said terrible things about us. We weren't allowed to enter restaurants. Some employers even beat their workers. But, as a bracero, you knew you couldn't complain.

Still, I expected to be treated poorly in the United States. From the moment I went on contract, I never thought that they'd treat me well. I knew I was going to suffer. I knew that to become someone in life, I would have to suffer. If I stayed in Mexico with my family, I would have continued to live in poverty. I have friends who stayed and they're still poor, very poor. They may have a place to live, but they barely earn enough to eat. They can't buy the things they want because they weren't willing to suffer. I'm proud of what I achieved.

Working as a bracero gave me hope. I always dreamed of one day having a house to live in and being able to give something to my children. I chose to go to the United States, knowing that I would suffer so my family could have a better life. When I left, I had absolutely nothing. Now, I have a house and a pen where I keep my animals—two hundred pigs, five cows, and eight bulls. Before, I didn't have enough money to buy a pair of shoes and now I have two cars. Then, I didn't even own a small radio and now I have four televisions, from a small one to a big twenty-seven-inch color set. I have a washing machine, a refrigerator, a stove, all of those things. When my wife was sick, I took her to a good doctor. I raised my children and put them through school. Now, one is a supervisor in a factory and another is a real estate agent.

I feel grateful to the United States, but the truth is, I never liked it there. Whenever I was up north, I felt closed in, imprisoned. I never felt free. To be a bracero is to be sold to the United States. You're sent north because of a contract between two governments. You're not free. You've been sold off to a boss you've never met. You feel bad, but you have to believe that, in the end, you'll get ahead. There are many braceros who lost their way and fell into vices, workers who made lots of money but didn't know how to save it. They didn't invest what they earned and now they've got nothing. There are others who left their families and never returned. They just disappeared and their families don't know if they're alive or dead.

As soon as I crossed the border back into Mexico, I felt different. I don't know why, but it's only when I'm here, walking on Mexican soil, that I feel free.

Beginning in 1943, the United States government required European prisoners of war to labor in the fields. POWs lived in special camps managed by the federal government and generally located in the rural South. Growers were supposed to pay POWs prevailing wages, although most of their earnings went to the War Food Administration to defray the program's cost. The POW program was marred by spontaneous strikes and labor unrest and criticized for allowing foreign prisoners to displace domestic workers. Still, as the war progressed, the numbers of POWs laboring in the fields rose from 41,000 in 1943 to over 120,000 by 1945.

On the East Coast, the federal government established a guest worker program similar in structure to the bracero program, but smaller in size and overall impact. In 1943, the British West Indies program allowed growers to bring workers from the Bahamas to labor in agriculture. Like the bracero program, this temporary-agricultural-worker program was originally justified on the basis of labor shortages brought on by the Second World War. In 1952, the program was revised and became known as the H-2 program, referring to the special visa issued to temporary agricultural workers. The program continues to this day, bringing thousands of West Indian and Mexican workers into the United States to labor in the fields.

After the Second World War, the federal government recruited Puerto Ricans to work as contract laborers in agriculture throughout the eastern states. Puerto Rican farmworkers quickly displaced the remaining Italian workers in New York and New Jersey and became an important part of the farm labor workforce through the 1970s. The program reached a peak in the late 1960s, when almost 22,000 workers were brought in on contract. Since then, the number of Puerto Rican contract workers has dropped steadily; there were around 10,000 in the 1970s and only a few thousand by the late 1980s.

From the 1950s through the 1970s, farmworkers were generally understood as traveling in one of three distinct migrant streams. The western stream was dominated by Mexican immigrants, although it also included some white workers (often the children of dust bowl–era migrants) and a variety of other immigrant groups, including Filipinos and other Asian laborers. The central stream was generally composed of Mexican Americans or Mexican-born immigrants, many of whom traveled in extended families. The eastern stream was dominated by crews of African American workers, Puerto Ricans, and some white Americans from the rural South.

Henry Dover ♦ *Fort Pierce, Florida*
We are sitting in a rooming house on D Street, the center of the city's African American farmworker community. It is late afternoon, the end of another workday. Outside, a street preacher yells into a microphone, his voice overamplified—loud, distorted, unintelligible. Vans carrying workers back from the fields pass by. Groups of men talk, laugh, and drink in a supermarket parking lot. Dogs root through garbage. People call out greetings to one another. The

orange-picking season is coming to a close, and already workers are heading north.

Henry Dover is six foot five with broad shoulders, large powerful hands, and long arms. While his physical presence is imposing, Dover has a gentle, soft-spoken manner.

I was born in a little town in Mississippi. I started doing farmwork back in the early sixties when I was nine years old. We were sharecroppers. We had about a hundred acres of land. The farmer planted the cotton and we picked it. We didn't get paid for working in the fields until the end of the year, when the farmer sold the cotton. All the farmers were white and all of the workers were black.

Back in those days, the black man was scared of the white farmer. The farmer could come along and do whatever he wanted to do. If the farmer's son was out there, a little white guy fourteen years old, I'd have to say "Yes, sir" to him. And if I spoke to the farmer's daughter, I'd have to call her Miss So and So. What did they call me? They'd call me anything that came to mind. Usually they'd call me boy—"Hey, boy, come here."

Back then, it was pretty rough in Mississippi. You might be walking down the street and three or four white guys would show up. They might throw something at you or hit you upside the head. Anything could happen to you down there, and nothing would be done about it. I remember a few of the older guys went out one night, and some white guys killed them—just for being out.

One day, I just up and left. I was trying to get away from the cotton, so I ran off and went to Arkansas. Over there, they were doing the same thing, picking and chopping cotton, so I saved up enough money to go to Chicago. I was seventeen. When I moved to Chicago, it was like I had died and gone to heaven. It was fantastic. I felt free. I didn't have to worry about a white man coming along. That fear had left. I didn't have to go out and work in no hot sun, work in the rain, no more pulling weeds. I found a job in a candy factory, making all types of candy—gumdrops, chewing gum. Then, I worked in a liquor warehouse. There were lots of good jobs. Later, I went back and got my mother. Things started looking up.

So, how did I get back into farmwork? That's a good question.

I have a brother who was living in Daytona Beach, Florida. I went down there one winter and started working in roofing. Roofing gets kind of slow at times and my brother told me about a guy, a contractor, who was doing farmwork, harvesting cabbages and potatoes. One day, the contractor asked me if I wanted a job and so I started working for him. I'd never been on a labor camp before. I thought it would be something different, something exciting. I didn't even know what a migrant worker was. I'd been working with the crewleader a couple of months before I heard someone say that we were migrant workers.

When I first started working, the contractor paid me minimum wage. I have pretty fast hands and I guess I'm pretty strong. I was doing the work of two men, so he started paying me extra. Most of the time I earned good money, about a hundred and eighty dollars a week, and I didn't pay rent. Also, he couldn't hound me like he did the others because I didn't drink his wine. I had my pride and I stood up for myself. I always felt that if a man don't have nothing he'd die for, then he's not a man.

The crewleader was misusing people. He'd slap workers to get them up in the morning, and then he'd give them wine. Most of the crew was addicted to wine. He'd make us work from sunup to sundown, the same way it was down in Mississippi. The people would work all day long every day. At the end of the week, most of them would only get a few dollars. It sure made you angry to work fifty hours a week and then have the man tell you that the only thing you got coming was eight dollars.

Those were hard times and the people on the camp didn't have no freedom. They were unhappy. They were lonely. They never had a chance to visit their families. Weekends on a labor camp didn't really seem like a weekend. You're out on the camp. You don't have transportation to go to town. So, the people would just hang around, drinking wine, listening to music, and fighting with each other. They'd fight because they ain't got no wine. They'd fight because they ain't got no money. People on the camp felt like they were in prison. They built up a lot of hate.

The crewleader had a Mercedes, a brand-new truck, and some kind of special car made from out of a magazine. He'd walk around with his fine clothes and shined shoes. His son had a Lincoln Continental. If a man on the camp had a woman, and the contractor liked that woman, he'd want to get with her. He might trick her up to his room and take advantage of her, and she wouldn't fight him because he was the boss.

Sometimes church people would come and bring clothes to the camp. Once, some people came to the camp to ask the workers how the contractor was treating them. The workers lied and said the crewleader was a good boss and a good man. They lied because they were afraid. They felt like they needed the contractor, like they couldn't function without him. The only thing most of them know how to do was farmwork. The crewleader had been taking care of them, feeding them, and clothing them for years. Even though most of them didn't have but one or two pair of pants and didn't earn more than seven or eight dollars a week, they felt like they couldn't function without the crewleader. He treated the workers like dogs, catching them by the collar and slapping them around. He picked on the weak.

There were some guys that had been working with the contractor for twenty-five years—guys like Jitterbug and Charles that couldn't read or count money. He'd work them for fifty hours and then give them a few dollars a week. That began to bother me. It bothered me to see someone treat another human being like that. I got to thinking about what would happen to those older guys in another ten years.

One day, I saw the crewleader hit three or four of the older guys and it was then I decided to call the labor board. By the time we got to Delaware that year, I decided that I was going to bust him wide open. So, I called the labor board people and told them about the contractor. They came out there and asked me what was wrong. I told them all the things that the contractor was doing.

Then, one of the investigators said, "I know that contractor. Him and I is good friends." He told me the best damn thing for me to do was to get my ass out of there. They went over and talked to the contractor, came back with my wages, and took me to the Greyhound bus station. You see, the farmer, the contractor, and the labor board guys all work hand in hand. The farmers are very powerful and the labor board people take money from them.

A lot of these contractors just steal the workers' money. They beat you out of your money and take it to the bank. To me, a contractor like that is a black man putting another black man into slavery. These contractors take advantage of other black guys that don't have any knowledge, that can't read. It's just like back in Mississippi. They put you in slavery.

Now, I'm picking oranges. In the mornings when I want to go to work, I get my fruit bag, lay it across my shoulder, and stand out there on that corner. People come by and pick me up and take me to work. I can pick fifteen to twenty bins of oranges a day. They pay around six dollars a bin, so I earn a hundred dollars a day. When I'm clipping honey bales—that's something like a tangerine and an orange mixed together—I earn a hundred and thirty dollars a day. You can go to work practically every day, but not this time of year, because the fruit's almost over. Now, watermelons are coming and lots of people are going north to do peaches.

Everything I do here is by the piece. If the fruit's kind of raggedy or if there's not much fruit on the trees, then you know it's going to be hard to make good money. So, you need to ask for a better piece rate. If we go out there and they won't pay us a fair price for a bin, we strike. We strike in a minute.

"You want to pay us eight dollars a bin? We're not going to pick it for eight. We want ten."

"We can't pay ten."

"Take us home."

Then, just like a pop of your finger, the crewleader will say, "Pay them what they want" and we win. Farmwork is nice if you're getting paid for it. It's good work if they pay you well and you're out there with a group of people that's happy. There's a lot of playing going on out in the groves. People are singing and talking about good things. They feel free. They feel like they're getting what they got coming.

Farmwork is kind of beautiful. It's peaceful. In the city, there's a whole lot of killing and shooting going on. Out here, you can breathe nice clean air. You can hear the birds. You can look up and see the sky. You're not cramped. Whenever I look up at the sky, I'll be thinking about God. That's what makes me happy, just seeing the plants, seeing how they change color, seeing the flowers. You can see all of God's nature out there.

Over the past three decades, the farm labor work force has undergone a steady process of Latinization. In 1965, less than half of California's farm labor force was Latino, but by the mid-1990s, Latinos represented over 97 percent of the state's farmworkers. In the eastern United States, Latino farmworkers are relatively new, first arriving in the late 1950s and concentrating in a handful of agricultural communities, generally in Florida. Since then, the percentage of Latino workers has steadily increased, displacing the traditional African American workforce. By the mid-1980s, the majority of migrants in the east were Latinos and by the mid-1990s, eight out of every ten farmworkers in the East were Latinos. If current trends continue, virtually all migrants in the region will be Latinos in the near future.

Over the last twenty-five years, several new waves of recent immigrants have entered the workforce. In the early 1980s, tens of thousands of Haitians arrived in Florida, many of whom found work in the fields. For several years, Haitian crews competed with African Americans in the Southeast, although many Haitian laborers subsequently left farmwork. Around the same time, indigenous Guatemalans— Mam, K'iche', Q'anjob'al, Q'ueqchi', and others—began to cross into the United States, fleeing state terror and political violence. By the mid-1980s, small communities of Guatemalan political refugees had sprung up throughout Florida, spurring the continued migration

of thousands more Guatemalans, many of whom continue to labor in the fields. In the late 1970s and early 1980s, large numbers of indigenous Mexicans—Mixtecs, Zapotecs, Triques, and others—began arriving in the Southwest, generally finding work in agriculture.

Demetrio Cuj ♦ *Lake Worth, Florida*

Demetrio Cuj is a Q'eqchi' Indian, one of Guatemala's twenty-three indigenous groups. Although his family was quite poor, they encouraged him to pursue an education. He worked during the day—selling newspapers and ice cream, shining shoes, and making jewelry—and attended school at night. Cuj became a teacher and was assigned to a remote village just as Guatemala entered the worst years of political repression, a period known simply as la violencia— *"the violence."*

In an effort to defeat a guerrilla insurgency, the Guatemalan military instituted brutal policies of state terror involving massacres, torture, "disappearances," and the destruction of entire villages. Two hundred thousand people were killed and hundreds of thousands forced to flee their homes. Anyone suspected of assisting the guerrillas could be hauled away by security forces, never to be heard from again.

Like tens of thousands of other Guatemalans, Cuj fled Guatemala and applied for political asylum in the United States. While his asylum case was being considered, he received working papers. In 1996, the Guatemalan government signed a peace accord with the guerrillas, formally ending thirty-six years of armed conflict. The future of Guatemala remains uncertain, as the nation has yet to reckon with its brutal past.

In 1980, the Ministry of Education sent me to a rural school in the department of Alta Verapaz. There was no electricity, no fresh water, no sanitation, nothing. The town was far away, in the middle of the mountains. The people who lived there were very poor. The houses had dirt floors, with walls of sticks stuck into the ground and roofs made of woven leaves.

I was the only teacher. I had one hundred and fifty students. In the morning I taught first through third grade—seventy-five students in one room. We started in Q'eqchi' and then translated the lessons into Spanish. In the afternoon, I taught fourth through sixth grade. I also taught literacy classes to adult students. The school, the chairs, and all the desks were built by the community. In the countryside, people don't know how to read or write and many can hardly speak Spanish. They consider a teacher to be a leader. They think that as a teacher you can do everything, so they turn to you to resolve all sorts of problems. Out in the countryside, teachers have to do a bit of everything. There were even times when people would call me to help women in labor.

The real problems began in 1981. People began to disappear, one by one. The army would kidnap people and kill them and we'd find their bodies. People would come to me at the school and tell me that their husband had been taken at night. Then his body would appear somewhere. They used to throw the corpses into a big river nearby and sometimes when you were bathing, you'd see dozens of dead bodies floating by. Sometimes, they left corpses shot up along the side of the road.

It got to the point where you had seen so many dead bodies and heard so many terrible stories that these things became normal. It upset your nerves. It affected you so much that it became impossible to really live. At seven or eight at night, most people would go out into the countryside. They were afraid to sleep in their own homes. Whenever you heard the sound of a car, you knew they'd come again to take someone away. You heard shots all the time.

I lived in a constant state of fear, of panic. How could anyone live through these experiences? Most of my friends were killed. I couldn't even tell you all their names because there were so many. Once I found the corpse of a friend of mine. He was our supervisor, the secretary of the literacy program. The army abducted him right out of the school, in front of all the teachers. They accused him of having collaborated with the guerrillas. They killed him and cut off his head.

Out of the thirty-two teachers in our area only five are still alive. They're all here in the United States.

The situation was so difficult that your nervous system changed. You became afraid of everyone you saw and everyone you spoke to. You never knew if the person you were speaking with was an informant. During that time, the majority of Guatemalans lived with so much nervous tension that it was difficult to endure, especially for those of us in the countryside. Whenever someone asks me about these things, I tell them the truth. So many terrible things happened, yet that's what we lived through. That's what happened to us.

One night, some friends invited me to a birthday party a few kilometers from my house. That same night, a friend came by to visit. Since I was planning to stay at the house where they were having the party, my friend stayed at my place and slept in my bed. When I returned in the morning, I went inside my room. My friend was lying in my bed in a pool of blood. They shot him fifteen times. The room was covered in blood.

I decided to leave the school immediately and went back to my home-town. When they realized they hadn't killed me, they came back to look for me, but I'd already left. I was hiding. They asked the man who owned the house where I was. He refused to tell them and so the army carried him away. They tortured him for six days and then killed him. One of my students came to town to warn me. He told me not to return because they'd burned down the house where I was living and were waiting for me. Fifteen days later, the student who came to warn me was killed. They cut off his head.

The army was watching me. I couldn't live in peace. If I went to a store, they knew. I couldn't rest. I could hardly sleep. I was afraid that at any moment they might come for me, break down the door, pull me out, and by dawn the next day, I'd be dead. My family has a house in town. The *campesinos* always came to our house when they needed a place to stay. One night when I was in hiding, the army came in, beat up my fa-ther, and took three people from within our house and killed them. In the morning, their dead bodies were found in the street. Then, we began seeing more and more corpses in town.

One day, four men grabbed me on the street and put me in a car. They beat me. They took me to a police station where they tortured me. They take a plastic bag and put glue in it and pull it over your face. It suffo-cates you. Then someone else came in and put a pistol in my mouth. First the police accused me. Then the army accused me. Then I was sent to jail. Finally I managed to get a message to my family. My sister paid a lawyer to get me out. As soon as I got out of jail, I decided to leave the country and go to the United States.

I took a bus to the Mexican border. There, I found a *coyote* who put me and fifteen others in the back of a truck. They placed boards down above us, and over the boards they loaded boxes of tomatoes and water-melons. We spent two days and two nights below the boards without get-ting out. If we wanted to pee or defecate, we had to do it where we lay. Finally we got to Mexico City. From there, we went by bus to Monterrey, where another *coyote* was supposed to take us across the border. They left us there and we never saw them again. Eventually I made it across the border. I got to know some other Guatemalans and we met a guy who needed people to pick tomatoes in Florida. I've lived in Florida ever since.

It's difficult to get used to living in the United States. If you can't speak English, then your voice is worthless. Even if you're educated, you have to work in the fields. You're never your own boss, and the *mayordo-mos* mistreat and humiliate you. You have to learn to accept it because that's the only way to survive. When I first came to this country, you could work every day of the week. Now there are so many people that it's hard to find work for more than a few days each week. And more people keep coming.

Still, it's much better to live here. I'm no longer afraid. In Guatemala, I could never sleep. My nerves were so frayed that I used to have to take pills in order to fall asleep. Here, I sleep calmly. I've relaxed. There are lots of Guatemalans here and almost all of them are indigenous people who've fled the violence. I'm no longer afraid someone will take me or a neighbor away. I can go to the store without worrying that someone might be waiting for me.

Beginning in the 1960s, public attention was again drawn to farmworkers' struggles. Renewed interest in farmworkers came at a time when the nation was growing increasingly concerned with questions of domestic poverty and civil rights. Viewers around the country were shocked by the Thanksgiving airing of Edward R. Murrow's documentary "Harvest of Shame," which helped stimulate a national debate on the plight of migrant workers. As part of an overall attempt to redress historical injustices, the federal government began providing farmworkers with most of the basic labor protections they had been denied since the 1930s. In addition Congress passed special labor legislation for farmworkers, beginning with the 1963 Farm Labor Contractor Registration Act (FLCRA), which required all contractors to register with the federal government, keep accurate wage records, properly disclose working conditions, and provide other worker protections. Twenty years later, the FLCRA was replaced with the Migrant and Seasonal Agricultural Worker Protection Act (MSAWPA), which provided farmworkers with a series of additional rights and extended liability to growers as well as contractors.

The federal government also instituted a series of assistance programs designed to reduce farmworkers' poverty and improve their access to basic social services. These programs provide health care, education, legal services, job training, loans, and other forms of assistance. Local, state, and federal inspectors monitor labor camps, transportation, field sanitation, pesticide application, and child labor practices and review employers' records. Farmworkers are also served by a number of private organizations, such as church groups, who provide outreach, counseling, and training as well as donations of food and clothing.

Despite the passage of special labor protections and the creation of a series of migrant assistance programs, the situation for America's farmworkers is still deeply troubling. Enforcement of protective legislation is minimal because of limited funding and the general difficulties of protecting a class of marginalized workers laboring in isolated areas around the country. While often beneficial, assistance programs are generally premised on farmworkers' continued poverty and have failed to challenge the structure of the farm labor system.

Jose Mendoza ♦ *Balm, Florida*

Jose Mendoza is a farm labor contractor who works in the fields and manages a small crew of workers, many of whom are relatives. In November 1989, he entered a cauliflower field with his crew. Nineteen hours earlier the field had been sprayed with a highly toxic insecticide called Phosdrin. The Environmental Protection Agency (EPA) requires a minimum wait of forty-eight hours before workers are allowed to enter a field sprayed with Phosdrin. The premature entry of Mendoza's crew and several others resulted in one of the most severe incidents of pesticide exposure in recent history. Before the end of the day, eighty-five farmworkers were taken to area hospitals.

The EPA estimates that farmworkers suffer as many as 300,000 acute illnesses and injuries from pesticide exposure each year. Studies reveal that farmworkers and their families are routinely exposed to dangerous pesticides, sometimes as a result of being sprayed directly and sometimes through pesticide drift or residues. Workers often experience eye irritations, respiratory problems, blistered skin, and swollen hands. While the most acute, obvious signs of exposure generally disappear rather quickly, pesticides and other agricultural chemicals are stored within the body, building up over years of continual exposure. Continual long-term exposure to pesticides, insecticides, and herbicides is associated with a number of serious, even fatal, illnesses.

Federal regulations require that employers carefully monitor pesticide application and post warning signs to prevent worker exposure. However, the enforcement of existing pesticide-application laws is sporadic, fines against employers are rare, and few workers are aware of the grave dangers presented by exposure to these chemicals.

I remember the day perfectly. I took a crew of about twenty-five workers to the field. We arrived at around eight in the morning. That day, we were tying cauliflower. Before picking, you have to tie the cauliflower so it doesn't get damaged by water or the sun's rays. There were three or four other crews in different fields, some tying cauliflower and others harvesting.

At about nine, one of my workers said to me, "Don Jose, I'm sorry, but I feel very bad. I'm going to the doctor. Look at how I'm sweating." It was true. The man was bathed in sweat. A moment later, another man came over and said, "I feel really sick." Then another man came up to me and said, "Don Jose, my head hurts. I feel nauseous." His son was also sick. Then two others came over. They had headaches, felt dizzy, and were nauseous.

I said, "Look, why don't you go sit in my van. Open the windows and the doors, let the fresh air in, and see if the shade helps you feel any better." I told my son to go talk to Deo, the *mayordomo,* who was cutting cauliflower with another crew. "Tell him to come here and look at the people. I don't know what's going on. Tell him the people are sick."

By the time my son came back, there were even more sick workers. The *mayordomo* told my son to let the crew stop working and to put them all in the shade and see if that helped them feel better. Then I sent my boy back to tell the mayordomo to come over because there were lots of sick workers. The people in the van were getting worse. Then other people began feeling weak. At around twelve, we took the first workers to the clinic. One woman was so sick she couldn't walk and we had to carry her.

The doctor in the clinic said that the workers were poisoned by a very strong pesticide. He gave the order that everybody should get out of the fields. One car after another was arriving, filled with workers. Soon, there were lots of people in the clinic, and they started sending people to nearby hospitals. The doctor at the clinic was wonderful. He saved the workers' lives. Later, he began to send those who weren't that sick back to their homes. Some of the workers who were very ill spent a couple of days in the hospital.

My crew was the most affected. There was one young woman in our crew who was the sickest of all. It was a miracle they saved her life. I went to visit all the people from my crew who were in the hospital. When I went to her room, I found her all alone. Her eyes were open, but empty. Her stare was vacant. Her mouth twisted. She was turned on one side, her body stiff and arched. It looked like she was in pain and I thought she was dying.

The poison is a powerful thing. The doctor gave us lots of advice about pesticides. He said that we had to be very careful and not go back to the fields where there was even a small amount of poison because if we did we could get very sick. He told us that when we felt dizzy, weak, and nauseous it was because the pesticides were in our blood, and that they gave people terrible headaches, made them weak and unable to walk. The laboratory tested our clothes and said the bosses had used a very powerful chemical. At that time of year there are lots of worms in the cauliflower, so to kill them they use strong poisons. You mix one quart of the pesticide with six hundred gallons of water.

The *mayordomo* was upset with the workers who didn't return to work. There were lots of people who didn't want to go against the boss. He said he would fire those who refused to return, and the people were afraid of losing their jobs. Of the eighty-five workers who were affected, there were many who kept on working even though they were sick. There were some women who went back to work, and a week later, they swelled up because of the poison. My daughter-in-law was pregnant at the time. She lost her baby.

The doctor told us that the workers who returned to the fields were crazy, that they didn't understand the risks they were taking. He said it could take years before you would see the effects of the pesticides. You could get cancer, go blind, or become sterile. Every eight days we had to go back to the doctor so he could check our blood. Each week, he told us that we still couldn't return to the fields.

We spent two or three months without working. At first, we were receiving workers' compensation. Then the insurance company sent us to one of their doctors who said that we were fine. He gave each of us a paper which we handed to the boss saying that we could go back to work. Then there was an argument between the doctor from the insurance company and the doctor at the clinic. The insurance company doctor sent us back to work, but the other doctor knew that we were still sick. He ordered us not to return to work, so I lost my job.

To this day I haven't gone back to that farm. The other crews are still working there, and the other crewleaders think we were just lazy and didn't want to work. I told them I wouldn't send my people back to the fields because the doctor said it wasn't safe. I wasn't about to send my people out to get sick and die just to be on the boss's side. There are some workers who still have attacks they say are caused by the poison. There are others who complain that they feel bad and get headaches when they work in the fields.

Before the incident, we knew that the growers were applying pesticides to the fields, but nothing serious had ever happened, so we didn't worry. We'd been affected by the chemicals before, but all that had happened was blurred vision and some swelling. Now all the workers are afraid. We've met with doctors and they've told us that every day you're in the field, you can absorb small amounts of poisons so that after many years the chemicals will build up and you can get really sick. Now the people are afraid because we've always worked where they sprayed pesticides.

When you're poisoned by pesticides, it makes you angry. You think, "Why didn't they tell me that they had just sprayed the field? Why did they put me out in the fields without letting me know about the pesticides? It was their responsibility. They're the ones who gave the orders to use the chemicals. If they knew about the danger, then why didn't they put up a warning sign?"

The grower didn't tell us they had just applied the pesticide. There was no sign, no paper telling us that it was dangerous to enter the field. Workers don't know when the pesticide's been sprayed. It's only the boss who knows.

We had some lawyers and the case went on for years. I don't know why it took so long, but five years later we got around two thousand dollars per person. After the lawyers took forty percent, that left each of us with around twelve hundred dollars.

Eventually the government did an investigation and fined the grower five thousand dollars.

Farmworkers remain the poorest of American workers. Enforcement officials, advocates, and workers generally agree that the situation of America's farm laborers has not improved over the last twenty years. The continued poverty and marginalization of farmworkers draws attention to the profound structural inequities that define our nation's farm labor system. The world of farmworkers reflects many aspects of contemporary American society—the social invisibility of production, the cultural and economic impact of immigration, and the widening gap between low- and high-wage workers. Despite various governmental and private initiatives, farmworkers continue to be members of America's dispossessed.

Maria "Cuca" Carmona ♦ *Pasadena, California*

Maria "Cuca" Carmona is a forthright woman who speaks her mind. She emigrated to the United States with her family when she was nineteen years old. She has worked in the fields all her life, and since the 1970s she has been involved with the United Farm Workers of America, having participated in several of the union's major strikes.

Carmona is one of the founders of the Farmworker Women's Leadership Project, a group of 200 farmworker women who run workshops, testify, lobby, and engage in a variety of organizing activities. In 1995, Carmona and several other women went to Beijing for the United Nations Fourth World Conference on Women.

Farmwork is hard. After working in the fields, you come home exhausted. As a woman, when you get home, you don't lay down and rest or turn on the television or drink a beer like the men do. You have to keep on working. When you get back home, you have to do all the housework—cleaning, sweeping, washing dishes, and cooking. Sometimes you have to keep on working until late at night. Then, you hardly have time to sleep before you have to wake up in the morning and do it all over again—making lunch for everyone, preparing things for the family, and going back to work. That's the experience that thousands of farmworker women live through every day.

In many ways, women are stronger than men. Whenever there are problems—sickness, family troubles—women stick it out longer. Women work to keep the family together. In a way, it's also easier for women to complain. There are lots of men who see injustice and just keep quiet. They think it's wrong to complain. My husband is like that. He's from Michoacán and the people there believe that a man shouldn't go around gossiping about his problems, "like some old lady." They believe that a man should tough it out, and that if he can't handle a job, then he should go and find a different one. Men don't want people to think they're a bunch of whiners. So, they don't say a word. They think complaining is something for women. That's one reason that there are very few men who go out and defend their rights.

A lot of times, the contractors and the *mayordomos* take advantage of women who work in the fields, especially single women, widows, and women without working papers. They tell them that if they don't have sex with them, they won't give them a job. Many women working in the fields are afraid. They're afraid to complain. They're worried that if they say anything, then they'll be fired. If they lost their job, then how would they support their children?

You see, the contractors don't care about you. They only care about making money. If I need a job, I have to go to the contractor's house to ask for work. If they want to give me a job, they will. If not, I won't work. The crewleaders don't like to hire people who know how to defend themselves. They prefer to hire someone who won't stand up for their rights, someone they can control, a worker who won't complain.

Many people try to impress the contractors. Even while they're deathly afraid of a contractor, they'll bring him presents and try to gain points with him. Some people will ask a contractor to be their *compadre* and let him baptize one of their children. They'll have a party, buy the contractor a bottle of tequila and a new hat. That way they bind the contractor to them and link themselves to the contractor. Having a contractor as your *compadre* gives a family some job security and helps the contractor have loyal workers.

I recently had a bad experience with a contractor while cutting grapes. The contractor started threatening us the moment we entered the fields, saying he'd fire us if we accidentally broke a branch or damaged the vine. Then he paid us only what he felt like paying us. He was cheating us on the hours.

When he gave me my check, I looked at it and asked him, "What's this?"

"Those are your wages."

"My wages? This is robbery."

"The problem is you don't work fast enough."

"What do you mean? I go home exhausted every day. I want to see my hours."

"Why?"

The man had changed all the hours. If you worked eight hours, he was only paying for six. So I brought a case against him with the labor commission. They forced the contractor to bring in his books. Then they made him pay me the money he owed me, the difference between what he paid me and what he should have paid me according to the minimum wage. I received sixty dollars. I was the only one in the crew to complain. All the other workers were afraid.

Another time, when I went out to the fields there was no water and the bathroom didn't work. When I go out to the fields to work, I'm not going to the beauty salon, but you need water to wash your hands before eating and a clean bathroom. So I told them I was going to make a complaint with the labor commission. The contractor told me no other woman had ever complained and that he'd never met anyone like me. I told the crewleader, "I'm a worker, not your slave." So he fired me.

Then the contractor spoke to the crew. He threatened them. He told them that if they wanted to keep working they'd have to tell the investigators that there were no problems and that everything was fine. You see, the contractors are afraid of the laws. They keep their crews under control. Farmworkers are afraid to complain because then word will get out to the other *mayordomos* not to hire you. So the workers just take it. When the investigators went out to the fields, the workers told them that they were happy and that everything was fine. When the labor commission returned from where the crew was working, they told me that they hadn't found any problems.

There's no future in farmwork. If you study a career, you can get ahead, moving up, from one position to another. In the fields, as you get older, it just gets harder. No one wants to hire you, so you have to suck up to the contractor, buy him little presents, or maybe try to become a *mayordomo*. I've been offered the opportunity to become a *mayordoma*, but I've always refused. If I was a *mayordoma* or a contractor, I'd have to oppress the workers just like the rest of them. You only become a contractor for the money. I've never met a good contractor. Not one.

Now, as farmworker women, we're educating ourselves. We're helping other farmworker women to know their rights. We have conferences where we teach women how to defend themselves, how to get legal assistance, how to sue. We analyze our situation and we've realized that what affects us most of all are the low wages. We're mothers and we need to earn enough so that we can provide for our families. We need the growers and contractors to pay us fairly. If I go out to work on a piece rate, I kill myself out there working and hardly earn enough to pay for a babysitter. We're educating ourselves and other women about our rights, so that we can fight for justice. We also have conferences on domestic violence, sexual harassment, pesticides, and AIDS.

I would like it if professional women would learn to appreciate the struggles of other women who are less fortunate. It doesn't matter what jobs women have or what circumstances they live in, they should all try to understand farmworkers' struggles. Women should unite to demand justice. Professional women should use their education to look after the well-being of women who have no voice, to help us defend ourselves because we don't always know our rights or know where to turn for help.

The situation for farmworkers is getting worse every day. The bosses are earning huge profits and the workers are left with nothing. They pay us the minimum wage while they're making millions. I wish that the bosses would understand that it's our labor that's made them rich and that each day the poor are getting poorer. What sort of future awaits us?

3. Growers
Somebody on Earth Has Got to Do This Job

TRAVELING THROUGH California's San Joaquin Valley, one is struck by the size, beauty, and sheer productive power of American agriculture. The Central Valley, as it is known, is the nation's most concentrated site of fresh fruit-and-vegetable production and stands as a symbol of the extraordinary magnitude and capacity of American agriculture. You can drive for hours along its interstate highways and narrow rural roads, looking out at the seemingly limitless expanse of fields and orchards. Acres of fruit trees line the road, their thin trunks passing by like repeating rows of fence posts; grape vines curl around trellises in enormous vineyards; parallel lines of lettuce merge to become a bright green mass at the horizon; blocks of citrus trees, their branches touching, appear as enormous hedges that continue on, mile after mile. Although the valley is flat, the road occasionally rises up above the plain and you can see that beyond the fields beside the road, there are more fields, and beyond those fields, still others.

For most of the year, the fields and orchards are largely empty of human presence. A tractor may pass, working the soil; a plane may fly overhead, applying chemicals; a small crew of laborers might be out pruning, weeding, or irrigating the land. It is only during the harvest that you see large numbers of workers in the fields, picking, climbing ladders, carrying buckets, filling bags, bins, and trays. Yet, even at the height of the harvest, when the fields and orchards are filled with laborers, the forms of workers moving through the fields are dwarfed by the enormity of the productive system that surrounds them. What one finds in the San Joaquin Valley is repeated on a smaller scale throughout the country in every region where fruits and vegetables are grown.

The productive capacity of our nation's agricultural industry is so great that for most of this century, the country has grappled with economic problems associated with food surplus rather than the more troubling concerns of shortage. American farmers produce 200 billion dollars' worth of agricultural products each year, over a quarter of which is exported throughout the world. Our country's agricultural industry offers an impressive variety of products at prices so low that Americans spend a smaller proportion of their income on food than consumers anywhere else in the world. Americans spend less than 9 percent of their income on food eaten at home, as compared to 14 percent in England, 20 percent in Japan, 50 percent in India, and still higher percentages throughout the developing world. The average American family spends only $400 per year on fresh fruits and vegetables, less than $10 per week.

Frank Banner ♦ *Southern Florida*

Frank Banner's father was a pioneer farmer. Banner remembers working alongside his father in the 1920s when mules were used to plow the sandy soil along Florida's west coast and workers earned $3 per day, laboring from sunrise to sunset. During the Second World War, Banner's father made a small fortune growing vegetables. Later, bad luck, mismanagement, and a drinking problem forced the Banners into bankruptcy, and the family lost their farm.

After graduating from high school, Banner thought seriously about leaving farming and moving out of the small rural town where he was born. He considered joining the U.S. Army or going on to college. One day, after passing his army physicals and receiving admission to the University of Florida, he attended an agricultural auction. On a whim, he spent his entire savings on used farm equipment. He rented some land, cleared it, and began growing vegetables. Over the years, Banner built his small vegetable farm into a multimillion-dollar company. The farm is still family owned and is run by Banner and his sons.

Banner is a large, soft-spoken man. Calm, measured, proud of his accomplishments, he speaks with a certain worldliness and cynicism. His office is attached to the farm's packinghouse and is filled with hunting memorabilia. Images of big game line the walls, and above his desk there is the stuffed head of a large bear, its teeth bared.

Back then, you had to live farming more than you do now. Farming was more skilled. You didn't have technology to help you. The only thing you could rely on was the fine-honed skills you'd developed over the years. You had to depend on your knowledge of the soil, plant diseases, weather patterns, and so on, your understanding of the trade winds, how deep to plant the seeds, the phases of the moon—information that was handed down to you, knowledge you picked up over time. You never want to set a plant out when there's a decrease in the moon. There's a full moon every twenty-eight days and a woman menstruates every twenty-eight days. There's a lot of things tied to these cycles.

It was backbreaking work. We used to load all our fertilizer by hand. First thing in the morning, you'd go out and load ten to twenty tons of fertilizer in hundred-pound sacks. Now we can do that with two little fingers. Technology has changed so much since then—hydraulic pumps, electrical machines, chemicals, and new varieties of seeds. Still, you got to have the feel of the soil and the earth. The knowledge and the feel of farming has got to be washed together with all this technology.

With all of these improvements, we've actually become too good at what we do. Back then, you'd open the land and get two to three hundred bushels an acre. Now, we get five hundred to two thousand bushels an acre. We're too productive. We overproduce and sell food cheap. That's the reason that such a small percentage of the population works in agriculture. We don't even market all of what we grow. When harvesttime ends, we've still got tons of vegetables and oranges left in the field. That food just goes rotten. There are people in New York hungry. People in Chicago hungry. It's hard. It's like we're throwing away our labor, discarding our time.

What drives me is being a productive man. I enjoy going out and planting seeds, crops, and trees; breeding cattle; producing food. To me, the most rewarding thing you can do in life is to produce food. The man that goes out and plants, cultivates, and harvests does more than anyone else. He's the one that goes out and gets it done. He's the one that spends the extra hours worrying about hailstorms, floods, droughts, and so on. The farmer.

People like me have a little more perspective on life. We know the value of a true quality job. These big corporate farms aren't like that. The owner doesn't have that kind of knowledge or feeling. He's separated from production by four or five tiers of management. Owner-operators like us are entirely different than the big corporate farms. We're hands-on owners. We get dirty every day. Right from the git-go, we've never asked people to do anything we've never done ourselves. Our workers don't have the franchise on hard work on this farm.

We're not coldhearted or unconcerned employers. The workers are part of farming, too. For us to survive, everybody has to take pride in what we do, including the employees. I see the workers as equals, as fellow human beings, no less. Although sometimes I think they're better off because they don't have the worries I have. I get aggravated when people curse out somebody for being a farmer. It's all blown out of proportion. There might be one bad apple in ten thousand. Well, the ratio's worse in the cities. The problem is we're a minority. Agriculture employs less than two percent of the population, so consequently we've got zero clout with the political people.

I remember what it was like before food stamps, government housing assistance, OSHA regulations, state and county regulations, the Farm Labor Contractors Act, all of it. Back in those days, you didn't worry about the health department coming around and checking the field toilets. You didn't worry about the Internal Revenue man looking over your books to see if you've been taking out Social Security. Back then, you paid people in cash. We didn't even have books. If you gave a man a check, he'd throw it back at you. Now, my time and my son's time is mostly spent dealing with regulations.

You see, these new rules and regulations have taken away people's rights. Now, a man can't take a job making less than the minimum wage, even if he wants to. After all, eighty percent of something is better than zero. His options have been reduced. Now, a schoolkid can't bag groceries after school or work in a packinghouse. What's wrong with that? It's better for a young person to work than be standing out on the street smoking pot. Well, we cured all that with the child labor law.

This is the 1990s. It's a different world. People now are ten notches above those 1930s' and 1940s' standards. We'll never go back to the times when the child labor law was enacted. We don't want to keep these restrictions on people forever and ever. You want to work? OK, get after it. You want to better your life? Go ahead, get after it. I don't believe that anybody should go hungry, but people shouldn't be given a free ride either. Now, we have generations after generations who are wards of the state. That's probably the main reason why we've got so many alien workers today. Foreigners are just a little hungrier. They don't have the government saying, "You don't have to work today because the government's going to give you a little check."

The people that come here are seeking to better themselves. Anything they can get their hands on is better than what they had back home. They're very conscious of the importance of a job. To talk with authority about this, you'd have to go down to Mexico, Central America, or Haiti to see where these people come from. If you were there, you'd be trying to get out, too. For them, it's either starving to death or coming over here and trying to get a job. They look at working entirely different than people who've been here for years and years. They come here wanting one thing and one thing only—to better their lives. They know what a job means to them.

You know, when I was a young man, I had to work. I bagged groceries. I mowed yards. I worked in the fields. But I didn't want to do that the rest of my life, so I'd go home and dream. Then I'd get up the next morning and try to initiate my dream. I was always a freethinker and a dreamer and that's what it's all about. The worst thing our society has done is to kill the freethinkers and the dreamers. Any kid, whether he's a Rockefeller, a Kennedy, or someone from a little town in south Florida, can go to sleep at night and dream of what he can do. Then, everything is all right. Then, it's still just great to be a migrant worker. There's nothing wrong with being a migrant worker as long as you have the spirit to dream, to think, and to make something of yourself. There's many migrants who over the years have brought their level up to second to none.

Society puts a stigma on agricultural workers. They stick this word *migrant* on them. It's unfair. They've degraded the word *migrant* so terrible bad. Nobody wants to be a migrant. Everybody considers him to be at the bottom of the barrel. When people hear the word *migrant* they think of a bunch of starving kids, or somebody standing there with a bullwhip making workers pick oranges or pick tomatoes. It's just not so.

After all, somebody on earth has got to do this job. Somebody.

When the United States was founded, 90 percent of all workers were involved in farming. While overall agricultural production has steadily increased over the years, farming has employed ever-smaller numbers of Americans. By the late nineteenth century, 40 percent of the American workforce labored on farms. Currently, only 2 percent of the nation's workers are on farms, producing more than enough agricultural products for hundreds of millions of Americans.

While few Americans have any direct dealings with agricultural production, farming has retained a special place in our national identity. From the words of patriotic songs to the imagery of political campaigns, American society holds farmers, particularly family farmers, in very high esteem. The popular vision of the farmer as independent, courageous, hardworking, and of strong moral character remains a powerful repository of our culture's values.

Each year, American farmers produce around 40 billion dollars' worth of fruits, vegetables, and horticultural products. It is this segment of the larger agricultural industry that hires the vast majority of seasonal farmworkers. For the last two decades, fruit, vegetable,

and horticultural production has expanded steadily. In the 1980s, sales more than doubled as a result of steady increases in domestic demand and a growing export market. While overall employment in U.S. agriculture continues to diminish, the need for farmworkers has increased.

There are many types of fruit and vegetable farms, from small operations of several acres set beside a family's home to giant agribusiness interests growing dozens of products on thousands of acres spread over several states. Fruits and vegetables are produced by grower cooperatives, family-run corporations, privately held investment farms, and publicly traded companies. Some farms are highly diversified, producing a variety of fruits and vegetables, while other operations rely on a single crop. Some farmers hire a handful of workers who labor for a few weeks, while others manage complex operations involving thousands of laborers, many of whom work year-round.

To stay in business, small farms are increasingly involved in growing fruits and vegetables on contract for large packing and canning companies or producing specialty items with small markets and high returns. Large farms are increasingly international operations or subsidiaries of agribusiness corporations that grow fruits and vegetables in different countries and sell brand-name produce.

Karen Dawson ♦ *Hartford, Michigan*
Karen Dawson lives in a comfortable home off a rural road facing a large field. Dawson and her husband, Steve, farm about 1,000 acres, combining machine-harvested grains—corn and soybeans—with hand-harvested crops, especially pickle cucumbers.

Currently, most of the farmworkers in Michigan are either Mexican immigrants or Latino families who travel north each year from Texas. There are migrant education, health, and legal services programs in the area.

We sit in a large living room, spacious and cool, beside a window that looks out across a green lawn to the road. There are family photos on the table, and Dawson's ninety-one-year-old mother sits off to one side, occasionally entering the conversation.

When I married Steve in 1966, everything on the farm was hand harvested. Everything. We started out with asparagus. We went to strawberries. Then we did black raspberries, tart cherries, blueberries, pickles, and tomatoes. It was totally labor-intensive.

In the 1960s, we had about two hundred workers split between a crew of Hispanics who lived on our labor camp and a crew of southern white itinerant workers who came into the area. We were always careful that everything was written out in both Spanish and English and that everyone knew the rules. We paid the workers directly, so we never had any horrible crewleader stories.

Over time, we changed the operation. We couldn't keep up with the regulations for hiring and housing that many people. Over the last thirty years, we've seen this one little economic unit go from a totally hand-harvested farm to a very limited hand-harvested farm. Now there's less people and more machines. The more you can take people out of the picture, the more efficient you become.

About twelve years ago, we began working with just one family, the Avilas. They usually come about the first of April and stay with us here on the farm until the end of October, when they go back to their home in Texas. They're a family that has always worked together. The mother and father are our age and they've been married the same number of years. They're just like us except they have more children.

The Avilas have rural values. That's not typical of American culture. Rural values means that you're concerned with the well-being of your family above anything else. Rural values has your elderly mother here in your house with you. It doesn't have her somewhere else. The Avilas' main concern is their family, and it shows in their children. Mr. Avila is the head of the family. Even his oldest son, Gustavo, who is extremely capable, always defers to his father. Gustavo talks about his father with a great deal of affection and respect. He's the oldest son and he fully expects to take care of his father and mother. He sees that as his responsibility. In American culture you don't generally find that kind of family unity. Maybe that's why we get along so well with the Avilas.

Gustavo is Steve's right-hand man. He plants, irrigates, and helps us with everything. Gustavo and Steve are very close. Steve taught Gustavo how to speak English. Since we don't have any sons, Gustavo would be the closest thing Steve has to a son. They have a very respectful relationship. They work together and look out for each other's best interests. I don't think that's typical of what goes on in the world today. Quite frankly, I don't know what we'd do without the Avilas. They know how we do things and we know how they do things. Basically, the Avilas work our pickles. We wouldn't even put pickles in the ground if the Avilas weren't here. We split the pickle contract right down the middle with them.

In southwestern Michigan, we have two migrant populations. We have the migrant population who comes here to work in the fields, and we have the migrant population who comes out of the city to enjoy the country. The farmers here know that we need workers in our area, but the tourists don't necessarily understand this. The community at large likes to look at farmers as landscapers who make everything pretty for them—our lush fields, our flowering trees, our bountiful crops. It's lovely for them to go out and take rides in the countryside, to feel like they're part of the country. Still, they don't want to see labor camps. They don't want to see us dirty. Most of those people don't sweat for a living.

If I hear anybody express anything about farming and farmworkers, it's that they feel guilty about us having to work out here in these fields. We get dirty. We sweat. We bend over. We work from sunup until sundown and the work we do isn't glamorous. It's hard, physical work. It seems that our country doesn't respect manual labor anymore. People look down on a man that works with his hands. They feel guilty our country still needs people who do physical labor.

It used to be that when you farmed, you knew the farmers. On this farm, Steve makes the decisions. If something is going on here that you don't like, you call Steve. Now, we have what I call "investment farms," where people totally outside of agriculture invest their money in a farm and then hire managers. These manager-run investment farms started in the seventies when family-held farms went bankrupt. The farms on both sides of us were bought out by investment firms owned by a holding company. Who put that together? Who's in charge?

Have you ever noticed how big businesses are never responsible for anything? Whether it's runoff into the water or pesticide drift, big businesses just write things off. We had a big company near here that completely ruined part of the water system. They finally moved out of town, but they left us with a big mess. So, who's responsible? It bothers me when I don't know who to get in touch with if I don't like what's going on at the adjoining farm. If I have a problem, who am I going to call? Now, they're all hired men, and hired men don't make decisions. If this trend continues, pretty soon, no one will know who's in charge. Maybe there won't even be anyone in charge.

I believe in entrepreneurs, family farmers who come up from the grass roots rather than investors who come down from multinationals and big banks. I don't like this trend of investment farms because it breaks down the fabric of the rural community. We're losing our community. Now, we have people running up and down the road that we don't know.

Family farms have always been passed on to sons or daughters. Farm-work is for young people. It's physical in nature and that's the way it's always been. As the Avila family ages, and as we age, there may not be a younger generation coming up. I don't encourage either of my daughters to go into farming. There's easier ways to make a living. I just don't think that family farms are going to be around much longer.

Throughout this century, particularly over the last thirty years, our nation's agricultural production has become increasingly concentrated in the hands of an ever-smaller number of growers. In general, family farms are being replaced by corporate farms, often owned by companies with diverse nonagricultural holdings. While there are currently 1.9 million farms in the United States, the majority are so small that they do not support their owners. Half of the nation's farms produce less than 10,000 dollars' worth of agricultural products each year. In order to make ends meet, more than half of America's farmers work outside of agriculture for at least part of the year.

The largest 1.5 percent of the nation's farms produce 38 percent of the country's agricultural products, while the smallest two-thirds produce only 5 percent. The concentration of production in the hands of large growers is especially pronounced in the fruit-and-vegetable industry, with almost 75 percent of the nation's vegetables produced by 6 percent of the farms and nearly 80 percent of all fruit produced by only 10 percent of the country's growers. Rising costs, increased competition, and basic shifts in the business of producing food have forced fruit and vegetable growers to enlarge, often increasing production substantially, in order to stay in business.

Fewer farms has not meant a reduction in farm acreage or diminished production. In fact, the reverse is true. Over the last several decades, production has steadily increased as farming has become more efficient and technologically sophisticated. New farming techniques have made it possible for an ever-smaller number of workers to produce large quantities of agricultural products. In 1965, each person employed in agriculture produced enough farm products for thirty-seven consumers; by 1975, each agricultural worker produced enough for fifty-eight consumers; and by 1989, each worker produced enough for ninety-eight consumers.

George Fisher ♦ *Southern Florida*
George Fisher is the president of the agribusiness group of a large corporation. He oversees three nurseries, a livestock operation with

5,000 head of cattle, three vegetable packinghouses, 6,000 acres of citrus, 2,000 acres of vegetables, and 20,000 acres of leased land.

Fisher grew up in Florida, served in the U.S. military, and then returned home to go to college and, later, graduate school. He spent most of his professional life as an international business consultant, working in South America, the Caribbean, Africa, Asia, and the Middle East. He accepted his current position after an executive-search firm contacted him about twelve years ago.

Agriculture is about as close as we come to "pure competition" in any segment of our economy. That means that any individual action that you make will have very little effect in terms of purchasing or selling. Farmers are as much the victims of external factors as farmworkers. The prices we receive for our crops have very little to do with what we spend to produce those crops. If there's a shortage, we have market power. If there's a glut, we have market weakness. Last year, prices in tomatoes fluctuated between two dollars a box and thirty dollars a box. It didn't matter that it was costing us between six and seven dollars to produce, pack, and ship each box. It's simple supply and demand.

Farmers feel hurt when they're portrayed as the bad guys. I'd like it if farmers and farmworkers could realize that we're both better off working together. Basically, our position—and I think that most farmers feel this way—is that if an individual works for us, we hope he'll have a decent standard of living, decent housing, adequate food to eat, basic health care, and so forth. It's our intent to address these issues in a variety of ways as long as we can continue to survive economically. Our company will only stay in agriculture as long as we're making a reasonable return. If we can't make a profit, we'll sell out, close down, and put our assets somewhere else.

Many doctors here criticize agriculture, saying that they have to provide emergency care for our workers because we don't provide health benefits. The other day, I was talking to one of my doctor friends who was getting on me about this. I asked him if he had a maid. He said yes. Then I asked him whether or not he had health insurance or a retirement program for his maid. He told me that he didn't because she only works for him two days a week. Then I told him, "Now you understand what we're facing out there." You see, some of our workers are only with us for a day or two. Others will work for a week or a month. Some will work, go away, and a month later they'll come back. We have between eight hundred and a thousand farmworker jobs, but we prepare four to five thousand W-2s at the end of the year. This means that on average we have five people for every farmworker job. How do you administer that? With this type of situation, just providing W-2 forms is a nightmare. What would it be like if we also had to keep records for a health care or retirement program? Our administration costs are six times what they would be for a more stable workforce. It's not that there aren't solutions, it's just that the solutions are difficult for a single company until they get to a certain size. We're moving in that direction in terms of size, but we're not quite there yet. Now, I think if we could work with a half dozen other firms, we might be able to put something together.

For some reason, agriculture seems to be the most visible industry regarding the general public's expectations of what employers should do for their employees. If you went over to the construction industry, you'd probably find that subcontractors there don't have retirement or health programs for their workers. They don't provide housing. They're struggling to cover their workers' compensation costs. Look at the food-service industry. What's their average wage? Probably not a lot different than ours. Look at the hotel industry, or the tourism industry. They employ somebody for six months out of the year and then fire him. They're not lambasted for paying low wages or laying people off every six months.

Farmers are like most businessmen. If enough people walk through the door to cover the number of employees needed to do the job, they're not going to develop affordable housing, provide health benefits, and so forth. Change comes because of economic necessity. Most farmers, like most businessmen, will only do more when workers don't show up.

A lot of the abuses that take place now involve the crewleaders and not the farmers. Very often what happens is that the farmer pays the crewleader the correct wages, but instead of paying the workers correctly and making the appropriate wage deductions, the crewleader pockets the money. Then the farmer is criticized. When I first came here ten years ago, we were still paying crewleaders in cash to pay the workers. Today, we pay each farmworker directly with a check.

In the past, abuses may have come from the owners, but I don't think that's the case today. My sense is that ninety percent of agricultural production is properly handled now. Today the question is not, Are you doing anything illegal? but, Should you be doing more for the workers? Should you be providing health care? A retirement program? Paid holidays? Better housing? Those things are not required, but should we be providing them?

The public feels that farmers should be doing more than we're doing. They say that we ought to pay farmworkers more. If you can show me how to make a reasonable return on my investment—given the inherent risks,

the freezes, the volatility, everything else—so that I can take somebody that I only employ four months a year and pay them for twelve months or so that I can pay seventy cents a bucket instead of thirty cents a bucket, I will do it. I am sincere about this.

I've gone through our numbers, and basically if we increase our wages, or any of our costs, by thirty percent, we eliminate our profits. So, if we raised the average wage from five dollars per hour to six fifty, we'd eliminate our profits. If we provided housing, health care, retirement benefits, or any combination thereof that increased our costs by more than thirty percent, we'd eliminate our profits. Once you eliminate your profits, there's no reason to stay in business. So we have to find ways to be more profitable or have greater labor efficiency if we're going to raise wages or increase benefits.

Today farmers are far more conscious and more legally inclined. Farmers are grappling with local, state, and federal governments who expect them to do more with less. There seems to be no one in government who's saying, "OK, we have these admirable objectives and these economic realities—how do we fit it all together?" What government seems to do is focus on the admirable objectives and then pass them on to us. Somehow they feel that we'll be able to survive, that we'll have the skill or the wherewithal to modify our businesses. In some cases, we will survive; in other cases, we won't. Some businesses in this country are already gone. Look at the industries that we've lost offshore. Maybe this will be one of them.

Unlike most commodities, fresh fruits and vegetables are highly perishable; their production is seasonal and dependent upon a variety of unpredictable factors, such as weather conditions. While farmers try to control growing conditions through soil treatment, irrigation, and the use of pesticides and other chemicals, each season's harvest varies in quantity and quality. Fresh fruits and vegetables need to be picked, packed, sold, and shipped within a limited time period and supply shifts constantly as harvests are brought in from around the country and imported from abroad. The prices growers receive for particular products rise and fall, sometimes substantially, throughout the season.

Often the key to making a profit involves harvesting during a production window, a short period of time either before or after the main harvest season, when the supply of a particular fruit or vegetable is limited. When the supply of a particular product is suddenly reduced by a freeze, drought, or excessive rains in one region of the country, growers in a competitive region often earn enormous profits. Similarly, a highly productive growing season in one or several regions can create an oversupply that drastically reduces prices, which, at times, fall below growers' production costs.

During the harvest season, growers are especially vulnerable to labor shortages and worker unrest. Each crop represents a large investment of labor and resources, which can be rendered completely valueless if it is not harvested in the right way at the right time. The success or failure of most fruit and vegetable operations rests upon the availability of harvest workers. Consequently, the agricultural industry, like any industry with difficult short-term labor needs, has two options—either create incentives to ensure that workers will accept difficult, temporary jobs, or find workers who have few, if any, other options. Historically, the industry has relied upon the second strategy, utilizing impoverished and vulnerable laborers who have been drawn to agriculture out of great necessity. American agricultural interests have consistently worked to reduce the risk of labor shortages by creating an oversupply of workers and supporting a farm labor system that discourages workers from organizing and suppresses labor unrest.

John Wagner ♦ *Southern Florida*

John Wagner has run a pepper farm for the past thirty-five years. He was born outside of Chicago and first became involved in agriculture when he managed a high school farm. He later studied agronomy and then moved to Florida where he sold fertilizers and chemicals, worked for a vegetable farmer who went broke, herded cows for a dairy farmer who also went broke, and later started his own farm.

Wagner and his wife began farming 5 acres. They now work 500 acres and continue to live in a house on the farm. Wagner employs about 100 workers. Unlike the majority of the growers in the area, his workers are employed year-round and live in housing located on the farm property not far from the Wagners' home. Wagner stands out among area employers, paying hourly workers in excess of the minimum wage, providing annual vacation pay, and covering his crew's medical expenses.

When we first started farming, there were still a lot of local blacks working in agriculture. The farm that we live on was a bean farm and the only building here was a large fertilizer shed open on two sides. They used to put a hundred and fifty bean pickers in there. The workers had to sleep on the floor. They had no toilets, no showers, and no electricity. The water came from a pitcher pump at the end of the shed. The workers would live there all winter and pick beans. That was not unusual when we came here in the 1950s. It was close to slave labor.

When we stated farming, people wanted to be paid every day. There was no weekly payroll. At the end of the day, the workers just lined up and got a five-dollar bill. By the next morning, they'd have spent it all on food or wine. The workers lived on rice, Vienna sausages, and wine that they bought in little country stores. Back then, workers couldn't save money, and if they tried, someone on the crew would take it from them. Looking back, you'd have to say that the situation has improved.

Although attitudes towards farmworkers have improved, the typical grower still views the workers with disdain. Relations are adversarial. They always have been. It's like a contest between the farmer and the laborer. Farmers are always looking at the bottom line and try to use as few workers as they can get away with. The only way that a grower can make money now—even at the present rates of pay, which are barely adequate—is to use workers very efficiently.

All the big farms place crewleaders between themselves and the workers. Each morning the crewleaders bring people to the farm, and when they leave, the farmer doesn't care where they go. They're just not concerned. I don't necessarily blame the farmers. I don't know of any industry that provides housing or looks into the family welfare of its workers. So farmers really aren't doing anything that isn't common in the rest of the economy.

Our operation is a little different. We don't use crewleaders. We've never used crewleaders. All our people work directly for the farm and most of them live on the farm. I know all their names.

We actually run a two-tiered operation. We have two crews: our crew, which earns considerably more than minimum wage and receives housing and benefits, and a crew in which we have a forty percent partnership. Our partners don't feel like we do at all. They've got about seventy people in their crew. Their workers get paid minimum wage and drive two hundred miles each day to and from work.

I always compare the unit costs between the two crews. Our unit costs are almost always better than the other crew, and they're doing exactly what we're doing. Our crew is definitely not made up of exceptional workers. Over the years we've had more women than men. Other operations don't generally hire women. We have some older women that are absolutely amazing, fifty-five-, sixty-year-old women out picking peppers eight hours a day. They're still more productive than our minimum-wage crew.

Over the years, we've tried to maintain a very low profile on this. For one thing, it doesn't help to be the only farm in this area to have a different pay scale. The only reason we've gotten away with it is that we're so much smaller than everybody else that we don't impact the overall labor supply. Also, since our help is steady, we're not hiring people away from other farmers. Any day we want, we could double our workforce. Most of the working people know our farm and we have no trouble getting help. It's kind of heartbreaking when we have to turn down people who are looking for work.

We've always hoped that the workers would manage their money optimally, but very few of them have. They manage to lose the money they make, which is little enough, in incredible ways—everything from playing the lottery to excessive drinking to a lot of other things that we really don't approve of. It's hard to watch them squander money on things that are no good for them, especially when they have such obvious needs, and we're trying to give them more money.

It's actually been a mixed bag trying to pay these people more. There's a definite limit to their ability to manage money. After thirty-five years, you get the feeling that they can't be given too much money. It just doesn't do them any good. There's some people that are very hard to mainstream in our society. This year, we gave out seventy thousand dollars' worth of vacation pay. That was totally optional. When I see what happens to the money, I think maybe I should have just kept it on the farm. Still, I try not to get discouraged. I know I'm not going to change the world.

There's very little cohesiveness in the crew. They're jealous of one another. Often the workers don't even speak to each other. In general, I have to be an intermediary between people. After thirty years, there's only one person working for us who knows the real names of everybody on the farm. They call their own neighbors by nicknames. Even the families don't want to have anything to do with one another. We'd always hoped that there would be a kind of union movement that would pull them together, but they don't want to know about each other. They just don't care.

We provide free housing for all salaried people and rental housing for everyone else at well-below cost. In a sense, the farm would be much better off if instead of having the quarters, we just paid them a dollar an hour more. A dollar an hour more would be forty dollars a week more per worker, and then we could just send them into town. We could do that to-morrow and even they'd be happy with it. If we held a vote, they'd all take a dollar an hour more, even though they're paying half what it would cost to rent their own place. They really don't understand the benefits they receive other than their wages. If it isn't in their paycheck, they just don't get it.

Our partner tells us that we're crazy to have a camp. We open our-selves up to castigation from the media and sometimes OSHA comes in with ridiculous fines. There's really no reason why any grower would want to house their labor. In our case, we've just done it for so many years. I think at this point if we had to close the camp, we'd just close the farm. I feel that the people are better off living here than in town. They're safer here. In town, they live twenty people to a house. Nobody inspects the housing. It's not regulated. Also, the housing we provide is probably better than anything they could find in town. They're better off on the farm so we've kept the housing.

When we started farming, it was just me and three Puerto Ricans. I knew right away that farmwork was not for me. The workers were better at picking, hoeing, and everything else. I knew I couldn't make a living doing the field work myself and it was clear I couldn't raise four kids and send them off to college working in the fields. We've depended on these people over the years, so our policies have actually been a kind of en-lightened self-interest. The workers have made our life what it is.

I feel a sense of gratitude. We've had a very good life. We feel very privileged at this point in life to be where we are and to have the crew we have. We just hope that there's some way we can better the lives of our crew. I certainly don't think we've given the workers anything they're not entitled to.

Agriculture has long been one of the most regulated and protected industries in the United States. Most government farm programs were developed in the 1930s, often with the intention, although not always the result, of protecting small family farmers. Growers receive billions of dollars each year in direct subsidy payments as well as benefiting from government-funded agricultural research, special tax laws, and subsidized irrigation projects. Still, with the exception of tobacco and sugar producers, direct farm-subsidy programs rarely benefit those growers who hire large numbers of seasonal workers. In fact, fruit and vegetable growers receive a smaller portion of their gross income from direct government payments than any other

American farmers. In general, the growers who hire seasonal workers operate within the least protected and most competitive element of American agriculture.

Nevertheless, the agricultural industries that employ farmworkers wield enormous power on the local, state, and national level. There are fruit and vegetable growers in nearly every congressional district, and there are countless growers' associations and organizations that fund campaigns and lobby politicians. Although the interests of growers may not coincide on many political issues, the grower community is unified in their goal of keeping labor costs low. Growers' organizations have consistently fought legislation designed to raise workers' wages, improve safety regulations, provide field sanitation, regulate pesticides and herbicides, and provide protections for farmworker organizing.

Harry Kubo ♦ *Fresno, California*
Until his recent retirement, Harry Kubo was the president and one of the founding members of the Nisei Farmers League, an association of small and medium-sized growers based in California's San Joaquin Valley. The Nisei Farmers League was formed in 1970 by a group of Japanese American farmers who banded together to respond to the United Farm Workers' efforts to organize their laborers. Today, the Nisei Farmers League represents about 1,000 family farms, some of which are still run by Japanese Americans.

My father came from Japan in 1906, when he was fifteen years old. He was the youngest of the boys, and in Japan the younger children emigrated because older sons inherited the property and continued the family business. In coming to the United States, my father had visions of grandeur. He thought that he would become rich overnight and then go back home to Japan.

My father had a minimal education and spoke no English. He worked as an itinerant farmworker, traveling from place to place, harvesting fruits and vegetables. The only possession he carried around with him was a blanket. My father returned to Japan to marry my mother. She came to California in 1920. Back then, it took three weeks by boat to get here. Two days after she arrived, she was out in the fields picking prunes.

When I was still real small, my father decided to settle down. He began working as a sharecropper. He would have liked to own a piece of property, but it was illegal for him to do so because of the Alien Lands Act, which wasn't repealed until the 1950s.

My earliest memories of working on the farm are from the early thirties during the Great Depression. Our family worked together to survive the depression years. We had no running water or sanitation facilities. There was no welfare program. There were no food stamps. You got nothing for doing nothing. Living under those conditions made us all a little more appreciative of what we have today. Farmwork molded what we do—how we think, how we live, and how we've raised our families. We learned to appreciate each other. We learned work ethics and family values.

As sharecroppers, we farmed forty acres of peaches, plums, nectarines, and pears. My father really loved farming. He loved to plant, to watch things grow, and to harvest the fruits he worked so hard to cultivate. We provided all the labor and all the expenses during the winter and spring. During the summer months, my father would hire Japanese, Filipino, or Indian workers to help us with the harvest. We fed and housed the workers. My father would sell the crop. We received sixty percent of the gross and forty percent went to the landowner.

I started school when I was five years old. I remember going to school the first day and not knowing what everyone was saying because I couldn't speak English. We only spoke Japanese at home. It was amazing because in two weeks I was able to start talking, and in a month I was just like the rest of the kids. My father had a strict rule: We spoke Japanese at home and English outside of the home. Even with our Japanese friends, we were supposed to speak English.

Discrimination against Japanese was rampant. It was a daily ritual to be called a Jap in school. There were parts of the school campus that were off-limits to Japanese Americans. A Japanese student couldn't run for any student body office. A Japanese American boy couldn't fraternize with a Caucasian girl or vice versa. I can remember going to a restaurant with a Caucasian friend and sitting there for a long time not being waited on. When my friend asked the waitress why we weren't being served, she said, "Well, you get that Jap out of here and we'll wait on you." That's just the way it was.

I graduated from high school in 1940 with the hope of going to college. I worked for a year in the fields and started college in September of 1941. Before my first year was up, the executive order came to evacuate. On May 12, 1942, our family was moved to an internment camp. I was nineteen. I was born in the United States, but I was categorized as an enemy alien. That really disturbed me. I wasn't born in Japan. The United States is my country.

I don't think any other nationality would have been able to cope with what happened to us. In the camps, we became a community. There were eighteen thousand people in our camp. We never rioted. Instead, we did things. We were self-contained. We had our own doctors, cooks, and teachers. We did all the work that needed to be done to maintain and sustain a community. For three and a half years, we lived in the internment camp.

In 1946, we left the camp. We had no money and so we went to work in the fields. We were happy just to have jobs and a place to live. My father was in his element again, farming. Our family set a goal of buying a piece of property. We earned seventy-five cents an hour. We never took a vacation. We never went out to dinner. In less than four years our family—my father, my mother, myself, a sister, and a brother—saved fifteen thousand dollars. We put thirteen thousand five hundred dollars down on forty acres of land. Since I was a citizen, I was able to buy the land. That's how we started our farm. We were fortunate. In 1950, we had one of our best years and we were able to pay off the balance on the farm and later buy an additional sixty acres. Today, we own the same hundred acres.

Despite what people say, there *is* a future in farmwork. You just have to set your mind on a goal. Anything that's sacred, you have to earn it. It can be done, believe me. The only problem with farmworkers is their inability to say to themselves, "I have a goal." Like we did. At seventy-five cents an hour, we saved fifteen thousand dollars.

When I was on the school board in Parlier, I addressed a group of junior high school students. After I spoke, they said, "Mr. Kubo, you're lucky. You have everything. In my house, my father and mother don't speak English. I don't even have a desk. We're discriminated against. We're not given opportunities. You're lucky."

You know what I said to them? "You're describing my life. We never had desks. We studied on the dinner table. We never had chairs. We sat on fruit boxes. My father and mother spoke no English, and we were discriminated against."

Two years in a row, I told this group of junior high school kids, "You have a golden opportunity. You need to understand that in the journey to success, you have to sacrifice. You can't be fooling around. You've got to prioritize your time. You've got to study." I tell my workers, "Your kids shouldn't be farmworkers. They should go on to school. They should become teachers or doctors."

I always talk about the lotus blossom. The lotus blossom is a beautiful flower in a pond, and it blooms out of muddy waters. That's also true with human beings. You might come from a dirt-poor environment, but you can rise above that. You've got to have a goal. You've got to have ambition. How do you teach ambition? That's your family values. It's got to be instilled in you when you're young, during your formative years. So don't ever think that farmworkers are being deprived. As a matter of fact, if I could start my life over again, I wouldn't mind being a farmworker at all.

The agricultural industry is complex and multilayered, employing ten times more workers in food processing, distribution, and sales than in actual production. After a product is grown and harvested, it has to be sent to a packinghouse to be sorted by size and quality and placed in boxes to be shipped to buyers. Federal regulations provide guidelines for the size and quality of different types of fruits and vegetables. Misshapen, undersized, or ugly produce is thrown away or used in processed food.

Individual growers often have their own packinghouses or use a packinghouse run by a growers' association or cooperative. In some cases, the packinghouse and shipping facilities represent a separate business. After the produce is sorted and boxed, it is sold to a produce buyer. Some buyers work directly for large chain stores, while others are middlemen who resell what they purchase to stores or other buyers. Fruits and vegetables are then shipped to the buyer, generally by truck or train, although international shipments are made by boat or airplane. Produce is treated in a variety of ways— iced, gassed, waxed, supercooled—to increase storage time and preserve freshness. The process by which a piece of fresh fruit or a vegetable gets from the farm to a consumer often involves a long line of intermediaries.

On average, growers earn about a third of the price that consumers pay for fruits and vegetables in the store, although this percentage varies widely depending on the product. Over the past decade, the percentage of the store price that growers receive has fallen, while store owners, shippers, brokers, and other middlemen take an ever-larger cut. In an effort to gain more control over the sale of their produce and to retain a greater percentage of profits, many larger growers have become vertically integrated, combining growing with packing and shipping in a single business. These grower/packer/shippers often market produce under their own brand names and sell directly to stores and brokers. The increased concentration of production and the control of the fresh-fruit-and-vegetable industry by a few large concerns has made it even more difficult for small and midsize farmers to compete with larger operations.

In recent years, the cost of machinery, chemicals, seed, and equipment has increased, while intense domestic and foreign production has kept the prices of fresh fruits and vegetables low. At the same time, the supply of farm laborers, particularly recent immigrants from Mexico, has steadily increased. A competitive market and labor oversupply have encouraged growers to pay low wages and offer few, if any, benefits. Over the last twenty years, farmworkers' real wages have dropped steadily.

Israel Baez ◆ *Belle Glade, Florida*

In 1963, Israel Baez's family left Cuba with sixty others, setting out in a small boat with the hope of arriving in the United States. A cargo ship found the boat and carried the passengers to Texas. Baez's family then migrated to southern Florida where his father found work as a mechanic at one of the large sugar companies. Since then, Baez has lived and worked in Belle Glade, Florida.

Until recently, Baez was the manager of employee relations for A. Duda & Sons, a large family-owned farm, which began operation in the 1920s. At peak employment, A. Duda & Sons employs 3,000 seasonal workers in vegetable fields and citrus groves throughout Florida and Texas. Like many growers in southern Florida, A. Duda traditionally depended upon local African American workers, many of whom worked for some of the roughest contractors in the nation. In the 1960s, the company began to hire workers directly and has gradually provided them with a number of benefits.

A. Duda is a family-owned operation. They are very religious minded. Since the mid-1960s, A. Duda has made a positive move toward improving the conditions for agriculture laborers. In addition to workers' wages, we provide employee benefits. Benefits have gone from a simple hospitalization plan to major medical with life insurance, retirement, paid holidays, and paid vacations. Every year something new is added to the benefit plan. We also have day-care services and a Migrant Head Start program. Nothing is withheld from the workers' checks to pay for these benefits.

Housing is probably the number one benefit we provide. A. Duda provides fine housing to out-of-state seasonal workers. Here in Belle Glade, we house close to fifty percent of our seasonal workforce. We have about a hundred trailers here and we have additional housing for up to seventy single workers. The housing is supplied to our workers at a minimal cost, about thirty-three dollars a week for families and eight dollars a week for singles. It's not really rent. It's more of a service charge. Housing is not easy to manage. It's what I call another gray hair on our heads. Tell me how many industries in this country besides the army supply housing? Some of my supervisors have been in the army and they say that our housing is a lot better than what they lived in. Still, in the long run, providing housing is very rewarding. It's rewarding to the workers because they have adequate housing, and it's rewarding to the company because we get a dependable workforce.

A. Duda used to hire contractors. Now, with the exception of one crew that harvests a six-week corn crop, all of our workers are A. Duda employees. We're big enough to manage our own workforce. Realistically, it would probably be cheaper for us to go with a contractor, but the company feels that in-house crews are better managed. I think we have a more loyal, dependable workforce now because they work directly for us. If they've got a problem, they come straight to the company.

The contractor system is still the cause of a lot of problems in the industry. To be quite up front, there are some contractors out there who are not businesspeople. Those are the ones that give the rest of the contractors a bad name. Still, crewleaders remain a necessity. You've got to remember that the majority of growers are small farmers. For example, let's say you're a small farmer growing strawberries. That's a very short crop, somewhere around six weeks. It's impossible for a grower that might have twenty or thirty acres of strawberries to put in a labor camp, provide a benefit package, hire a personnel manager—to have a lot of things that we have—for a six-week period. There ain't no way in heaven they can do that. It's too costly. So your crewleader is still needed.

In general, we have a very long season with vegetables and citrus. Workers start coming this way around October and go back home around the last week of June. So, there's only a small window when they're not going to have employment. When the season ends, a lot of people go back to Texas and Mexico and draw unemployment.

Over the years, we have developed such a good relationship with our employees that our turnover is minimal when you compare us to other agricultural employers. Turnover varies depending on families or singles. We have approximately ninety-five percent return into our trailers in Belle Glade. We have a bit of a higher turnover on our singles workforce because they have no roots. In the citrus we have a lot of single young Hispanics or blacks. If we have a good citrus crop and the workers are making good money, they'll stay with you. If you have a bad crop for a week or so, they'll leave you and go down the road to work for whoever has the better crop.

One thing that helps us reduce turnover is that we stay in communication with our employees. Every year we meet with the workforce, everyone from seasonal employees to full-time clerks. We break them into groups. We send out surveys. We see if they have questions for the management team. We hold meetings. We remind them of their benefits. We try to get them to tell us of any problems they might have had. It's quite interesting the questions they ask: Is the company making money? Will there be a bonus this year? Will there be a pay increase? We encourage communication both ways, management to employees and employees to management. It's not unusual to see the general manager walking through a packing plant and talking to a celery stripper or a packer.

We've spent a lot of time and a lot of money on training, from foremen to upper management. Labor management training. Labor relations. We bring in a consultant every other year to do attitude surveys all the way across the company from the seasonal employees all the way up to management. We learn a lot from the surveys. We see what our weak areas are. We have preharvest meetings for all the supervisors and foremen. We go over the regulations. We go through communication training, how to deal with people problems, how important it is to follow up on Joe if he hasn't shown up to work in two or three days. We tell them, "Treat them like you want to be treated." When you're off sick, we make a point to call and see what's wrong with you. If you're in the hospital, we make it a point to go and see you. If a person gets hurt or killed on the job, we roll out the red carpet.

You know, A. Duda is not the only company that's doing good things in agriculture. Every year you've got lots of companies that are doing more for their workers. Overall, the agricultural industry has taken a step forward, but it still needs to improve. My belief is that the people making the positive moves are going to stay in business. You can't operate in the nineties like you did in the sixties. If you do, sooner or later, you're going to get busted, and when you get busted, you're going to have problems.

Most people look at farmers as the bad guys: We're slavedrivers. We work people for below minimum wage. We overcharge them for goods. We're terrible. That's the message that America hears just because a small group of people—who may not know any better—might not be doing the right thing. You have companies that are doing lots of positive things, but they get attacked because they're big. If we have a small accident and unfortunately one or two people get killed while we're transporting them to work, I guarantee you, we'll make the front page of the paper. Agriculture gets picked on.

Agriculture needs to get together as a big team and start sending positive messages to the people of this country. We need to educate people, to help them understand where the tomato they get comes from and what's done to get it produced. Our message to the public is, "Stop and ask questions." If you see a farm that you want to visit, stop and see if you can go in. That way you'll understand a little more. Agriculture is just like any other industry.

For most growers, farm labor is an extremely touchy subject. Farmers are generally upset at the media's portrayal of the agricultural industry as unconcerned, uncaring, and even brutal employers. Growers feel frustrated, misunderstood, and picked on. They complain that no one wants to hear their side of the story, and claim that media exposés often blame the entire industry for the actions of a handful of bad employers.

Growers often say that the conditions that make farmworkers' lives so difficult are largely beyond their control. They claim that farm labor contractors are generally responsible for the worst abuses and that workers' low annual incomes are more a function of temporary, seasonal employment than improper treatment. To some degree, the growers are right. The temporary, seasonal nature of farm labor is an inherent part of the industry and the average hourly wage for farmworkers is not generally lower than what is found in other low-wage industries. Still, the agricultural industry has lobbied diligently and consistently to deny farmworkers access to basic labor protections, to block legislation designed to improve the lives of workers and their families, and to ensure that there is an oversupply of laborers.

Many older growers complain bitterly about how the agricultural industry has changed over the last thirty years. Growers resent the increase in state, federal, and local regulations and the proliferation of government agencies that monitor their businesses, particularly in regards to farmworkers' rights. Since agricultural workers were exempt from virtually all basic labor protections up until the 1960s, growers were accustomed to employing farmworkers without having to make Social Security deductions, purchase workers' compensation insurance, adhere to basic safety standards, or even keep written wage records. As farmworkers began to be included under basic labor, health, and safety provisions, and as special legislation and regulations were written to improve the living and working conditions of farmworkers, growers were forced to treat farmworkers in more or

less the same way most businesses treat their employees. Growers were required to comply with labor laws, keep accurate records, and allow enforcement agents to investigate their farms and issue citations and fines.

To many growers, the passage of protective labor laws, media exposés, and Legal Services' litigation represent a concerted attack on the agricultural industry, an effort to discredit and even humiliate farmers. To avoid problems with inspections, fines, and lawsuits, many growers have stopped providing workers with housing and transportation. Most significantly, growers have become increasingly dependent on farm labor contractors, often passing all labor management responsibilities on to intermediaries in an effort to limit their own liability.

Even when growers comply with the law—guaranteeing laborers the minimum wage and following basic labor and safety standards— farmworkers' annual wages often fall well below the poverty line. Although there are individual growers who, for a variety of reasons, have decided to pay workers improved wages or institute benefits programs, they represent a small minority. There is little pressure for growers to use workers efficiently or to take it upon themselves to keep workers employed for extended periods of time. The poverty and marginalization of farmworkers remains a key element of our nation's agricultural system.

American agriculture presents a fascinating case of modern technology and business management combined with a dependence on a poor immigrant workforce with few options. The actual production of fruits and vegetables is increasingly wedded to the latest developments in high technology—genetically engineered seeds, laser-leveled fields, optically scanned sorting, computer-controlled soil analysis, the use of satellite systems to position tractors and map fields. Storage and shipping involves the use of special gases, packaging, and quality controls. Sales are tracked by computer, marketing is supported by consumer-preference studies, and both are managed by a professional class similar to that of any other major industry. Growers study at universities and rely upon the professional services of lawyers, agents, consultants, and specialists of all types. The farm labor force, on the other hand, is still composed of the most vulnerable laborers in the country, who are increasingly poor Latin American immigrants.

The combination of American agriculture's modern infrastructure and its dependence upon poor workers, laboring in an informal, shadowy world, reveals the extraordinary disparity of power that defines our nation's farm labor system.

Kevin Conway ♦ *San Joaquin Valley, California*

Kevin Conway's father started the family farm in the 1930s. Since the early 1980s, the farm has increased in size and now covers thousands of acres. The Conway farm grows, packs, and ships all of its fruit and is one of the area's largest operations, selling over 150 million pieces of fruit each year. At peak harvest season, the farm employs several thousand farmworkers.

The Conway's farm has been investigated several times by the United States Department of Labor, repeatedly sued by California Rural Legal Assistance, and targeted by the United Farm Workers union. After several organizing efforts and a series of elections, the farm's workers eventually voted for union representation. Although the farm has been involved in negotiations for some time, to date no contract has been signed.

It's my job to oversee all the ranch operations. I have foremen, crew bosses, and field labor working for me. I don't have an office. I go from ranch to ranch, supervising. I check to see that the job that they're doing is being done the right way. This is a very specialized industry. There is no one that can teach you how to do it. If you're going to be on the cutting edge, you have to get there through experience. You have to stay on top of new varieties and new techniques in the field—pruning, cleaning, harvesting, processing, packing, and handling the fruit. Things are changing all the time.

Since we started, our goal has been to be the biggest and the best—not only to put out the most fruit but also the highest-quality fruit, which we can sell for more than our competitors. We're in business to make money and bankrupt our competitors. That's why we exist. We don't exist for the benefit of the farming community. We don't give a damn about the farming community. We don't believe in promoting agriculture in general, so that all may benefit. We believe in promoting our label.

A fast worker picking on a piece rate makes seven to eight dollars an hour depending on the job. Everybody else just falls right in line, except for the people that can't make minimum wage. They have to be laid off, even when they want to work. Right now, our base wage is five fifteen an hour. I don't think that there are any other growers with a base hourly wage over five dollars. Since half of what the workers earn will be piecework, they average around six fifteen an hour. Based on the amount of taxes we pay, providing benefits is impossible.

There's no question that farm labor is skilled. Anybody who says that farm labor is unskilled has no idea what they're talking about. The more precise you want the job done, the more skill it requires. We only want to pick the fruit that's ready. Whereas the average farmer will pick a tree three to five times a season, we'll pick a tree eight to ten times on average. Sometimes we'll pick a single tree up to twenty-five times. A common block has over five thousand trees with different soil types and different size trees. The maturity of the fruit varies considerably throughout a block. There might be twenty peaches to pick off one tree and two peaches to pick off the next three trees. A farmworker working for a competitor who says, "Pick the top third of the tree" doesn't need a lot of skill. That same farmworker who comes to work for us, where we say, "Just pick the fruit that's ready for today," needs a lot of skill.

I know the term *farm labor* needs to be used, but to me farmworkers are employees. I wouldn't classify them as any different than somebody who's a welder or works on a ship or does data entry. They're laborers. They want to work. Farmworkers are all individuals. They all have their own individual needs and desires. Every last one of them is different, just like you and I are different. Farmworkers are not members of a group that thinks alike, wants the same things, or has the same aspirations in life. You may have someone who wants to work four months a year and then go back to Mexico to be with his family for the other eight months. You might have a guy who's got a job in Oregon in August, but he's going to stop here for a month in July. You might have a young guy who wants to be a crew boss, and so he'll work as much as he can.

There's no question that farmwork is an entry-level job. It's up to every individual farmworker to decide what he wants to do. Does he want to acquire the skills to better his life? To get a job that has fringe benefits and higher wages, you have to give something up, you have to give up the freedom of being able to come and go as you please. You have to give up your homeland. You may have to give up your family, or part of it. Those are an individual's choices based on what direction they see their lives going.

The press has done an incredible job of portraying farmworkers as hopeless people who are being exploited on a daily basis. That's just a total falsehood. Farmworkers are seeking to better themselves. They don't look at farm labor as drudgery. There are many farmworkers that enjoy farm labor. It can be very rewarding. There's a lot of freedom in farmwork that you don't get in any other business. You can look at the system and see that there isn't enough work and so the workers have to migrate, or you can look at it—the system—and say that the workers want to be able to come and go as they please. They don't get into farm-work thinking that they're going to work forty hours a week and get two weeks' vacation each year. Farmworkers enjoy their freedom. They enjoy the fact that they can send money home and improve things for their families.

It's a positive thing for a young man in Mexico to have the opportunity to come up here and make more in one hour than what he would make at home in a week. He can stay in Mexico and earn five dollars a day, or he can come up here and improve his family's chances for a better life—Do you call that desperation? If so, then desperation is a great motivator. The desire for something better is what moves society forward—in your life, in my life, in everybody's life.

It's convenient for people to think of farmworkers as exploited people. This country is controlled by guilt. People feel guilty for not being farmworkers, for not having to do that kind of work. People think, "It must be hard work out in the field" or "It's hot" or "They don't make a lot of money." Well, they don't make a lot of money, but that doesn't mean that it's not honorable work. It doesn't mean that they're not skilled. It doesn't mean that they're not ambitious. It doesn't mean that they don't love their families. There's no other connotation that goes with being a farmworker other than that it's an entry-level job.

There are a lot of new laws that have created an incredible amount of rights for farmworkers. Well, I don't trust people who say, "I want to pass this law because it will help the farmworkers." Farmworkers are not lob-bying for these laws. Farmworkers know what they want. They're not looking to be told what they want. We have to follow these laws and they cost a lot of money. There's record keeping, administration, fines, penal-ties, lawsuits. The most controlling aspect of agriculture, or any business, is that the workers can leave me and go to work somewhere else. I sug-gest that we let their personal choice regulate me and let my personal choice regulate them.

One thing I've found out after numerous encounters with agencies who claim to represent farmworkers is that they have to pick an enemy and the best enemy is the farmer. I don't understand why the farmer is held up as the person that is exploiting this labor. I had some numbers run for me the day before yesterday. The taxes that the government takes from the workers' checks and the matching taxes we have to pay equals thirty cents of every dollar the workers receive. Thirty percent. If a farm-worker works fifty weeks a year, averaging six dollars an hour, that's about forty-four hundred dollars a year that that farmworker doesn't get. That money comes right out of the farmworker's pocket. Farmworkers are being exploited—by the government.

If the farmworkers aren't getting their due, it's because of the do-gooders who try to create a system to give them everything that they could get for themselves if they were just left alone. If you gave the farm-workers back the money that's been taken from them, they could pay for all those benefits themselves. I believe that many of the extra protec-tions are created by people who are using the farmworker to pursue an anticapitalist agenda. When the government says it can do for you what you can't do for yourself, that's socialism. When they say that you're not capable of running your life, and that they're going to do it for you, that's socialism. Let the farmworkers keep what they earn. Let them take care of themselves. They're producing enough to live well, but the problem is, it's being taken away from them, and not by the farmers.

We've got an incredible amount of guilt-ridden liberals who've em-powered an army of bureaucrats to take the farmworkers' money and re-distribute it. They've created millions of nonproductive citizens that are living off the back of the producers. The farmworker is a producer, the classic producer. Everything they do is production. This country has cre-ated an entire class of people who do not produce. At the end of the day, they have nothing to sell. They produce nothing to eat, they produce nothing to wear, and they haven't helped anybody to produce anything. Not only do the bureaucrats not produce, but they hinder the producer, which is even worse. I would be all for paying them to stay home.

There's an army of bureaucrats out there whose sole job is to try and run our business in the name of helping someone else. Bureaucrats are self-sustaining. Taxes are not enough. They've been empowered with the ability to sustain themselves with fines and penalties. The laws are writ-ten in such a way that you are always in noncompliance. The only ques-tion is, Do they want to enforce them at your company at this time? We're a big target and so they come after us. They look at our big buildings, our landscaping, our packinghouses, the amount of people on the payroll, and they figure this is where the most money is. Why would they spend a day with a farmer with twenty farmworkers when they can go to someone with two thousand? A couple of days ago, I figured it out that two cents of every dollar our farmworkers earn goes for legal fees. Even though we win, they keep suing. They just keep coming at us. It never ends. As long as the agencies are out there that are funded to attack us, we're going to be under attack.

If the liberal bureaucrats and the people who empower them ever want to do anything for farmworkers, they should quit living off the farmworker, quit taking their money, and get off of the farmworkers' backs. It's disrespectful and it's immoral.

4. Contractors
Between Workers and Growers

IN THE EARLY MORNING, before the sun has burned off a thick fog that lies close to the ground, groups of men wait in a gravel parking lot beside a row of old school buses, whose rectangular forms glow a soft orange under the streetlights. When the farm labor contractors are ready, the buses fill up with workers and head out to the fields. Those who are left behind won't work that day. They drift off alone, disappearing into the mist. A pickup truck with a camper pulls up to a house, honks the horn and several men in work clothes and baseball caps pile into the back. Forty minutes later, the *ritero* enters an orchard where there are dozens of other cars and trucks. The workers step out, talking and joking among themselves, until the supervisor, the *mayordomo*, arrives to assign them to their rows. A man approaches a soup line beside a homeless shelter and asks if anyone wants a good job picking fruit, promising good wages and a chance to get off the street. There are a few takers and a few knowing glances.

Both farmworkers and growers depend upon intermediaries known as farm labor contractors or crewleaders. Essentially, contractors connect growers looking for workers with workers looking for jobs. They may also take on many, if not all, of the responsibilities for managing seasonal workers. At a minimum, they establish agreements with growers and then make sure that enough workers show up at the fields at the right time. Along with their assistants—*mayordomos*, field walkers, *riteros*, crew bosses—contractors supervise crews of farm laborers and keep track of their hours and production. Contractors also transport workers to and from the fields and house crews in labor camps that they control.

Farm labor contractors have long been associated with many of the most severe abuses in agriculture. Because of this, growers' continued reliance on contractors is one of the most controversial aspects of the farm labor system. Contractors often make false promises when recruiting workers, house laborers in substandard conditions, transport crews in dangerous vehicles, intimidate farmworkers with threats and violence, and use a variety of schemes to control workers' wages.

Growers commonly pay contractors a lump sum for their services, leaving the middlemen with both the responsibility of paying individual workers and the opportunity to cheat their crews out of their earnings. Some contractors pay farm laborers for fewer hours than they actually work or siphon a couple of dollars off each picker by underreporting their piecework earnings. Others loan money at high interest rates or require workers to pay for food, rent, tools, and transportation, often at artificially elevated prices. One of the most common scams involves pocketing wage deductions that are supposed to be presented to state and federal governments. Stealing wage deductions takes advantage of workers' ignorance about how Social Security, unemployment, and similar programs function. Workers only discover that their wage deductions have been stolen months, if not years, later when they seek to benefit from these programs.

Contractors often wield enormous authority over their workers, sometimes running their crews like small fiefdoms, hiring and firing workers at will, and displaying constant favoritism. They commonly play off of farmworkers' basic vulnerabilities—their poverty and limited options, their lack of working papers, their inability to speak English, their minority status, and their addictions. The worst abuses typically occur at isolated labor camps, where contractors control virtually every aspect of their workers' lives.

Ralph DeLeon ♦ *Santa Paula, California*
Ralph DeLeon was born in Mexico, just below the border. His parents were schoolteachers who crossed into the United States in the late 1950s, when he was nineteen years old. DeLeon worked in the fields and then helped local growers' associations manage the large numbers of bracero workers who were brought into the area to harvest citrus and vegetables. In the seventies, he became a manager of the only area labor association that resisted unionization. In 1976, he became an independent farm labor contractor.

DeLeon's company, SAMCO, works almost exclusively in citrus and avocados—pruning trees, caring for groves, and, above all, harvesting. At peak season, between May and July, he has as many as 500 workers, who earn between $60 and $80 per day. In December, the slowest time of the year, his payroll drops to about 150 workers. Although the majority of DeLeon's workers are in California, he also manages a crew in Florida. Outside DeLeon's offices, there is a collection of trucks and harvesting equipment. Inside, there are computers to keep track of payroll, posters detailing workers' rights, and stacks of cardboard boxes filled with wage records.

After the bracero program ended in 1964, the same workers kept coming. They were used to having us as their employer. I knew the workers personally and that created a certain loyalty. Back then, workers and contractors understood their jobs. The contractor would go out of his way to make workers' lives easier. We knew the workers came from a different country and we wanted to make sure that they didn't get into trouble. We were the intermediaries between the workers and all the problems they faced. We were their attorneys, marriage counselors, and loan officers. Workers expected contractors to help solve their problems and we did the best we could.

As time went on, the workers realized that they had the freedom to travel wherever they wanted. So they started to go from contractor to contractor looking for the best jobs. Now, after I hire a worker I might never see him again. I never know if someone who's working here today will still be around tomorrow. Workers no longer turn to the contractors for help. There's a barrier between management and labor. We've lost the loyalty, the mutual respect that was created when we had a stable workforce. There's no more trust, no exchange of feelings between the worker and management like we had after the bracero program ended. Farmwork is less human than it used to be.

I don't think the abuses are significant these days. Workers have the freedom to work for whoever they want to. If a farm labor contractor is abusing a worker, there's lots of other contractors he can go to. If I'm abusing these guys, who's forcing them to stay here? When farmworkers talk about abuses, they're just telling you what you want to hear. It's a fantasy world. A worker might tell you about abuses, but deep inside, they're not interested in those things. Farmworkers come to this country to work, save some money, and go back home. They don't care about taxes and Social Security. Why should they care? They're going back to

Mexico in a few months, after they save a couple thousand dollars. What they really want to know is where they can work and how much money they're going to make. The rest is incidental.

These days, workers aren't afraid of the supervisors. That's a fallacy. During the bracero program, workers labored under the threat that they could be sent back to Mexico at any time. Back then, crewleaders were tough. Even ten years ago, workers were afraid of the foremen. Today, it's the foremen who are afraid of the workers. Supervisors can't discipline the workers anymore. The young kids who are coming over now aren't afraid of anything. What's there to fear? What's the supervisor going to do? There's no more discipline. We're losing control.

Farm labor contracting exists for the grower's benefit. Most of the contractors in California do their own payroll, pay their own workers' compensation, and pay their own taxes. By using a contractor, a grower avoids having to deal with the labor laws. If I don't do the job the way he wants, he'll just call another contractor.

Still, a farm labor contractor can provide more stable employment to a farmworker than most growers. A good contractor can schedule a crew to go from one grower to another. These days, it's becoming more difficult to keep your workers busy because there's been a proliferation of farm labor contractors. In 1976, there were two farm labor contractors working citrus in Ventura County, myself and one other guy. Today, we have three thousand fewer acres of citrus and fifty-seven farm labor contractors. Now, when my crew finishes with one grower, I may not have another job for them.

In order to compete, new contractors come in and charge growers less than established contractors like myself. To do this, they pay lower wages, don't pay taxes, don't have insurance, and often don't even register as farm labor contractors. Over forty percent of workers' wages goes to taxes, workers' compensation insurance, unemployment insurance, and all those other expenses that, legally, you have to pay. So, if you don't report workers' wages to the government and don't buy insurance, you can end up with a pretty good profit. That makes it very enticing to break the law. As more new contractors come in, more rules are going to be violated. The laws are only imposed on the contractors that are visible. The ones that are invisible continue to be invisible no matter what you do. The more laws you pass and the more difficult it becomes to comply with the law, the more contractors will become invisible.

As a contractor, there are so many things that you want to do for the workers. In 1980, I used to provide my workers with transportation, vacation pay, health insurance, and a retirement plan. I used to help my workers buy homes. You could see the tears in their eyes when you said, "This house is yours." Today, we don't offer any benefits. There's no way I can do what I did for workers ten years ago. I simply can't afford it.

Workers are absolutely worse off now than before. The main reason for these changes is the availability of labor. If we could close the border, it would benefit my workers tremendously. Then, in order to compete for labor, the prices growers pay would rise. I'd pay my workers more and farmworkers throughout the nation would earn the high wages they deserve. As long as we have the influx of people coming across the border, farmwork cannot become a respectable job.

Since 1963, federal law has required that farm labor contractors register with the United States Department of Labor. There are currently around 16,000 registered contractors in the country, a significant increase over the early 1990s. There are also countless others who provide a variety of contracting services yet remain unregistered. In general, farm laborers working for crewleaders are poorer, more vulnerable, and more likely to migrate than those who work directly for growers. Farmworkers working for contractors earn an average of $6,000 per year, about three-fourths of the average farmworkers' annual wages.

Farm labor contractors are a diverse group. Some contractors run small operations with fewer than a dozen workers, while others hire hundreds of laborers and work several jobs at the same time. Some contractors operate as modern employment services, with ID cards and computerized payrolls, while others keep no records, paying workers in cash at the end of each day. Small-scale contractors generally manage their crews directly, whereas large operations may have several layers of supervisors. Some contractors live day to day with their workers, while others have little direct contact with the laborers they hire. In addition to providing growers with workers, many larger contractors also haul the produce their crews harvest to packinghouses, processing facilities, and juice plants.

The contractor system has a certain obvious logic in an industry that needs large numbers of workers for relatively short periods of time. Recruiting, hiring, and supervising workers are difficult, time-consuming tasks, particularly where the season is short and the workers must travel long distances from their homes to the fields. By using a contractor, growers can get several hundred workers to show up for a short-term harvest anywhere in the country by contacting a single intermediary. Contractors generally speak the same language as their crews and can take responsibility for every aspect of worker

supervision, from record keeping to quality control to housing and transportation, leaving the grower free to manage the farm.

Manuel Gomez ♦ *San Joaquin Valley, California*

It is a cold, gray Sunday and Manuel Gomez and his sons are drinking beer and cooking in the yard behind his office. We sit on benches across from a row of small houses that Gomez rents to farmworker families. To one side of the small boxlike homes, there are rows of tractor trailers that Gomez uses to haul citrus from the groves to the packinghouses.

Orphaned as a young child, Gomez was raised by his grandparents in a small town in central Mexico. After his grandparents died, he crossed into the United States without papers in the late 1940s. For over twenty years, Gomez picked fruits and vegetables in California. Eventually he worked his way up to become a supervisor for a large citrus grower. In the early 1970s, he asked the grower to help him become a contractor. The following year, he began managing a crew of forty workers. His business grew rapidly. At one point, Gomez had 800 farm laborers working for him, harvesting asparagus.

Ninety-nine percent of all contractors work outside of the law. Not one, not two—all of us. You have to break the law. Breaking the law is the only way you can make decent money.

There aren't a lot of contractors who steal bins from the people or cheat the workers on the hours. What we do is keep part of the payroll off the computer. We enter eighty or ninety percent and keep the rest off the records. By keeping some workers off the computer, we don't have to pay their taxes or Social Security deductions. We pay the workers out of our pockets and keep the taxes we should have paid in for their work. Deductions and taxes add up to large percentage of the workers' wages. You can't take that money from every worker because you have to report your payroll to the government. Still, if you bring a hundred people to the field you can hide the wages of ten or even twenty workers. If you pocket a hundred dollars for each of those workers, you can make some money.

Of all the contractors I know, there isn't one around here that's on the level. Any contractor can tell you this. If the contractors don't tell you that they're breaking the law, it's because they don't want you to know the truth. That's all. They're afraid the government will catch them. Everyone knows we're doing this.

The truth is the worker hardly notices. He doesn't mind what we're doing because he still gets his money every week. He doesn't realize that nothing went into his Social Security. When he gets old, and he needs the money for his retirement, then, it will be bad for him. Still, most of our workers are undocumented so it doesn't really matter. They don't even use real Social Security numbers, so we're not stealing from the workers, we're just stealing from the government. I don't see it as all that bad.

You have to break the law if you want to get ahead. It's difficult for a contractor to get by if he works within the law. There are a lot of jobs that don't work out—where the *ranchero* promises to give you four weeks of work and then he only gives you two. You might spend three thousand dollars and only earn fifteen hundred. You've lost money. You've fallen behind. Then, you've got to replace the money you've lost, or you'll go under.

There are lots of contractors and lots of competition. In this town there used to be only four contractors. Now there are twelve. It's difficult to work when there's so much competition. Contractors are always arriving at a farm to look for work. If you have a job somewhere, every season forty or fifty contractors will come by trying to steal your job. And you'll do the same at the farms where they work. You've got to be very careful with the jobs you have because every farm has got ten contractors waiting in line for your job. If you don't do a good job for a good price, the *ranchero* will just hire someone else. There are always more contractors than there are jobs.

In citrus, they pay me by the bin. Since I know all about the work, I know how much to charge the *ranchero*. Right now I'd pick oranges for about nineteen dollars a bin. That means I'll pick the oranges, take them out of the groves, put them in a truck, and bring them to the packinghouse in good condition for nineteen dollars a bin. Let's say you pay the worker ten dollars to pick, a dollar to the forklift driver, two dollars to the truck driver, and two dollars for the *mayordomo*. By then you've spent fifteen dollars. That leaves you with four dollars for your equipment and commission. If you pick three hundred bins a day, that's good money.

The most money I ever took in during one year was about a million dollars. Out of that million, I kept about ten percent, say, a hundred thousand dollars.

It's not easy being an intermediary. Working between the bosses and the workers is hard. You have to fight with the boss all day long, telling him that the people aren't making any money and he needs to raise the piece rate. Then, he'll say, "That's your problem." You're always out there struggling to get the workers another hour of labor or a better price so they can take home some money. It's hard.

It's always the workers who suffer, and farmworkers suffer more than other workers. The farmworkers' labor is valuable, but the pay is bad, less than in a factory and less than lots of other jobs. The product is plenty valuable, but there are five or six layers of people between the worker and the consumer. Look at an apple. Two apples cost about a dollar. A worker makes around ten dollars for a bin of apples. There are about two thousand apples in a bin, so a worker makes a hundredth of what you pay in the store.

Farm labor isn't fair, but that's how it is and that's how it's always been.

The contractor system is fundamentally a mechanism of labor control. By hiring farm labor contractors, growers not only avoid the responsibilities of managing seasonal workers, they also insulate themselves from dealing directly with the men and women who labor in their fields. Contractors act as a buffer between growers and workers. In fact, many growers who use farm labor contractors have no direct contact with the workers their businesses depend upon. Similarly, many farmworkers who labor under contractors have never spoken to a grower or even a grower's representative.

By isolating workers from growers and by passing along all managerial responsibilities to a middleman, the contractor system reinforces farmworkers' powerlessness and their marginalized place in society. Contractors protect growers from having to deal with farmworkers, and they force farmworkers to become dependent on an informal, shadowy world that offers limited options and few protections.

Gordon and Billy Earle ♦ *Arcadia, Florida*

Gordon Earle and his son, Billy, built their business on crews of "fruit tramps," mostly white workers recruited out of homeless shelters and soup lines, or picked up off of street corners in skid row neighborhoods. These workers wander from one place to another, harvesting fruits and vegetables, riding freight trains, drifting in and out of missions and labor camps. Fruit tramps are a dying breed. They are growing too old to keep traveling and too slow to earn decent wages working the fields.

The Earles now spend most of their time managing a labor camp that often houses several different crews at the same time—Mexicans, Haitians, African Americans. Workers live in three parallel rows of rooms, with each row facing a thin strip of dirt and grass, littered with cigarette butts and crushed beer cans. When the camp is full, it is a loud, raucous place. There are dice games and dominoes; music played at top volume on cheap portable radios, the constant rise and fall of voices—yelling, laughing, swearing. The camp is a self-enclosed community with a kitchen, dining room, camp store, and parking lot that is filled with vans and pickup trucks during the harvest season. A chainlink fence surrounds the property, which is located a few blocks from a shopping plaza.

GORDON I was born in Mississippi in 1921. Our family had a truck and we started going from place to place, working the fields. My father always found jobs for us. We worked hard and didn't ask nobody for nothing. Traveling around was tough on my schooling, but it was its own kind of education. I learned things a lot of people never learn. I learned the ways of people. I know if a man is a horse's ass from the time he opens his mouth.

I got married and worked in defense plants until the war was about over and then went out to California. I was working nights canning peaches and sleeping during the daytime. It was hotter than hell. I had three kids and my wife was pregnant with another. I knew there had to be a better life than what I had, so I lay there and figured out what to do. I got an old bus and I made some seats for people to sit on.

Hell, I had no trouble loading up fifty people who wanted to go pick cotton. You'd just pull up to the corner where the migrant guys were waiting, load up, and away you'd go. I got fifty cents from each of them and made me twenty-five dollars. Then, I went and bought me some cotton sacks. I'd rent a man a cotton sack for a quarter a day. That was seventy-five cents per man. I was running about fifty men, so I earned thirty-seven dollars a day. Back in the forties, that was big money. I'd also go out in the field myself. I was a pretty good cotton picker, so I made me another fifteen dollars a day.

Then, I started carrying ham sandwiches and candy. Every man out there was spending a dollar or a dollar and a half on that. By then, I was making a hundred dollars a day. You never earned a whole lot for any one thing, but when you put it all together, you came home with a good day's pay. And, it was a lot better than what you'd earn just picking.

As I went along, I bought more buses. I got to where I was running five buses. At one time, I was the biggest watermelon contractor in the state of California. In a single day, we handled eight hundred and forty tons of watermelons. When cotton picking by hand went out and machines came in, we started to work in Florida picking oranges. We'd pick oranges in Florida in the winter, and in the spring, we'd go back to California to work in cantaloupes, watermelons, onions, and alfalfa. Eventually, we just settled here in Florida.

BILLY In every town in the United States, there's always a place where the migrants, the transients, hang out. You just go into town and start asking, "Where are the winos at? Where do your migrants hang out?"

If a man worked for us, we'd bring him to the camp and feed him good. We don't bullshit nobody. If there's good picking, we'd go out there on the street and say, "We got some good picking. It's so much a box if you want some." If the picking's bad, we'd say, "We've got some sorry picking. It ain't worth a damn, but we've got it. If you want some, let's go get it. If you don't, I can't blame you."

We got a good name, from the West Coast to the East Coast. We've never shortchanged or cheated nobody. If you owe me a penny, I want it, and if I owe you a penny, you're gonna get it. It's that simple.

GORDON The migrant worker is a two-week worker. When you hire a man, he'll stay a couple of weeks, get him a little money, and go back into town. He'll get drunk, stay drunk a week or two, and then come back. The workers are always flowing in and out. If you're working a hundred men, you got to be ready to go get thirty or forty more by the second week. The third week, you'll need another thirty or forty, and the fourth week, it's the same thing. They rotate, just keep coming and going. Some years, we see the same guys three or four times. Pretty near every man we've worked has had a job that beat migrant pay. But nothing beats migrant worries.

BILLY We've always kept our men right here on the camp. They didn't have to go downtown for nothing. We'd have a big house full of things—shoes, socks, everything. For a period of time, even the law didn't come in here. They knew we could take care of the migrants. You don't have to whup or beat a wino, all you have to do is show him you can.

GORDON If ours got into a fight, we settled it. You go up there and shake him a little bit, look him in the eye, and say, "Now, you know you're wrong." You see, the migrant only wants to make enough money to drink.

In the old days, the migrant didn't get no food stamps, no welfare, no nothing, so they had to work. Since the government came up with unemployment and food stamps, a lot of migrants quit working. There's plenty of work, but now the migrants will draw unemployment and food stamps for as long as they can. They sell their food stamps at fifty cents on the dollar, and, along with their unemployment check, hell, a migrant can sleep in a mission and stay drunk for half a month.

BILLY I grant you some of your missions and goody-goody people mean well. They really do. But if they'd just come out of the clouds and come back down here to earth they'd realize they're doing a lot more harm than good. If you leave the migrant alone, he'll go to work; but if you give him something for nothing, he's not going to work.

GORDON That's the problem with your government and your churches. They're on the migrant kick. They got their nose too damn far into it. They just don't understand that you can't upgrade the migrant. If you stick a migrant in a nice place, in thirty days, he'll put holes in the walls and knock the windows out. It's his nature. The government wants to upgrade the migrant, but it's just not possible.

BILLY About six years ago, black workers started to replace white workers. We specialize in whites, but now the old whites are dying off. We don't hire blacks if we can get away with it, because blacks are more trouble, always have been, last hundred years.

GORDON The older blacks ain't trouble, the ones that are around forty or fifty.

BILLY The older blacks are good people. A lot of them have been mistreated. Coming up through life, folks would look at them and say, "There's a nigger, I'm gonna kick him in the ass." Now, the young blacks are different. They're all looking to get something for nothing. You go over there across the tracks and see them standing all over the place, on welfare or crack.

GORDON If you got half a dozen quiet younger niggers, and one agitator comes in, that agitator can get the whole bunch stirred up.

BILLY We always let them know right quick that a man's a man and an asshole's an asshole. It don't make a difference if you're black or white. They know that we don't give nobody no shit and we don't take none. Once in a while when we'd get a smart-ass nigger, I had blacks working for me who'd get his ass, or I'd get his ass, or, if it took both of us, we'd straighten that nigger out and we'd put him on the highway. If you've got a troublemaker, you got to put him on the road and get him out of there.

GORDON Now, the government's come in and made it hard on the contractor. These days, a labor contractor can't run a legitimate business, even if he wants to.

BILLY What it boils down to is that the government makes a crook out of you. You can't run a legitimate business and be honest with the government. Why? Because the farmer will stick you in a bad orchard and then say, "Pick it." What are you going to do? You're sitting there with forty or fifty men. You can't quit, so you start picking, even though you know the workers won't make minimum wage. It happens all the time. It's "pick it or else." In a bad field, only ten or twenty percent of the migrants can make minimum wage. Then, the government comes in and says it's the contractor's fault.

Ninety-nine percent of all contractors break the law. They lie on the wages. If you work eight hours a day at four twenty-five an hour, that's thirty-four dollars a day you're supposed to make. If you only earned twenty-five, the contractor turns around and writes down that you worked six hours. If your workers can't make minimum wage, you've got to lie on your payroll. The government don't know you, but they say you're a damn crook because they make you lie. They squeeze that damn contractor to where the contractor ain't got no choice.

If you quit, then what are you going to do? You gonna come home? You can't afford to come home and do nothing. You got fifty men and maybe fifteen of them have been with you for twenty years. What are you going to do with them? Some of those guys are fifty years old or older. Twenty years ago they could make minimum wage, but hell, now they're old. Your government says, "Get rid of them." Well, we've known these guys for years. Would you fire a guy you've known for fifteen or twenty years? So, we just lie on our damn payroll.

GORDON Now, the Mexicans can make the minimum wage. They're twenty-five years old and all they've ever known is hard work. They're the cream of the crop. They can go out there and pick them some peaches. Our workers are old white guys. We've had guys close to seventy picking fruit. What should be done about these Americans? You can't just run 'em off. Pretty soon, there won't be no more American migrants, 'cause the sons of bitches are gonna die off and your younger ones won't work in the fields.

BILLY Right now, without a labor camp, a crewleader just can't make it. With a camp, you can charge your workers for room and board. Hell, we only charge seven dollars a day, which ain't shit, but it's something. The government says the contractor's not supposed to make a profit off his camp. Well, if a contractor can't make money out of the field, he can at least sell cigarettes and beer. I don't force the workers to buy anything, but the migrant wants wine and beer. These days, there are a lot of contractors selling crack. That way they get all the workers' wages back. Your straight contractors are gettin' out of the business.

You know everyone loves the migrants when they're out there picking oranges, but no one wants them to get too close. The growers want the migrants when they need 'em, but they don't want 'em up the hill near their fine homes. The contractor's just like the migrant. We're in the same boat. Growers need the contractors to bring in the migrants, but they won't invite a contractor home for supper. No grower has ever invited me

to supper. There's still a line there, just like the line between the blacks and the whites. You know, way down deep, I hate growers.

You see, we work with migrants every day. We deal in migrants. We live with migrants. We are migrants—poor white trash, just like the rest of 'em.

Contractors are almost always ex-farmworkers who know how to deal with the workers in their crews. Most contractors manage crews composed of workers from their own cultural and ethnic background—African American workers usually work for black contractors, Latino workers for Latino contractors, and so on. Contracting is a highly competitive business. Successful contractors are usually strong leaders—ambitious, clever, and, at times, ruthless. Although crewleaders run their crews in a brutal, domineering fashion, they frequently view themselves as well-intentioned leaders operating as best they can within a tough and uncompromising environment. Contractors often express a confused combination of warm paternalism and cold suspicion regarding their workers, viewing their crews as childlike and in need of guidance as well as wily and duplicitous. This combination of a stern leader and a heartless confidence man expresses both the power and vulnerability of the contractor's situation.

Contractors generally have limited formal education and virtually no business background. Whereas most contractors speak English, many are only partially literate. Still, what contractors lack in modern management skills they make up for in firsthand knowledge of the farm labor system. Traditionally, contractors have played an important social role in the lives of individual farmworkers and within farmworker communities. Contractors often provide advice and assistance to workers, loaning money, helping relatives get jobs, and acting as key intermediaries between their crews and the larger society. African American contractors operating in the rural South sometimes help their workers in dealing with white society, interceding with police, landlords, and others. Latino contractors are often asked to become *compadres*, that is, to baptize one of their worker's children, and thereby establish a formal relationship of trust and long-term assistance.

While contractors wield enormous, often brutal, authority over their crews, they are ultimately at the mercy of the growers who employ them. Contractors rarely control significant wealth. When things get tough and growers refuse to pay more, contractors can only bear down harder on their workers. In the end, contractors remain small operators within a large system; the abuses they commit are symptoms of a larger problem, a sign of the profound inequities that define the farm labor system.

Robert Wilson ♦ *Pahokee, Florida*

As a young boy, Robert Wilson carried drinking water to workers in Florida's vegetable fields. When he was nine, he began migrating north with his family. At twelve, he started traveling on his own. By seventeen, he was a farm labor contractor. Wilson is six foot four and in his prime, he weighed over three hundred pounds. Several years ago, he retired from contracting.

I migrated such places as Florida, the two Carolinas, Virginia, Maryland, Delaware, Pennsylvania, and Vermont. I've been in the Midwest, the far West. I've gone all the way from Florida to Washington State. It takes a special breed of person to be a crewleader. You got to like people. You got to want to better yourself. Most of all, you got to want money.

To tell you the truth, being a crewleader is a hell-fired life. I liked traveling around, working with people, and having responsibility. A crewleader without a crew is nothing, and a crew is no better than their leader. They were my black boys, and I treated them in that manner. We were close, like family. I felt like they were my relatives. I loved them and I helped them.

To get a job, the first thing I'd do was find out from the Employment Service office where crews were needed. I'd look for a good guy and do what they call "breeze his palm," give him a little under the table—buy his liquor for him, have a big cigar for him, or have a gal for him—and he'd tell me where to go. Other times, I'd just ride up north and go lookin' for a farmer. I'd drive out on the farm, catch a guy out in the field on his tractor, and talk with him to see what he needed. That's the best way to negotiate, face-to-face. He'd either trust me or he wouldn't. If he didn't trust me, I'd keep going. You see, he only had one little farm and I had a whole state to cover. If I didn't like New York, I had Pennsylvania. If I didn't like Pennsylvania, there was always New Jersey. I always had another possible job lined up. There's always someone else out there on the highway who needs you.

To find workers, I'd go to a migrant town. The first thing I'd do is find what we call a "know-it-all nigger." A know-it-all nigger is a black guy who knows everyone's business in town. He know who's got the biggest farm or the most money. He's one of the biggest wine drinkers you ever looked at and one of the biggest damn liars you could run into, but when you find your know-it-all and buy him his drinks, cigarettes, and eats, he'll help you get labor.

To tell you the truth, life on a migrant camp is a pleasant life. Most camps had recreation halls, where everyone would go to gamble or drink after the payoffs, or on a rainy day. On the weekends, we used to have dances. Everyone would get together and have a hell of a good time. They'd get to drinking that booze and dancing. They'd show off a little bit, let their wig down, and raise a little hell. The cook would be frying fish, making pan-fried chicken and homemade pies. I'd go in there and buy three or four quarts and sit them on the table and let the workers drink. Then they'd say, "Now, there's a damn good nigger." See, I was one of them. I was part of them. I come up with migrants, and I was a damn good leader.

You have to use a different type of language in a migrant camp. A crewleader on a camp has got to make passes at the women. You need to say things like, "Come here, baby, let me talk to you, you damn good pussy bitch." When she walks over, you got to go patting her hips and trying to feel her up front. You got to tell her, "You look like you got a damn good pussy. What you doing tomorrow? You want to go with me to the field?" It makes no difference if she's got a husband, if she's in your camp, you got to wink at her and say those things. They'll laugh about it and say, "Old John there, he sure got a nasty mouth. Guess what he told me?" That way they'll go out there and work with you. Somehow, that's a way of being nice to them, letting them know you watchin' them and care for them. Their husbands have to talk to the other women like that, too. It's just play. Sure, some of 'em will slip around with you, but they just like anything in the city.

Now with the men, it's a lot different. When you need to get them to work, you say: "Get your damn black ass on that bus and let's go." "You're a no-good son of a bitch." "You simple nigger, you ain't worth a damn." This is the language you have to use on migrants. That's what they understand. Every day you got to keep shoving them, pushing and pushing, to get them to go to work. Some guys just lay around and say they're sick. You tell them, "Hell, I'm sick, too. Get your ass out of here." That's just the way camp life was.

Usually before I'd go into a camp, I'd check it out. Lots of times you'd go into a camp and you couldn't get out. One time, I carried a load into a camp in the state of Virginia. When I got in there, there was no work. So, I wanted to go. We was way back there in the woods, on a lake next to an old colonial graveyard. The guy who was running the camp and his henchmen told me he wouldn't have work for a couple of weeks, but I couldn't take my crew out. He had a couple of guys standing behind him. Well, what do you do? You got to leave the workers there. You just keep on riding. I didn't even think of going back. You go back there and you'd get killed, or get whipped damn near to death. You'd get what they call a labor camp ass-beating.

I've known camps that had some rough henchmen. If you got stuck in one of those camps you had reason to worry, 'cause they'd whip your ass. That's all there was to it. They'd beat you the old-time way, just smack you right upside your head. I've seen guys leave a camp quick, fast and in a hurry. They weren't traveling by bus or car. They were traveling by the will of that damn swamp. Out there, you'd be scramblin' for your life.

It was tough going up through the northern part of Florida, on into Georgia and the Carolinas. They just hated blacks, period. It wasn't only us guys going north, all the blacks around there was catchin' hell. I've seen guys come out of Alabama and Mississippi who'd never seen money until they got out of there. White folks didn't give a damn about you. They saw you as nothing, nothing but a no-good, stinkin' nigger. That's the way they booked you. Oh, man, it was rough. I felt like I was on a damn plantation. People were downright nasty to you and you couldn't do a damn thing about it. You had to put up with it day after day, year after year. I learned not to get mad. When a farmer gave me a fucking, I never got angry at him. He was the white farmer and he had the money. The farmer controlled you.

I studied the white man. I know his ways, his steps and his doings. Once I got to know the white man's likes and dislikes, I learned how to get around him. Many times, a white migrant was helpful to me, especially going up through the South. Sometimes I'd go out huntin' white workers. I'd buy the white migrant a big Western hat and some boots, put three hundred dollars in his pocket, and pay him to go up the road with me. Because of his white face, he could go places I couldn't go. He'd be the big bossman. When I jumped on the bus, I'd say, "Hey, boss." We'd laugh and talk and he'd pay for everything. He'd go on up the road and get a store to fix us sandwiches and stuff and they wouldn't bother us. When we made it up north, I'd give him a hundred dollars and a ticket to wherever he wanted to go.

A lot of times, the best part about camp life was leaving the son-of-a-bitch, gettin' the hell away from there when the season was down. You made that money, and you're figuring to change states. You're going someplace else, a new environment, a change of scenery, a breath of fresh air.

In the early sixties, growing public concern over the treatment of farmworkers led to a series of congressional hearings that revealed that farm labor contractors were responsible for many of the worst abuses of agricultural workers. In 1963, Congress passed the Farm Labor Contractor Registration Act (FLCRA) to regulate the activities of crewleaders. The FLCRA required all contractors to register with the United States Department of Labor and provide workers with accurate information about the jobs being offered—the type of work, location, wages, transportation, and housing. Contractors were obligated then, at least in theory, to fulfill their recruitment promises.

The Department of Labor was given the responsibility of investigating contractors for alleged abuses and enforcing the law through fines and the possible revocation of contractors' licenses. Congress amended the law four times in the 1970s, expanding the definition of a contractor, increasing contractors' responsibilities, and providing for stronger enforcement. Growers were held responsible for hiring unregistered contractors, and workers were given the right to sue contractors who violated the law.

Both growers and worker advocates were frustrated with the FLCRA because it failed to produce significant improvements in the lives of farmworkers. In 1983, Congress replaced the FLCRA with the Migrant and Seasonal Agricultural Worker Protection Act (MSAWPA). The MSAWPA outlines specific protections regarding the recruitment, employment, transportation, and housing of workers. It requires contractors to keep accurate wage records for their workers and disclose wages and working conditions to laborers in writing. It also requires that worker housing and the vehicles used to transport workers meet certain standards and be inspected and registered. Further, under the MSAWPA's "joint employer" doctrine, growers and contractors can be held jointly liable for violations of the law.

Eva Silva ♦ *Immokalee, Florida*
Immokalee is an agricultural town—flat, hot, and desolate. The road into town is bordered by newly planted orange groves and large fields of tomatoes and peppers, which give way to a grass airstrip for crop dusters and a long row of packinghouses and farm offices. Much of the worker housing is south of the main street—rows of old trailers, clusters of wooden cabins, and flophouses, where one can rent a bed for a few dollars a night.

Eva Silva lives on the north side of the central dividing street, beside a clinic and the local high school. Her home is modest, shaded by trees. The bus she uses to carry workers to the fields is parked just outside the fence surrounding her property. Silva is one of the few women crewleaders in the area. She is slight of build, polite, and soft-spoken. She stands out within a profession dominated by men.

It is summertime, the off-season. In a few weeks, workers will begin arriving in town, gradually swelling the local population from 8,000 to nearly 30,000 during the peak winter months.

I tell my daughter that I was never a child. A child plays outside and goes to school. Back then, nobody was a child, because we were always out working in the fields. We were always sick and tired, always traveling in the back of the truck, always working.

I used to work so hard I would cry. When we'd come back from the fields, we'd go inside the house, take a bath, and stay shut inside. We never went out. My mother wouldn't let us get involved with anyone, talk with anyone, or have anybody come to our house. We didn't have friends. We never went to the movies or to dances. That's just the way our parents were.

My mother and father told us that we had to work because we didn't have enough money. They didn't care about learning or school, so I only went to school for a few weeks at a time. When I went to school, I was always afraid. When the bell rang, the other kids would run to lunch or gym class, but I didn't know what the bell was ringing for. The other kids knew how to read. They dressed differently than I did. They had everything they wanted.

When we were in the fields, guys used to send someone over to tell us they liked us because we weren't allowed to talk with them. One day a girl told me that her brother had seen me and that he wanted to know if I would be his girlfriend. I said, "Yes," but told her to tell him that we weren't allowed to date. She told me that the boy didn't care and that he liked me. The first time we met, he asked me to run away with him. I was afraid. I'd never met him before, never talked to him. Still, I didn't care. I would have run away with anyone. I was sixteen when we got married.

After we left, I told my husband all the things that I'd gone through. I told him that I didn't want him to be like my father. We were married for twenty years and he never once came home drunk. I told my husband I never wanted to go back to my family, and we never did.

For four years, my husband and I worked for a farmer, pruning and tying tomato plants. We worked very hard. I'd even work while I was pregnant. Then, I'd have my baby and be back at work two weeks later. The farmer liked how we worked. We were responsible. We did a better job than anyone else. Then, the farmer asked us to become crewleaders.

First, we bought a van. The farmer paid us forty-five dollars each day per van and five fifty an hour. With the money we made, we bought another van. We didn't earn much until later, when the farmer agreed to give us a nickel for every hundred feet of tomato plants the people worked. Then we started making money. We used to make a thousand dollars a week from September through May. Three years later, the same boss man wanted us to buy a truck to pick tomatoes. We didn't want to pick tomatoes because we'd never done it before. We were only used to tying and pruning. We didn't like picking, but we made good money. That's what I still do. I take people out to pick tomatoes.

There are a lots of crewleaders who have money. They have everything they want and so they don't understand the workers. They talk to the people as if they're stupid. They get mad and yell at their workers. Some crewleaders will fire the workers right there in the field. They think they're so important.

When we were workers, the crewleaders treated us like animals. They laughed at us. Because of this, my husband and I always tried to be different. We cared for our people and talked nice to them. We were always patient. I'd always tell my husband, "Let's not be hard on the workers. Remember how they treated us." You have to help the people learn how to do the work. They're poor people, just like we used to be.

Then, my husband passed away. It was hard. He was the crewleader and he ran everything. I cried for him all the time. I'd call out to him, asking him why he'd left me. I'd asked him to come back and tell me what to do. I knew he wasn't around, but that's what I used to do. Nobody stayed with me. Nobody came by to ask how I was doing. They left me by myself because I had money and they thought I had everything I needed. You know, money is really nothing. What I needed was somebody to stay with me, to tell me that everything was all right, to let me know that I was going to make it.

When my husband died, people tried to take advantage of me. Other crewleaders wanted me to go down. So I told myself that I had to be strong, to continue with my work. I never let other people know that I was crying. I didn't have a man to help, so I had to do everything myself.

Well, I was strong enough to show them and now they hire me everywhere that I ask for a job. That's why so many crewleaders here don't like me. If I ask for a job, they give it to me. A lot of men think that I get jobs because I'm a woman. They think that I get work because the growers feel sorry for me or because I sleep with the bosses. That's not it at all. I always do a good job. I don't sit around and act the pretty woman. I'm out there with the people, getting dirty. A lot of the men are afraid of me.

Women are actually better crewleaders than men. The men are just playboys. They're always thinking about being with a lady. Many crewleaders have two or three women. That's why they don't save any money. They come to town and pick up their lady and spend all the day with her, leaving the people alone in the fields. They don't really care about their workers. They don't care about how their people are picking. A woman crewleader cares more about the workers.

I'm proud of myself. I have four kids right now, and they each have property for when they grow up. I'm working for my children. The husband I've got now says that I worry too much about my kids. He says that I want everything for them. Well, I don't want my kids to be like me. Kids today have choices. They can finish school. They can be whatever they want to be.

I'm the smallest of the family, yet I'm the one that's got more than everybody else. I got what I wanted working in the fields. A lot of people think that I've got schooling, but I don't. I can't even write. I'm smart just because I'm smart. I don't have an education, only some things that got into my head. Now, I understand things.

Although protective legislation has now been in place for several decades, abusive contractors continue to operate with impunity. In part, this is a result of the enormous difficulties of enforcing the law. Farmworkers labor throughout the country, often in isolated rural areas. Contractors, in turn, are always moving, shifting addresses, and operating businesses that are highly informal and possess few assets. Those few contractors whose licenses have been revoked rarely stop working. The appeal process allows contractors to continue operating for several years using the license in question. Even if a contractor is placed on the Department of Labor's revocation list, he or she can have a spouse, relative, or supervisor obtain a new license, and the operation will continue as before. If the "new" contractor also gets in trouble, yet another relative or associate will take out the contractor's license.

Contractors who operate outside of the law are often difficult to track down. Their camps are hidden. They may have no official address or fixed office. Investigators cracking down on the most abusive contractors have to seek out illegal labor camps, interview workers after normal work hours, and provide migrants with protection and assistance in leaving the most dangerous situations.

Federal and state legislation regulating farm labor contractors has not produced the intended improvements in farmworkers' lives. In fact, in some instances, more rigorous protective regulations have led law-abiding contractors to stop providing certain services, particularly transportation and housing. This has forced farmworkers to become increasingly dependent on a growing array of unlicensed, unregulated subcontractors.

Traditionally, contractors transported workers to and from the fields and, at times, from their homes to fields located hundreds of miles away. For years, old school buses filled with workers, and often bearing the contractor's name, were a common sight in many rural areas. Federal legislation requiring contractors to register their vehicles and purchase insurance requires contractors, like other commercial transport services, to provide reasonable protections for their passengers. Since current regulations require minimum liability coverage of $100,000 per seat in a vehicle, many contractors either refuse to purchase insurance or no longer transport workers.

Currently, over 90 percent of federally registered contractors do not have authorization to transport farmworkers. In California and Arizona combined, there are fewer than 200 contractors with legal authorization to transport workers. Since farmworkers still need to get to and from the fields, an underground, unregulated system of transportation has evolved. Small unlicensed operators, known as *riteros*, now transport workers to and from the fields, generally charging laborers a few dollars a day. *Riteros* are farmworkers who have saved enough money to buy a car, truck, or van. They are unable to afford the required insurance, and few of the vehicles they use could pass mandatory safety inspections. While contractors and growers are well aware of the *ritero* system and often use *riteros* to recruit workers, they generally claim that how workers get to and from the fields is not their concern. They insist that the *ritero* system exists beyond their control and supervision.

The housing situation for farmworkers is similar. Until recently, many growers provided farmworkers with temporary housing in labor camps, which were typically owned by growers, growers' associations, or contractors and managed by crewleaders or camp supervisors. This housing was generally provided free of charge or at reasonable rates. Labor camp conditions varied considerably and many were dangerous and unsanitary, with leaking roofs, unsafe water, or inadequate sewage systems. Federal regulations were then passed, outlining detailed minimum requirements for farmworker housing. Federal, state, or local officials were made responsible for

inspecting and approving labor camps and issuing fines to camp owners whose housing was in violation of the law.

Following lawsuits, investigations, fines, and bad publicity, many
growers decided to close down or even demolish the housing they had
previously provided to workers. Since migrant laborers still needed
temporary housing, they were forced to find rental housing or live in
illegal labor camps, creating another dangerous and informal business. In areas with a high concentration of seasonal farmworkers, it
is not uncommon to find old trailers or crumbling shacks rented to
farm laborers at exorbitant weekly rates.

Ricardo Porras ✦ *Selma, California*

*Ricardo Porras was born in a small town in the state of Guana-
juato in Mexico. He crossed the border when he was twenty-eight
and has spent over fifteen years working as a farm laborer. Like
many farmworkers, Porras dreams of getting ahead, moving up,
and becoming a farm labor contractor. Unable to save enough
money to break into contracting, Porras has spent the last five years
working as a* ritero, *carrying workers to and from the fields in order
to supplement his income as a laborer.*

*It's a cool early evening in a migrant neighborhood of small one-
story houses. Groups of men sit on the front steps, drinking beer, listening to music, and talking. Porras leans against a pickup parked
in front of his house. Occasionally a car passes by, its occupants
shouting out greetings. The town is known as the "Raisin Capital of
the World."*

A *ritero* is someone who takes people to the fields to work. We're
farmworkers like all the rest. Here in California there are lots of workers
without vehicles. Since the fields are far from where the workers live, you
can't work without transportation. That's why the workers need *riteros*.

Contractors call *riteros* and tell them to go out and find workers. After
you've lived one place for a while you get to know a lot of workers. You call
your friends and let them know you're looking for workers. Then, one person talks to another. That's how we get a group of workers together.
There are also apartments here where single workers live. When you
need people, you can go there and ask if anyone wants to work. I feel useful as a *ritero*. I'm doing something necessary for society, something
which helps farmworkers.

Workers usually want to know how much a job pays and whether it
pays by the hour or by a piece rate. It's important to work for contractors
who pay well. You need to have a couple of different bosses because when

one boss doesn't have work, another one might. We charge the workers four dollars a day, to and from the fields. The more people you carry to the fields, the more you earn. The best vehicles are big vans that hold eighteen workers. If you carry eighteen people at four dollars each, that's over seventy dollars. With the forty dollars you earn working in the fields, you'll make over a hundred dollars a day. Even after expenses, you earn double what a regular worker earns.

When you're working as a *ritero,* you're always worried about the possibility of an accident. The vehicles are often overweight and unstable. You have to drive slowly. I know lots of *riteros* who've had accidents, including some pretty bad ones, where vans filled with workers have gone off the road and crashed. Many workers have died in these accidents. In one accident, eleven people were killed. You can get in serious trouble when people get killed. All the *riteros* I know who've had serious accidents have gone away. Some go to Florida or Texas or back home to Mexico.

The law says that to transport agricultural workers you're supposed to have what's called a "permission to transport." To get this, you need to have your vehicle registered and have insurance coverage of a million and a half dollars. These are good laws. Farmworkers should be protected. The problem is that the insurance is too expensive. Unless you transport a lot of people or work for a big company, you can't pay for insurance. There are some companies that pay for a contractor's insurance, but *riteros* work outside of the law. We drive without insurance and without a permission to transport. There are lots of *riteros* who don't even have a driver's license.

The bosses know what's going on. The fields are far away, so without *riteros,* how could people get to work? There are even some bosses who give the *riteros* a bit of money at the end of each season to thank us for taking the people to work. They know the transportation isn't free. The contractors are responsible to provide growers with workers and *riteros* are responsible for getting people to work. If we don't fulfill our obligation, then nothing would get done. If we don't get to the fields, then the workers don't get there, either. It's impossible for the growers not to know about the *riteros.*

Now, I'm using a van that carries nine people. My van isn't registered, and at four dollars per worker, I can't afford insurance. So, I work outside of the law. Before they began enforcing the laws, we didn't even know we were doing anything illegal. Now that we know about the laws, we feel guilty. Now we work with a certain anger. We're poor. We have to work, yet what we do is illegal. The law makes us feel ashamed.

It used to be easy to be a *ritero.* The government never used to bother us. Now, in California, it's getting difficult. They're always watching us. If

they stop you and your van isn't registered to transport workers, they'll take the van from you. These days, the most popular vehicles are trucks with campers where you can hide the workers or vehicles that only hold six or seven passengers because they don't attract much attention.

The future for *riteros* looks grim. We don't know what's going to happen. I'm thinking of leaving California and going to another state where there aren't so many regulations, some state farther north, maybe Washington. We all come here to work. We take what we can get.

Growers run businesses that are increasingly large and complex. As agriculture becomes dominated by large producers, growers' operations have come to resemble other modern businesses. They pay taxes; sign contracts; deal with banks, insurance companies, and government agencies; and follow a variety of rules and regulations. Contractors, on the other hand, often operate in a largely unregulated and informal world. They recruit workers from street corners, in bars, by word of mouth, rarely establishing formal employment agreements. Despite regulations to the contrary, contractors often pay crews in cash and keep no records. Those contractors who abide by the law either charge more for their services or turn to a variety of subcontractors—*riteros* and others—who operate informally.

In many ways, the use of farm labor contractors in agriculture reflects upon larger issues in the changing American economy. Farmworkers' marginalization and poverty has long been linked to the institutionalization of the contractor system. Growers have used farm labor contractors to distance themselves from a minority workforce, to keep wages low, and to avoid legal and moral responsibility for farmworkers' poverty. With ever greater frequency, American employers of all types are turning to contractors and subcontractors to provide them with workers. Whether they need janitors, secretaries, clerical staff, or factory workers, American businesses are hiring intermediaries as a way of reducing costs and avoiding a variety of employer responsibilities. As in farm labor, the use of contractors, or layers of contractors and sub-contractors, allows employers to insulate themselves from certain liabilities and to distance themselves from responsibility for the workers who play a key role in their company's economic success. Increasingly, workers find themselves laboring in an informal, unprotected environment with few, if any, benefits. As more employers turn to intermediaries to provide them with laborers, many American workers are beginning to look more like farmworkers.

Franck LeGrande ♦ *Immokalee, Florida*

Franck LeGrande, known as Ninety-nine, was born in Haiti to a prosperous family. His father owned land, stores, and a cargo ship. LeGrande is now an established farm labor contractor. We speak in LeGrande's office, which is attached to the living room of his pleasant one-story home. He has five children. The oldest is eighteen and recently entered college. LeGrande is thinking of leaving contracting and studying to become a real estate agent.

I had to leave Haiti in 1980. At that time, Haiti was a dictator country. You had to be careful of your speech or you could be arrested and killed by a government agent. Nobody could say anything against the government. If someone heard you say the words *politics* or *communism*—just the words—that would be your life. Speaking those words was equal to death. There were no trials, no going to court.

My father was very well off in that part of the country so people always took care of him. When one of my friends was arrested, someone told my father that if he wanted me to stay alive, I had to leave the country. In a dictator country, when they come and arrest your friends, it means you're next. We never heard from my friend again.

A family friend who owned a boat took me to Miami. Then, most people paid two thousand dollars to go to Florida. He brought me over for free. I was twenty-five years old.

I had no family in Miami and no friends. I was alone, all by myself—lonely. I wanted to go back to Haiti, but I was afraid of being killed. In the daytime I worked at a golf course, mowing lawns. At night, I washed dishes. I worked seven days a week at the golf course and six days a week at the restaurant. Working sixteen hours a day, I brought home less than two hundred dollars per week.

In Haiti, I always had money. I worked for my parents in the store. I knew nothing about hard work. I had never done manual labor. There were always servants at home so I had never even washed the dishes. If you come to the United States from another country where your parents are wealthy, you have to forget who you were in order to survive. In Miami, I would run into people who used to work for me in Haiti. There I was, washing dishes, just like them. I decided to get away from anyone I knew from home, so I went to the country, to Belle Glade where no one knew me but a cousin who was working in the cane fields, pulling corn, and cutting celery.

In Belle Glade I made it my will to do any kind of hard work I could find. For me, the United States was like some kind of adventure. I wanted to prove to myself what I could do. I made it my goal to do every

type of hard work I could put my hands on, to give it my best shot. I tried everything—cutting cane, celery, cabbage, and lettuce; picking oranges, grapefruit, apples, and peaches—if it was hard work, I wanted to try it. Whether you work by the hour or by the piece, farmwork is hard. If you work by the piece, you really have to run, to sweat. You have to fight yourself to make money. You get tired. You feel like you can't go on, but you have to continue. You have to keep working.

While I was working in the fields, I was going to school four nights a week to learn English. I bought a book that came with a practice tape. Where I worked, none of the bosses spoke Creole. Since I spoke English better than the other workers, my crewleader made me a field walker and a translator. They had me walk behind the crew and check on their work. At first, I didn't know what to do, but they taught me.

Three years later, I bought a van and became a crewleader. I started planting cucumbers and harvesting watermelons. I carried ten people in my van. I was working for a small farmer. When he quit farming, I went to work for a bigger farmer, picking peppers. Then, I worked with an American crewleader who had a bus. We had about sixty Haitian workers. I spoke Creole, so I supervised the crew. When the other crewleader left that farmer, I stayed on. Then I bought my own bus.

Being a crewleader is hard. I get up at four o'clock in the morning and by five I'm at the store where I load my crew. What time I leave depends on how far I'm going, but I've got to be in the field with my crew ready by seven. I have to make sure that sixty people are doing what my boss wants them to do. I have to show the workers how to do things right. You can show some people how to work, come back, and they're still doing it wrong. So you show them again and again. It's an all-day job. You've got to spend the whole day out in the fields to make sure they're doing things right. You have to teach people how to work in the field— how to plant, how to shovel, how to lay plastic. Teaching people is a big part of being a crewleader.

To make money as a crewleader you have to have a lot of workers and a lot of jobs. If the job is big enough, a crewleader can make good money, but a crewleader that only works small jobs can barely survive. Crewleaders have lots of expenses. If a hundred thousand dollars comes through a crewleader's hands, he's got to spend a third on taxes. The rest pays for a good truck or goes to the insurance company. A lot of crewleaders think that when they get paid, the money's all theirs. Crewleaders see a lot of money and many go out gambling or spend what they get. Then, later, they can't pay their expenses. There are a lot of crewleaders who end up with nothing.

This country is like a big machine, and the machine has tires, a driver, and an engine. The farmworker is part of the transmission of this machine. Farmworkers do the hardest work in this country, yet they're always belittled. The farmworker is forgotten, unknown. Back in Haiti, I never looked at nobody low. I always looked at the guy who worked for my family as equal to my father's friends who had money and owned their own stores. It's hard if you believe that everybody is equal because life is just not that way. Not in Haiti. Not here. Nowhere.

5. *Pasando al otro lado*
The U.S./Mexico Border

THE U.S./MEXICO border stretches 2,000 miles from Border Field State Park, California, on the Pacific Ocean, to Brazos Island, Texas, on the Gulf of Mexico. Like all borders, the line that separates the United States and Mexico is both real and imaginary, a formal boundary that divides and defines. In marking the space between two deeply connected nations, the border reveals powerful contradictions between legal systems promising order and the complex lives of people whose identities are bound to their passage back and forth across the dividing line. Physically the border is deeply unassuming, an almost uniformly bland passage of empty brush and dry desert— hot, generally flat, and largely uninhabited. Symbolically, the border stands for the division of two worlds: the wealthy, industrialized United States of America to the north and the struggling, less-developed nations of Mexico and Central America to the south.

For migrant farmworkers, over half of whom are recent immigrants from Mexico, the border is a site of conflicting emotions. By crossing to the other side—*pasando al otro lado*—foreign-born workers enter a land that promises economic opportunity as well as confusing, often alienating, difference. For those with proper documents, entering the United States is little more than a formality. For those without papers, crossing the border is illegal.

Thousands of prospective immigrants cross the U.S./Mexico border each day. Migrants float their children across rivers in inner tubes, sprint across California highways, and wind their way through the empty expanse of miles of desert. They follow high-tension wires, walk along abandoned dirt roads and across hills, guided by the stars. Crossing the border can be as simple as a quick sprint across a highway or so dangerous as to be fatal, as immigrants fall victim to unscrupulous smugglers or find themselves wandering alone, lost in the desert.

Jorge Urroz ✦ *Kennett Square, Pennsylvania*

Jorge Urroz is the third oldest child in a family of fourteen children. Although he was a good student, he left school when he was eight years old to take a job herding goats. Since then, he has worked to support his family.

Urroz has spent virtually his entire adult life as a migrant laborer, harvesting crops throughout the United States. Several years ago, he moved from California to Kennett Square, a small town near Philadelphia, which is known as the "Mushroom Capital of America." After trying to unionize other Mexican laborers at the farm where he worked, Urroz was fired. He has now devoted himself full-time to the struggle to organize local mushroom workers.

I began to understand things when I was five years old. That's when I realized that we were very poor. Some nights when we sat down to dinner, we'd start crying. We were hungry. We wanted more to eat. Sometimes, my father would leave the house because he couldn't stand to watch us suffer. Other nights, he'd get drunk and beat us as if, out of desperation, he wished us all dead. There were times when we were so afraid that we'd sleep outside. When we came back to the house in the morning, our father would beg our forgiveness, saying that when he drank he changed and didn't know what he was doing.

We learned about the United States from an uncle who worked as a bracero. One year, he brought back a radio and we used to gather around and listen to it. We were so poor that we thought owning a radio meant you were rich. My uncle also brought back new clothes for my cousins. When they came to visit us at our *rancho,* they were always so well dressed. They teased us because our clothes were torn. We had no sandals, no shoes, nothing. We walked around half naked. It was humiliating.

Because of my childhood, I always wanted to go to the United States. I thought about it all the time. It was my dream to go north to work and then return home with clothes for my mother and all my brothers and sisters. I used to pray to God, "Lord, give me the chance to make it north so that my family won't have to suffer anymore, so that they'll no longer spend days without eating."

When I was eight, I asked my father, "Why don't we cross over to the other side to work because here we suffer too much?"

He said, "The other side of what?"

You see, he was stuck in his world. He was one of those people who never understood how to open up new opportunities.

When I was fourteen, a *coyote* came to the *rancho* to tell us that there were farmers in the United States who needed workers. He said he had contacts with people who could get us work and that if we paid him a commission, he'd help us cross the border. To pay the *coyote,* I needed to find someone who would lend me money. Since I had nothing of my own, my father signed for my debt, putting up our small plot of land as collateral.

My parents were worried because I was young, undernourished, and very thin. My mother cried and cried. She was afraid I'd never return. She knew that people died crossing to the other side. She knew that there were criminals along the border who stole from migrants and sometimes killed them. I calmed my mother, telling her that I was going north because we were so poor. I told her I wanted to help my brothers and sisters go to school and that I was ready to lay down my life for them. My mother was upset, but she gave me her blessing: "I pray that God will help you."

When I left, my mother and all my little brothers and sisters were crying. I've always carried that image in my mind. I left feeling very sad, sad but grateful. I prayed to God, asking him to help me to pay back my debt.

The *coyote* told us to meet him in the central bus station in Mexico City at a certain time. The *coyote* had contracted a bus to take us to the border, near Tijuana. People from all over Mexico arrived to fill up the bus. My grandparents had given my mother a little corn and she made me some tortillas for the trip. I passed out my tortillas to the other travelers. It was the first time for all of us.

On our way north we passed through a police checkpoint. They stopped us and made us all get off the bus. An agent asked me, "Where are you going?"

"I'm going to Nogales to visit relatives."

"Where do they live? Give me the address."

"I don't know the address, but I have it written down somewhere inside my suitcase."

"You can't go on. You've got to stay here or go back where you came from." They wouldn't let me continue north unless I paid them a bribe. I told them I didn't have any money, not even enough to buy food to eat.

Then, a woman whose husband was already in the U.S. came over and said, "This is my nephew. How can you make him stay here if he's traveling with me?" They began to talk, and in the end, the woman paid my bribe and they let us continue on.

We stopped in a small town in the middle of the desert and got off the bus. We spent three nights there. On the third night, the *coyote* said, "Tonight at eleven o'clock, we'll cross, but first we'll go out early and hide." There were three guides for forty of us. We went out to the desert, hid ourselves, and waited for nightfall. Then we started out. The guide went ahead. At one point, Immigration passed right by us. They had a helicopter with searchlights, but we threw ourselves on the ground and hid. We backtracked and found a new route. Then it began to rain. We walked through the countryside all night long. We were soaking wet. Around seven in the morning, we reached a town. We had crossed the border. We were in the United States.

The *coyotes* took us down a narrow street where there were two vans waiting for us. They packed us into the vans, back-to-back, crushed together, and took us north to Washington State to pick apples. They didn't feed us for three days and only let us out to use the bathroom. The *coyotes* kept telling us, "Now you're in the United States. Don't make any noise because they'll catch you and send you back." When we got to Washington State, they dropped us off in a barn and said, "We'll come back to take you to work."

It was the beginning of October and it was very cold. There was no heat in the barn and we had no blankets. We had nothing to wear but the clothing we'd crossed in. We were freezing. For two days, we waited. The *coyotes* never returned. They'd abandoned us. I kept thinking about my family and my debt. I thought we were going to freeze to death.

There was a church near the barn. Finally, some people in our group went out to ask for help. They were Jehovah's Witnesses and they invited all of us into the church. They gave us food to eat, warm clothes, and a place to sleep. Then they helped us find jobs.

As soon as I could, I mailed my family a letter and a money order. I didn't want them to know about what had really happened, so I told them everything went well and that I was busy working. I sent them enough money to pay off my debt, with a little extra to buy food. I was picking cherries, working as hard as possible. For every box of cherries I picked, I earned a dollar. While I was in Washington, I sent my family three money orders.

Several months later, I returned to Mexico with most of the others. I bought clothes for my mother and for each of my brothers and sisters. I

left the United States with a suitcase filled with clothing. I also bought a radio.

The bus from Mexico City let me off at around nine at night. It was still a two-hour walk to my family's house. I wore new clothes and new shoes. It was the first time I'd ever owned real shoes.

I arrived at my house around eleven. It was dark and everyone was asleep. I called out, "Mama. Mama, are you there?"

No one spoke. Then, I heard my mother crying.

"Mama, it's me. I'm back."

My mother wasn't sure if the voice she heard was really me. She didn't know if I was real because for three nights she had been dreaming about me. She was afraid.

Then, my younger brothers and sisters woke up. They rushed outside and ran to embrace me. When my mother heard my brothers and sisters shouting, welcoming me home, she came outside. She looked at me, smiling. She hugged me and gave me a kiss. We stayed up all night talking. I took out the radio and opened the suitcase, showing them everything I'd bought. We were very happy.

I returned home with dollars. I took my mother to a doctor. I bought food for my brothers and sisters. I also bought a small piece of land, just big enough for a house. I was fifteen years old. When I was sixteen, I went back to the United States to work.

While there are no exact statistics on undocumented immigration, it is estimated that each year, between 1.5 million and 2.5 million people enter the United States illegally, primarily by crossing the U.S./Mexico border. While most undocumented immigrants cross over to work and then return home, about 275,000 settle in the United States each year. It is believed that there are now a total of 5 million undocumented immigrants in the United States, over half of whom are Mexicans. There are also more than 335,000 undocumented immigrants from El Salvador and 165,000 from Guatemala. Undocumented immigrants are concentrated in several states, with 2 million living in California, 700,000 in Texas, 540,000 in New York, and over 350,000 in Florida.

While undocumented workers take on a variety of jobs, many are drawn to farm labor. The general informality of agricultural labor makes it relatively easy to work in the fields without legal papers. Jobs are seasonal, workers rarely labor under formal contracts, and employment is usually found through personal contacts. Many contractors and growers keep workers off the books and pay in cash. Nationwide, about half of all farmworkers are undocumented, and each year, the percentage appears to be rising. When farmworkers receive work authorizations or discover other employment opportunities, they commonly abandon agriculture for jobs offering greater stability and higher wages.

Within farmworker communities it is both easy and relatively inexpensive to obtain false working papers or fake Social Security cards. There are few Immigration raids in rural areas, and it is difficult to monitor farmworkers as they move from place to place, passing from one employer to the next. For many undocumented farm laborers, the hardest part of working in the United States involves safely crossing the U.S./Mexico border.

Roberto Suarez ♦ *Clinton, North Carolina*

In El Salvador, Roberto Suarez worked in a textile factory. As political tensions increased in the early 1980s, the factory was shut down. Work was hard to find and the violence extreme. Suarez left El Salvador, traveled across Guatemala and Mexico, and eventually arrived in Matamoros on the U.S./Mexico border.

Before coming to the United States, Suarez had never worked on a farm. Since crossing the border, he has labored almost exclusively in the fields, spending the winter and spring in Florida picking tomatoes and bell peppers and traveling north with different farm labor contractors during the summer and fall. We speak one late afternoon in a labor camp, while sitting on cramped bunk beds in a cabin overlooking a field. Suarez is the only Salvadoran in a labor camp whose crew is composed of undocumented Guatemalan workers, the majority of whom also fled their homes to escape political violence.

I left El Salvador because of the war. I was afraid of being killed. So many of my friends are dead. Down there everything is politics. I didn't want to join the army and I didn't want to fight with the guerrillas.

I didn't know anything about crossing the border when I arrived in Matamoros. I didn't know where to go or who to talk to. I didn't even know where the river was. I was afraid that someone would trick me or turn me over to Immigration. After wandering around the streets, I finally asked a taxi driver how to get to the other side. He took me to a *coyote* who told me that he would take me across the river for a hundred dollars. I paid the *coyote* and he showed me how to cross the border. It was easy. We crossed around noon, in the middle of the day.

When I got to the other side, the *coyote* took me to a store. I walked inside and bought a soda. Then, the *coyote* found a taxi which took me to the Casa de Oscar Romero, which is a place for Central American refugees. I spent two weeks there. Sometimes Americans would come by to hire people to do yard work or wash cars. For a full day's labor, they paid ten dollars. I worked hard and earned almost nothing. So, I decided I had to go on a little farther—farther north, farther east. I didn't really know. I just wanted to keep pushing on.

I was worried, nervous, and afraid. I didn't have a guide. A *coyote* could help you, take you by the hand, but you had to pay them. Also, some *coyotes* were crooked. I'd heard stories about how they'd take you somewhere and steal your money; tell you one thing and then drop you off in the middle of nowhere. Then you'd be completely lost. Lost and alone.

So I decided to travel by myself. I found a taxi and headed north. Immigration started following the car and pulled us over. They caught me. They asked me where I was from. I told them I was Mexican. I was afraid that if I told them the truth, they'd send me back to El Salvador. They sent me back across the border to Mexico. When I got to the other side, I just turned around and came back. By then, I knew how to cross on my own.

So, there I was back on the other side of the border. A *coyote* came up and said he'd take me to Houston for four hundred dollars. I told him I didn't have any money, but that in Houston I could pay him because I had some friends who were living in Los Angeles who could wire the money. Then he asked if I had any money to cover the gas. I had seventy dollars I'd saved from working seven days at ten dollars a day. He agreed to take me and I gave him the money. We arrived at a small town and he told me to get out of the car. "I have to go around the corner to pick up a friend who can help us get past the immigration checkpoint."

I got out of the car. He told me to wait. I waited. One hour passed. Two hours passed. He never returned. He had abandoned me. I felt terrible.

So, I just started walking. I wanted to go north, but I got lost. The road I took went west and I walked all night long. The next day, an American stopped and gave me a ride to a bus station. I had forty dollars hidden in my clothes, which I used to buy a ticket. I knew I couldn't continue north because I'd been warned about an immigration checkpoint fifty miles north of Harlingen. I stepped off the bus when it seemed we were getting close.

Then, I walked into the countryside. I went away from the road for several miles and then headed north. I walked through the brush. I brought a cloth bag with some apples and a container of water. There were so many rough bushes and thorns that the container tore and I lost all the water. I spent three days and three nights without water, wandering alone in the countryside. There was no shade and all I had to eat were the apples. The juice from the fruit helped ease my thirst.

By the third night, I couldn't stand it anymore. My feet were bloody. I could hardly move. I was just dragging myself along. At around three in the morning, I heard the far-off sounds of cars passing on the highway. I went out to the road and just stood there. I decided to leave myself in God's hands. I walked along the road. If Immigration passed by, they would have grabbed me. Finally I reached a gas station. I asked the guy who was working there where the immigration checkpoint was and he told me it was several miles back.

I'd made it. I felt so happy. From the gas station I spent the last of my money on a bus ticket to San Antonio and from there to Houston, where there was another house for refugees. I spent a month there working for Americans who would come by to find people to clean their homes and cut their lawns. In Houston, they paid more than in Brownsville, around thirty-five or forty dollars a day. I saved two hundred dollars.

Then, one day, a man arrived at the house. He told us that he needed some people to work in Georgia. He said they'd give us a nice house to sleep in and free food. He told us there was lots of work and that we'd earn three hundred dollars a week picking vegetables. He said a lot of nice things and so, along with ten others, I went to Georgia. When we got to Georgia we found out that the work was terrible. They had us pick squash for forty cents a bucket. We made less than ten dollars a day. He had lied to us.

Still, by the grace of God, I made it. I crossed the border. I was working in the United States. One day, I dream of returning to my country, if only to visit my mother.

To lessen the risks of crossing, many undocumented immigrants pay smugglers—known as *coyotes, polleros,* or *pateros*—to help them enter the United States. Smugglers charge immigrants different rates, depending on the services they offer and the distance traveled. Some smugglers help migrants cross the border, following well-worn paths through the brush or hoisting immigrants onto their backs and wading across the river. Others transport workers from their homes in Mexico directly to job sites in Texas and California or as far away as New England or the Pacific Northwest. Still other smugglers transport workers thousands of miles from small villages in Central America on buses, in cars, or hidden in trucks, often crossing several international borders before arriving in the United States. Some *coyotes* operate alone or with family members, while others work within sophisticated underground networks involving crossing guides, multiple drivers, and special "drop houses," where workers are hidden until friends or relatives can come by and pay off their smuggling fee.

Most undocumented immigrants, especially those arriving for the first time, borrow money to pay smugglers' fees, which are often quite costly. Some prospective migrants borrow money from family members already working in the United States, while others turn to local moneylenders, who often require poor families to put up their homes or small plots of land as collateral. While immigrants who successfully cross the border generally pay off their debts rather quickly, the possible loss of a family's home or land makes migration extremely risky. Immigrants with limited resources, or those whose friends or relatives never arrive to pay the smugglers' fees, are sometimes "sold" to farm labor contractors who force new arrivals to work off their debts by laboring in the fields.

The illegality of crossing the border has created a violent underworld of smugglers, bandits, and thieves. Along the U.S./Mexico border, immigrants are often robbed or beaten and sometimes murdered. Women are commonly raped. Each year, tens of thousands of prospective immigrants fall victim to criminals operating along the border. Those who fail to cross the border on the first or second attempt may find themselves living with little or no money in border towns, where they become particularly vulnerable targets for abuse.

Tomas Robles ◆ *Matamoros, Mexico*

Tomas Robles sits on a mattress drinking beer in a small apartment near the central bus station. The door to the apartment is a large wooden panel that opens onto a narrow street. To enter the apartment, you unfasten a steel padlock and unwind a thick, yard-long metal chain.

Robles is a patero, *a smuggler who helps undocumented immigrants cross the border to enter the United States. When he was seventeen, he left his home in Veracruz and traveled to the border town of Matamoros. He stayed with a cousin who gave him a job selling tacos that paid about ten dollars for each twelve-hour shift. The taco stand was across the street from the bus station where people traveling north from other parts of Mexico arrived each day, intent on crossing the border. Stepping off the bus, with their bags and suitcases in hand, travelers often asked Robles if he knew anyone who could help them cross the Rio Grande and enter the United States.*

He began sending recent arrivals to smugglers he knew. For each re-ferral, he earned fifty dollars, a week's wages selling tacos.

Later, Robles quit working at the taco stand and became a patero, *working for one of the largest smuggling operations in Matamoros. He claims to earn as much as a doctor. He is twenty-four years old.*

First, I look at you. I study you. Then I know whether or not you're going to cross to the other side. You see, there's a lot of competition and it's the *patero* who talks the best that gets the most people.

When people arrive, they're afraid. If I see that you've just stepped off the bus and I ask if you want to go to the other side, you're not going to say yes. You're uncertain. You'll think to yourself, "Who is this guy? Is he a criminal? a policeman?" So you'll tell me, "No, I'm not going to cross. I'm just here to visit some relatives." Now, when a lot of *pateros* hear this, they'll just walk away. Not me. I say, "You know what? What-ever you want to do, my job is to cross people over to the other side and I won't charge you a nickel until we get there."

I just keep talking. I don't stop. I say, "It doesn't matter to me if you've got no money. All you need is a telephone number of someone over there, a relative or someone else who can pay your way. Here, I'll cover your food and lodging. I'll give you a place to sleep and everything. I won't charge you a penny until we've crossed over. Do you have the num-ber of someone on the other side?"

Then, you'll look at me and say, "OK, I want to cross. How much do you charge?"

"Six hundred dollars from here to Houston. Everyone charges the same. But, listen, we can't talk here. It's dangerous with all these police. I live just a block away. Let's go to my house. You can wash up. I'll buy you something to eat and we can talk some more."

Then you follow me, see, and we keep talking. Once you're at my house, you're mine. That's how it works. Before we cross the border, you give me the telephone number of someone on the other side, and we call. If they say, "We don't have any money," or "We don't know him," that's it, there's no deal. That's how we arrange things.

Then we put you up in a hotel until we've gathered ten, twelve, or fif-teen people. Sometimes it takes two or three days. We won't carry just two or three people across. It isn't worth it. We need at least eight be-cause we never work alone. We usually cross over with three or four *pa-teros.* When we've got everyone together, we tell them, "You know what? At four o'clock we're going to cross the river. You'll have to leave your suitcases here. This isn't a vacation. You're going to cross with just a shirt and a pair of pants, OK?"

Then we say, "If they catch us, don't tell them who's carrying you across. If they ask who helped you cross or which one's the *coyote,* you just say, 'Nobody's carrying us across. We're all just looking for work.' That way, if Immigration finds us, they'll just send us back across the border, back to Matamoros. They won't jail us and we'll cross over again. If Immigration catches us, they'll ask for our names. We'll give out fake names, and if they catch us again, we'll give them different names. They never remember us."

Once we've talked this over and everyone understands, we take a taxi that drops us off close to the river. On the Mexican side, the police patrol the river on horseback. If they see us, they'll come over to check us out.

"Listen, we're just going over to Brownsville to earn a little money."

"OK, just give us a little something so we can buy a drink."

So we give them a little money and they'll let us pass. If we're caught by police who know we're *pateros,* we're screwed. They'll make us pay them one, two, maybe three hundred dollars. If we don't pay them, they'll arrest us for some crime we've never committed. They won't just charge us with being *pateros,* they'll charge us with assault and really screw us. They're tough assholes, so we have to work with them. After we give them their *mordida,* they'll let us pass.

Then we go on to the river. We take off our clothes and put them in a bag. We get in the water and cross the river naked. If we crossed wearing clothes, when we got to the other side, we'd be wet and people would notice. If *La Migra* sees that, they'll say, "Look, there goes another wetback," and they'll nail you.

Sometimes we cross people who don't know how to swim. Then, we buy inner tubes and put the people inside. They get nervous, but I tell them, "Don't worry if you can't swim. Just hold on tight to one of my feet." They'll grab on to my foot and I'll swim across the river using my hands. It's about thirty feet across, but when the water's high, the current gets strong. If you know what you're doing, it's easy, but if not, it can be dangerous. Lots of people drown.

On the American side of the river, there are bandits who carry knives and guns. They'll wait for you and catch you as you get out of the water, naked. They'll tear open your bag looking for money. They'll check your socks and your shoes. They look everywhere. If you're wearing good boots, nice pants, or a decent shirt, they'll steal them. Sometimes they take everything you've got. Other times they beat you up or threaten you with knives. That's happened to me many times. I've got a knife wound on my leg, another one over here, and another here. Look at all these scars. Look at how they've sliced me up.

Once we've crossed the river, we walk calmly into Brownsville. Then we call up some friends who drive taxis. We put five people in each taxi and carry them to a hotel. We get one room for everybody. The next day, around three or four in the morning, we wake everyone up. We divide the group up between three cars. That way if the police or Immigration stop us on the way, they'll only catch one group and the other two will make it through to Houston. We lose less money if we split up, because when they catch you, they arrest the drivers, confiscate the car, and send everyone back to the other side.

Before we get to the immigration checkpoint, we get out of the car and let the driver continue north. The drivers have their papers, so they can pass through the checkpoint. Then we walk into the countryside. It's dark, but we know where we're going. There are power lines that we use to guide us. We go on together, walking and walking, for five or six hours. There are lots of rattlesnakes and you can die if they bite you. We walk on through the brush until we get to a place to rest. Then one person— only one—goes out to the road to see if the others are there. When they arrive, we get back in the cars and off we go to Houston.

Then we drive to a special house. Our boss meets us there. We gather everyone into the house, park the cars, close the door, and then start calling the phone numbers, one by one. "OK, we've got your nephew here—or your son, your brother, or whoever. Come on over with the money." They come over and pay us. We give them the person and off they go. There's times when they don't want to pay or when they only have three or four hundred dollars. Sometimes they'll give us rings, watches, or bracelets. If they don't have anyone who can pay and nothing to give us, we take the people back to Matamoros. If there's someone who'll buy the people off of us, we'll sell them.

Our boss collects the money and when everyone's gone, he divides it up. He takes his cut and everyone else gets a share. Then we go to the best bar in Houston and get drunk. We take a lot of chances on the road—the police might catch us, Immigration might send us back. Who knows? We might drown in the river or someone might kill us. So we celebrate to make up for everything we've gone through. We drink and drink until the table is covered with beer bottles. We have girls on all sides of us, sitting on our laps, dancing. We have a great time. Nothing but *pateros* and women. There in that bar, for one night, we're all kings.

I know that what I do is illegal, but it's men who invented these laws, not God. It's the American government that doesn't want us to pass people to the other side. They don't want us to be with you, the *gringos*. I'm not doing anything wrong. I'm not robbing, beating, or killing anyone.

I'm not working against God. Where these people are from, they earn so little they can't even support their families. So even though what I do is illegal, in the end, it's actually good. I'm helping people to better themselves, to realize their dreams.

I'm ready for whatever might happen. If today or tomorrow they kill me, or a snake bites me, or they crush the life out of me, my kids will have money in the bank. Every day, I risk my life for my family. It's an adventure being a *patero,* a beautiful life—to know the road, to cross the river. If tomorrow something were to happen to me, who cares? In the end, every man suffers for the life he leads.

On the American side of the border, Immigration and Naturalization Service (INS) agents work day and night to prevent undocumented immigrants from crossing into the United States. They use helicopters with searchlights, infrared sensors hidden in bushes, motion detectors buried in the desert, and miles of fences. INS agents cruise border-area roads searching for suspicious vehicles and patrol the open range in four-wheel-drive vehicles painted the agency's trademark light green. There are nighttime patrols that search the countryside for the traces of undocumented immigrants winding their way through the desert and across the border. Every major road north of the U.S./Mexico border has a twenty-four-hour checkpoint where passing vehicles are inspected, often by dogs specially trained to find immigrants hidden in truck beds or behind false seats.

The INS employs 9,000 Border Patrol agents, 90 percent of whom work along the U.S./Mexico border. The INS spends over $1 billion per year on border control in the Southwest, nearly triple the amount spent in the early 1990s. INS agents have sometimes been found to abuse their authority through illegal apprehensions; threats; and the use of excessive, occasionally lethal, force. Concerns regarding INS actions have risen as the number of agents working on the border continues to increase.

Each year, the INS apprehends over 1.5 million people trying to cross the border illegally. Ninety-eight percent of those caught are Mexicans and virtually all agree to return voluntarily, waiving their rights to a deportation hearing. Typically immigrants sent back to Mexico make another attempt at crossing as soon as possible, sometimes only hours after being apprehended. According to official estimates, for each individual who is caught crossing the border, between two and three undocumented immigrants successfully enter the United States. Many nongovernmental sources believe the success rate is far higher.

Hernando Benavides ♦ *Laredo, Texas*

Hernando Benavides has spent the last eight years trying to prevent undocumented immigrants from entering the United States. He works for the INS as a Border Patrol agent.

As a shift supervisor working out of the north Laredo station, one of Benavides's key responsibilities is determining how to deploy a limited number of agents in the most effective way possible. For each eight-hour shift, he must decide how many agents to send out to patrol the highways, investigate the train yard, or go out on "sign duty," combing the countryside for the telltale marks of men, women, and children trying to slip into the United States across miles of open ranchland.

Benavides was born in the Rio Grande Valley. He graduated high school, served in the military, and then spent several years as a local police officer before signing on with the U.S. Border Patrol.

We have one shift that works the Missouri Pacific train. That's an exciting shift because all we do is run around down there in the yards. You open up boxcars, grain hoppers, and check the engines—you get in every nook and cranny. You check around the rail tracks, grassy areas, and bushes. The aliens are everywhere to be found.

Aliens are desperate. Desperation, hunger, and the need to feed your family will make you do strange things. Sometimes they take risks I'd never dream of taking. Of course, if I was in their position, I might consider doing the things they do.

We've caught groups of aliens that are locked inside boxcars by smugglers. The smugglers place them inside and then seal the boxcar so the train looks perfectly normal from the outside. During the summer, temperatures of one hundred degrees are fairly common, so those boxcars are like ovens. The aliens just sit there with jugs of water and sweat it out. When the train reaches its destination, the smugglers find the boxcar, unlock it, and let the aliens out.

Unfortunately, things don't always work out that way. Sometimes the smugglers' car breaks down, or they don't make it through the border checkpoints, or they think they're going to get caught and just leave the aliens locked inside. There have been several cases here in south Texas where we've found a bunch of dead aliens in those boxcars. I guess for them it's just part of the danger involved, part of the journey.

Normally, we sterilize the train, so to speak. We go in there and get everybody off before it leaves the yard. Many of the aliens hide along the railroad tracks and then when the train starts to move, they come out, and that's when we lose a lot of them. They run toward the train from all directions just like mice. Once the train gets going, we don't normally stop it, so they take a chance and jump on while it's moving. That's where the majority of accidents happen. A lot of men are cut in half and killed by trains. Many aliens lose legs and arms. I've seen quite a few of them, and it really sticks in your mind.

As dangerous as it is, working in the train yards is probably one of the most fun things we do. It's like a game of cat and mouse. You can see the aliens in the dark moving. They hide from you. You hide from them. It's a game of strategy, a question of who's more clever. We catch a lot, but a lot get away from us.

On average, we'll catch thirty or forty a night down in the train yards. There's nights when we catch over a hundred and nights when it slows down. It depends on the weather and on the level of the water in the Rio Grande. If the water's flowing fast and the current's strong, you don't have as many crossings. I've personally caught groups as large as sixty. Normally, they'll be hiding from you, laying on the ground. You walk up to them, identify yourself, and tell them not to move. Then you pick up the radio and call transport: "Come to such and such a place, I've got twenty-five up here."

They don't scatter. There's no need to. They're not down here to cause trouble. They just want to get to the interior to work. Like I said, it's a game. They know the rules just as well as we do. You take down their names, biographical data, and whatnot. You do an I-213, a very brief arrest report. The majority of them sign a Voluntary Departure and, if nobody gives you a hard time, they'll all be put in a van and taken down to the bridge to cross back into Mexico.

You know the majority of those people—and I'm talking ninety-nine percent of them—will turn around, come right back, and try to get on the train two or three hours later. That's probably the main reason they don't give us a hard time. I've caught the same group as many as three or four times in a single eight-hour shift. You catch them real early, you send them back, and an hour later, here they come again. Then, at dark you might catch them once or twice more. Every time you catch them, they'll give you a different name, but we recognize their faces. There's nights that it's funny and nights that it's not. It depends on your frame of mind.

Sometimes we have a group of people that we'll catch eight or even ten days in a row. Then, all of a sudden, you don't catch them anymore. They've gotten away from you. I'd bet you my last penny that they didn't just turn back and go home. They managed to get through.

Still, they're numbers. If I catch thirty and send them back across and then catch all thirty of them again, that's thirty more. I haven't caught thirty, I've caught sixty. If I catch them two hours from now, I'll have caught ninety that night. I know my bosses will get upset at me for saying this, but it's a numbers game. The more aliens you catch, the more equipment and manpower you can justify. The more you produce, the more your needs are.

Sometimes I feel good about my job, and sometimes I don't. I'm from this area so I've been exposed to illegal immigration all my life. As a youngster, my grandfather had aliens on his ranch. My father had them too, and before I got into the Border Patrol, I worked alongside them. My first brush with Border Patrol was when they raided our place to take the workers away. Heck, those guys would be back later that same night.

When I started working with Border Patrol, I did things I wasn't supposed to do. I can remember going up to farms where we'd find ten or fifteen aliens and the farmer would come out and beg and plead with us not to take them because he needed them for another three or four days. He was supposed to bring his crop in and if we took the aliens, we were pretty much going to ruin the guy. So I'd gather the aliens and say, "Look, I want to give you guys a chance to work for three more days. I'll come down to pick you up on Friday afternoon. That way you can get paid."

Let me tell you, partner, ninety percent of the time they would stay there. You'd go up there on Friday afternoon and, man, they were all cleaned up with their little bags, ready to go. They'd been paid and they were going back to Mexico to spend a weekend with their families. On Monday morning, or maybe four or five days down the road, they'd come back.

Some of the folks we catch come across with their kids. Sometimes you'll have a family with four or five kids, and the father will rig up a tire tube and put the kids inside and bring them across the river, one at a time. I've seen them bring infants, you know, just weeks old, and float them across in an inner tube. A lot of times our officers will sit on the riverbank and watch them with binoculars. When they finally get the whole family across, you jump out and sack them up. You can see the frustration and pain in their faces. I mean, you've got to throw them back across the border. You've got to send them back to Mexico.

Still, sometimes you give out advice: "Don't cross here. The water's dangerous in this area. Go down about half a mile where the water's knee-deep and you can walk across safely." Sometimes I'll catch a group on the train and I'll walk them over to one of the cars and say, "You see this picture right here with the skull and crossbones? Don't get in these cars." A lot of the trains carry chemicals and even if the cars are empty, there's still a residue which can be deadly. There's other cars that are easier to get out of, so I'll tell the aliens, "See these cars? Climb into one of these 'cause if you get locked in, they're easy to open." Are we supposed to do that? I don't know. I do it and I know my guys do it. We can save their lives.

There's a human side to our job. There has to be. The human element is very important, because as small as the things we do may seem to us, they affect people's lives. You can't help but get involved. I've bought food for them out of my pocket and probably everybody else has too. I've called my wife numerous times and told her, "Hey, make me about ten sandwiches and put a bunch of apples or peaches in."

Still, you develop a thick skin. You hear things and you see things, but they don't register. You become hard. Injured aliens in a train yard are a perfect example. I can go up there and see 'em all cut up and everything and come back to the office, type up a little memo, and then go home. For a long time it bothered me, but you have to program yourself to put it aside. If you worried about every single person that you came across with a hardship story, man, you'd go nuts. Everybody's got a hardship story. That's why they're here.

Even though it's our mission on the Border Patrol to catch every single alien, I don't think we'll ever stop them.

The roots of the current wave of Mexican migration can be found in the labor policies of the United States government, particularly the bracero program, which operated between 1942 and 1964 and allowed for the entry of millions of Mexican guest workers. For twenty-two years, the bracero program let growers avoid competing with other industries for domestic workers, kept agricultural wages low, and ensured that farm labor would be a job attractive only to workers with few options. The program also established direct links between thousands of rural communities in central and northern Mexico and agricultural centers in Texas, New Mexico, California, and other southwestern states. The program acclimatized Mexican workers to seasonal migration as thousands of communities grew economically dependent on migration back and forth across the U.S./Mexico border, setting the stage for continued, expanding labor migration.

After the program ended, both legal and undocumented Mexican workers generally took over the jobs previously held by braceros. Many ex-braceros continued migrating, often working for the same employers. Others gained legal residency, later sponsoring relatives and spurring an increase in legal immigration from Mexico. The end of the bracero program coincided with a general reform of U.S. law governing legal residence. For the first time ever, numerical limits were imposed on Mexican immigration. Subsequent restrictions on

Mexican immigration in the 1970s laid the groundwork for the current massive backlog of Mexicans on waiting lists for U.S. visas. There are now over 1 million Mexican nationals qualified to immigrate to the United States on these lists; and close to three-quarters of those qualified are spouses and young children of Mexicans legally residing in this country.

Undocumented immigration grew rapidly in the 1960s as Mexican workers began to labor in a variety of nonagricultural industries. The number of undocumented Mexicans has continued to grow steadily for the last thirty years. Although there are no exact statistics on illegal immigration, it is widely believed that in 1970, there were fewer than 1 million undocumented immigrants in the United States. By 1980, the number had grown to around 3 million, and now, there are an estimated 5 million undocumented immigrants in the country.

In an effort to curb the growth in illegal immigration, Congress passed the Immigration Reform and Control Act (IRCA) in 1986. IRCA legalized the status of many undocumented immigrants living in the United States and tried to discourage employers from hiring unauthorized workers. The law required all employers to check the legal documents of potential workers and created a system of fines and penalties for hiring those without appropriate papers. Prior to 1986, American employers faced no penalties for hiring laborers without legal working papers.

When IRCA was being negotiated, agricultural employers were concerned that the combination of legalizing undocumented workers and penalizing growers for hiring unauthorized immigrants would create a serious labor shortage on farms across the country. In response, they lobbied for the creation of a new guestworker program similar in structure and scope to the bracero program. Eventually, a compromise was reached through the Special Agricultural Worker (SAW) program which provided undocumented farmworkers with an expedited means of legalizing their status and gaining work authorization. Overall, more than 1 million undocumented farmworkers were legalized through the SAW program out of a total of 2.8 million immigrants legalized through IRCA.

While some farmworkers who gained legal status through the SAW program remain in agriculture, many drifted from the fields to find more stable, higher wage employment. Partly because of this trend, the percentage of undocumented farmworkers has continued to rise throughout the 1990s. This has led to the current situation in which the agricultural industry finds itself highly dependent upon laborers who cannot legally work. While IRCA did not decrease undocumented immigration, there are renewed calls for a new amnesty program, highlighting the continued problems of our nation's immigration policy, especially as regards the U.S./Mexico border.

Alan Nelson ♦ *Sacramento, California*

From 1982 through 1989, Alan Nelson was the commissioner of the United States Immigration and Naturalization Service. He ran the INS at a time when American society was growing increasingly concerned with the impact of undocumented immigrants. Nelson supervised the implementation of IRCA, the denial of political asylum claims for many Central American refugees, and increased policing of the U.S./Mexico border. Until his death in 1997, Nelson continued to work on immigration issues as an independent consultant.

One of Nelson's most public activities was his support of Proposition 187, California's controversial 1994 ballot initiative. Proposition 187, which Nelson helped write, prohibited undocumented immigrants from receiving social services, non-emergency public health care, and banned undocumented children from attending public schools. Although the ballot initiative was approved by fifty-nine percent of the state's voters, Proposition 187 was never implemented because of a series of legal challenges. Nearly five years after it was initially approved, a mediated settlement was reached removing almost all of the ballot initiative's controversial proposals.

I think what you are seeing now is a change of attitude. People realize we have a sovereign right to try to prevent illegal crossing. There has been a public recognition that illegal immigration is wrong and that it needs to be dealt with. Now it's not such a terrible thing to put up a fence, install a lighting system, or dig a ditch. It's good to see that happening.

The other side has been very effective for the last number of years in blurring the distinction between legal and illegal immigration. Since it's hard to come out and say, "I think illegal immigration is wonderful," they'll say, "Immigrants are good for the country. They contribute more than they take out. They take jobs nobody else will take." The people that try to blur the distinction between legal and illegal immigration are not having the success that they used to have. The public now understands that there is a huge cost to illegal immigration. That is making it easier for politicians to deal constructively with the problem. This is not a partisan issue.

We are a nation of immigrants. We are generous and that's fine. We should be generous. We've got a good system for people who legally immigrate, but we cannot tolerate undercutting that by excusing or accepting illegal immigration, which violates our laws, morals, and everything else. If you're an illegal immigrant, you're in violation of the law. You're subject to arrest and deportation. You can't work. You can't get benefits, and so forth.

Well, if the law means anything, we cannot in any way justify illegal immigration. I think the major driving force is a matter of principle. If you've got a law on the books, it has got to be enforced. Allowing for illegal immigration fosters a disrespect for law. We are a nation of laws. If people want to change the law, let them come along and try to change it. With IRCA, we changed the law to allow three million people who were here illegally to stay legally. It was done through the law.

There's no shortage of legal agricultural workers now. A lot of times when contractors or growers say that they can't find legal workers, what they mean is, "We want the illegals because we can work them harder, pay them less, abuse them, and get away with it." I often analogize it with slavery. A lot of people say that the economic benefits of slavery were positive and that slaves helped the economy and did a lot of good. Well, nobody now says that we should have slavery. I think the hiring of illegals is parallel. What people who favor hiring illegals mean is, "We are now getting by with cheap, subject labor that we can rip off. We can charge outrageous amounts for food and housing and they can't complain." More often than not, employers know when they're hiring illegals. It's not a big secret. Because of this, I'm a strong supporter of employer sanctions.

Sanctions are the stick, and the carrot is these jobs. When an illegal is apprehended, a vacancy exists. Let's fill those vacancies with citizens or lawful aliens. Here is where we can get the state employment services, the county welfare departments, and other state and federal agencies to work together so that when an illegal alien is pulled off the job, they should fill that position with a legal worker. If we did that, we'd do away with the "recycling" of illegals, where one illegal alien gets pulled off the job and deported, and another one often comes in and takes that same job. If you gave those jobs to legal workers, then you could cut down on unemployment and welfare.

Another thing I've pushed for a long time is full interior repatriation. That is, send the Mexican illegal aliens back to their homes in the interior. If you just dump them back across the border, as they do now, then they'll just keep coming north until they make it.

If the law worked as it should, it would be difficult for an illegal to get a job or to keep it. Same with the benefits. Under the law, the illegal is not entitled to benefits. Still, a lot of times, they slip through the cracks and get benefits. So you have to make the system work better than it does. The illegal alien has got to see the evidence out there in front of him. He's got to say, "I'm going to have a harder time getting across the border. It's gonna be more difficult because they're more likely to catch me. If they catch me, I'm going to be sent back to my home and then I'll have to make another thousand-mile trip to the border. That's going to cost me. So, is it worth all the risk?"

Can we afford these changes? Well, can we afford to let things continue as they are? Can we allow something to occur that is undercutting our whole system?

While IRCA succeeded in legalizing the status of many undocumented immigrants living in the United States, it did little to discourage the arrival of new immigrants. Workers continued to cross the border as wages and benefits in seasonal agriculture remained stagnant, decreasing in relation to rising costs of living, and making farm labor even less appealing to domestic workers. New arrivals now had to present documents testifying to their legal status, creating a large black-market industry in fraudulent papers. Farmworkers who legalized through the SAW program often took advantage of their new status, leaving agriculture for better jobs. IRCA failed to curb undocumented immigration because employer sanctions were relatively easy to avoid and the law was superimposed on an economic system already premised on the flow of large numbers of workers back and forth across the U.S./Mexico border.

Over the last decade, American society has grown increasingly concerned about the impact of legal and illegal immigrants. In many regions of the country, there is a growing fear that immigrants are abusing public services, flooding public schools with children who don't speak English, and costing society far more than they contribute. In fact, immigrants, both legal and illegal, contribute to American society in much the same way as citizens. They earn wages, pay income tax, Social Security, property tax (often as rent), and sales tax. Until recently, legal immigrants were provided with virtually the same access to social services as citizens, with most categories of legal immigrants allowed access to Aid to Families with Dependent Children (AFDC), Social Security insurance, unemployment benefits, Medicaid, food stamps, Head Start, and federally funded housing programs. About 5 percent of working-age immigrants received some type of welfare, a figure equal to that of U.S.-born citizens. Undocumented immigrants, on the other hand, have long been denied virtually all nonemergency social service benefits.

Changes in immigration and welfare laws in 1996 and 1997 radically reduced legal immigrants' access to medical and disability programs, food stamps, and federal housing benefits. Most new immigrants are banned from receiving benefits for their first five years in the United States. These laws strengthened the Border Patrol, increased penalties for entering the country illegally, and made it easier for a variety of agencies to police immigration status. In addition, the legislation imposed higher earning requirements for U.S. citizens and residents seeking to sponsor the legal immigration of relatives, and enacted bans on legalizing the status for undocumented immigrants who remain in the country, or who have been deported. While it is unlikely that these laws will reduce undocumented immigration, they are likely to further marginalize an already vulnerable population.

Concerns about immigration cut to the heart of American identity. The United States has long viewed itself as a nation of immigrants, a democratic society formed of diverse people from distinct cultural backgrounds. Still, this vision of America has always been balanced against strong fears about the negative impact of new arrivals that have periodically produced harsh, often violent anti-immigrant movements. In the 1990s, new nativist movements appeared, beginning in California, the state with the largest percentage of foreign-born residents. Populist anti-immigration movements often seek to increase Border Patrol activity, restrict immigrants' access to a variety of social services, and establish English as the official language.

William King ♦ *Newport Beach, California*
William King began working for the United States Border Patrol in 1957. Over his long tenure with the Border Patrol he held a variety of positions, working in rural and urban areas throughout the country. He was director of the Border Patrol Academy and chief patrol agent, and he was responsible for running the IRCA amnesty program in the western region. King is now the executive vice president of Americans for Responsible Immigration, a group that lobbies for stricter immigration controls.

Illegal aliens are just that. They are people who cross the border, break the law, and are subject to criminal prosecution. There is no way that you can attach the term *immigrant* to an illegal alien. The legal definition of an *immigrant* is an alien lawfully admitted to the United States for permanent residence. You can't link an illegal alien to an immigrant in any way, shape, or form.

I see illegal aliens as similar to burglars. Burglary is a crime; illegal entry is a crime. In both cases, there's trespass with criminal intent. The burglar who gets in your house is going after your personal possessions. The illegal alien who makes it into the United States is going after your job, your education. He's going after welfare.

I've arrested thousands of illegal aliens in my lifetime. I could tell you stories all day long—chasing people, fistfights, arresting seventy people by yourself in a drop house, catching people in the desert, tracking them by snowshoe on the northern border, working the lofts in the New York garment industries.

I've rarely met an alien I didn't like. I don't blame them. If I was one, I'd be doing the same thing they are. If I was a poor and destitute citizen of Mexico looking north to the land of opportunity and hearing from everybody else who goes up there that there's no price to pay for breaking our laws, hell, I'd be one of them too. But the question is, How much of this can we reasonably stand? I am totally opposed to continuing to see this country as a release valve for Mexico's poor and unemployed.

Somebody has to take care of them and it's going to be the taxpayer. It just doesn't make sense. We can't afford to support ever-growing numbers of people coming here with low skills and no education. These people are destined by one means or another to access public education, social services, welfare programs, and long-term medical care that's available to them. Hell, they're even competing for jail space. There are over nineteen thousand illegal aliens serving time in California state prisons right now. Well that means that there are nineteen thousand victims out there too. I'd say fully sixty to seventy percent of the murders we read about in Orange County every day are attributable to illegal aliens. Most of that, thankfully, is against other illegal aliens, but they are the people that are pulling off this stuff.

I think we will be witnessing a tragedy unless something is done to regain control of the border and do something about the illegal aliens who are here. This state is just about broke, and the cost attributed to maintaining the illegal population just grows every day.

Here in California we are being overrun. And when I say overrun, I mean that literally. They are everywhere. There are job pick-up points all around Orange and Los Angeles Counties where the illegals collect on a daily basis to be picked up and taken to work by a variety of construction businesses, drywallers, gardeners, and that type of thing. My eyes are better trained than the average citizen to spot these people, but I haven't spoken to one guy off the street who isn't fed up with it. If you go into parts of Los Angeles, you'd think you were in Tijuana. Spanish is spoken everywhere. I'm told that in some places, there are more windows open in welfare offices for Spanish speakers than there are for English speakers.

When I came to El Paso in 1957, it was practically impossible to find an illegal alien. I think I was in for two months before I arrested one. For the first fifteen years that I was in Border Patrol I never lost an illegal alien once I laid my eyes on him. Then it progressed to a point where I just said, "The hell with it." You know, I'd pick them up on my way to work and I'd pick them up on the way home. I've even arrested them while playing golf.

When I started working with Border Patrol in the 1950s, we caught fewer than fifty thousand aliens a year. In San Diego alone, every year for the last eight or nine years, Border Patrol has made around five hundred thousand arrests.

Originally jobs were what attracted everybody. Years ago, it was single guys who came up here long enough to make a buck and go home. They generally worked in agriculture and then went back home to take care of their families. Then, they saw how easy it was and what a bunch of real saps we are. They began to say to themselves, "Why should I go home? Why shouldn't I just bring my family up here?"

Years ago I worked in what they called Anti-Smuggling in San Diego. I infiltrated alien-smuggling rings and I saw firsthand how these people were treated once they introduced themselves into the alien-smuggling pipeline. Every crime imaginable is committed against these people. I've seen murder, rape, robbery, kidnapping, beating, extortion. We've picked up young girls who've been gang-raped and kicked loose in the desert.

I've seen enough of it to know that this government should flat be ashamed of itself for allowing this smuggling to continue. It is a multimillion-dollar business and it's been going on for years. I've arrested second-generation smugglers and they make a good buck at the expense of their own people. Oddly enough, I never arrested an Anglo who was the head of an alien-smuggling ring. It was always them doing it to their own people.

I am absolutely concerned about the type of people that are coming across the border. The border is wide-open to every dirty punk that wants to cross over and do whatever damage he can up here. The average illegal once he crosses the border has no idea that there is any kind of a price to pay because INS is no longer on the street. We used to do factory checks, raids, and street sweeps. Hell, at the job pick-up points that I'm talking about you'll sometimes see fifty or sixty of them. Citizens complain because they urinate, defecate, and hold everybody in total contempt. They know nothing is going to happen to them.

I think the biggest mistake we ever made was killing the bracero program. If we need foreign workers, then we should have a guest worker program because that would provide the government with some control. We'd have the assurance of knowing who we were getting rather than taking whoever comes up the pike, breaking our laws through illegal entry. With a guest worker program, we'd have control over them while they were here. We could guarantee them safe passage and fair wages while they were here and everybody would be the winner.

When the illegals come here now, they're not adapting to our ways. They're not assimilating. They insist on maintaining their culture. They insist on speaking Spanish. California is no longer a melting pot. To say that this state is still a melting pot is a damn distortion and a lie. The illegals have no desire to assimilate. For that reason, they're going to affect our culture. Now, I don't mind immigrants affecting our culture, as long they do it legally. If they can come here legally, that's fine. But to allow them to come here illegally, take advantage of everything we have, maintain their own culture, and encourage more to come is a stupid policy.

Could we close off the U.S./Mexico border? Sure. We did it in 1954. All the border needs is the attention of Congress and whatever administration is in place. I don't think we need any more legislation. There's plenty of laws on the books to take care of the illegal problem. We just have to approach this from a sensible, logical position. It won't take a hundred thousand Border Patrol agents to seal the border. We need more agents, but that's not the only answer. We also need access to some military technology. Border Patrol needs to be modernized.

I'm too old to have any young kids to worry about, but I've got grandchildren. I want my grandchildren to have the same opportunities, the same quality of education, that my children had and that I had. I don't want their childhood to be overshadowed by what is taking place in this state today, which is largely attributable to illegal aliens. I want my grandchildren to be able to live a decent life.

The United States is experiencing a new wave of immigration. Currently, legal and illegal immigration adds 1 million people per year to the nation's population. Half of the country's foreign-born population arrived over the last two decades, and the 1990 census revealed that 8 percent of the population was foreign-born, more than any year since 1940. The majority of new arrivals come from Latin America and Asia, unlike earlier waves of immigrants who generally came from Europe. If current immigration trends continue, by the year 2050, the percentage of non-Hispanic whites will fall from three-quarters of the nation's population to slightly more than one-half, as one in five Americans will be Hispanic, one in eight African American, and one in ten Asian.

The U.S./Mexico border represents a powerful symbolic space through which immigration, both legal and illegal, is understood. For some, the border is a battleground, a vulnerable physical weakness which must be protected from a literal invasion from the south. For others, the border is an imaginary division between two interconnected nations, an anachronism within the context of a global economy premised on massive international flows of people and things. For prospective immigrants, the U.S./Mexico border is a transitional space, the gateway to a different, distant land—a lonely place of hard labor, opportunity, dislocation, and frightening risk. For hundreds of thousands of undocumented immigrants, many of them farm laborers, crossing the border—*pasando al otro lado*—is the first step toward the promise of a new future, however uncertain.

Douglas Massey ◆ *Philadelphia, Pennsylvania*

Douglas Massey is a sociologist and demographer, the director of the Population Studies Center at the University of Pennsylvania, and one of the nation's leading experts on labor migration from Mexico to the United States. Working with a team of U.S. and Mexican researchers, Massey has assembled a database on the labor migration patterns of residents from over thirty communities in western Mexico. To date, the research teams have collected data on the migration histories of thousands of workers, documenting the ways in which traveling to the United States to work has transformed social and economic life in many parts of Mexico and further bound the two nations to each other.

Immigrants don't just suddenly appear when the economy goes bad. They've been there all along. However, when you build up public hysteria, these issues acquire lives of their own and they are hard to control. People get victimized and ugly ethnic prejudice comes to the surface.

It's virtually impossible to stop undocumented migration through police action. The cost of closing off the border would be exorbitant and people will always find ways to cross. The U.S./Mexico border has to be permeable because of the economic relations between the two countries. People have to cross that border. It's not like Berlin where you had two completely separate and disarticulated economic systems on either side of a wall. You can't build a wall between two systems that are completely integrated and becoming more so every day.

The actions on the border are mainly for political show. Everyone realizes they're not going to be very effective. In fact, the agencies that are in charge of suppressing the border are so underfunded that they can't even begin to carry out their mandate. Nobody really expects them to be effective. They are there for political consumption in a very cynical fashion.

I think that both the Border Patrol agents and the migrants realize that they're playing a game. They have a tacit understanding. If the migrants don't resist arrest, passively go to a holding cell, and don't request a deportation hearing, then they'll get a chance to try again. In fact, it would be an unmitigated disaster for the Border Patrol, the INS, and certain courts if every Mexican that was caught exercised his right under U.S. immigration law to a deportation hearing. It's not in the Mexicans' interest to do so. When they're caught, their immediate goal is to get back to the Mexican side of the border as soon as they can so they can try to cross over again. They waive their rights to a hearing and undergo voluntary deportation in which they are quickly processed, transported back to the border, and turned loose.

That way the INS benefits because they get to arrest a lot of people. The more arrests they make, the better they look. The INS gets to show that they're out there fighting against "the hordes" coming in. At the same time, the Mexican knows that he can get back. He might have been unlucky this time, but he can try again as soon as possible. Everyone knows this is going on. It's a complete charade.

It's very difficult to explain the upswing in migration strictly in terms of wage differentials. The fact that Mexico is poorer than the United States is nothing new. There have been big differentials in average income, average wages, and economic opportunities for years and years. Nevertheless, it's only relatively recently that migration flows have increased dramatically. What really explains the dynamic increase in the migration process is the formation of networks which link workers in Mexico to jobs, people, and resources in the United States. The general public, policy makers, and people who should really know better do not understand the important role that social networks bring to the whole migration process.

To get an idea of how this works, consider a person in a community where no one has ever gone to the United States. For that person, traveling to the United States is a daunting prospect. He doesn't know what to do or where to go. He doesn't know how to get across the border or how to get a job. He doesn't know how to get around in the United States or how to speak English. Migration is costly and very risky. It takes money to transport yourself to the border, to cross into the United States, to get settled and find a job. If you're not wealthy to begin with, you may have to turn to a local moneylender who charges very high interest rates. If the trip isn't successful, you may return home in debt. That could put your family in great financial risk. So, for that person, traveling to the United States is a very discouraging idea.

However, if you come from a community where fifty or sixty percent of the residents have been to the United States, it's very easy to find someone who can tell you where to go, how to cross the border, how much it's going to cost, how to find a *coyote,* what places to seek work, and who to stay with when you get there. All this information is readily available. So, as more people go to the United States, the costs and risks of migration fall and the potential benefits rise substantially.

Once one person in a community goes to the United States, then the community begins to be transformed. After that person comes back, everyone to whom that person is related has a social tie to someone who's been to the United States. That social tie is a resource that enables people to gain access to the United States, which opens up further avenues to still more people. Over time, you see a very rapid change in communities, so that twenty years after the first person migrates to the United States, ninety percent of the households in a particular community will have someone working in the United States.

Migration is energized through the dynamic expansion of social networks which interact with the wage differential between the United States and Mexico. The wage differential stays the same, but because of the expansion of social networks, the ability to make that wage differential pay for you increases dramatically. Gradually, migration to the United States becomes a part of the normal course of events. In many communities in Mexico, a young man coming of age is expected to go to the United States. I've sampled more than thirty communities in Mexico and I've never found one without migrants. I don't believe they exist.

Whenever people ask what the United States should do about Mexican immigration, my answer is, "Forget about it." If you wanted to do something about Mexican immigration you should have thought of it in 1942 when the bracero program was set up. Our economies and societies are so integrated, the process so well advanced, the networks so well developed, that the cost of ending immigration would be prohibitive. So, don't worry about Mexican immigrants. Immigration is going to do what it's going to do and the best course of action is to recognize that and to try and channel migration in a legal direction. Increasingly, Mexicans see the border as a blur, something that isn't sharp and clear, something that is disappearing. Perhaps Americans fear this and want to prevent it from happening.

We are now witnessing forces that are producing immigration on a global scale. Immigrants and multiethnic environments are basic structural features of modern postindustrial society. It's happening in the United States and it's happening in every other industrial country in the world. One way or another, we have to learn to grapple with this issue, face the facts, and deal with it. Immigrants are not going to go away. Most Americans have a completely jaundiced and mistaken view of the whole migration process and what's driving it. They also have misconceptions of the effects of Mexican migrants on American society. They tend to forget the contributions and dwell on the costs. Americans actively recruit Mexicans during times of economic growth and prosperity and then, suddenly, when we hit a recession or a period of economic dislocation, we become obsessed with the costs of immigrants, both real and imagined.

This is symptomatic of a broader problem in American society. Americans want to have their cake and eat it too. We want to have a high level of consumption, but we don't want to pay for it. We want to have a high level of economic growth, which requires immigrant labor, but we don't want the immigrants that go with it. People feel overwhelmed by the numbers of people wanting to come north to take our wealth away. This idea is driven by their view of Mexico as an impoverished and corrupt place with limited opportunities and no social mobility. This is a completely ethnocentric view. The reason that migrants come to the United States is not so much because they are poor and we are rich, but because our economies are intertwined.

I don't think Americans realize the extent to which our nations are already completely integrated. I would like to help Americans to see the degree to which we are all part of the same economy and society. Western Mexico is part of the U.S. labor market and certainly all of Mexico is part of the U.S. capital market. We use their labor pool as our own, and increasingly, our labor is going there. This is not something that you can prevent because it's already happened.

6. Slavery in the Fields

IT IS COMMON knowledge among African American farmworkers that there are places throughout the rural South where you can be taken, forced to work in the fields, and paid no wages for your labor. The crewleaders who run these labor camps typically send family members or trusted henchmen to homeless shelters, soup kitchens, and poor neighborhoods to find new workers. Recruiters strike up conversations with men and women who have fallen on hard times, promising good jobs with free housing, cheap food, and high wages. For those seeking a break from the day-to-day struggles of life on the streets, the offer seems almost too good to be true. Some workers are drawn in by the possibility of a decent place to live, the opportunity to save a little money, and the dream of starting life anew. Others are won over by the promise of easy access to wine, beer, and crack cocaine. For alcoholics and drug users, labor camp life provides a chance to slip anonymously into the numbing comfort of addiction, safe from the violence and uncertainty of the street.

Workers who accept the recruiters' offers are loaded into a van or an old school bus and driven to the crewleader's labor camp, which is usually located in a remote, rural area, sometimes hundreds of miles away. Upon arrival, it becomes clear that each of the recruiters' promises was either a gross exaggeration or an outright lie. Instead of a clean bed in a newly furnished house, prospective workers discover that they must sleep on dirty mattresses in crowded barracks with holes in the floor, leaking roofs, and filthy outhouses. Instead of home-cooked meals, workers find themselves eating endless meals of bologna sandwiches, rice and beans, and turkey necks.

New recruits quickly learn that labor camp life revolves around "the line," where workers can purchase wine, beer, cigarettes, or drugs from either the crewleader or an assistant. Even those without money can go through the line, since virtually everything at the camp is sold on credit at highly inflated prices. In some cases, crewleaders also lend money to workers, typically charging 100 percent interest.

On the first payday, workers unfamiliar with labor camp life begin to understand the nature of the world they've entered. At the end of the week, the cost of food, rent, loan payments, and credit purchases of wine, beer, liquor, and drugs are deducted from each worker's wages. As a result, migrants living on these camps rarely earn more than a few dollars a week for their labor. In fact, many workers end each week owing money to the crewleader. Since what was owed from the previous week is carried over to the following week and then added to that week's purchases, few workers can pull themselves out of debt.

Those unfamiliar with this system are outraged at what they find. Workers find themselves stranded in labor camps, which are often located far from town, surrounded by fences, and watched by guards. Some workers try to pay off their debts in order to leave as quickly as possible. This is difficult, since the crewleader controls the books, marking down all credit purchases, real or invented. Crewleaders are generally armed and often rely on groups of thugs, known as henchmen, who police crews, threaten workers, and assault those who refuse to cooperate. Workers who want to leave a labor camp while still in debt to the crewleader must deal with the henchmen. Occasionally workers are beaten as an example to other members of the crew, and there are cases where farmworkers have died at the hands of crewleaders and their henchmen. To leave this type of labor camp, it is usually necessary to escape, to slip away in the middle of the night, winding one's way along rivers, railroad tracks, and back-country roads.

Fred Sampson ♦ *Augusta, Georgia*

Fred Sampson sits on a bench at the Greyhound bus station. He is on his way to Atlanta to see his family for the first time in years. Two nights ago, he escaped from a labor camp in the ridge country of South Carolina, the heart of the state's peach industry.

Sampson is forty-five years old. Until a few years ago, he was building houses outside of Atlanta and earning over $400 a week. When the project was finished, he lost his job. At first, he lived on his *savings, but he was unable to find another job and couldn't collect unemployment since he had been working off the books. After a few months, he had spent all his money. He lost his apartment, became homeless, and spent nearly a year living on the streets.*

I am not going to tell no lies because lies come back to haunt you. I don't have to lie about what happened to me.

I was smoking. I was getting high. But I took care of myself. I paid my rent, never got evicted, never sold anything out of my house. It's just a weak person that uses crack as an excuse for crime and violence.

After I lost my job, things fell apart. I ended up homeless. I spent a year on the street. I was about to give up. I was looking for anything to get me off the streets, to get me some money and a place where I could sleep.

I was on a soup line in Atlanta. The crewleader's son recruited me. He looked like a regular guy. He wore a T-shirt, jeans, and sneakers. He talked real good.

"Any of you guys want to go to work?"

Someone asked, "What are you doing?"

"We're going to South Carolina to pick peaches."

A lot of people shied away from him, but no one tried to tell me what was up. So he started talking to me and a few other guys, and we started listening. One of the guys asked him, "Hey man, y'all run rocks?"

He said, "Yeah, but you have to talk to my mama about all that. You know, you can get you some beer, some wine, cigarettes, run that line."

At the time, I didn't know what a line was, but I knew what rocks were, so when he said, "run that line," I just put two and two together. I figured that the line was where you could go to get you a little something to smoke. Then he told us that just for coming, his mama would give us a rock for free, to recruit you. He said anything after that comes out of your pay.

I figured making minimum wage for forty hours a week, that's roughly a hundred and sixty dollars. He said my food bill would be about forty-five dollars a week. I figured that would leave me with over a hundred dollars. I'd spend a little of that and have some money left over each week. So I went with him to Johnston, South Carolina, to do peaches.

The first week they didn't let us work too much. They put us out in the field, but they wouldn't let us pick for more than two or three hours each day. At the time, I didn't know what they were doing, but now I understand. See, when you first get to the camp, the crewleader won't let you make enough money to clear that first week. That way, you go into debt. Even before you get a chance to put your own self in debt, she gets you in the hole, and she won't let you out. I felt used, but, shoot, I couldn't turn around and go back to the streets. That's what I was running from. Man, I needed money. I needed a place to stay.

We left Johnston around August to go to Benson, North Carolina, to pick sweet potatoes. You'd fill up a bucket of sweet potatoes, put it on your shoulder, and walk across the rows to the truck. You'd lift the bucket up to the guy in the truck and he'd give you back your bucket with a ticket. That's your count. That's to show that you dropped. Then you go back to your row. They paid us thirty-five cents a bucket.

After sweet potatoes, we left North Carolina and went to Glennville, Georgia, to plant onions. We were sticking little Vidalia onion plants in small holes. It was getting cold. Man, there were times it was so cold that the ground froze hard as a rock. You'd make a fire and they'd come and put the fire out. They'd say, "Get your ass back to work. You keep warm by working."

What can you do, man? You're out there. You're alone. You're some-where way out in the fields. You can't buck the man. You ain't gonna fight him.

Man, the camps was really bad. In Glennville, we lived in a chicken coop. It was a big place with wood boards for the walls and tin for the roof. Everybody lived in there together. The roof leaked and there were rats everywhere. Mice used to get up and watch television with me. The bathroom and the showers were in the same place with the sinks. Some-times it would all back up and the human waste would come out through the shower. You couldn't stand on the shower floor because of all the mess that was there. If you wanted to keep clean, you had to go outside and bathe with a bucket.

We spent the winter in Georgia, and then in the spring we picked and cut onions. It would take two big buckets to fill up a sack that weighed sixty to seventy pounds. You'd get seventy cents for a sack. It was hard work, but if the onions were good, I could fill about eight sacks an hour. Still, I never made minimum wage. Never. One week, I earned ten dol-lars. Other weeks, I was paid two dollars, three dollars, four dollars. Some weeks, I got nothing.

Saturday was payday. The crewleader would call your name: "Send Fred in." I'd go in and she'd say, "Well, Fred, you have so many dumps and this is what you made. Sign this." That was the check. Sometimes it was the right number of dumps and sometimes it wasn't. I kept a record mentally. At one time I kept it on paper, but it didn't do no good. I heard guys sit and argue with her saying they had more dumps, but what could they do about it? Ain't nothing they could do.

Once I signed the check, she'd say, "What you want?"

"The usual." On Saturday, it was a pack of cigarettes, a beer, a pint of wine, a rock, and a few dollars. There were times when I got no dollars.

It was a mean life with those people. I can't say about other camps, 'cause I never went to but one camp. For thirteen months and two days I stayed with that crew. I was there so long because I didn't have nowhere else to go. A lot of times, I wanted to leave, but then I'd look at the television news and see that the economy was bad. I figured there were no jobs. So I hung on in there and took it.

A lot of times I was so far from everything that I didn't know how to get away. Then, when we were in Trenton, South Carolina, I found out that I could go to Augusta and get some assistance. The night before I left, I asked the crewleader about taking me back to Atlanta. That night in the wee hours of the morning I was awake and I saw her husband standing in his trailer watching my room.

I left the night before last and made sure the crewleader didn't see me. I left between midnight and one o'clock. I wasn't scared when I left the camp. Once I made up my mind to leave, I wasn't going to work for them again. I didn't run. I walked. I walked away and didn't stop. I walked all the way from Trenton, South Carolina, to Augusta, Georgia. It took twelve hours. My back hurts. The instep of my feet hurts. Last night, I had to sleep on the floor at the Salvation Army.

It's been an experience, I'll tell you that. I'll never forget it. Never. It's nothing that you'd put your worst enemy through. I mean, they work you to death. They just don't care. Man, the way they treat people? It's miserable. That ain't even living. You're just existing. A lot of times I kept going by telling myself, "I ain't going to let it beat me. I'm going to find a way out."

For a person to be a migrant worker and continue to be a migrant worker, his mentality has got to be low. Either that or he just done gave up. So this is where I am today. It makes me feel mean and bitter. Mean and bitter. Right now, I got two quarters in my pocket. I don't feel sorry for myself because this experience is going to make me stronger. I hope it makes me strive to get something and then keep it. Before, I took everything for granted. Now I'll be more aware because I could fall again.

I've been thinking of telling everybody that I've been in jail, but I can't do that. I'm going to tell my children the truth. I hope it don't make them feel that I was weak. I'm going to tell them everything because it might happen to them. I am going to tell the truth.

In 1992, a federal task force was formed to investigate abusive contractors working in the South Carolina peach harvest. About a year after Sampson fled the labor camp, his crewleader, her husband, and their son were arrested for peonage, criminal violations of the Migrant and Seasonal Agricultural Worker Protection Act (MSAWPA), and drug-related charges. All three plea-bargained, the crewleader pleading to MSAWPA violations and the son to conspiracy to hold workers in peonage. Only the son received a jail sentence.

Over the last three decades, a number of courts have established that the conditions of debt peonage under which thousands of farmworkers live and work violate federal antislavery statutes. Farmworkers living in camps where they are held in debt peonage are forced to labor against their will and subject to threats and acts of extreme violence.

Since the mid-1970s, the federal government has periodically organized task forces to investigate allegations of debt peonage among farmworkers. Between 1977 and 1990, the Justice Department filed twenty cases charging seventy-one defendants with holding workers in involuntary servitude. Eighty-five percent of these defendants either pleaded guilty or were convicted of enslaving migrant farmworkers. Nevertheless, most crewleaders convicted of holding farmworkers in involuntary servitude serve limited sentences, often leaving jail to continue operating labor camps.

Debt peonage represents the most extreme form of farmworker abuse. Although it is increasingly uncommon, until quite recently, large numbers of African American farmworkers labored under conditions of debt peonage throughout the South. There are also isolated cases of immigrant farmworkers who are forced into debt and held against their will. Most of these situations involve recently arrived undocumented immigrants who have no knowledge of their legal rights and limited contacts with established migrant communities. In some cases, Latino immigrants fall into debt to *coyotes* who then pass workers on to contractors. These contractors hold crews in labor camps where they are forced to pay off their smuggling fees as well as additional debts for transportation, housing, food, and liquor. In several cases, contractors have been found guilty of holding immigrant farmworkers in involuntary servitude.

Debt peonage among African American workers has a distinct history that illustrates the direct link between the development of the farm labor system in the rural South and the legacy of slavery. While the Civil War led to the emancipation of America's slaves, the post-

bellum southern economy remained dependent on a docile agricultural labor force whose freedom was limited through a variety of legal
and economic mechanisms that controlled workers' mobility. In the
early years of Reconstruction, a series of laws known as the Black
Codes authorized local authorities to jail freed blacks or place them
into forced labor if they violated poorly defined vagrancy laws or
failed to pay special taxes.

The Black Codes were quickly replaced by a series of special contract laws that obligated workers to labor for particular employers
for a complete agricultural season, from planting through harvesting.
Special clauses in these laws allowed employers to withhold workers'
earnings for a variety of mild offenses, such as arriving late in the
fields or missing a day's work. The objective of these laws was to keep
workers from leaving their jobs until the harvest season had ended.
At the completion of each season, workers and their families would
often seek new employers. Since they had few other options, African
Americans generally signed new contracts that were equally demanding and similarly repressive.

Workers typically borrowed money and supplies from their employers and were often prevented from leaving because of their debts
or forced to transfer existing debts to new employers. The use of debt
to control workers was the logical extension of an agricultural system
built upon slavery and then forced to deal with laborers who were
legally free to live and work wherever they chose. By encouraging
and often forcing workers to fall into debt to their employers, growers created and maintained a docile workforce, justifying their actions on the basis of workers' decisions to borrow. In this way, many
areas of the rural South retained a plantation culture in which large
landowners continued to exercise considerable control over African
Americans who labored in their fields.

The use of employee debt to control worker mobility was further
perpetuated by the sharecropping and land-tenancy systems that
dominated agricultural production in the South from the late nineteenth century through the 1920s. Farming land they didn't own,
sharecroppers and tenants borrowed money, seeds, and supplies
from landowners in return for a portion of the harvest. If there was
a poor harvest or the crops were destroyed by drought or disease,
tenants often had to borrow additional money and supplies, forcing
workers and their families deeper into debt.

In the early twentieth century, improved technology reduced the
number of tenant farmers and sharecroppers needed for preharvest
labor. As fruit and vegetable farms increased production and

acreage, farms required significant numbers of workers for short periods of time, particularly during the harvest season. Many white and black workers who remained in rural areas drifted from sharecropping into migratory labor. Some traveled in their own vehicles and worked independently, while others worked in crews managed by contractors, many of whom used debt peonage schemes to control their workers.

The use of debt to control workers is cynically premised on workers' freedom. Employers claim that employees who fall into debt do so of their own accord, as a result of a series of free, rational decisions. Of course, workers rarely have the freedom posited by opportunistic employers or the intermediaries they hire. Systems relying on employee debt generally involve tricks, threats, and physical violence. Workers may be drawn in by false promises, fooled by hidden charges and excessive interest payments, and ultimately threatened with beatings or police action. For African Americans in the rural South, the violence associated with employers' threats was real and the barriers to defending their rights were often insurmountable.

By the 1940s, the majority of migrant farmworkers in the South were African Americans as most white farmworkers found better jobs during the economic expansion of the war years. The threat of violence and the use of workers' debts to control African American farmworkers was standard practice on migrant crews in the South from the 1940s onward.

Hazel Filoxsian ♦ *Fort Pierce, Florida*

Hazel Filoxsian began working in the fields when she was seven years old, helping her family pick vegetables in Florida. She first traveled north on a migrant crew when she was thirteen. For years, she drifted in and out of farmwork.

After divorcing her first husband she took her last trip "up the road." Following this experience, she decided to work as an advocate for farmworkers' rights. For several years, she worked as an organizer for the Florida branch of the United Farm Workers of America. Later, she founded the Migrant and Immigrant Assistance Center, a nonprofit organization dedicated to serving the needs of area farmworkers.

Filoxsian is a striking woman with an open, expressive manner and a broad, welcoming smile. She stands six foot three and has long hair and green eyes. She is extremely articulate and speaks with great care.

The last time I went north was in 1984 when I went to Wilson, North Carolina, with a white Haitian crewleader. His entire crew was Haitian. Since I was the only single woman in the camp, I had some problems. There were lots of men there and I couldn't speak Creole. I didn't understand them and they didn't understand me.

I left the Haitian crew and moved to another camp that was run by Irene Taylor. This camp belonged to the same farmer as the first camp I was on. Taylor's camp was like a nightmare. If someone had sat down and told me that there was a person as cold as Irene Taylor, I wouldn't have believed it. I can't imagine anyone, especially a woman, being that bad.

Taylor had a room that she would force women into. Whatever man earned the most money that week could choose which woman he wanted to sleep with. Taylor would force the women to do it. She'd lock them in the room, and if anybody came to their aid, she'd warn them off with her gun. She'd say, "If anyone interferes, I'm going to kill 'em." We all knew that she meant it.

I wasn't among the women that were forced into that room because I told Taylor that I was going to work, earn my money, and leave the camp. I'm the kind of person that can make people understand that I'm serious about what I say. Maybe she saw that I was different from the other girls. I don't know. Taylor didn't fool with me too much.

Also, I had a gun, a little gun. Nobody on the camp knew I had it. I kept the gun in my bra. It was a raggedy little .22 pistol. The firing pin was missing and my friend Razzie from the other camp had taken a piece of clothes hanger and pushed it in so that the revolving mechanism would stay in place. If you fired it, you had to pull out the piece of metal, rotate it, and reset it in order to fire again.

There was a guy on the camp whose street name was Mule. He was a twenty-three-year prison veteran and they said he'd killed his stepfather and a deputy in Gainesville. He was out of jail, on parole, I suppose. That particular week, Mule had earned the most money and we were all in the kitchen getting paid off. He was laughing and everybody was joking, "Oh, he's going to have a time tonight." "Oh, Mule's got all that money tonight, but he'll be broke in the morning."

Then Taylor asked him, "Well, Mule, which one do you want?"

The man looked over at me and said, "I want that one, the girl with the green eyes."

I started looking around to see if there was anyone else among the women who had green eyes because I figured he couldn't have been talking about me.

Then Taylor came over to me and said, "You got to go with him."

"What do you mean I got to go with him?"

"Well, I promised him a piece of tail if he earned the most money."

"Well, then you go with him. You promised him. I didn't."

Then Mule reached out to grab me by my shoulder and I pulled out my little gun. When I pulled out the pistol and it went, *pow!* and nearly blew Mule's finger off—the finger was hanging from his hand by just a thread—I knew right away that I better take advantage of the situation because I wouldn't have time to adjust the gun for a second shot.

"Listen, I want you to know that I'm a crack shot and the next one goes right through your heart."

I was so scared. Oh my God, what if he didn't believe me? What if he saw that I was scared? What if he heard my knees knocking, my teeth chattering, my heart pounding? I ran back to my room and tried to get my clothes and stuff to get away. Meanwhile, the crewleader was sending guys over to find me, to stop me from leaving. One came with a bat and the others had these big belts. The one with the bat hit me and I lost all feeling in one arm.

I fell. I was trying to scramble away. They were beating me. I lost the little gun and left all my clothes. Finally I managed to get away from them. I ran as fast as I could. I had no idea where I was going, absolutely no idea. I didn't know anything about the area, so, I just went down the road. I remember going across a bridge and there was a sign that said TAR RIVER. There was a river there with muddy, muddy water.

During the day I would sleep in the woods. Jesus Christ, I had the worst case of chiggers and red bugs. At night, I would walk along the road, dodging the car lights, ducking in and out of the woods because at that time they were hijacking people and selling them to the contractor who bid the highest.

I finally ended up on a labor camp which was all Haitians. That's where I met my present husband who turned out to be the best thing that ever happened to me.

The institutionalization of debt peonage to control black farm-workers in the South was founded upon racism. Virtually all of the region's growers were white and the vast majority of the workers were African Americans, who generally labored under the supervision of black crewleaders. Growers benefited from a docile, low-wage workforce, and they commonly isolated themselves from the brutality and violence of camp life, a world of black workers controlled by black crewleaders. In general, it was the crewleaders who engaged in the most direct abuses—running the line, fixing the books, threatening and disciplining workers.

The cruelty of the system was self-perpetuating. Growers hiring these types of crews generally paid the crewleaders a single lump sum, thereby avoiding the responsibility of keeping records or paying workers individually. By recruiting desperate individuals with few options and then enticing them into debt, the crewleaders who ran these camps managed to pocket most, if not all, of their workers' wages. These crewleaders could thereby underbid legitimate crewleaders. The more distant, difficult, and uncontrollable workers seemed to growers, the more likely they would be to hire tough crewleaders who could handle unruly laborers.

Local residents rarely dealt with the African American farmworkers who passed through their communities, and residents generally knew little about migrants' lives. To the degree that locals dealt with migrants—in stores, gas stations, or passing in the street—they usually viewed the workers with suspicion and fear, particularly within the white community. The more isolated the workers were, the easier it was for crewleaders to exercise extraordinary, often violent, control over their crews. Workers fleeing camps would often be returned to their crewleaders by local police, who were generally uninterested in investigating cases of possible abuse or wrongdoing. The use of debt peonage by African American crewleaders reflected and reinforced the social division between whites and blacks. Black workers knew they couldn't turn to white authorities for assistance, and growers and local residents allowed crewleaders to run their crews however they wanted, so long as farmworkers arrived for the season, worked hard, and were kept generally hidden from view.

African American crewleaders were usually ex-farmworkers who had moved their way up from field workers to supervisors and, finally, to contractors, having gained enough experience to manage a crew and saved enough money to buy an old truck or bus. For enterprising blacks, becoming a crewleader represented one of the few available business opportunities in the rural South, one of only a handful of ways to pull oneself up out of poverty. Consequently, African American crewleaders played a complicated role within black communities. On the one hand, most crewleaders were brutal, abusive, and domineering, using tricks, false promises, and violence to control their workers. On the other hand, crewleaders were among the wealthiest local blacks and were often important local leaders. Even as they lined their pockets with workers' wages, they provided farm laborers and their families with advice and protection, often acting as key mediators between the divided worlds of black and white society.

Robert Wilson ♦ *Pahokee, Florida*

Robert Wilson grew up in the migrant stream and became a crewleader in his late teens, when debt peonage was common throughout the South. He continued to work as a crewleader until an illness forced him out of the fields. He now lives alone in an apartment and spends most of his days indoors.

The first thing a crewleader's got to have is something for the workers to drink. If a black don't have a sip of wine or a good drink of liquor in the morning, he won't go to work. Hell, with some of these guys I worked with, you had to drink to put up with them. The second thing you got to have is somewhere for them to eat. Those are the two main things you need to run a migrant camp. Without liquor and food, you got nothing.

If you're the crewleader, you keep your hands clean. Selling booze is illegal. You don't sell it. That's so you don't get in trouble if the state revenue service comes in. The farmer's not going to put up with me if they get me for illegal booze, so I always had someone else sell the wine and liquor. If they got put in jail, me and my farmer would get him out. Still, I was the daddy of it. It wasn't wrong 'cause if they didn't get liquor from me, they'd go right on down the road and get it. I'd mark up the price, but not more than the others.

You had to be ironfisted with the men. If you didn't, you couldn't handle them. I'd carry a big gun and sometimes I had a couple of fellows there with me. I carried what we called a hogleg—a big old Colt .45 automatic. I'd walk in the camp sometimes and just blast up the top of the house. Then it would get real quiet and I'd throw some language at 'em: "Hey, all right, you motherfuckers. Straighten up in here. Now, goddamn it, I ain't gonna have any more of this motherfuckin' shit."

You know what I mean? Thing's quiet down in there and they'd say, "Now, that's a good crewleader. That's a good one." Now, if you go in there all spit and polished and say, "You boys, please lay off of things. Don't do that," they'd say, "Where'd that pussy come from? Get that pussy-assed nigger out of here."

You had to be rough and tough, because you'd meet some of the damnedest people you ever looked at. You can believe that. To be honest with you, most of the guys in this business were wanted somewhere. They'd be running from wives or running from the law or done screwed over some farmer or crewleader. On a camp you'd never call anyone by their real name. It's always Baldy, Big Butt, Pretty Gal, Eighty-five, Big Mama, things like that. Still, there's one name you get on a camp that you wear from the time you get it until the day you die. That name is mother-fucker. You're going to be motherfucker if you don't be nothing else. That's how we talked: "Hey, come here, motherfucker." There was no use trying to fight it.

Most migrants are gentle and you can handle them. But, wherever you find money being passed around, with payday every day or a nice payday at the end of each week, you're gonna find robbery. A guy might pick string beans as fast as a poor horse is trottin', but if you didn't watch him close, he'd run off with that payroll. He'd have a .38 in your head and say, "Give it up," and you either give it up or he leads you down and takes it. That's just the way it was.

Now, generally speaking, a lot of what you hear about in camps isn't as bad as they say. The workers never give you the reason why things happen, you know? If you hear talk of some guy being clipped or being stabbed, there had to be a reason why it happened.

Let me clear some of this up. Here you are, a crewleader. I come to you and you load me up. You give me twenty dollars to put in my pocket and you feed me all the way up the road. When I get to the camp, maybe there's a week before work starts. So, you feed me for a solid week, you wine me and you dine me. Now, when the work time comes, what do I do? I want to leave. Now, you know I'm a nasty motherfucker. Why? Because, I owe you maybe fifty, sixty, or possibly a hundred dollars. When I get ready to go, you say, "Hey, where's my money? I gave it to you in good feed."

Then I tell you, "Kiss my ass."

Well, what are you supposed to do about that? You're responsible for the blankets and sheets and now I've got them in my bag and I'm taking them with me. I haven't done a lick of work and I'm telling you to kiss my ass. Well, what would you do about it? I'll tell you what you'd do. You'd beat my ass. That's exactly what you'd do. There ain't no "if you felt like you could."

If a man bucked up against me, he'd go straight to hell. That's what you'd do, too. It's not that crewleaders are nasty. It's the migrant that's responsible. He don't give a damn about you. You only got one job and one little farm you're working on, and he's got a whole state he can go around to.

Now, not all migrants are thieves. Most migrants are nice people. What makes them bad is that nobody gives a damn about them. Nobody give them any respect. I don't give a damn how good they work, mi-grants have never been thought of as anything but a piece of trash, a waste. They know there ain't nobody looking out for them, and that no-body cares. They're just out there working from one day to the next, from one state to the other, and everyone that comes along gives them shit to eat.

If a migrant can work and make him a few dollars so he can get his cigarettes, a few drinks, and some eats, then he's all right. He'll sleep in a shit house, a country shit house. He don't give a damn. He's a migrant and he knows that no one's going to make it no better for him, so he just don't care. That's a migrant's life. That's his state of mind.

If you put the average psychologist out there, the migrant would drive him nuts. They'd drive him nuts 'cause he couldn't figure them out. I put a good thirty-five years right straight down at it, and I never figured them out. I learned their ways, how they operate, but every migrant's different. You'll never figure them out. Never. Not in a lifetime. It's impossible. *Impossible* is the word of a damn idiot and that's the word I'm using—*impossible.* It's idiotic for me to say so, but I'll just have to wear that idiot name. Once you know you'll never figure out the migrant, then you can go to work.

Here's something a farmer once taught me. He said, "Robert, if you catch one of them damn niggers down on his knees eating shit, you leave that black motherfucker right down there eating that shit. 'Cause if you take him out of there and feed him a steak, as soon as that son of a bitch gets going, that black motherfucker'll push your head right down there to eat that shit, and then he'll laugh at you." That's the natural truth.

You cannot satisfy them sons of a bitches. I don't give a damn what you do, you cannot satisfy a migrant. You can give him the shirt off your back, and you still won't satisfy him. They'll laugh in your face. That's the life of a migrant. You just can't trust them.

You see, I studied the migrant just like I studied the white farmer and the other white overseers. There's something that most of them don't realize and if they do know it, then they don't want to admit it. You see, there ain't but two kinds of people that run things on this earth, the people with the money and guns and the people without the money and guns. Now, the ones who've got the money and guns are going to damn sure make them bastards that ain't got the money and guns do what the hell they want done. When you come down to it, you either got the money and guns, or you don't. If you got the money and guns, then that bastard that don't is going to damn sure let you boss him around, at least if he wants his black ass to stick around.

While the Civil Rights movement transformed many aspects of racial inequity in the South, rendering segregation illegal, providing remedies for employment discrimination, allowing blacks to vote,

these changes by no means signaled the end of debt peonage for African American farmworkers. Debt peonage remained a central element of the black farmworker experience up through the 1970s, gradually diminishing in the 1980s, and to some degree continuing up until the present.

Improved opportunities, continued migration from rural communities to urban areas, regional economic shifts, and the institution of a variety of social benefits have steadily drawn African American workers away from farm labor. By the 1970s, the black farm labor force was growing older and fewer young African Americans were willing to work in the fields. Increasingly, the most abusive African American crewleaders were forced to recruit workers out of urban missions and homeless shelters, often hiring men and women with no previous farm labor experience. Most recently, crewleaders have moved away from the traditional alcoholic workforce and have begun employing crack addicts recruited off the streets in large cities.

Crewleaders sometimes justify their actions by arguing that no one else is willing to provide these workers with housing, food, and employment. In fact, many homeless workers stay in abusive labor camps not only out of fear, but because they have few options other than returning to the harsh reality of life on the streets. Some of the worst abuses of farm laborers continue in part because these workers have been abandoned by society. Workers who escape from one violent labor camp often find themselves back in skid-row neighborhoods, sleeping in missions or in parks, sometimes biding time until another recruiter comes along, offering them work in the fields.

Over the last several decades, the number of black crewleaders has steadily diminished as African American farmworkers are being replaced by Latino immigrants. Currently, over 80 percent of migrant farmworkers in the South are Latinos, most of whom are recent immigrants—young, experienced farm laborers who are preferred by agricultural employers. Recent Latino immigrants are generally willing to work for low wages and accept difficult living conditions without having to be coerced through systems of debt peonage, intimidation, and violence. Consequently, the most abusive African American crewleaders are disappearing, not because of a concerted law-enforcement campaign to eliminate debt peonage, but as the inevitable result of the arrival of large numbers of vulnerable immigrant workers.

Bob Jameson ◆ *Central Florida*

Bob Jameson was raised on a family farm on the Eastern Shore of Virginia.

"We had tenant houses all around the farm. You really got to know those people. They'd work in the fields, baby-sit for your family, they'd do anything. You never locked your door. You didn't even have keys. Everybody lived together, sort of like a family."

In the early 1960s, Jameson moved to Florida and began working a 35-acre vegetable farm. Since then, the farm has grown to 1,200 acres. Jameson grows cucumbers, potatoes, cabbage, onions, and sweet corn.

Like most growers in the area, Jameson obtained seasonal workers by hiring African American crewleaders. For twenty-five years, he worked with one of the area's most successful and notorious crewleaders, a man known to be both charming and brutal, who, over the years, held thousands of workers in debt peonage.

I'm a farmer. That's what I am. I see farming a whole lot differently than a guy who's a professional in New York City or a condominium owner in Naples or someplace like that. I have a different, more realistic understanding of farming. Agriculture has always relied on the poorest people. Farmworkers don't make a lot of decisions. They just do a job and get paid for it.

Some contractors are bad. They're mean. They have to be mean to keep this crowd together. These people are their children, and they treat them just like children. Contractors give the workers everything because they don't have the ability to take care of themselves.

In order to recruit and keep workers, a crewleader has to give them what they want. They're fed, sold wine, sold cigarettes, and made happy. They may not be real smart, but they damn sure know what they want. They demand wine and whiskey. If there are drugs involved, they demand that. Workers won't stay on a camp if they can't get what they want. For two bottles of wine you can get these people to work all day long. What the hell are they going to do with money? They just want a few bottles of wine. Farmworkers are happy because they have no decisions to make. They have nothing to do except what the crewleader tells them to do. They go to work and live day by day.

Some contractors were pretty ruthless. Usually, they'd have bodyguards, big old boys that they'd tip. If you came in, borrowed money, and ate food for a week, then you had to pay the contractor back. Contractors took advantage of the situation. Getting out of debt was just about impossible and there was no easy way to get off a camp.

I knew those things went on. I had to know. Still, as a farmer, you really didn't want to know too much about it. You couldn't change it. I guess you could have become the labor contractor and hired all those people yourself. You'd have had a heck of a time recruiting those people each season. With a crewleader, there were always people standing in line to come work for you.

If a guy happened to be on the farm, it was his responsibility. I didn't have anything to do with it. I just relied on those people to harvest the crop. You'd see some people out there that you felt sorry for, but they didn't necessarily feel sorry for themselves. They were like a herd of cows. They were led in and led down.

If you didn't spend the night in one of those camps—which I never did and never would have consented to do—you couldn't really know what was going on. You see, there's two sides to every story. You can't trust a wine drinker or a dope smoker. He may not intend to harm you, but he's sure as hell not going to be what you call dependable. If you bought those people a brand-new house and put 'em in it, they wouldn't have it in two days. They ain't gonna put up with that. They're not gonna clean it and take care of it. If you gave them a bunch of money, they couldn't handle that either. In thirty minutes it'd all be gone. They would have given it to somebody or somebody would have stolen it from them.

Once in a while, you'd find people in those crews who'd been somebody, a sergeant in the army or something. People who'd come out here after their wives had left them and they'd started on the wine. You'd see them out here in the morning, reading a newspaper. They were intelligent people, but they'd just given up on life. So they'd work all day in the fields and drink wine all night, and that's probably what they'd do for the rest of their lives. You couldn't buy those people back into the life they'd left—the real life.

I think the crewleaders are given a bad break. Some of those guys did a remarkable job to keep their people busy and give them a little self-satisfaction. You know, most people like to work. There's no satisfaction in being paid welfare every month, just sittin' on your porch waitin' for the mail to come. These people had jobs and those crewleaders saved the government a lot of money by working these people, by giving them a sense of being someone instead of just wandering around, living on the streets, and sleeping in a park.

I had one labor contractor for twenty-five years. He was one of the biggest-hearted guys you could ever find. Those workers were his life. He did everything for them. He was their papa, their mama, their doctor, their savior, their everything. If they didn't have him there, you know, they'd be laying in a ditch or sleeping on the street. They couldn't even get welfare because they'd never stay in one place. Now you couldn't go to our contractor, tell him you wanted to work, borrow fifteen dollars, and then say, "See you later." He wouldn't let you do that. You had to stay long enough to pay him back. He couldn't have survived if he let everybody take advantage of him like that.

A lot of folks called our crewleader a bad guy, but he was actually pretty nice. He did a lot of things for a lot of people. He had people that followed him all the time, workers that just thought he was God. Whenever he said, "Do," they did. Some of those people had been with him ever since they were young, and they loved him to death. Hell, he kept them alive, kept them going. They'd work all day and drink wine at night. Then they'd work the next day and drink wine that night. That was their life. You try to give them more, it ain't gonna work.

Sometimes life is brutal. It's not the crewleader who's the cause of that. The crewleader is just doing a job, like everybody else. He's not the reason why a man doesn't have a great job and live in a brand-new house. The crewleader's got nothing to do with that. The worker is down at his rung of the ladder doing what he chose to do.

Our crewleader was trying to keep his people working, and they were just as happy as they could be until a Legal Services lawyer came in. He started putting ideas in their minds, sending nuns into the camps, and telling the people how badly they were being treated. When he started doing that, the workers listened, particularly when they thought they were going to get something for nothing.

We were sued by Legal Services. I knew we hadn't done anything wrong. My father always taught me not to accept responsibility for something I didn't do, so we decided to fight it. We spent two hundred and eighty thousand dollars for attorneys. We were found innocent. We hadn't broken any rules. My crewleader was an independent contractor. He had plenty of opportunity to do bad or good for himself. Even if he broke the rules, we didn't. It's a pretty dangerous precedent for the federal government to say that you've got to be responsible for your brother. I mean, how can I be responsible for you, or you for me?

Anyway, the lawsuit just about broke us, but we paid our bill. We also fired our crewleader. We had to let him go.

The Labor Department kept telling our crewleader to change, to keep books and all that, but he didn't pay attention. He just wouldn't change. Maybe he didn't know how to change. I don't think he went any further in school than the fifth grade. So, they broke him and took everything he had. At one time, he owned a lot of land and had plenty of money. Maybe it was his money and maybe it was money that he took from his people. I don't know. He was real big and now he's broke.

Our crewleader is still at it. He hasn't got many people in his crew, but he's still working. It's kind of pitiful, but crewleading is all he knows how to do.

The results of all these changes turned out pretty good for the farm. We don't use crewleaders now. We pay each worker individually and now our crew is about ninety-five percent Mexican and Haitian. They're more disciplined and more motivated. These guys know how to keep their money. They're not going to spend it on getting drunk every night. They keep their money and pool it together because they've got their minds on buying things. If they've got two or three family members working, they'll get a pick-up truck a few weeks after they start. The blacks could never keep their money. Those old people just didn't have the brains. They were good-hearted people, but we just had to let 'em go.

I know what's going on. I know this state doesn't want to put up with migrant labor. They don't want the farms anymore. They're tired of it. They've made their money and they don't want to be down here with us in the real world of producing the fruits and vegetables that keep them happy and fill their restaurants and kitchens with good food. Look what's happened to food over the years. Go into a grocery store now and look at an apple. It's beautiful. I mean, it looks like a picture. A head of cabbage? A sweet potato? Absolutely perfect. When people go to the grocery store and see all those beautiful fruits and vegetables, they should know that they're harvested by people.

You can feel sorry for the workers who are out here cutting lettuce and pulling corn, but those people are basically OK. There's nobody in the world that doesn't wish he could be somebody else or be a rung farther up the ladder. Farmworkers are basically happy people. They aren't chairmen of the board or business owners or nothing like that. They don't know anything about those things. You and I can go out to eat dinner in a restaurant and be waited on or take a small vacation or spend the night in a motel, but these people don't think about that. That's not what they expect. Most of them have never lived like that, so it's not a problem for them.

The trouble today is that people think that the government should take care of everybody. They don't realize that there have always been poor people and rich people. Once we realize that everybody can't live in a two-bedroom, two-bath house with two automobiles in the garage, then we'll have learned a great lesson. Everybody is not the same, and everybody is not going to be the same in a good society where people are free.

It is an extraordinary experience to enter a labor camp where workers are held in debt peonage. Some camps are unassuming, small clusters of wooden shacks or rows of rusting trailers, while others are long barracks-style buildings surrounded by chain-link fences and signs warning visitors to keep out. There are often piles of garbage everywhere, broken bottles, and crushed beer cans. Old school buses and rusting vans used to transport workers are parked to one side, and beside them, the crewleader's car—often a white Cadillac or a newly purchased four-wheel-drive truck. When workers are not in the fields, they have little to do. They hang around in groups talking, watching television, or standing around a fire drinking. Some listen to portable radios, while others are passed out in their rooms or sleeping under the trees. Many workers look beaten down, their eyes glazed over. There are often several old men wandering around, their hair gray and clothes tattered.

Few outsiders enter these labor camps, and visitors quickly draw the attention of crewleaders and their henchmen. People stare. Conversations die down. At the toughest camps, the crewleader and his henchmen arrive almost immediately, eager to find out who you are and what you want, since visitors usually mean trouble. Henchmen often dress like urban gangsters, flaunting gold jewelry and baggy clothes, alternately threatening and evasive. If you are well dressed or white, you're likely to be treated with deference, though it's always clear that the crewleader wants you to leave as soon as possible.

What is most memorable about a visit to one of these camps is the visceral sense of workers' fear. When the crewleader is nearby or the henchmen are listening, workers nervously tell you that the work is good, the housing fine, and the wages fair. Left alone for a moment, workers will draw you aside and whisper stories of abuse or slip notes into your hand pleading for help. Legal advocates, church groups, and others who visit these camps grow accustomed to the fear and hopelessness of these migrants. They often receive midnight telephone calls from workers who have managed to escape and are hiding in the woods, desperate for assistance.

Farmworker advocates estimate that there are currently between fifty and a hundred crewleaders who rely on debt peonage still operating in and around the rural South. These crewleaders provide employment to several thousand workers each year and represent a small percentage of the total number of farmworkers in the United States. Consequently, growers often claim that focusing attention on cases of debt peonage unfairly brands the agricultural industry as corrupt, criminal, and anachronistic. While it is true these situations are now the exception rather than the rule, the fact that involuntary servitude and debt peonage remain serious issues among America's farmworkers in the 1990s is extraordinary, raising deeply troubling questions about both the history and structure of our nation's farm labor system.

Calvin Douglas ♦ *Orlando, Florida*

It's springtime, midafternoon at the Orlando Rescue Mission. The floor of the main building is divided into rectangles, like small parking spaces. Each rectangle can be claimed, like a room, by one of the hundreds of homeless people who find shelter here each night.

For years, Calvin Douglas was a successful barber working in Tennessee. He had his own business, a house, and two cars. His wife at the time worked in the local school system and his daughter was finishing a degree in chemical engineering. Almost by accident, Douglas discovered the lucrative business of dealing drugs and started selling painkillers out of his barbershop. Gradually, he expanded his business to cocaine. Two years later, Douglas found himself driving south to Miami with two young women and $200,000 in cash in the trunk of his Oldsmobile.

Douglas began using cocaine, and within eighteen months, he'd spent all his money. Addicted to crack, he found himself living on the streets of Orlando. A "road man" met Douglas at a shelter and offered him a job, hinting at the availability of drugs and women. Later that day, Douglas and several others were transported to a labor camp in central Florida. The labor camp was run by the crewleader who had worked for Bob Jameson for twenty-five years. The day after Douglas arrived at the labor camp, he was working at Jameson's farm.

The thing that astonished me most about living on the labor camp is that they didn't care about your name. You had no name. You just had a number. My number was seventy. They called you by your number. "Number seventy, come here."

Every day, we'd go to work. We worked from sunup to sundown. We'd get up in the dark and come back at dark. The work was hard. You're out in the field and there's this long row that looks like it will never end. You think you won't finish, but finally you get there. Then, you have to turn around and come back.

After work, you'd stop by his house. He had a real nice house with a swimming pool and all that good stuff. That's where they ran the lines. Every day you could charge stuff—liquor, beer, cigarettes, things like that. That's also when the cocaine came into it. If you had no bad habits then they really didn't want you there. If you were the type that could save money, they found some way to get rid of you. They only wanted people with drug and alcohol problems.

They were also skeptical of white men. They'd only take a white guy if he was a real drunk. If not, they wouldn't mess with him. I heard the crewleader talking once. He said he didn't like to hire white workers because he didn't want to hire the wrong one, someone whose father or relative might come down on him.

When they figured up your paycheck, you almost always owed them. Sometimes I got a few dollars, maybe twelve or thirteen dollars for a week's work. If you had money, he'd take you to a special store, owned by some white guy. He'd load up the bus and everybody would go to this man's store and spend their money.

I had no control over my life. I had no money. I had no clothes to speak of. With the way they talked to you and the way you were dirty all the time, I felt like a slave. If you wanted anything, you'd have to ask the crewleader and he'd tell you, "No." The cook wasn't allowed to feed us until the crewleader got to the camp. It didn't matter when the food was ready, we had to wait until the crewleader arrived, because he served us all himself.

"Number thirty-six, Number fifteen, Number seventy."

He'd pile your plate real high, and then I'd come behind you and get just a spoonful. It was like the way you'd train a dog. You're the only one that feeds your dog, so your dog is beholden to you. That's the way he felt about the people on his camp.

One day, a guy was sick. At four-thirty in the morning they started blowing the horn on the bus. The guy was sick and the crewleader took his foot and just kicked the door in—*bam!*—right off the hinges. "Get up, you going to work. You done ate my food, drank my beer, and smoked my dope. You going to work."

Another day, there was a guy who went to the fields with a hangover. He was laying halfway in and halfway out of the road. The crewleader came through and ran over the man's leg in his Bronco. I saw it with my own eyes. He wouldn't take the man to the hospital. He just left him there. The man lay there all day long. "Ain't nothing wrong with him. He'll be all right." But the man wasn't all right. There was something wrong with his leg. He never once took a worker to the doctor.

I've seen his gun and I've seen him reading the Bible. He says he reads the Bible because somewhere in there it says that if you don't work, you shouldn't eat. I'll tell you, that crewleader is one of the worst men I've ever met. He was evil.

I wanted to get off the camp, but the only way you could leave was to run away. If you tried to get away, they'd send somebody after you. Then they'd take you back to the camp and beat you up. I saw people being beaten after they tried to escape.

Still, there was one time when I left.

They wanted us to pick seven bins of oranges each day as a quota. I wasn't a good orange picker, so one day I didn't get but three bins. The foreman told me that since I didn't make the quota, I wouldn't get to eat when we got back to the camp. They served everybody food except me. So the next morning, when we stopped at a store to get gas, I got off the bus and hid. After the bus left, I started walking towards Orlando. About forty minutes later, here comes the crewleader in his big Bronco.

"Hey, Number seventy, come here!"

"Naw, man, I'm through."

"Come here, I want to talk to you."

"No, I'm on my way to Orlando."

"Get in, I'll take you."

"No, that's all right." I kept on walking.

He was driving and talking to me through the window. "What's wrong, Number seventy, you scared? Come on, get in and talk to me."

I don't know why, but I got in his car. I was scared. I knew he wasn't going to take me to Orlando, but he said he just wanted to talk to me. "You mess with that thing, Number seventy?"

"What thing?"

"You know what I'm talking about. You mess with cocaine, don't you?"

"Yeah, sometimes."

"Tell you what. Let me catch up to the bus and put you back on. You go out there and work. It don't make no difference how many bins you get. You go out there and work and when you come in tonight, you come around to the garage and I'll take care of you."

"OK."

When we got back that night, I went around to the garage, and sure enough, he had a hundred dollars' worth of cocaine for me. He gives me the cocaine and says, "Don't worry about a thing." That's how the crewleader stopped me from leaving.

Everybody in town knew about the labor camp. The sheriff, the farmers, and the crewleader were all in cahoots. The farmers knew how we were treated. You could tell they knew by the way they'd talk. There was one farmer in particular I talked to. He owned an orange grove. Once he told me, "I know you guys are working for next to nothing, but I can't do anything about it." He said he didn't like what was going on, but then why was he using that contractor? I didn't ask him, but I knew the answer—he got cheap labor and made more money.

This is going on today, right now. It keeps going on because of the way our society works. The farmers want cheap labor and they know they can get cheap labor with the right contractor. In order for the contractor to provide cheap labor, he's got to find people that have no hope. They capitalize on people's problems. The farmers know what's going on. They just turn their heads the other way.

When I was out there in the fields, I'd think a lot about air-conditioning. I thought about how I'd lived pretty good for a lot of years. I used to go from my air-conditioned house to my air-conditioned car to my air-conditioned barbershop. I never had to sweat. I didn't know nothing about hard work. There I was out in the blazing sun. I'm sweating. I'm dirty. I'm nasty. I thought a lot about what I'd lost. Still, I feel lucky to have survived. There are lots of people that don't survive. I'm fifty-five now.

I'd say that living on that labor camp was the worst experience I've ever had. It's hard for me to believe that kind of stuff is still happening. It shocked me. Most people wouldn't believe that it's true, but I know it's real because I lived through it. I guarantee you that the same things are happening right now, as we sit here, on somebody's labor camp. The road men come through here all the time and they always leave with people.

7. When Main Street Looks Like Little Mexico

IN EVER GREATER NUMBERS, Latino farmworkers are settling in small towns throughout the rural South. In local bars, one hears the lilting polka melodies of Mexican dance music; at weekend flea markets, farmworkers and their families browse for bargains and socialize; in area supermarkets, one can now buy tortillas, *chiles*, and canned mole sauce. For longtime residents of these communities, Latino immigrants seem to have appeared almost overnight, and to many, their growing number feels something like an invasion.

Up until the late 1950s, the majority of migrant workers in the eastern United States were African Americans. At that time, there were also significant numbers of white Americans working the fields, and in some areas, crews of Puerto Rican workers who were brought north each year for the harvest season. Beginning in the 1960s, many domestic workers left farm labor for more-stable jobs with higher wages and safer working conditions, or they were freed from their dependence on migrant work through antipoverty and social service programs.

The first Mexican American farmworkers began working in the southeastern states in the 1950s, generally migrating from the Rio Grande Valley in Texas. As these workers settled in Florida, some established themselves as crewleaders and hired more-recent Mexican American arrivals and increasing numbers of Mexican-born immigrants. From the mid-1960s through the 1970s, Latinos steadily displaced the traditional African American labor force in many areas of Florida and in a handful of other isolated locations throughout the South. By the early 1980s, Latino farmworkers were working throughout the eastern United States, rapidly making inroads in specific regions and crops, and gradually expanding their presence from one community to another. By the mid-1980s, the majority of East Coast migrants were Latino, and by 1990, fewer than one in ten migrants in the region had been born in the United States.

Nearly 70 percent of Latino farmworkers in the Southeast are undocumented immigrants. As a rule, there are relatively few INS agents working in the rural South, and many *coyotes* now send workers smuggled across the border directly to contractors in rural communities throughout the Southeast. Largely as a result of the rapid influx of undocumented workers, migrants' wages on the East Coast are now among the lowest of any region in the nation.

Lucy and Reina Quintanilla ◆ *Faison, North Carolina*

Maria Lucila Quintanilla—"Lucy"—was born in Mexico and grew up traveling back and forth between the border towns of McAllen, Texas, and Reynosa, Tamaulipas. She married at fifteen and moved to Texas in the late 1970s. For years, Lucy, her husband, and their children traveled north out of Texas to work in Michigan and Indiana during the summer and into the fall. In January, they would take advantage of school vacation to migrate east to Florida to harvest strawberries, always returning back to their home in Texas's Rio Grande Valley.

We sit on a sofa covered with crocheted doilies inside the family's trailer. It is a comfortable home with family photos on the walls and a pleasant, relaxed look. While we speak, Lucy's teenage daughter, Reina, joins the conversation.

LUCY One year, when we were working in Florida, there was a really bad freeze. The growers lost all their strawberries. If we'd gone back to Texas, we would have had to live off food stamps because we had no money and there was no work. Our *compadres* said, "Let's go to North Carolina." So we came here and began working in tobacco and sweet potatoes.

At first we were scared to be in North Carolina. Since there weren't many Mexicans here, people looked at us as if we were strange. Then we began to bring up nephews, brothers, and cousins. Other Mexicans also brought their families, and we began to fill up this little town with Mexicans.

A lot of Americans look down on us. They see Mexicans as beneath them. They think that we're uneducated or that we steal. They think we've come here to take things from them. It isn't like that. You don't travel the way that a migrant travels, wandering from one place to another, coming here from so far away, without a good reason. We've come here to work. All of us work in *la labor.* We come here because we want to earn money to buy things—a sofa, a refrigerator, a stove—to fix up the houses we've left back in Texas or Mexico.

REINA If a Mexican kills someone, they think all Mexicans are killers. If a Mexican robs someone, they think all Mexicans are thieves. Even though they see all these Mexicans working in the fields, they never think of Mexicans as workers.

It's hard not to get upset by how you're treated here. I'm an American citizen. I have the same rights as any other American citizen, yet people here look at me as just another Mexican, and that upsets me.

Still, what really bothers me is that here they don't want us to get ahead. In our culture, we're taught that if I have something good, then hopefully you'll have something good, too. In their culture they believe that the more I've got, the better it is for me, and whatever happens to you is your problem.

LUCY If I have a nice house, I want you to have a nice house. If I eat well, I want you to eat well, too. If I have good children, then I hope that you'll also have good children. All the positive things that happen to me, I also want to happen to you. The Americans in this town live well. They have nice houses. So why don't they want Mexicans to live well and have nice houses, too?

We know the Americans don't like us. It's rare that an American will say hello to a Mexican. It's much more common for people of color to greet us than the Americans. My children have more black friends than American friends.

REINA Blacks are in the same situation that we are. In the end, the Americans don't like them, either.

LUCY We come here and buy cars, beds, furniture, everything we need. Still, even if all we're buying is a hairbrush, it's still profit for them. Whatever we want here, we buy with our money. So why they don't like us?

REINA They don't even call us Mexicans. They call us wetbacks. You hear them say this all the time. "Look, there's some more wetbacks." Why do they call us wetbacks? It makes me angry. We've come here to work. Right now there's no work in Texas and the people who stay there have to live on food stamps. Those of us who come here are the ones who want to work, the ones who are willing to sleep on the floor and suffer through cold and hunger.

Still, not all Americans dislike us. We've worked with Americans that have treated us as equals.

LUCY Who knows? I think the Americans who help us only do so because they need us. There's two classes of people here, those with farms and those without farms. The Americans who have fields to plant and harvest like the Mexicans. The other group, the ones without land, are the ones that don't want us here. That's where people's interests come in. It's out of personal interest that some Americans accept us. They know that they need Mexicans to work. I don't think that there are a lot of bosses who really like us. They only want us here because they need our labor.

REINA The Americans feel that they've been invaded. They think we represent some type of danger. Now that they see more Hispanic people here, they think that things will get worse.

LUCY I don't think that the Americans are actually afraid of what we do. They're afraid they won't be able to get rid of us.

If current immigration trends continue, in less than thirty years, Latinos will be the largest minority group in the nation. While Latino immigration to urban areas is now a widely recognized aspect of contemporary American culture, Latino immigration to rural America, particularly in the South, has received surprisingly little attention. In cities, Latinos can take advantage of the anonymity of urban life, setting up immigrant neighborhoods that blend into an existing multiethnic society. Latinos settling in rural areas face an entirely different situation. They are unable to assimilate into local culture and clearly stand out.

Latino farmworkers who settle out of the migrant stream and take up permanent residence in rural towns in the South represent a serious challenge to local society. They speak Spanish in a world where everything is in English. They eat different foods, listen to different music, and are largely unfamiliar with the local culture. Enormous mistrust exists on all sides. Many local residents, both black and white, fear that if Latino immigration continues at its present pace, their communities will soon be composed largely of Spanish-speaking foreigners.

Eastern North Carolina is a case in point. For years, North Carolina has drawn the largest numbers of farmworkers of any state on the East Coast, employing over 44,000 migrant workers each year. The majority of farm laborers work in eastern North Carolina, harvesting tobacco, sweet potatoes, pickle cucumbers, squash, apples, and a variety of other fruits and vegetables. In the late 1970s, the first Latino workers began to find their way to the fields and labor camps of eastern North Carolina. From 1981 to 1990, North Carolina's Spanish-speaking migrant population nearly doubled, from 14,000 to at least 27,000. In the 1990s, increasing numbers of Latino workers have arrived in the area, steadily displacing African Americans. It is inevitable that in the near future virtually all of North Carolina's migrant workers will be Latino.

Mary Watson ♦ *Eastern North Carolina*
Mary Watson is in her late fifties and has lived all her life in a small town in eastern North Carolina. She is closely involved with the affairs of her community. She goes to church regularly and is a member of the Rotary Club and a number of other civic organizations.

Over the last several years, she has had many encounters with Mexicans working in the area. Until recently, she rented several small houses to migrants, and as a member of the local rescue squad, she periodically administers first aid and emergency medicine to workers injured in fights or accidents. Watson also works in local government, where she deals with people—migrants and others—accused of a variety of crimes, from shoplifting to murder.

Watson has graying hair, a calm voice, and a genteel manner. A string of pearls hangs around her neck.

I guess most people would think a woman in the position I'm in would be afraid all the time. There are women who might be afraid, but I'm not. I get along real good with people of all races and all walks of life. I can get down and talk with the lowliest criminals as well as the society folks.

You've got to have compassion, and I have a lot of compassion for the migrants. It's like they're caught in the bottom of the barrel, like they just can't dig themselves out of a hole. There's just a whole element of humanity that's down there, and if it wasn't them, it would probably be somebody else. The farmers need these people to harvest their crops. Poultry, livestock, and farming is the lifeblood of this whole area of the state, and the black and the white people who used to do that kind of work just won't do it anymore.

Farms here used to be small. They were family oriented. A farmer, his wife, and their children would work the farm. I can remember how in the fall, when it was cotton-picking time, they used to close the schools at noon and let all the kids go home so they could pick cotton in the afternoon. In the spring, they'd do the same thing. Child labor laws did away with that.

Now there are big outfits—big farmers, we call them. They go out and buy several million dollars' worth of equipment, rent several thousand acres of land, and get a large tobacco allotment. It's big business now. Since the farmers still can't do without manual labor, we need these people.

I don't think the Old South population understands. They just don't want the Mexicans here. I see people's attitudes getting more and more negative. People here are very hard-nosed about change. It's sort of like back before school integration, when resentment built up until finally our national Supreme Court had to rule on it and force integration. In a way, it's a similar situation. The federal government is going to have to get involved and help the states. It's a big problem and we can't deal with it alone. People's attitudes have got to change.

I've always been proud of myself for being nonprejudicial, but I guess I'm getting older and less patient. This is just a whole different world from when I grew up. The community has changed and I'm worried about it.

We don't know exactly how many Mexicans are here right now, but there's probably around two hundred. If you took all the Mexicans in the labor camps in the surrounding community and brought them into town, you could hardly get in or out of the grocery store. They stick together, play together, drink together, and socialize together. With the number of children they're having, soon the whites are going to be outnumbered. I can see a little town like ours, with a population of about six hundred white people, becoming almost totally Hispanic.

This used to be a nice town. Everybody kept their houses all neat and trim and pretty. Now, it's just an instant slum wherever the Mexicans go. Every place that they move into becomes a junk hole almost overnight. Their lifestyle is instilled in them from the time they're born and that's not going to change when they get here. When a Mexican family moves into a house, the first thing they'll do is knock out all the windows and the doors. Then they'll nail up some boards and put two or three padlocks on it. They know how to keep somebody out, but they don't seem to care about other people's property. I've been to Tijuana and our town is getting to look just like that.

Go on up to the Piggly Wiggly on a Saturday afternoon, park the car, and sit and watch. The Mexicans have their food stamps and their rolls of hundred-dollar bills. They peddle their food stamps among one an-

other and then go in and buy tons of food. They're sitting all over the sidewalks. Main Street looks like Little Mexico.

Right now, there's a big flap going on because the Campbell family, who are big farmers, applied to the town board for a permit to put a trailer park inside the city limits on some property which is now zoned for agriculture. Well, you should have gone to the town board meeting they had the other day. People were saying: "We don't want the damn Mexicans sitting in our back door and that's what's gonna happen if you let them put a trailer park there." "There are many little widow ladies afraid to even walk down the street. They're afraid to go to the grocery store or the Post Office." "Instead of making more places for them to live, we should be shipping all the Mexicans that are here back home."

People in town don't want to prevent the Campbells from putting in a nice trailer park, but they know—just as sure as I know that I'm sitting here—that in a few months' time the migrants will turn the trailer park into a dump. Then the town would end up having to hire another full-time police officer as well as a maintenance person to look after the waterworks and trash removal. Soon, it would be a new little ghetto, right in town. The Campbells have got plenty of property outside the city limits where they could put up a migrant camp.

The Mexicans are ruining the community. It's like they're little children. They work hard from all I can see, but they're just sort of floundering around in society. They know how to work, and they know how to eat, sleep, and drink, but they don't know how to manage things.

I don't think I'm angrier than most others. I just see a lot more in this job. I see a lot of the Mexicans getting into the court system. The people who come here are not willing to follow our laws. They don't even know what the laws are. They're living by their standards from back home instead of our standards. They want to come here and reap all the benefits, but they don't want to live according to our laws. They'll buy an old car for two or three hundred dollars, get a license plate from somewhere, and stick it on and drive. They'll never get the title in their name, if they even bother to get a title. One old car might be sold a dozen times among the Mexicans. When they want to get rid of the car, they just abandon it. They'll park it by the road and that's where it stays.

With the Mexicans, there's not a care in the world. They don't try to keep or maintain anything. They like money, freedom, and no responsibility. They ignore the laws and they use their ignorance as a crutch. In America, it's just free and wide-open. It's like a promised land.

Friday afternoon is payday and they're lined up in front of the post office getting money orders, up to five hundred dollars. Some of them buy several. They send the money back to Mexico to support their families there. Over here, a man can make as much in a week as they make in a year in Mexico and he sends his wages back home. They earn good wages, but they send it all somewhere else instead of putting it back in our tax base. The bottom line on business is the tax base. The population we're supporting is growing by leaps and bounds, but our tax base isn't getting any bigger. Taxpaying people are fed up with this transient element. They get on the welfare rolls for food, housing, and medical care, and then they stay. It's just bleeding us to death to care for these people and look after them. It's expensive and the costs keep going up and up.

To me, I see that there are givers and takers in this world. The whites have always been the givers, and the blacks and the Mexicans have always been the takers. If they don't get it handed to them, then they'll take it. They're taking away from our quality of life by the way they live.

It's going to get worse. It might get better many years down the road, but it is going to get worse before it gets better. Somehow this country has got to put a stop to this influx of needy people. We cannot take them all in. It's as if I opened up my house and said, "I've got four bedrooms here. Tell all the needy people in the county." I'd have a thousand people in there in two days. Well, that's what the federal government is doing to this country.

From the beginning, this country was built by immigrants. After a while, you get to a saturation point. We've reached that, but we're still laying back and bringing them in. Those of us that are working to support them all have just about burned out.

In the South, the first Latino immigrants to arrive in a particular community were generally brought there by farm labor contractors hired by area growers. Like the African American crews that they replaced, most of the first Latino crews lived in isolated labor camps, generally owned by growers and located on farm property away from the homes of local residents. The first wave of Latino farmworkers spent much of their free time in the labor camps and usually had a limited impact on the communities where they worked. Crews of Latinos would arrive in an area, work until the season ended, and then leave, continuing north, or returning to Florida or Texas. Local residents had few direct dealings with these crews and were often only marginally aware of the growing number of Latino workers passing through their communities each year.

Gradually, individual workers and immigrant families began to settle out of the migrant stream, deciding to stay in particular communities after the season ended. Many of the first settled-out migrants

found year-round employment with large growers. Some learned enough English to work as supervisors and translators, helping local employers communicate with the growing number of Spanish-speaking workers. Others left agriculture for better jobs in construction or the rapidly expanding poultry industry. For many employers, settled-out migrants were ideal workers since they were willing to accept difficult jobs for relatively low wages and no benefits. For these workers, virtually any nonmigrant job was an improvement over farm labor.

As ever-larger numbers of Latino immigrants passed through the South, the population of settled-out migrants continued to grow. Workers rented trailers and small houses, found jobs for friends and relatives, and gradually built up fledgling Latino communities. The first communities were small, insular, and largely invisible to non-Latino residents. As workers sent for their wives and children, and as families told others about opportunities in the area, rural Latino communities grew in both size and visibility. Often local residents remained largely unaware of the sizable presence of Latino immigrants until restaurants, bars, and stores catering to migrants began appearing in town and Spanish-speaking children began entering the schools.

Lou Carter ♦ *Mount Olive, North Carolina*

While growing up, Lou Carter spent her weekends on a farm not far from the house where she now lives. After high school, she went to college and then worked as a high school teacher in a nearby city. She married a fifth-generation tobacco farmer and left teaching several years ago to work full-time on the farm.

It's early morning. The sky is overcast, and a heavy fog lies close to the ground, settling in low places and covering the tobacco fields with a thick, gray mist. As we talk, Carter's son drives a tractor back and forth across a field beside the house. Her daughter is out back with the migrant crew, barning tobacco.

Farming for us is not necessarily an occupation—it's a way of life. Farming has to be in your blood. If it's not in your blood, you can't take it. It's hard and time-consuming, but it's a wonderful life.

Our day normally starts about six-thirty in the morning and runs until around ten-thirty at night. Basically, the work is hard. It's not mind-boggling and it's not always backbreaking, but it's tiresome. It's steady, muscle-developing work that the average American just doesn't want to do. They've found easier ways to make a living.

We started hiring Mexicans around 1984. These people were hungry, scared to death, and spoke very little English. All they wanted was to go to work, period. They wanted a job and it didn't matter what it was, they'd do it. That's really what prompted us to start using Hispanic workers.

We started by hiring crewleaders. We had some good ones and some bad ones. There are some horror stories in every situation and we decided that given what crewleaders were doing at the time, we'd be better off hiring our own workers and living with them on a day-to-day basis. So we built a labor camp. That way, we could get to know the workers and they could get to know us. We'd be aware of their comings and goings and make sure that they were OK. The first crew came to stay with us in 1989. So far, it's worked out pretty good.

The migrants start coming by as soon as the orange season is over in Florida, which is around the end of March, beginning of April. They come knocking on our door in droves. We have to turn a lot of people away.

I've dealt with the workers for the last four growing seasons. I've learned a lot of Spanish and they've learned a lot of English. To some people it might seem like I'm a plantation owner, but I don't ever get the plantation feel because I'm in the fields with them all the time. I don't ask them to do anything I don't do. I don't feel that I'm any better than they are, and I don't act like they're any lower than me. Ours is an unusual working relationship. From April to October, I feel like a mama. These boys are my babies. I have two children of my own, and normally I have anywhere from five to seven workers. We sit out there and discuss everything under the sun. I have to look after them. I feel responsible.

I won't tell you that I don't get mad at them. I won't tell you that there aren't some very heated arguments in slang Spanish and that I haven't called them "a child of God" and that they haven't called me that or worse. Still, out of all the resentment and frustration that you feel, you develop a sense of a love for them. My workers are very aggravating. I can talk about 'em all I want to, but I get very angry if somebody else does, just like with my own children.

I try to put myself in their shoes. I have to respect anybody who goes four thousand miles away from home to make money to feed his family. I don't know how many so-called American people would go that far to feed their family. The Mexicans have a very strong sense of community and a very strong sense of family. If people don't believe that, all they have to do is stand over at the post office and they'll see just how family oriented these boys are. They'll get a phone call from Guatemala or a letter from Mexico saying, "We need money and we need it bad," and on Monday morning, they're at the post office. These men leave their mamas, their wives, their children, everything they've ever known, to come to a country where people don't like them because they're different. I may not always agree with the migrants, but I certainly respect them.

Now there are places where the workers are treated horribly and conditions are really bad, but the majority of them have nice houses which they tend to tear up. Why? I don't know. It's a bad assumption to make about an entire group of people, but it's true. I really don't understand it, but year after year, we have to spend a lot of money to repair the camp. Every year we have to replace screens. I don't know why it is, but they'll kick the screens out like it's just a big thing to do. You also have to replace bathroom fixtures and smoke alarms. Lightbulbs? My God, they carry off lightbulbs by the thousands. I also furnish linens and blankets for all our boys and they disappear from season to season. You get real irritated with things like that, but then you have to consider that these people haven't had the advantages we've had. It's like a kid who's never had a piece of candy going into a store filled with candy jars. Invariably, that child's going to have to take a piece of candy.

The majority of these people make good money. Our boys get paid four dollars and a half an hour, a bit more than minimum wage. They don't pay rent, their electricity is furnished, and they're given a vehicle to drive, along with insurance and gas. So these boys have it pretty well made. I think that's where a lot of the resentment's from. The community gets upset because they've worked here all their lives and now they see people coming in from another country and getting all these advantages that they don't have.

This puts us in a strange position because we understand both sides of the situation. In the South, we're all brought up knowing our place. People who cross the lines of place—the boundary lines—tend to cause friction. For generation after generation in the South, people have placed value in one's station. Also, people tend to be afraid of what they don't know. Ignorance is a strong force in deterring people from accepting others into their community. You're going to have a lot of friction any time that you have different cultures living together. People just don't understand.

When these boys first come, they're starving to death for work and money. When they first arrive, they're afraid to ask you for anything. Then they start to become Americanized. They learn about food stamps and other programs. After they've been here awhile they become very demanding. You get real irritated with that. It's like a bunch of children who have learned how to manipulate their mama or daddy. Still, they're very tenderhearted and sweet. If you work with these boys every day, you get to like them. You develop a friendship and a real sense of family.

In fact, I'll tell you this little story.

Last year, one of our workers wanted to go to Guatemala to see his mother, who he hadn't seen in around five years. So we went to a travel agent in Goldsboro, bought his ticket, and got everything situated. Then I carried him to Raleigh-Durham to catch the airplane.

It was like sending my child off to a foreign country. I walked in with him, and I talked to the lady at the ticket counter to make sure that there would be somebody to meet him in Miami so he'd get on the right plane to fly to Guatemala City. We were discussing all this stuff, and the lady at the ticket counter looked at me and said, "Are you his mother?"

After getting over being irritated because I didn't think I looked that old, I told her, "No."

Then she said, "Well, you must be one of those nice ladies that works with the churches around here."

"No."

She looked at me and said, "Well, you sure are real concerned about him. What do you do, if you don't mind my asking?" In a roundabout way I think she was trying to find out if he was my "friend," so to speak.

I told her, "He works for me."

So we got him situated and he was going to have to wait on his plane, and he came back and said, "You need to go home, people here are very crazy and drive much too fast."

"I'll be OK."

"No, you go home. Go back home. No stop, no go shopping. Go home."

So I walked him into the terminal to make sure he got in all right. When I got him in and started to leave, I turned around. He looked at me with tears in his eyes and I looked at him with tears in my eyes and we had to hug each other. I had to pat my baby on the back to make sure that he was going to be OK. "Are you sure that you want me to leave you here?"

"I am OK, no problem, no problem."

So I left him, and I started out the door. Then, I turned and watched. He was following me back to make sure that I got to the car, and that I was OK. After he turned around, I had to run back to the terminal to make sure that he got back inside and was situated. We were playing cat and mouse, chasing each other across the parking lot at the airport in Raleigh-Durham, so I could make sure he was in the terminal and he could make sure I was in the car. It was like he was my child who I was sending off to this foreign godforsaken place that I knew absolutely nothing about. There was that sense of loss, that empty-nest feeling because I had pushed this baby bird out and was sending him on his way. It sounds so ridiculous because he was twenty-five years old. Still, in so many ways, he was such a baby.

The change in the ethnic composition of the East Coast farm labor force occurred around the same time as a general restructuring of fruit-and-vegetable production. Due to a variety of economic pressures over the last twenty-five years, small produce farmers have found it increasingly difficult to stay in business. Small farms that provided the social and economic foundation of rural society in the South traditionally relied on family members, neighbors, and local laborers to work their fields. As thousands of small family-run farms went out of business, growers who wanted to stay in agriculture were forced to expand, becoming increasingly dependent on the seasonal labor of migrant farmworkers.

Until relatively recently, the majority of white families in eastern North Carolina owned small farms. Farmers' children grew up laboring in the fields, and not long ago, schools closed during harvesttime so young people could work. Many farmers developed arrangements with neighbors and relatives, taking turns helping one another with labor-intensive jobs, from building barns to butchering animals to bringing in the harvest. Farmers also relied on local black workers to labor in the fields. Now that many smaller farms have shut down and surviving operations have grown in size, traditional work-sharing relations have disappeared, and an increasing proportion of hand labor is provided by Latino immigrants.

Virtually everyone in the rural communities of eastern North Carolina recognizes that Latino migrants take on difficult jobs at wages that few domestic workers will accept. From the perspective of African American farmworkers, Latino immigrants are often seen as working too hard for too little. Some workers complain that immigrants have the unfair advantage of using their wages to support families living in distant countries, where the dollars they earn go further than in the United States. For many local residents, the increased dependence on foreign-born workers exemplifies the dissolution of a traditional work ethic, a sign that young Americans are pampered, lazy, and self-indulgent. For older residents, the influx of Latino migrants stands as a sad reminder of the passing of traditional rural life.

Angela Denise Rodriguez ♦ *Faison, North Carolina*

Angela Denise Rodriguez grew up working on her grandfather's vegetable farm. She picked peppers and squash, drove a tractor, and tended the fields. At fifteen, she married and dropped out of high school. She had a daughter, got divorced, and later completed a GED and went on to college. She married again and had another child before her second husband passed away.

I was running a booth for my mother at the flea market. One day, he just walked over. I didn't know Spanish at the time and he didn't know English. It was Valentine's Day, and for some reason, he brought me roses.

I had never seen him before. I never had any dealings with the Spanish because I was afraid of them. I come from a middle-class family and I was always raised to believe that the Spanish were bad people, you know, with their knives and their drinking.

And he brought me roses.

I couldn't understand a thing he said. He was standing there speaking to me, and I didn't understand a word. Every weekend he would come back to the flea market to see me. That went on for two or three months. One Friday he walked up to me, right in front of everyone, and kissed me. I was shocked. It went from there and Martin and I started dating.

"I love you," was the first thing I learned to say in Spanish. He wrote it down on a piece of paper—"*Te amo.*"—and he got one of his friends to tell me what it meant in English. Then it was numbers. Then, words like *eyes, nose, ears, mouth, teeth, hair*—the body parts. Then words like *cat, dog, house.* We would see a chair and I would say "chair" in English and he would say "chair" in Spanish. That's how we taught each other to speak Spanish and English.

The first year, Martin and I were very secretive. We didn't let many people know about our relationship. My parents didn't know. My grandparents didn't know. Mostly, I would go to the labor camp where he lived and we would sit and talk. We just weren't seen together in public.

Then we decided to get married. When we were first married, we lived in separate homes. We talked a lot on the phone, and we would see each other at night. We were married a whole year before my mother ever found out. It was all secret. I didn't want to hurt my parents. I was scared that my mother would disown me because I was married to a Spanish man. I was afraid of hurting her because she had always brought me up not to associate with the Spanish.

Then we took off and went to Mexico and my mother knew something was up.

When I went to Mexico for the first time, I was amazed by the countryside—all the crosses on the sides of the mountains and on top of the stores. We were there at Christmastime and on Christmas morning, instead of opening presents like we do over here, everybody walks to the churches with lit candles. We're busy buying houses and cars and expensive toys for our kids, but the Mexicans are different. It takes less to make them happy. They look at life differently. They value life itself, not material things. I always tell my grandmother that today in Mexico it's like it was here a hundred years ago when families were closer.

After my parents found out we were married, we moved to the farm. Martin moved in with me and then we started helping out my grandfather.

For over thirty years, my grandfather had blacks working for him on the farm. It got to the point where he just couldn't get them to work anymore. Then my grandfather asked me if I could get him some help for the farm. So I went and got my crewleader's license. We started out with six people.

My grandfather knows a lot of older gentlemen in the neighborhood who also needed farmworkers. They wanted to use the six I had and so we went from one farm to another. I tried to help everybody in the community, six workers here, four over there, two over here—whatever they needed, I tried to help. That's how it started.

The next year, more workers came back and our business tripled in size. As word got out, it just got bigger and bigger. At the time, I didn't realize what I was getting into. That six people turned into a very big business. This makes the fourth year that I've been a crewleader, and I now have two labor camps, two apartment houses, and one hundred and thirty-six workers. My workers call me *La Reina de Trabajo*—"The Queen of Work"—because I work all year long. I've always got a job for my people somewhere.

There is a lot of conflict in the town about the Spanish people. The community wants their money—when they go shopping at the grocery stores or eat at Hardee's—but they don't want to deal with them. More than half the community simply doesn't like the Spanish and I don't think it's going to get any better. The main reason they don't like the Spanish is that they can't understand them. It was the same way for me when I was first involved with the migrants. I'd be in a crowd with Martin and they'd be talking in Spanish. I wouldn't know what to think because I couldn't understand what they were saying. How can you judge a person you don't understand? How can you know what they're thinking and feeling?

We have very few facilities for the Spanish. There are so many migrants here and hardly anybody here knows how to speak Spanish. We've only got one clinic where the doctor speaks Spanish and there's nobody at the hospitals or courthouses to translate. There's just a general lack of communication. What keeps people from seeing the migrants as human is that they don't spend any time with them. They see the Spanish in the grocery stores, but they just pass by in the aisles. They don't take the time to get to know the migrants. They don't go to dances together. They don't associate with them, so how would they know what they're like? Nine times out of ten, the only time the Spanish are recognized is when they're in trouble. To the community, the migrants are like aliens. The community is afraid of the unknown, afraid that people from another country are coming here and taking over.

Every year, there are more Spanish people coming into the area. The migrants are here and they're not going to leave. As long as there's work here, there are going to be migrants. The community needs to realize that instead of rejecting these people, they need to figure out a way to help them. They've got to learn to live with the migrants.

The Spanish are more devoted to their families than our own people. They come over here and work for months and months to send money home to their mothers and fathers. How many of our own people send money home to help out their parents? They're also more devoted to their work. They rarely get sick, they're always on time, and they always want to work more hours. They come here to try to better themselves, and our people are trying to pull them down.

My husband was a farmworker, so he knows how crewleaders treat the people. That's why he treats workers better than the other crewleaders. He's been cheated out of money. He's lived in houses with no lights and no water. He came here illegally and two of the people that crossed with him drowned in the river. Even now, my husband is afraid of water. He still won't go swimming.

Sometimes I want to get out of the business because there's just too much going on. You see so many people get hurt, not just physically, but mentally. There are so many crooked crewleaders who cheat the people, stick them in beat-up houses, and steal their money. It's hard for workers. They have to travel from one place to another just to make a living. When work ends here, they go off to somewhere else. They have no destination, no idea where they'll be from week to week. They carry very little clothing and own so few things. It's hard to understand their way of life and it's very sad.

Being a crewleader hasn't been easy. For me, it's more than a job. I live with these people on a daily basis. We're like a family. It's as if there's two of me, one that's with my community and one that's with the migrants. It's like there are two different worlds here and I have to bring them together.

They say that God has your life planned. I wonder. I think it's my destiny to do what I'm doing. I believe that my life had to be planned because my husband and I were thousands of miles apart and we were brought together. With two different languages and two different cultures, we were joined into one. It's amazing.

As growing numbers of Latino families settle into small towns in the rural South, local residents often complain about the social and economic costs associated with the new immigrants. Many residents believe that Latino workers and their families demand excessive services while providing the community with little in return. They feel unfairly burdened with the costs of treating workers' illnesses, providing social service benefits to migrant families, paying for increased law enforcement, and educating growing numbers of Spanish-speaking children. Community leaders complain that workers avoid paying taxes and send their earnings out of the area to family members living abroad.

The arrival of Latino immigrants in small towns is creating a crisis in local identity. Throughout the rural South, race relations have long been based on a clear demarcation between black and white residents, who rarely share the same neighborhoods or attend the same churches. Still, most local residents, whether blacks or whites, know each other or know of each other, having lived in and around the same area for generations. As a general rule, people know their place within an insular, familiar world. The arrival of Latino farmworkers has forced rural communities to respond to a new group of neighbors who do not fit easily into the existing social system.

Francisco and Sofia Cordero   ◆   *Warsaw, North Carolina*
Sofia Cordero first arrived in North Carolina eighteen years ago, when she was eleven years old. Her family had been traveling north out of Florida to do farmwork in New Jersey. Their truck broke down in North Carolina, and so they decided to stay in the area and look for work. Since then, Sofia and her family have traveled back and forth from Florida to North Carolina each year.

Francisco Cordero entered the United States in the early 1980s, swimming across the Rio Grande, riding a freight train to San Anto-

nio, hitching a ride to Dallas, and later making his way north to Chicago. He met Sofia in Florida, where they both worked in the fields.

Two years ago, Francisco and Sofia decided to settle in North Carolina. Recently, Francisco left the fields to work in construction and Sofia left farm labor to work at the local migrant health clinic. She is studying to become a nurse's assistant.

SOFIA Everyone says that we were the first Hispanic family in the area. North Carolina has changed a lot since we first came. Back then, there was nothing for us in the stores. Now, they've got *chiles,* tortillas, and Spanish-language magazines.

Things are changing, but truthfully, I don't think they're changing for the better. There are so many people here now that growers no longer have problems finding help. Now it's easy for the growers to take advantage of the workers, and now they're paying workers even less than before.

FRANCISCO Here, the life of a Mexican is pure work. You need to work all the time. We earn more working here than in Mexico, but that's the only advantage of living here.

SOFIA What image does the *bolillo* have of the Mexican? They think that in Mexico people are dying of hunger. The *bolillos* really believe that. They think people come to the United States because they're starving.

FRANCISCO They think that in Mexico we're all hungry, that we've never eaten meat, and that we should be grateful for whatever a *bolillo* gives us.

SOFIA They think we're desperate, and because of that, they feel justified in abusing us. There are many bosses here who steal workers' Social Security or pay workers below the minimum wage.

FRANCISCO The other day a friend told me that the *bolillos* were lazy. I think it's just that the *bolillos* have the upper hand. They're the ones with the money. It's not that they're lazy, it's that they have enough money to pay other people to work for them. If Mexicans had money, we'd probably do the same thing.

The ones who are lazy are the *moyos.* They're the ones that don't work, the ones who live off food stamps. They spend their time stealing. I've heard that when they get out of jail, they'll steal things right in front of a policeman so they'll be put back in jail where they get three meals a day. I don't know if that's true, but that's what I've heard.

Before the whites used to have the *moyos* under the whip, no? They were beaten down. And now they're the ones who refuse to work.

SOFIA We had one boss who was a very good person. His wife was a registered nurse. He had plenty of money and a nice house. When you'd see him in the street, he'd always come up and talk with you. He'd come over to our house and eat with us. If the dishes were dirty, he'd clean off a plate, sit down, and grab some tortillas.

FRANCISCO There was another *bolillo* who invited us to eat at his house. He served us first and then served his family. He understood how Mexicans do things.

SOFIA Still, it's hard to be friends with the *bolillos*. I've always felt that even if you don't like someone you should speak kindly to them and respect them. But to be real friends? That's difficult. You can never really be friends with someone who's your boss. You can't get past the relationship of boss to worker.

Also, the *bolillos* have their own culture, their own way of thinking. They're very different than us. Whether you like it or not, people really are different. I think it would be very difficult to have a truly intimate friendship with a *bolillo*.

Mexicans always look for Mexicans, *moyos* look for *moyos,* and *bolillos* look for *bolillos*. Everyone speaks differently, listens to different kinds of music, and has different ways of having fun. We don't all have the same culture. We can't have the same conversations. It's easier to talk to someone who's more like you. We understand each other better.

The arrival of Latino immigrants in the rural South is the product of a farm labor system that has historically relied on successive waves of new workers. In this sense, Latino farmworkers in the rural South represent the latest chapter in a long history of agriculture's dependence on vulnerable immigrant labor. Still, the impact of Latino workers on the rural South also represents something new, particularly as workers and their families settle out of the migrant stream and take up permanent residence in small communities. Migrant farmworkers are pioneers in a social process through which Latinos are settling in rural areas unaccustomed to foreign immigration. As these new arrivals find stable, nonmigrant jobs and set up growing Latino communities, other workers—often recent immigrants with no working papers—are replacing settled migrants laboring in the fields. In this way, Latino farmworkers are changing the face of rural America.

Dora Medina ♦ *Faison, North Carolina*
Dora Medina has spent most of her life as a farmworker. Several years ago, she began cooking food and carrying it out to the fields to sell. With the money she saved, she bought a small restaurant from a woman who had fallen on hard times. Medina fixed up the place and now works full-time managing the restaurant, a one-story

cinder-block building, with a flat blue roof and two potted plants by the door. The small building is topped by a large sign, featuring the portraits of two men and the name of the restaurant, El Valle.

I decided to call the restaurant *El Valle*—"The Valley"—to honor mom and dad for putting up with me for all those years. It was my way of saying thanks. The restaurant sign has two circles—one circle represents Mexico and the other circle represents Texas. The Texas side has a profile of my dad's face, with his wrinkles and that firm smile, wearing a ten-gallon hat. Dad represents the Texas side. The Texas side always dreamed of a better life. When we went out to Ohio, Michigan, and Florida, Dad always dreamed of having something. When I thought about my life, I thought a lot about the border and about Mexico. My husband represents the Mexican side. I couldn't leave him off the sign because he's the one I love.

The first time I drove up and saw that sign, I felt like I had finally arrived. I felt that all my struggles, all the pains that I'd gone through, were worth it—all to get to that point. I remember feeling like something was washing the inside of me, carrying everything away. There I was, me, Dora—the one who wasn't good enough for nothing, the one who was always making mistakes, the one who never got it right—it was me that had accomplished this. I parked my car and I cried. I cried like a kid, like a little baby. Now, every morning when I drive up here and see the sign, I feel proud.

Before I had the restaurant, my husband and I would go to the bank to cash his checks and the tellers would say, "Thank you." That was that. They'd never talk with us. Now that I have the restaurant, I'm somebody to them. Now that they have my account, I'm noticed. I matter. These days, I can hardly get inside the bank doors before everyone's saying, "Well, hello, Dora!" "How are you today?" "Dora! How you doing?" It puzzles me. I tell my husband, "That's strange, honey. Remember when we used to walk in there, and they hardly even said, 'Hello'?" Now, they call me by my first name. I think, "My Lord, what's going on? What did I do?" I guess you've got to do something to be recognized.

Here, Latinos usually go unnoticed. It seems that the only time people pay attention to us is when something bad happens, like when there's an accident or if someone goes to jail. Then the locals read about it in the paper and for a couple of minutes we're noticed. That's bad for the whole community. It affects all of us. It sets up a barrier.

I remember reading in the paper about some lady who lived across the street from some migrants. She said, "The whole time that they're here, I panic because I never know what they're going do. What if they're stealing

my things? While they're here I'm always scared." The woman was imply-
ing that for the six months that the workers are here, it's chaos, like you
never know what's going to happen from one minute to the next. But she
never even crossed the street to say, "Hello, my name is so-and-so."

The local people here are guarded. They never take the time to go
out of their way and learn who the migrant workers are and what they're
all about. Don't they realize that the same people they're afraid of are the
ones that pick the salad they eat? We're not here to harm them.

I'm just one of countless migrants who's wasted years in the fields. I
remember when we'd be driving to Ohio and the fields would be green.
It looked beautiful, but for us that meant work. Now, when I see that the
fields have been picked, I say, "All right, it's finally over." I know somebody worked hard in those fields. I feel good when I see empty fields because I know that no more migrants will have to work there until next
year.

I feel sorry for farmworkers. I feel like they'll never be noticed. I
would be thrilled if someday the newspaper would say, "We would like to
thank the farmworkers, the pickers. We appreciate the hours, the days,
the weeks, they've spent harvesting our produce." I wish somebody
would finally say something like that. Migrants need to be recognized.

Now, with this restaurant, maybe I have a little bit of a right. Maybe
I could be the one that makes everyone realize, "Lord, have mercy, those
tomatoes I ate yesterday? Somebody picked them with their own
hands." I might be the one that says that.

8. Farmworker Politics
Some Measure of Protection

IN THE LATE twentieth century, it's often difficult to remember that many of the uncertainties and abuses that farmworkers currently experience were common in other industries in the not-so-distant past. Virtually all of our nation's key worker protections did not exist until the 1930s. The minimum wage, the forty-hour workweek, child labor provisions, unemployment insurance, Social Security, and legal protections for union organizing all evolved out of complex, turbulent struggles between organized labor, industry, and the federal government, which culminated in legislation passed during the Roosevelt administration's New Deal. The 1930s' labor laws expressed a basic philosophy that the federal government bore a responsibility to guarantee minimum protections for workers in order to serve the greater social good. Agricultural workers, however, were specifically excluded from every major New Deal–era protection.

By denying farmworkers the basic protections extended to virtually every other American, the federal government officially accepted and, in fact, institutionalized the second-class status of agricultural laborers. Employment practices unimaginable in other industries remained common, acceptable, and even legal within agriculture.

Beginning in the 1960s, farmworkers gradually came to be covered by most of the key protections of the New Deal labor laws, although many important exclusions continue to this day. Around the same time, particular legislation, regulations, and social programs were enacted to compensate for prior exclusions and to minimize the impact of farmworkers' poverty. Despite these efforts to ameliorate the effects of decades of exclusion from basic labor protections, farmworkers remain the nation's poorest workers.

Mark Schacht ♦ *Sacramento, California*

Until recently, Mark Schacht was the key lobbyist for the California Rural Legal Assistance Foundation (CRLAF). CRLAF is a nonprofit spin-off of California Rural Legal Assistance, an organization that receives federal money to represent farmworkers and other poor residents in rural California. CRLAF was created in part because formal Legal Services funding cannot be used for lobbying and other political activity.

Before moving to California, Schacht worked in Washington, D.C., as the legislative director of the Migrant Legal Action Program and as a legislative aide who helped write the farmworker provisions of the Immigration Reform and Control Act.

A few months after this interview, significant cuts in Legal Services' funding reduced Schacht's job to a half-time position.

After all these years of legislative effort, you can candidly say that the situation is not much better now than it was in the 1960s. Despite repeated state and federal legislative efforts to deal with these problems, the situation has not improved.

The growers understand their legal and political needs and they're very well organized. When a bill is introduced in the legislature, there's an aura created around it by both its proponents and opponents. The California legislature has a significant agricultural lobby and a significant contingent of rural members in both houses. So often the worst thing that can happen to a bill is for it to be described as a farm labor bill. When that happens, then everybody instantly knows how everyone else will line up.

Often our strategy is to not characterize a particular bill as a farm labor bill, but as an issue that affects all employees. Over the last decade, we've managed to get a number of bills signed into law that way. Still, we've also presented bills where we take the industry head on. That's where the big lobbying money comes in. Everybody knows that a farm labor bill matters to the Western Growers Association, the Farm Bureau, Agricultural Producers, the Grape and Tree Fruit League, the Wine Institute, the tomato processors, the cotton growers, et cetera. They know that there's money to be made and campaign contributions to be won. There is intense lobbying on the part of agriculture to peel away the votes needed to pass the bill. The big money comes out with every bill that's considered a farm labor bill.

All of the farm labor bills start from real, tangible social wrongs that can be righted without a lot of money being spent and without a lot of disruption to honest business people. These bills are the right thing to do and you can often convince people to talk about farmworker issues in public in a way that's favorable to you. Still, an appeal to what's the right thing to do won't convince legislators to overcome the politics that are swirling about the bill and actually vote for you.

Legislators know that when you're going up against agriculture, all the power of a multibillion-dollar industry will be arrayed against you. If it looks like you're about to be run over, they'll vote against you. Here, politics is the only reality. Everything that's done in the legislature is done for a political reason. So when everybody sees that the growers are going to kill a particular bill, then that bill is dead on arrival and no one wants to spend any political capital on it.

When we propose legislation, the typical response of the agricultural interests is, "Why is agriculture being singled out?" Well, agriculture *is* the great exception. Everywhere you look, agriculture has an exemption, from labor standards to environmental standards. When you get around to cleaning up a mess in a special industry with special protections and privileges, you inevitably end up crafting industry-specific solutions. Agriculture is special because they made themselves special.

You talk to growers and they'll show you statistics that the average wages in agriculture are six dollars and twenty-five cents an hour. What they don't show you is that field workers' wages—the people at the bottom of the rung who've been doing stoop labor in this state for a century—are far lower. There's a subclass of workers who are illegally paid less than the minimum wage, and virtually everybody working close to the minimum wage is almost certainly earning below the minimum wage some of the time. Still, the state of California never finds these violations. The California Department of Labor has cited slightly over fifty growers in the last ten years for minimum-wage violations. This is astonishing. This industry has eighty thousand farms. We have cases for groups of workers involving hundreds of thousands of dollars in unpaid wages and the state can't seem to find these violations.

We've got litigation against some of the largest agricultural producers in the world, as well as the sleaziest, lowball, cheating contractors. You find the same kind of violations—they're stealing people's wages, they're charging them for tools when it's illegal, they're transporting them in substandard vehicles. All of these things have to do with money. It costs more to run a decent operation that's up to code than one where you have lousy broken-down buses and don't pay the workers what they're entitled to.

The solutions involve making growers responsible for the workers who are brought onto their property and making sure that there's enforcement against those growers who behave irresponsibly. The agricultural industry could be cleaned up and it wouldn't take a lot of money. What it would take is political will, and that's not something you'll find in either party. If you gave an enforcement agency the ability to really address the problem, to assess fines and penalties, to have the enforcement authority to focus on the bad guys, you could create a climate in the agricultural industry where it would no longer be acceptable to break the law.

There are legislative solutions to the problems of illegal conduct. Of course, that's not where farmworkers' real problems lie. The real problems of American farmworkers come from being Third World workers earning Second World wages and living in a First World economy. The only way that situation can really be addressed is if those workers were to get paid for the value of what they do, which is certainly not what's happening now.

The agricultural industry is the best-organized, most powerful, ruthless, unscrupulous special-interest group in America. They've successfully defeated the whole wave of industrial unionism that swept the country in the 1920s and 1930s. The industry stopped the clock and kept it stopped. We're defeated through money, slick lawyering, lobbying, and the worst sorts of duplicity and ruthlessness. The agricultural industry calculates what its interests are and then goes out and targets what it needs to do. It is a corrupt scheme in that it subverts lawful enforcement activities by defeating budgets, amending laws, and keeping both public and private enforcers weak and underfunded. Agriculture wants to keep in place a system with an oversupply of workers, low wages, and antiunion conditions.

The farm labor supply is like a barrel that the growers make sure is always brimming over. There are lots of hungry people out looking for work, just like the old days. The Joads from *The Grapes of Wrath* are still here, only in recent years they've become foreign-born, Spanish-speaking Mexicans. They're still on the move, still looking for work. These workers are pretty much invisible. You may not see them, but it's a huge labor force that's here every day, working the fields.

People should know that their food is heavily subsidized by what is essentially a corrupt production scheme. You can drive by a farm and see the big house, the swimming pool, the Volvos, and the kids with their gold jewelry. If the brown workers were stooping in the rows right next to these houses, you could maybe catch the glare of the disparity between the two realities. Still, as a consumer, you really don't see these things. We've been seduced by modern agribusiness.

In 1938, Congress passed the Fair Labor Standards Act (FLSA), which created a national minimum wage, a forty-hour workweek, mandatory overtime wages, and child labor provisions. Farmworkers were excluded from all of these protections until 1966—nearly thirty years after the law was originally passed—when about 30 percent of farmworkers were provided with minimum-wage protections. The law was amended twice in the 1970s to cover most farmworkers, although the current version of the FLSA specifically denies farmworkers the right to overtime pay, excludes laborers on small farms from any protection, and allows children as young as twelve to work in the fields.

Farm laborers were also excluded from the Social Security Act of 1935, denying them unemployment, old age, and disability benefits. In 1950, the law was amended to provide most agricultural workers with old age and disability protections, but the informal, transitory nature of farm labor has allowed thousands of employers to pocket Social Security payments and made it extremely difficult for workers to benefit from these programs.

Since farmwork is inherently seasonal—like construction and tourism—unemployment insurance represents an ideal mechanism for protecting workers during slow periods of employment. Nevertheless, unlike all other workers, farm laborers were excluded from unemployment insurance benefits until 1976—over forty years after the law was first passed. Even now, migrants have a difficult time qualifying for and receiving benefits when moving from one state to another. Because of these difficulties, less than a third of farmworkers even apply for unemployment benefits.

Libby Whitley ◆ *Washington, D.C.*
Libby Whitley worked as a lobbyist for the American Farm Bureau, one of the oldest and most-established national growers' organizations. She walked the halls of Congress daily, meeting with legislators and their aides, testifying in committees, and presenting growers' perspectives on various proposals. Over the last fifteen years, she has represented growers' interests in discussions of key farmworker legislation, including the Migrant and Seasonal Agricultural Worker Protection Act, the H-2A program, and the Special Agricultural Worker provisions of the Immigration Reform and Control Act.
Whitley is cheerful, upbeat, folksy, and earnest.

Up to the 1950s, almost everybody in Congress knew somebody who was attached to a farm. Their parents or grandparents were still farming, they had grown up on a farm or spent summers on a farm, or they had aunts and uncles who still farmed. They had some connection to rural

America. They had a basic understanding about some of the hard issues farmers are confronted with when the rains don't come or prices are crummy or the bull dies and you don't have the money to go buy a new one. They understood those things.

As congressmen become more representative of urban areas, they lose an understanding of agricultural production practices. They lose their connection to the farm and that makes it a lot harder for those of us in the agricultural industry to communicate with them about the realities of life on the farm.

For years, farmers have argued that we faced unusual circumstances and should be exempt from certain laws, like minimum wage. While it's undeniable that farmers face challenges that other employers don't face, our arguments that we're different and deserve specialized treatment have come back to haunt us. We're quickly becoming more regulated than any other industry. I have a sixty-five-page book that talks, in a *summary* fashion, about the laws and regulations we're subject to—Occupational Safety and Health Administration, the Migrant and Seasonal Agricultural Worker Protection Act, the Fair Labor Standards Act, regulations governing pesticides administered by the EPA, full-reporting requirements under the Immigration Reform and Control Act, et cetera. In terms of labor issues, we are probably the most regulated industry in the country. The farmer feels a sense of despair when he thinks of complying with labor laws. They do what they can and then they cross their fingers and pray, because you can't be in full compliance one hundred percent of the time.

I think that the average farmer considers that he has a close working relationship with his workers. In all the years that I've worked on these issues, I have never heard a farmer speak disparagingly of his workers. He will tell you that his workers are his single most important resource. Without his workers, he can't get his crop in. Without good workers, he can't sustain the quality and productivity that he needs. A farmer values his workers. In order to attract good workers and keep them through the season, he'll provide good housing, high wages, productivity bonuses, end-of-season bonuses, awards, and incentives. Most farmers will tell you when they have a good year their workers have a good year as well.

Worker advocates seem to think that, by definition, growers are evil. Unlike them, we don't take the position that farmworkers are evil. Farmworkers are valuable. They are one of the most valuable commodities a farmer has. The media always focuses on the worst-case scenarios. The annual reprisals of the "Harvest of Shame," the horror stories of housing problems and wage violations, the constant harping on how farmers are all bad employers— this tends to reinforce a negative perception of agriculture. Those cases are not the norm for the industry. They're the rare exception. There are good employers and bad employers. That's just as true in agriculture as it is anywhere else.

The Department of Labor's own statistics show that seasonal employment in agriculture is not the lowest-paid industry. We pay better than many other entry-level-type industries. We pay better than the fast-food industry. We have to compete for our workforce.

There are some very valid questions about farmworkers' quality of life and human dignity, but you cannot just blithely shove off all these problems on the productive sector of the economy and say, "You're making a profit, so you deal with it. You pay for all this stuff." At some point the productive sector isn't productive anymore and the whole system collapses in on itself. There is an attitude that farmers should be a social services agency, that if a farmer wants farmworkers he should pay for their transportation, their housing, subsidize their meals, take care of their children, and provide a greatly enhanced wage to compensate for the fact that they're not going to be employed twelve months a year. I suspect the farmer would be more than happy to do all of that if the price that he was getting for his commodity would permit him to do it. But, you know, it doesn't work that way.

Fruits and vegetables and other horticultural specialty crops are one of the areas where American agriculture is economically strongest. They are not price-supported industries. Arguably, if there is a free market in the agricultural industry, it is in the labor-intensive industries such as fruit-and-vegetable production. Congress doesn't understand the basic economics of agriculture. If you're getting four dollars a box for bell peppers, you can't force new labor costs on the bell pepper farmer that will raise the harvest cost to six dollars a box. That extra two dollars has to come from somewhere. If the money's not there, the next year, that farmer is going to stop growing peppers. That's what farmers are doing all the time.

In order to have farmworker jobs, you have to have farmers able to hire workers. That doesn't seem to me a perspective that many of the worker advocates share. If you make it impossible for a farmer to get labor or to hire labor, the industry will die and that's a definite possibility. I hear a number of people say if the farmer can't afford to do certain things for his workers, then he shouldn't be in business. Well, that's fine. Then America should not be in the business of producing fruits and vegetables domestically. In a very paternalistic and arrogant fashion, that is simply exporting problems abroad that we don't choose to deal with here. That's saying, "Well, I couldn't possibly eat a bell pepper that was produced in the United States and sold for four dollars a box, because we

Marissa González
Jorge Luis Hernández
Ignacio Gonzalez
Jennifer Garza

Martin Valdez Jr.
Belinda Villarreal
Sandra Esquivel
Jairo Alvarado

Juan Manuel Garcia Jr.
Blanca Estela Jaramillo
Roger Sandoval

Noviembre

NOVEMBER

Flor Estela Alaffa
Patricia Lorena Garza
José Antonio Guajardo
Hilda Martinez
Jose Alejandro Barrera
Arnulfo Gonzalez
Jorge Luis Silva
Brenda Hazel González

Erika Safia Hinojosa
Juan Manuel Alvarado
Adolfo Javier Cerda
Victor Manuel Ramirez
Michael Alonso Reyes
Domingo Martinez
José Alberto Vargas
Karina Elizal

David Miramontes
Pedro Lira
Brenda Vargas
Hector Mercedes Cant
Juan Manuel Garza Jr.
Blas Manriquez Jr.
Veronica Adriana Vargas

weren't housing the workers, transporting them, and paying them adequately. But I am more than happy to buy a green bell pepper that was produced in Mexico and sold in America for two dollars a box where the worker was living in a cave, paid five bucks a week, and bathed in chemicals over which we have no control." So what they're saying is that we're happy to let things be done abroad that we would never allow here.

Today, we have a horrible, adversarial situation, an us-versus-them mentality. We line up with our friends on the Hill, and they line up with their friends on the Hill. We build these ramparts and then take potshots at each other across what seems like a no-man's-land. Farm labor is an issue that nobody likes to handle. It is a tough issue. It is kind of a no-win issue. Farm labor doesn't make anybody happy. The farmer isn't going to be happy. The worker advocates aren't going to be happy. The issues just never get resolved.

Farmers are very resilient people. They truly believe that when God closes a door, he opens a window. They always find a way to hang in there and keep on keeping on. We've seen a pretty significant decline in the number of farmers and I'm not certain that the trend is reversing itself. The median age of farmers today is fifty-six, and there are very few farmers who encourage their children to go into the business. Farmers are good guys. They do the best they can, given horrendous challenges. They confront things that most Americans wouldn't tolerate for a minute.

Farming isn't a job, it's a way of life. It is hard not to get emotional because I see the potential for the end of this way of life, the end of an industry that has made America great and still represents a lot of values which Americans hold dear. I see the growers as victims. I really do. Growers' suffering and pain probably motivates me as much as the suffering and pain that the worker advocates see on their end. I see growers put out of business. I see families who've been on farms for two hundred years end up on the breadline. I see people commit suicide over class-war litigation. There are bad apples in every bunch, but farmers are really the salt of America.

One of the most significant pieces of New Deal legislation was the National Labor Relations Act (NLRA), a response to decades of active, and at times militant, labor organizing. The NLRA affirmed workers' rights to organize, strike, and engage in collective bargaining, and created the National Labor Relations Board to arbitrate labor disputes. Excluding agricultural workers from the NLRA dealt a harsh blow to struggling farmworker unions, which were quite strong during the 1930s, and further distanced farmworkers from industrial workers, whose unions grew in size and political influence. Although proposals to include farmworkers within the NLRA have been repeatedly presented in Congress, farmworkers remain excluded from federal protections for labor organizing.

Farmworkers were also specifically excluded from a variety of state worker protection laws, most notably workers' compensation, which covers medical treatment and lost wages for workplace accidents. While farmwork ranks as one of the most dangerous occupations in the nation, only eleven states provide farmworkers with the same workers' compensation coverage as other workers. In twenty-five other states, farmworkers have limited coverage, and in fourteen states, agricultural employers are not required to provide workplace insurance for their laborers.

The 1930s' legislative record reveals a striking lack of discussion regarding the rationale for excluding farmworkers from fundamental labor protections. There is some mention of the political obstacles to protecting agricultural workers, a few comments about the government's intention to include farmworkers in the future, and the occasional remark that excluding farmworkers from basic worker protections is simply unfair and unjust. Ultimately, the decision reflects the gross imbalance between the political influence of agricultural interests and the powerlessness of farmworkers.

Beginning in the 1960s, media exposés, congressional hearings, and popular pressure produced a growing awareness that migrant farmworkers labored under oppressive conditions and that their exclusion from basic protections was unjustified. Both the Democratic and Republican presidential platforms of 1960 included promises to improve the lives of migrant workers. Congressional hearings revealed that many of the most consistent and troubling abuses—low wages, terrible housing, dangerous transportation, false promises— occurred at the hands of farm labor contractors. In 1963, Congress passed the Farm Labor Contractor Registration Act (FLCRA), which required all farm labor contractors to register with the federal government, keep appropriate wage records, and provide accurate information to their workers regarding promised employment. The FLCRA sought to improve conditions for farmworkers without having to directly confront the question of grower responsibility.

In 1983, out of frustration with the FLCRA, Congress passed a second piece of special farmworker legislation, the Migrant and Seasonal Agricultural Worker Protection Act (MSAWPA). The MSAWPA expanded protections regarding the recruitment, employment, transportation, and housing of farmworkers. Employers are required to keep accurate wage records, provide workers with written terms of their employment, have labor camps and vehicles inspected and approved, and provide workers with informational postings outlining the conditions of work and housing. The most significant and controversial aspect of the MSAWPA is that it allows both growers and contractors to be held liable for violations of the law.

Although each piece of protective legislation has included an enforcement system involving complaint procedures, investigations, and possible sanctions, there is universal agreement that the Department of Labor has never been provided with enough investigators or adequate resources to respond to farmworkers' needs. The cases are also hard to investigate—the workers labor in isolated locations throughout the nation, move from one place to another, often speak no English, and are difficult to contact during normal working hours. Workers are unlikely to file their own complaints since they are generally unaware of their legal rights, unused to turning to authorities for help, and rarely believe that voicing their complaints will have any real impact on their lives. Most employers realize that the chance of being investigated is slim and that the penalties are relatively minor, often far less than the money they save by not following the regulations. Advocates complain that investigations of farm labor abuses are a low priority for enforcement agencies and that when investigations are conducted, they rarely target growers.

Saul Sugarman ♦ *Washington, D.C.*
Saul Sugarman began working at the United States Department of Labor in 1962 after serving in the military and finishing law school. In the mid-1970s, Sugarman was sent to southern Florida to prepare a report on the conditions of West Indian H-2 workers brought into the United States each year to hand harvest sugarcane. The Sugarman Report became a controversial document because it revealed that large sugar companies were cheating tens of thousands of workers out of their wages each year.

Sugarman was asked to retract his report. He refused. The Department of Labor sent another investigator to Florida who prepared a new report that found no significant problems with the sugar companies' treatment of their workers. West Indian workers continued to be brought into the country for another eighteen years until a series of media exposés and lawsuits proving Sugarman's allegations to be true led the sugar companies to disband the program and replace the workers with machines. A number of people in the Department of Labor have described Sugarman's report as "career affecting."

The true Saul Sugarman is someone who never forgot the lessons his Hebrew-school teacher taught him a long time ago. The first recapitulation of the Ten Commandments says, "The wages of the day servant shall not remain with the master overnight." Here we are some four thousand years later still struggling with that. You wonder where society is going. We're fighting the same battles over and over without making a whole lot of progress. Change is so incremental. How can a people get anywhere like this? How can a nation advance? How can we expect to better ourselves if we continue to treat other people the way we do?

When I started working in the Department of Labor, I thought that the Wage and Hour Division wouldn't last more than five or six years. The minimum-wage laws seemed like such a simple thing. I figured there couldn't be too many employers who would continue to violate minimum-wage protections. Boy, was I wrong.

It's actually very simple for growers to comply with the law. A lot of people in other parts of the economy are in compliance with these laws. Still, the growers are always pointing to the contractors as being responsible. That's ludicrous. After all, it's their farm labor contractor. There's no farm labor contractor if there's not some grower to employ them. They created the role of the middleman. It didn't grow out of nowhere. It would be better if we could hold the grower responsible for abuses, but the agency leadership has been holding back because of a sensitivity to the grower lobby. The growers have tremendous power over the Department of Labor.

Nobody in the department wants to get burned. They're all working for a living. They have families and children. They're careerists. Civil servants can try to change things, but generally they're beaten back or disciplined in some way. Civil service is not independent of what's going on in the politics. People here take orders. You can push, but you pay a price for that. There is a layer of people over us who keep things constrained.

At times, the Department of Labor has wanted to lead, but it's never really had the resources. We don't have what it would take to really do the job. We use the equivalent of twenty-seven full-time employees to ensure compliance nationwide. It's a pittance. We're not a threat to anyone. The political leadership that comes from up top could really make a difference—if they wanted to. No one in the Department of Labor has ever wanted to know what it would really take to improve the situation of farmworkers. We've had little drives, small efforts here and there, but there's never been an interest in developing a long, continuous program that would help farmworkers. For thirty years we've been grasping at straws.

Why do growers allow workers to be mistreated? You know, I've never asked a grower that. It's not part of our enforcement procedure. It wouldn't hurt to ask, although I don't think you'd get an honest answer. I hate to think that growers mistreat workers because they have a low opinion of them, but that seems to be part of it. Farmworkers are different than growers. They're from a different socioeconomic class. They're not members of the growers' churches or of the growers' communities. If the growers' own sons and daughters were the migrant farmworkers, things would get better pretty quick. We all know that. If next year, all our country's migrant farmworkers were college students from middle-class America, the situation would change.

Farmworkers' problems are a moral issue. The larger society ought to be embarrassed by what's happening to farmworkers. Still, farmworkers always seem to be someplace else, far away, out of sight and out of mind. It's not only the growers who see farmworkers as being "other people," the larger society sees them that way, too.

These are issues that no law can change. That's what this is really all about. Beyond all the legalisms, getting down to the very root of the whole thing, we all have to be willing to see other people as part of the same human race. If we see other people as less worthy than ourselves, we're never going to get anywhere. There's no hope for all of us if we can't get beyond that, not just as far as farmworkers are concerned, but in everything else. We have to get beyond narrow legalisms.

Farmworkers are poor people that work for a living. They're not on welfare. They get very few social services. Who's going to help them? There has to be someone who's willing to say this situation is awful and we have to do something about it, that we're a civilized country and we're not going to tolerate the way farmworkers are treated. Nobody could seriously argue that farmworkers don't deserve better than what they have. The few pennies it would actually cost to improve things is insignificant in relation to the benefits we would gain.

Growers can't really believe that the way things are is the way they're supposed to be. They know better. We all do. The growers have to see farmworkers as their responsibility. I think that things could change if we could get the growers away from all the legalisms and just say, "The answer is to do the right thing. You know in your heart what it is that you have to do." Surely the growers know the answer.

I think if I could get a grower alone—if I could spend eight days hiking the Appalachian Trail with him, climbing up and down mountains and along those ridges—then perhaps I could change one employer. He might also change me a bit, and then we'd both be better off. Maybe in the end, the world is changed one person at a time. Maybe that's all there is.

For growers, the fundamental problem of farm labor has never been workers' rights, but access to a steady supply of low-wage labor. The U.S. government has helped agricultural employers gain access to workers both through general immigration policies and through the creation of special guest worker programs that allow agricultural employers—and only agricultural employers—to import foreign workers into the United States. Traveling north from poor countries where there are few opportunities, these workers are far more willing to accept difficult conditions and low wages than Americans. Since temporary foreign workers can be sent home at any time at the employer's request, they are unlikely to complain and virtually impossible to organize.

The bracero program was the nation's first major guest worker program. It lasted twenty-two years and allowed for the entry of between 4 and 5 million Mexican workers. At the beginning of the Second World War, western growers were worried about labor shortages brought on by the expanding war economy, which was drawing domestic farmworkers away from the fields. The growers appealed to the federal government to create a legal mechanism to bring Mexican workers into the United States to labor in agriculture as a special wartime policy. Without public debate or legislation, a bilateral agreement between Mexico and the United States was signed: Mexican workers would be recruited by U.S. government agents and then sent north to labor for growers who were required to feed, house, and employ them for a set period of time. During the war years, the bracero program imported no more than 50,000 workers per year.

By 1947, with the war over, the program was set to expire. At the insistence of western growers, the bracero program continued. Undocumented immigrants were passed over to farms as "paroled" contract workers and new provisions allowed U.S. employers to contract directly with Mexican laborers. In 1951, the program was given new statutory basis through Public Law 78, and the number of workers brought into the country rapidly expanded. By the mid-1950s, over 400,000 braceros were being brought into the United States each year, nearly double the number of legal immigrants allowed entry. The bracero program was coupled with a crackdown on illegal Mexican immigration and the passage of federal laws making it illegal to recruit and transport—although not to employ—undocumented immigrants. The federal government also instituted mass expulsions of illegal Mexican immigrants culminating in the militarized "Operation Wetback" roundups of 1954 and 1955. The bracero program continued through 1964 when it was finally terminated because of vigorous opposition from labor unions, religious organizations, and community groups.

Agricultural interests on the East Coast also petitioned for the creation of a temporary-labor program during the Second World War. Between 1943 and 1947, around 66,000 West Indian workers were brought to the United States through the British West Indies program. After the war, growers recruited workers and established contracts, and in 1952, the importation of West Indian workers became known as the H-2 program, in reference to the special H-2 visas that allowed workers into the country. Every year until the early 1990s, about 20,000 H-2 workers (later known as H-2A workers) traveled from the West Indies to the East Coast: 10,000 sugarcane workers in Florida; 6,000 apple pickers in the Northeast; and the rest in a variety of other agricultural jobs.

In theory, the H-2 program was designed to provide adequate protections for domestic workers. Foreign workers were only supposed to be recruited for jobs where no domestic workers could be found, and the wages and working conditions for H-2 workers were not supposed to depress the local market. The Department of Labor was responsible for approving growers' requests for H-2 workers, ensuring that growers had done an adequate job looking for domestic workers, establishing fair wage rates, and approving housing, working conditions, and contracts.

Virtually every aspect of the H-2 program has been the subject of litigation, generally pitting federally funded Migrant Legal Services' attorneys against both the Department of Labor and a number of growers and growers' associations. In several cases, the litigation has led growers to hire domestic workers instead of H-2 workers. The largest employers—Florida-based sugar growers—brought the last group of H-2 workers into the country in 1994, after which hand-harvest laborers were replaced by machines. Despite legal obstacles and protracted litigation, the H-2A program has grown substantially in the late 1990s. Currently, over 34,000 H-2A workers enter the country each year, including increasing numbers of Mexicans. There are signs that the program will expand considerably, possibly becoming a new bracero-style institution, allowing large numbers of foreign guest-workers to labor in America's fields.

The history of special federal programs that bring immigrant workers into the United States to do agricultural labor reveals just how politically powerful growers are in comparison to farmworkers. Any industry that relies on large numbers of manual laborers could benefit from access to specially selected young workers from poor countries who can only work for a single employer, can be fired at will, and are easily replaced with workers in a similar situation. However, a large-scale program of this type within the United States would be politically impossible for any industry other than agriculture. While there are temporary-foreign-worker programs that allow a limited number of nurses and other skilled foreign workers into the country, one can imagine the public response if convenience-store owners, automakers, construction companies, or fast-food restaurants were allowed to bring workers from the developing world into the United States to be housed and fed by their employers and promptly sent home if they complained.

Delroy Livingston ♦ *Brooklyn, New York*

Delroy Livingston was born in rural Jamaica, where he grew up raising fruits and vegetables on a small farm. He worked four full seasons hand harvesting sugarcane in southern Florida. He now lives in Brooklyn where he is married and works in construction.

One year, a number of workers at the Okeelanta Corporation refused to cut the cane at the row price that was being offered. The workers walked back from the fields to the labor camp, hoping to negotiate a better rate. The following day, Livingston and several hundred others were rounded up by law enforcement officers using police dogs. The incident became known among cane cutters as the Dog War.

"The police came in with the dogs who mash down and bite everything. They were barking and trying to grab you. The police rush in, kick over everything, and forced you out the door and into the bus."

All of the workers in the barracks, including many who had not participated in the strike, were taken to Miami. From there, they were put on planes and sent back home without their belongings. Some workers left the United States wearing only shorts, while others went home barefoot.

From when I was eighteen I always tried to get a farmwork card to go and cut sugarcane in Florida. I go to the MP office and ask if they give me a farmwork card. Them always promise me. They take my name and say they call me.

I knew a lot of people who cut cane. They told me that it was hard work. I always like hard work. I like rough work. I like my clothes dirty. I'm not a person who dress in a necktie and those things. So, I always want to try cane cutting, to experience it. I respect a hardworking person more than a easy-working person. When you come in with a necktie, you're sitting all day, but when you're out there in the field, you work hard and appreciate your money better.

When I was twenty-four, they finally give me the card. Then they give me a date to go to Kingston where the men who come from the U.S. test you to see if your body fit enough to cut cane. When you get there, you form a line with two or three hundred others.

Then the man question you. They want to see if you're tough. Them ask you if you feel that you can manage the work, and you answer, "Yes." Them tell you that over there it is very hot, and you say, "Well out here it very hot, too." Them say that over there it cold and you say, "Well, I try it." So, them say, "OK."

Then they look at your hand and your build. They take your hand, hold it, and squeeze the palm to see how soft it is. If your hand is soft, they say you cannot manage it because you have to hold that bill—the cane knife—and it mash up your hand. They say if your hand is too soft, the bill mess it up and then you can't work. If you tell them you're a farmer and you have a soft hand, they know you tell them a lie. When they look at my hand they say, "OK, that look all right." My hand look very tough, man, lot of corn in it, lot of roughness.

Then, they look at you. If you're too skinny or too fat, they don't want you. If you're fat, you cannot work fast, and if you're skinny, then you easy to die because the work is very hard. And if you were skinny when you go to work, you're gonna get more skinny because over there that work is hard. The first man stamp your paper and he send you on to another man who ask you the same questions or other questions. If you fail the questions, he send you out. They only select a certain number of men. I was a lucky one to go through.

Then they tell you that you have to go to a medical test in Kingston. There they test your blood, urine, pressure, and those things. They check you for sickness with a chest X ray and everything, to see if your body fit. If you pass the medical, then they sign all the papers, saying which camp you going to. Then they send you back home and say wait for a telegram. When the telegram arrive, you go back to Kingston, and they take you on a bus to the airport. Then they put you on a plane.

The first time I came on contract was my first plane ride. I was very excited. I tried to be calm, but the plane lift up off the ground, and then shoot up in the air. When I come off of the plane it was at night so I couldn't see a thing. We went straight to the bus and then off to the labor camp. I expected the camp to look good, but when I got there, it was just cane fields. As far as I could see, just sugarcane. I wonder what type of a place is this? All we can see is cane, the camp, and the sugar factory. It was like being in a desert of cane.

The camp is a long building with an upstairs and a downstairs. You sleep in bunk beds, one bed on top of the other. There are hundreds of workers on each floor. All you see are the same guys that you leave Jamaica with. Once in a while you see a white guy driving a truck, or a police officer. You're on a plantation, just praying for the five months to be up, praying to go home.

They wake you up at four o'clock in the morning to go to the mess hall. They give you two slice of bread, some porridge, and a cup of tea. Then you go to the field. Your rice trucks supposed to come there at eleven o'clock, but sometimes they don't reach you until one or two o'clock. In the fields, you don't have no time to even eat, not five minutes, man. You don't come back until maybe three-thirty. You rest, make some rice, eat, play domino. It lonely, but you try to make friends. You sit around and talk. Sometimes you play cricket on a big playing field. When it Christmastime, you get up in the morning and they give you a ripe banana, an orange, and a piece of cake. That's your Christmas.

Cutting cane is rough work, man. I think it's the hardest work in the world. You have to keep your bill, your cane knife, real sharp. You have to have a hat because the sun too hot. You have to wear a iron hand and foot guard. Without the foot guard, you'd cut your foot off. You have to bend down and grab hold of the cane. You hold as much as you can in your hand and then you chop the root and lay it down. Then you cut off the leaf and put it on one side, and lay the cane on the other side. You have to do it all fast, very fast. If you don't cut fast, you don't make money.

When I was out there cutting the cane, the only thing I'd think about all the while I was working is, "I'll get some money, go back home, and buy a piece of land." That's the only thing I thought about. I always wanted a three-bedroom house. I never built it. I did achieve a lot of things by cutting cane though. I buy furniture, a television, a VCR, a stove, a fridge, and a stereo.

While we were there, all the people we saw were black. The only white is the big man in the office. And we don't see them. The big bosses is white and the white is not going to have other white men cut cane. The work is too hard for the white. The white can't manage it, so he have to

get a black man. White people are weaker than the black. They use the black because the black can go all day long. White man will be boss, but he won't be cutting that cane.

In Kingston, they tell you they going to pay five dollars thirty an hour. This is what it say on the contract. When you get to Florida, they don't pay you by the hour, they pay you by how much cane you cut. They might pay fifty dollars for a row of cane, so a half row is twenty-five dollars and quarter row is twelve dollars fifty. When you come out of the fields, you get a ticket from the ticket writer that says how much cane you cut and how much money you earned. If you can cut fast and the row is fifty dollars, the ticket writer will write that you worked eight hours. But if you work all day and only cut a quarter row, the ticket will show that you earned twelve fifty and only worked for two hours—even though you were out there for the full eight. The company rob you. You see, if they put you out for eight hours and you only make ten dollars, they supposed to build up your pay to about forty dollars, to make the eight hours' money. That's called "build-up pay." But the company don't want to do that, so they tell the ticket writer to put down the same hours as the money you earn. I always ask the ticket writer about it and he say that's what the boss tell them to do and they got to do what the boss say. You can't complain, because if you do, they send you home the next day. They'll claim you called Legal Aid on them. So you have to just go up there and learn to work fast.

When I just start to cut the cane, I used to earn a hundred and fifty dollars for two weeks. When I start to improve on cutting the cane, I would earn two hundred, maybe two hundred and fifty, that's after they take out the rice bill, the saving, and everything.

The workers are mistreated. You don't get a good bed or a proper meal. They don't respect you and they don't pay you right. They're very greedy, man. They make millions off the sugar, but you're the one in the field, doing the hard work. The companies don't care who you are. All they're interested in is that you get their work done. If you can't cut the cane good, they send you home. They told us that if they sent back a thousand today, they can get two thousand tomorrow, so it's no matter to them.

Now they've stopped bringing workers in to cut cane. I think that they should give us farmworkers some benefit like a pension or something. I'm not talking about people that spend a year of their life cutting cane. I'm talking about all those people who spent fifteen or twenty years, getting nothing money and then going back home. They should get something from all that work. Just give them something, and they'll feel all right. But, they'll get nothing, man.

The 1960s' War on Poverty created a series of social programs specifically designed to improve the lives of migrant farmworkers and their families. Farmworkers' poverty, isolation, and their constant mobility were recognized as obstacles to accessing social services and key problems for migrant children, who rarely finished school. The problems of farmworkers were also understood as a federal responsibility, since state governments were seen as unlikely to spend money on transient workers with limited ties to local communities. The laws established four key programs: Migrant Health, Migrant Education, Migrant Head Start, and the migrant provisions of the Job Training Partnership Act (JTPA), all of which continue to operate.

Migrant Education and Migrant Head Start are designed to help farmworker children succeed in school. Migrant Health allocates funds to serve farmworkers' health needs, often providing outreach services to labor camps and working to coordinate care for workers who move from one place to another. The JTPA program trains farmworkers in job skills to help them leave agriculture and find higher wage employment. Other federal programs help migrants gain high school equivalency degrees, offer assistance with the first year of college, and provide funds to build affordable housing.

Government assistance programs for farmworkers are premised on the idea that the farm laborers' poverty is a permanent feature of American agriculture. The goal of educational and job-training programs is to try to improve the lives of farmworkers and their children by helping them get out of agricultural labor and find more-stable jobs. Health care, legal assistance, and poverty relief programs all try to lessen the impact of farmworkers' poverty and vulnerability. Although some of these programs are more successful or better run than others, they all reflect a basic vision that the poverty and powerlessness of farmworkers is inevitable. None of these programs seeks to transform the farm labor system itself and none addresses the economic structure that defines farm laborers as the epitome of America's working poor.

Ed Zuroweste ♦ *Chambersburg, Pennsylvania*
Dr. Ed Zuroweste is the medical director of a community health center in Pennsylvania. The center receives federal funding to serve migrant farmworkers. Zuroweste grew up on a farm. In high school, he picked sweet corn, green beans, and strawberries alongside migrant farmworkers. While in college, he harvested tobacco in Kentucky.

When I left my residency in Ohio, I decided to come to a small town in Pennsylvania. I had no idea there were any farmworkers here. One of the first patients I took care of was the area's migrant nurse. She was the only person who had a job through the state Health Department to care for the one thousand farmworkers that came through this county every year. There was no clinic. There was no provision for the farmworkers except for this one nurse. I lived in Mexico for a couple of years and spoke Spanish, so I told the nurse to let me know if she ever needed any help. The next day five farmworkers showed up in my office.

Farmworkers exhibit the type of health status that one sees in the Third World. We see a lot of infectious diseases because of poor sanitation, poor nutrition, and exposure. Whenever you have a population that lives in poverty, with poor sanitation and poor access to health care, then you have a public health problem. Farmworkers are very susceptible to diseases that are out there— tuberculosis, cholera, leprosy—things that we haven't thought about much in recent years. Since farmworkers' access to health care is very limited, they often present in a more advanced stage, which makes them difficult to treat. It never ceases to amaze me how advanced farmworkers' medical problems are. We see lots of undiagnosed, untreated chronic diseases—hypertension, diabetes, advanced cases of cancer. If you have hypertension that isn't picked up and treated, then you have complications such as heart disease and kidney disease. Farmworkers' dental problems go way past what we normally see, even in poor populations. We had a volunteer dentist tell us that farmworkers' dental health is even worse than what he finds in the Third World countries where he works.

I went to medical school to become a family doctor. It was only after I got here and saw the first farmworkers that I became intensely interested in migrant health. When I saw some of these horrendous problems, I went to the state legislature and asked them what they were doing for farmworkers. They told me that they didn't do anything. To this day, the state of Pennsylvania provides no health-care funding for farmworkers, except for emergency Medicaid if someone is in the hospital. So, when I got nowhere with the state, then I went to a national meeting and got involved with a national organization called the Migrant Clinicians Network.

The first year I treated farmworkers in my office. The next year, I set up a night clinic. After two or three years, we got some federal funding to pay the salaries of the nurse practitioners, the physician's assistants, and the outreach workers. A lot of the care we provided was free, although sometimes I would get a small stipend. If we got a patient on emergency medical assistance, then I'd get paid the medical-assistance rate.

Around ten years ago, we became a nonprofit organization and then the cost of treating migrants stopped being a drain on my private practice. Still, I always felt torn. Our migrant program was a separate thing we did at night. I would spend the day seeing middle- and upper-class patients—the president of the local bank and well-to-do people—then, at night, I would treat farmworkers. I always felt closer to the migrant population. I felt like they needed my services more than the people I saw during the day. It was a struggle.

Finally, I realized I could treat my private-practice patients and farmworkers at the same time. Around three years ago, we set up a community health center. It's a primary-care health center with a midwife, two nurse practitioners, three physician's assistants, and four family doctors. It was cathartic for me to move to my new practice. A lot of what I did before was at night, so it was kind of invisible. Many of our private patients weren't exposed to farmworkers. Now, it's all out in the open.

When I transferred to my new practice, some of my patients didn't come with me. They didn't want to sit in the waiting room with poor people or migrant farmworkers. Still, I was pleasantly surprised that most of my private patients, from every economic walk of life, came with me. Now I work at a place where our philosophy is to turn no one away. If a patient can't pay, we give them free care. I feel better at night going to sleep knowing that we treat everyone and that we don't send collection agencies out to harass patients who can't pay their bills because they're poor or unemployed. I like having a waiting room with patients that are multidimensional, multiethnic, and economically diverse. In our health center, we treat millionaires just the same as we treat the homeless.

In the summertime we gear up for the migrant population. The only way you have good migrant farmworker health care is if you have outreach workers who go out to the labor camps. Nurse practitioners and physician's assistants go out every night to interview workers and do health screenings. If they find a worker with a serious problem, they'll either send them to our night clinic or have one of us see them during the day. They make sure that nobody falls through the cracks. You can't meet farmworkers' health-care needs unless you do outreach and have doctors who speak their language and know about pesticides and Third World infectious diseases.

I challenge anybody to tell me that the health status of farmworkers has improved significantly in the last thirty years. I've been involved with migrant health for fifteen years. I went into it thinking that we could make a difference and improve farmworkers' health. I have yet to see that happen. Migrant Health funding is still low. What we have so far are

Band-Aid programs that reach maybe fifteen percent of the farmworker population. I'll see somebody with dangerously high blood pressure and over three months I'll get their blood pressure normal. I'll give them enough medicine to last them four months or so, but when they come back the next July, their blood pressure is back up again. In the seven months they've been away, they've had no access to health care. It happens over and over, and it's very frustrating.

Still, we're on the verge of making some major changes. There is an infrastructure now, and with current technology, we can coordinate care not only between migrant health centers here in the United States, but also across the border into Mexico. We should have more clinics which would track workers and transfer medical data. If someone had active tuberculosis and started treatment in Pennsylvania, we could assure that they would get treatment all the way down to Florida and even into Mexico. We have the technology and we have the national expertise to do this. All we lack is the enthusiasm from Congress and the funding to make a difference.

Farmwork is still the most dangerous occupation in the United States. There are lots of physical injuries because of exposure to heavy machinery, pesticides, and accidents. Do you know how hard it is to get workers' compensation for a farmworker? In many states, farmworkers are excluded from workers' compensation. Even when there's insurance, the insurance company puts up a lot of roadblocks. Because of the transitory lifestyle of the farmworker, if the insurance companies hold out long enough, the workers will never get their money.

Did you know that three hundred kids die every year in farm-related accidents? Now, they're not all migrant farmworker kids, but these are children under the age of sixteen who die every year in work-related injuries. There are also an estimated twenty-four thousand kids who are injured on farms in work-related injuries. Now, what if I told you that in the fast-food industry every year, three hundred children under the age of sixteen died on the job and twenty-four thousand were injured? There would be a public outcry the likes of which we've never seen, right? But these kids die from work-related injuries in farm labor, and nothing's ever done. These children remain excluded from a lot of the child labor laws. My kid couldn't go work in a steel mill or a mine. No way. But they can work out on a farm and they can pick from dawn to dark around pesticides and heavy machinery, and that's legal. This is all because of the lobbyists for the agricultural community and the pesticide industry. It's all economics, as always.

I have a great respect for farmworkers. I like working with the kind of people who put in an honest day's work. Even though they have very difficult lives, they have a lot of pride and a lot of self-respect. They're not looking for a handout. They're not sitting on a welfare line. They travel all over the country to work, and all they ask for is to be respected, paid a decent wage, have a roof over their head, education for their kids, and access to decent health care. They give us much more than they ask for. Although emotionally and spiritually, farmworkers are sometimes extremely strong, politically they are very weak. Farmworkers have been excluded from basic protections because they have no political voice. So they can be abused and exploited. That makes me feel guilty and ashamed.

The health care of farmworkers is an issue of human rights. We're exposing farmworkers to work-related health problems. We're exposing them to these dangers and then not providing them with access to health care to identify and solve their problems. The health of farmworkers is a moral issue.

Perhaps the most controversial federal program provides migrant workers access to free and low-cost legal assistance through the Legal Services Corporation (LSC), which began providing special grants to serve migrants in 1977. Unlike health, education, and training programs, which are rarely confrontational, LSC grantees use federal money to prepare complaints and fund lawsuits against state agencies, contractors, and growers.

Since few private attorneys are willing to take on farmworkers' legal claims, virtually all labor-law cases alleging employers' mistreatment of farmworkers have been brought by Legal Services attorneys. To a large degree, the controversy surrounding Migrant Legal Services is evidence of its considerable success. As farmworkers were gradually brought under the protection of basic labor standards, many contractors and growers continued to run their businesses as before. Growers and crewleaders were often unaccustomed to business practices that were normal in virtually every other industry, from keeping written payroll records or paying minimum wage to making Social Security deductions and following basic safety guidelines.

Growers often claim that Legal Services' lawsuits are a form of harassment. During the 1980s and into the 1990s, a concerted political campaign against Legal Services claimed that farmworker lawsuits were based on insignificant technical violations and overzealous advocates using taxpayers' money to engage in antigrower crusades. Agricultural interests have lobbied fiercely to deny funding for Migrant Legal Services programs, and while the programs continue, increasingly severe restrictions have been placed on the use of federal money to defend farmworkers' rights. New regulations prevent Legal Services employees from representing undocumented workers, even with nonfederal funds. Since undocumented workers are often the most vulnerable members of the labor force, some advocates have left Legal Services to form private nonprofit organizations to represent farmworkers.

Greg Schell ♦ *Belle Glade, Florida*

Greg Schell is a Legal Services' attorney who has spent his entire career defending farmworkers' rights. For a number of years, he has been involved in several large lawsuits against sugar companies in southern Florida. Schell is a model of tenacity. He works seven days a week and has refused vacations for years. He is famously despised by growers and their attorneys up and down the East Coast.

Migrant Legal Services has been the only protection that most farmworkers have had over the past twenty-five years. I am proud that we've had some impact, but I feel terribly frustrated knowing that our limited resources are being used to do the job that an enormous federal agency has money to do. If we received a fraction of the money earmarked for enforcing these laws, we'd really see some changes.

Growers hate Migrant Legal Services because we've been effective. Unlike the Department of Labor, who can be politically pressured, Legal Services has always been independent. That was the whole point of the Legal Services Corporation. By empowering farmworkers who normally have no political influence, we've presented a direct challenge to the social and economic structure of many rural communities. Allowing farmworkers to sue farmers, showing that growers are often unscrupulous employers, destroys the moral superiority most farmers are accustomed to, the sense that they are the pillars of their community. That represents a threat to the whole social structure, especially in rural areas where hand-harvest agriculture is the principal source of local income.

Unlike large industrial employers with plants all over the country, farmers view lawsuits personally, as an attack on their personal moral stature. So they're often willing to spend any amount of money to fight these cases. They often hire the biggest firms and pay any price on cases that they are ultimately going to lose. We're always right in these cases.

When Legal Services says that the workers weren't paid right or the housing was bad, the number of cases where the court found that the workers were paid right or the housing wasn't bad is almost nil.

Our problem is that the legal system allows a well-funded defendant to delay, harass, intimidate, and harangue long enough to avoid liability unless our side is willing to dig in for the long fight. The farmers have figured out that in many cases it's a pretty good bet that Legal Services won't be able to survive that sort of protracted legal warfare. We've generally had one to three attorneys and maybe a paralegal or two. The big growers hire the biggest firms who put ten lawyers on a case. We don't have resources, but we have the tenacity to hang on and keep pounding them over time. We've only been successful when we've hung on like bulldogs.

The Department of Labor has never engaged in sustained enforcement against farmers. This is totally the result of growers' political power. Whenever there is an investigation or the suggestion of a substantial penalty, growers contact their congressman, senator, or governor, who then leans on the Department of Labor, which has proven enormously sensitive to such pressure. A single congressman shouldn't be able to deter the Department of Labor from its mission, but all too frequently that's how things happen. The Department of Labor, like all federal agencies, responds to political pressure, and there is probably no greater disparity of power than what exists between agribusiness and farmworkers.

If the current laws were enforced, things would be significantly better for farmworkers. Workers would get paid properly, have their Social Security and unemployment benefits paid. Now, if farmworkers were treated like other workers, then we'd see real changes. Some farmers might go out of business, get out of hand-harvest agriculture or leave the country. The rest of agribusiness would start using modern employment practices—begrudgingly. Kicking and screaming, they would raise wages and improve working conditions, make jobs more steady, and bring farmworkers closer to the economic mainstream.

In my eighteen-plus years as a farmworker advocate, I've seen some positive changes, but overall I'd say farmworkers are even farther from the mainstream economy then when I started. It seems extraordinary to me that in the final years of the twentieth century we're having serious discussions about why the person who picks the lettuce that goes on the buns at McDonald's doesn't deserve overtime while the person who serves the hamburger receives overtime. It seems rather remarkable to me that in half the states in this country farmworkers are the only major group of workers not protected by workers' compensation. It took eleven years of screaming and yelling, lawsuits, and everything else to force a very reluctant Department of Labor to issue regulations requiring toilets and clean water at the job site for farmworkers.

There is no area where the Department of Labor has failed more miserably than in administration of foreign-labor programs, which now show signs of growing to levels not seen since the bracero years. The Department of Labor has failed to enforce the law with respect to protecting both domestic workers seeking jobs and foreign workers brought in under H-2 contracts. Review after review, study after study has shown widespread violations in the foreign-worker program. In my experience, which is pretty extensive, I have never seen the foreign-worker program properly run.

The H-2 program is essentially a system of mail-order workers. It's perfect for growers because it keeps them from having to recruit domestic workers or raise wages to keep workers from going to another farmer who might pay more. The regulations designed to protect domestic workers from the adverse effects of the program have not been enforced. The growers never suffered any lasting repercussions for violating these regulations, even though the law prescribes a whole range of penalties for such actions.

It was only with the advent of Migrant Legal Services in a few areas, that workers were able to successfully sue growers who had improperly denied them jobs. In fact, as a result of repeated lawsuits that were quite costly, that growers in several states voluntarily elected to get out of the foreign-worker program and now have gone back exclusively to domestic crews. If they can find domestic workers now, weren't those workers there before the H-2 workers were brought in to do the job? Of course, they were. Bringing in foreign workers in any large number over a period of time produces a large displacement in the domestic job market, which will result in unemployment. I have yet to see the job that is so bad that no domestic worker will do it at some price. If a job is so bad that only Third World workers will do it, or so poorly paid that no domestic workers will accept it at that price, that raises the question as to whether those jobs should be allowed in this country.

If the H-2 program has proven anything, it is that the government is totally inept, unable, or unwilling—because of political pressures or otherwise—to enforce any protections for domestic workers. The H-2 program is scandalous in that it points out just how powerless the workers are. This is particularly true for workers brought to the United States to hand harvest sugarcane. For decades, not one major premise of the sugar contract has been consistently honored. The amount of money that workers were cheated out of varies from company to company. In some companies, the workers were cheated out of a quarter to a third of their wages. An average worker earning six thousand dollars a year would have been cheated out of about two thousand dollars each season. A company who employs a thousand workers would be cheating the workers out of two million dollars each year. Over thirty years, that's sixty million dollars, just for that one company. The bigger companies have a couple of thousand workers. We're talking about an industry that cheated cane cutters out of hundreds of millions of dollars.

It's extraordinary. And, it's extraordinary that nobody cared. We may have had a jaded view of government, but we weren't jaded enough. We spent a great deal of time suing the government trying to get them to do the right thing. We somehow thought that the government would do something about this. We even succeeded in convincing midlevel people to do something. Still, the bottom line was the political folks would get involved and at higher levels any action to get the sugar companies to follow the law would be squashed.

It's entirely politics. The growers call their congressman. They call their senator. They send in their lawyers, who are all former government people. Even people in the Department of Labor who were very much committed to protecting the workers couldn't control the program. There were no profiles in courage. The reality is that there are compromises people make in government. They convince themselves that it's better to be on the inside and have some modest influence on curbing the monster, rather than trying to be pure and literally falling on their sword. Given the political pressures, I don't think it matters who's in government. No effective action was ever undertaken by the United States Department of Labor. Even after congressional hearings and government accounting office audits which confirmed these abuses, the bottom line is that the government never did a thing.

Because of the ineptitude and inaction of the Department of Labor, tens of thousands of farm labor jobs that were filled by domestic workers for years have been given over to foreign workers. Those jobs will probably never be returned to domestic workers. Of course, domestic workers could be farmworkers. Domestic workers do all kinds of crappy jobs. They lay tar, dig coal, and do all sorts of difficult labor-intensive jobs, but they get paid, receive benefits, and have rights. To make farm labor attractive enough to a sufficient number of domestic workers, you'd have to restructure the system and pay higher wages. You wouldn't be able to

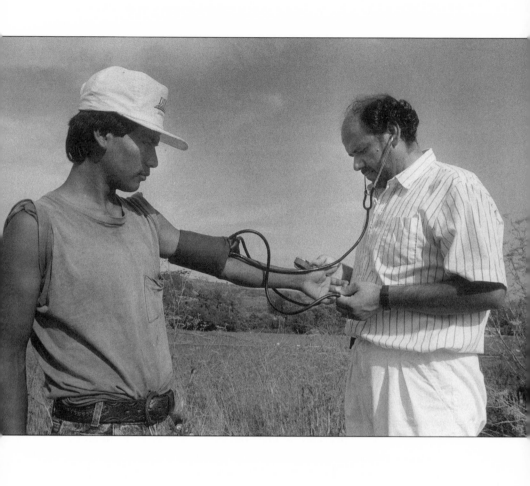

view workers as completely replaceable. The truth is, until there is a control on the supply of labor, there will never be significant pressure to increase wages or allow for farmworker organizing.

I think what drives Legal Services advocates, above all, is a deep sense of the injustice of this whole situation. Some advocates are driven by the David versus Goliath, rich versus poor dynamic, but what motivates most of us is something far more basic: a sense of the enormous injustice of what has occurred to farmworkers in the United States and the need to correct it. There is no group of clients you could care more about than farmworkers. They are remarkable. They're not looking to blame anyone, or seeking big judgments. They only want what they've earned. Even more than money, what farmworkers want is for someone to listen to their story, to listen to them as human beings. To have clients like that makes this job pretty easy, and when you win, it makes the job all the more rewarding.

Federal immigration policy is currently the single most important influence on the farm labor market. In almost every region in the country there exists a significant oversupply of farmworkers. In some areas, at some times during the year, there are two, three, and even four workers for every available farm labor position, and large numbers of recent immigrants, especially from Mexico, continue to enter the farm labor market.

In 1986, the federal government passed the Immigration Reform and Control Act (IRCA), which legalized many undocumented workers living in the United States and created mechanisms designed to discourage employers from hiring unauthorized workers. IRCA allowed all undocumented workers who had lived continuously in the United States for five years to apply for permanent residency. The law also required employers to ascertain that all their employees had working papers, and it instituted the first meaningful sanctions against employers who hired undocumented workers.

Since agriculture relies heavily on documented and undocumented immigrants, growers were nervous that the law would reduce their access to workers, forcing wages to rise and, growers claimed, possibly threatening the industry's viability. With this in mind, agriculture lobbied for the institution of a large-scale temporary-agricultural-worker program. Worker advocates and organized labor protested, claiming that a temporary-worker program would simply repeat the bracero program's abuse of workers while depressing agricultural wages and displacing domestic farmworkers.

In the end, a compromise was reached known as the Special Agricultural Worker (SAW) program, which allowed anyone who had worked ninety days in agriculture during the previous year to receive temporary residence for two years, followed by permanent residence. Grower interests also pressured Congress to include a second special farm labor program within IRCA, known as the Replenishment Agricultural Worker (RAW) program, which would allow a certain number of laborers into the country if the Department of Labor determined that there was a shortage. After three years' participation in the RAW program, workers would be eligible for permanent residency. To date, no RAW workers have been approved because the Department of Labor has not found a shortage of available farmworkers.

To receive legal residence under the SAW program, workers had to submit proof that they had worked for three months in agriculture, which usually consisted of copies of employment records. However, since farmwork is highly informal, workers were allowed to legalize through SAW on the basis of letters from farm labor contractors and growers. One unintended result of the law was a short-term underground market for letters from employers. The ease of registration for the SAW program produced an ideal situation for the agricultural industry, allowing for the mass legalization of young, male immigrants and spurring further undocumented immigration as recently legalized workers encouraged their friends and families to join them in the United States. More than 1.25 million people applied for legalization through the SAW program and over 1 million of these applications were approved.

Farmworkers are continually referred to as a special group, yet their special status is ultimately a function of the structure of our nation's farm labor system. What lies at the heart of farmworkers' special needs is their poverty and their position within a system that ensures that they remain poor. Government interventions in the lives of farmworkers have sought to improve workers' lives without addressing the system's fundamental structural problems.

Jim Handelman ♦ *Southern Florida*
Jim Handelman is a farm labor specialist for the United States Department of Labor. Along with several other investigators, he is responsible for enforcing the federal laws that protect the employment rights of southern Florida's estimated 150,000 farmworkers. Handelman began enforcing farmworkers' rights almost thirty years

ago when the Department of Labor first instituted regulations to protect migrant workers.

"They created the position of farm labor specialist. They asked me to apply. I chose not to, so they appointed me."

Agriculture is a giant business. Sometimes the growers talk about the high cost of labor, but labor is just a small part of the overall cost of agricultural production. The cost of chemicals has soared, the price of fuels has gone up, but the farmer doesn't have a handle on those costs. You can't tell the chemical company, "If you don't lower the price of your pesticide, we're going to have people pinch the caterpillars off the leaves." You can't tell Standard Oil, "If you don't lower the price of gas, we're going to burn wood in our tractors." The farmer can't dictate those prices. He doesn't produce the chemicals or own the oil or gas. But he owns those laborers just as surely as if they were his slaves—"These are my terms. This is what you'll do and if you don't like it we'll get somebody else." It's all a matter of who the growers can control and who they can't.

You ask what percentage of growers and crewleaders are in full compliance with the law? I don't think that any one of them is in full compliance. At least fifty percent of crewleaders and farmers are in serious noncompliance with the law. While there are some employers who have made great improvements in the way that they house and transport their workers, the other side of the coin are the farmers who have simply buried their heads in the sand. A lot of the violations occur when farmers ignore things that should be done. I don't sympathize with growers who talk about how difficult it is to be in compliance with the law.

Still, there are some corporate employers and some individual growers who have finally reached an awareness that farmworkers really are at the bottom rung of a ladder and that we need to do something about it. Some people have a conscience, others do not. Unfortunately, there are a lot of growers who don't have a conscience.

The piece rate for harvesting tomatoes has not gone up in the last twelve years. We're talking about forty cents per bucket. A good worker could probably earn six dollars per hour in a five- to six-hour day, so they may earn thirty to thirty-six dollars for the day. The thing is, they may only have three days of work that week, so they end up earning only a hundred dollars a week. Cheap labor, cheap labor for big business—there's no other way to explain why the piece rate for tomatoes is still forty cents per bucket.

My response to growers who say that they can't afford to pay more is that forty cents for a thirty-two-pound bucket means that it costs about one and a quarter cents per bucket to pick a pound of tomatoes. So if you doubled the price to two and a half cents per pound for each bucket picked, you would double the workers' wages. Now, if you paid another one and a quarter cents per pound for tomatoes, would you quit buying tomatoes in the grocery store? Other crops are basically the same. There's no other way to explain how the piece rate for beans is two dollars and fifty cents per hamper. At that price, workers involved in the bean harvest can't even earn minimum wage. I think that there's enough shame for everybody to share some of it and enough responsibility that everyone should accept some of that as well.

As long as we allow large numbers of illegal aliens to come into this country, they are going to keep the farm labor wages from rising. Illegal aliens are willing to work for less than what the law requires and under conditions that are below what the regulations impose on their employers simply because it's a job, and it's either that or starve. You can hardly blame them. They're trying to earn whatever they can. They're at the mercy of the people who employ them. I don't think that agriculture is more attractive to illegal aliens, I just think that work in agriculture is more available. Agriculture is more remote. The American worker, the legal worker, is not going to work in agriculture and suffer what these people have to suffer. The only way to stem the tide in agriculture is to raise the wages and get Americans back in the jobs. It's possible.

I'm not very popular here. I have very few friends who are farmers and I've kept it that way on purpose. I have some farmer acquaintances who I respect because I think that they're doing their best to do what's right, but there aren't a whole lot of them. I consider them honorable people and I think that they know I'm trying to do what I do as fairly and reasonably as I can.

In many cases farmworkers don't want to see us any more than the farmers do. Farmworkers see us as an adversary. We disrupt their ability to work for unregistered contractors. We look after their transportation to make sure that it's safe and insured. In most cases, it's not. If we interrupt that in any way, then they think we're the bad guys. It's the same with housing. Largely, the worst housing is populated by migrants who have essentially no voice, no say at all. In many respects, it's worse today then it's ever been. If we get into their house to inspect for safety requirements, they're afraid that they're going to be evicted. They know that we're not going to let twelve people live in one room, sleeping on pieces of cardboard on the floor. Therefore we're the bad guys because we're putting a halt to those conditions.

You sometimes wonder who you're helping and who you're representing. Without our help, I'm sure that things would get even worse for the farmworkers, but the farmworkers fail to recognize that. It's hard to do this work when there's so little appreciation. I used to be emotionally involved in my work, but now, after years of frustration, I'm burned out. I don't feel bitter, just frustrated.

I understand that politics plays a very active role in the labor market. Sometimes I look very critically at what I've done. I often feel that it's not much of an accomplishment for a career. I feel as if I haven't left much of a mark. Then I speak with other people and they say, "If it hadn't been for you, it might be ten times worse. You might be the only force that's kept any balance at all." The worker has got to have something. He's got to have some measure of protection. He's got to have somebody looking out for him.

9. Farmworker Unions
A Sense of Their Own Power

FARMWORKER ORGANIZING in the United States is the story of a continual uphill battle in which workers with limited resources and few allies have struggled against politically powerful employers in an effort to improve the living and working conditions of one of the nation's least desirable jobs. Considering the extraordinary obstacles they face—the enormous disparity of power between farmworkers and growers, the inherent problems of unionizing seasonal workers, and the general oversupply of laborers—it is striking how consistently farmworkers have organized themselves into unions. While farmworker unions' difficult, often violent, struggles have produced meaningful improvements in workers' lives, they have generally been unable to impact the structure of the overall farm labor system or create sustained industry-wide change. Nevertheless, the history of farm labor unions shows how farmworkers have continually taken an active, often courageous, role in challenging powerful economic interests in an effort to improve their lives.

The production and harvest of fresh fruits and vegetables is extremely vulnerable to labor unrest. Since many crops spoil if not picked and processed at just the right moment, worker unrest, especially the refusal to harvest, represents a powerful threat to growers. With some crops, the failure to harvest even for a limited period of time—a few days or weeks—can severely impact a grower's business. Because of this, growers and their associations have continually sought to discourage and disrupt farmworker organizing by firing organized workers and their leaders, hiring strikebreakers, and resorting to threats and violence. Growers have also used their political influence to repeatedly deny farm laborers legal protection for organizing. They have also worked hard to ensure a steady over-supply of laborers by lobbying against immigration restrictions affecting agriculture and for the creation of special guest worker programs.

While agriculture is extremely vulnerable to labor unrest, the nature and structure of farm labor makes it inherently difficult to organize workers. Most farmwork is unskilled, requiring no formal education and limited training. Workers need not be literate or even speak English. This means that almost anyone can be hired as a farm laborer, from recent immigrants to children to the elderly, greatly expanding the pool of potential workers. Since farm labor is generally seasonal, it is difficult for workers to engage in long-term organizing or exert steady pressure on employers to improve conditions. Whatever gains might occur in a given season can easily be lost by the next season when a new group of workers is likely to arrive in the fields. The situation is even more complicated for migrant workers, whose constant movement makes organizing especially difficult.

Dolores Huerta ◆ *Santa Cruz, California*

Dolores Huerta founded the United Farm Workers union—the UFW—with Cesar Chavez. Huerta was born in New Mexico, where her father was a miner, union leader, and state assemblyman. When her parents divorced, Huerta's mother moved to California where she ran a restaurant and boardinghouse. Huerta began working as an organizer at a young age and was a founding member of the local Community Service Organization (CSO). In the CSO, Huerta led voter-registration drives, challenged segregationist policies, lobbied for improved protections for farmworkers, and met Cesar Chavez.

When the CSO refused to support Chavez's efforts to organize farmworkers, Huerta and Chavez formed the National Farm Workers Association (NFWA), which eventually became the UFW. Huerta rose to national prominence while directing the union's successful grape boycott that resulted in contracts for most of California's table-grape workers. She also directed the lettuce and Gallo wine boycotts of the 1970s and served as the UFW's key contract negotiator.

Huerta is now in her late sixties, has eleven children, and continues to work long hours as a labor organizer and public speaker. Huerta remains youthful, wildly energetic, and passionate about the union's dream of fundamental social change.

One day, Cesar called me over to his house and said, "You know, farmworkers are never going to have a union unless you and I start it."

I thought he was kidding and started laughing.

He said, "No, I'm serious." Then, in the next breath, he said. "We won't see it built in our lifetime."

"Why, Cesar?"

"Because the growers are too rich and too powerful."

Then he asked me if I would help him. When I saw he was serious, I felt honored. Cesar knew that a real farmworkers' union was my burning desire.

We started by doing a census of farmworkers. We split up the Central Valley and went door-to-door, Cesar and his kids in the north, and me and my kids in the southern and eastern counties. We leafleted the whole area and did a census. Then we organized in the communities and signed people up. We had a convention with delegates and elected officers. At first I wasn't going to be an officer, but Cesar said, "You have to be an officer. The people who actually do the work are going to run this union."

We've pretty much followed that philosophy. The people who do the work in our union become the decision makers. Lots of outside groups offered to help, but Cesar wanted a union that was led and directed by farmworkers, a union made up of our own people—a true farmworkers' union. Cesar's dream of having farmworkers run the union is an important part of what we do. All of our field offices are run by farmworkers, all of our radio stations are run by people who've come out of the field, and we have several negotiators who used to be farmworkers.

What made us successful where so many other organizations failed is that we took the fight from the fields to the cities. We took the fight from Delano to New York, Canada, and Europe. The vast majority of people don't like to see injustice. Farmworkers' poverty is so extreme and the growers are so wealthy. People look at the way farmworkers live, they see the things the workers don't have, and they ask, Why? Why aren't these workers paid fairly? It's not the consumers' fault. Consumers shouldn't feel bad, but they should be concerned. They should help ensure that the people who are feeding them are not exploited or abused.

The only way workers can defend themselves from abuse is through a union. Because of our work, millions and millions of dollars have gone into farmworkers' pockets. Our workers earn higher wages than non-union workers. Our workers are covered by a pension plan. Our workers and every member of their families are covered by our major medical plan. Unionized workers have a grievance procedure so we can get people back to work if they've been fired unjustly. Workers on contract have seniority rights so they'll be rehired when the season's over. The union helps farmworkers stabilize their lives, settle down in a community, and send their kids to school. Through the legislature, we were able to get unemployment insurance for farmworkers and pass the Agricultural Labor Relations Act.

There's no security without a union. Being unionized means that you can stand up on your own feet. You see the difference if you compare a union company to an antiunion company. Workers who have a union contract aren't abused, yelled at, or treated like animals. Unionized workers are relaxed. There's a sense of freedom in a union company. Workers listen to the radio and talk. They're not oppressed. They're treated like human beings. Workers will tell you that being unionized gives them self-worth, it gives them a sense of their own power.

When you go to a company without a union contract, the workers are afraid to talk. They're afraid to even look at you. Workers without a union feel helpless. They think it's their fate in life to be victims. They need their jobs and they know that there are always more workers waiting to take their place. They know that they can get fired just like that. If workers ask questions—*boom*—they get fired. Growers fight tooth and nail to keep the workers from organizing because a union is the only way farmworkers can improve their situation.

I've negotiated with hundreds of growers. A lot of them are good people. They don't see what they're doing as wrong. It's a lifestyle. Growers are good people, but they're racist. They've grown wealthy, fabulously wealthy—become millionaires and billionaires—by exploiting people of color. They don't give a damn about their workers and that's hard for me to understand. Growers dehumanize their workers. Why would you refuse to give workers a toilet? Because if you don't give them a toilet, then they're not human beings. Why would you allow workers to be sprayed with pesticides? Growers view farmworkers as tools. Workers give the growers their entire adult lives, yet they won't even pay them a fair wage for all their hard work. They don't consider the horrible poverty these workers suffer. Why? Because their goal is profit and they don't care about the people.

I speak heart-to-heart with the growers, but it doesn't do any good. I'm at the table with these guys and they're arrogant and bigoted. They think they're above the law. These guys have hearts of stone, literally. How do you talk to people who are racist? You have to use force. You have to force them into contracts. You have to make them into better people by forcing them, just like in the South during the time of the civil rights struggle.

If you dehumanize people, then they lose their self-worth and they won't fight for their rights. The union gives workers self-worth, it gives them faith in their ability to really change their situation. Some of these companies will sign contracts with other unions, but not with the UFW. They don't want to give any power to farmworkers. Growers fear their workers. That's part of their racism. When you're exploiting people, you fear them. When workers strike, you can see the growers' fear.

Things have gotten worse for farmworkers. Workers know what's happening to them, but they still have to go to the fields. A couple of weeks ago, I saw a woman in a tomato field during a school day. She had three of her kids out there with her and when she saw me she started apologizing. She said, "I had to take them out of school because we didn't have enough money to buy groceries." They're out there every single day, little kids picking tomatoes with their hands too small to even cover the damn tomato.

The big question for the workers is, How can we survive? You go to their homes and you see that they're barely making enough to feed and clothe their children. When I visit workers in their homes, I feel as if I'm back in the fifties when we started. People are still being exploited in the same way: little kids carrying twenty-five-pound buckets; twenty workers sharing a house just to pay the rent; women who have to meet the foreman in a motel to get a job.

Farmworkers work very hard. They pick tons of fruits and vegetables—not pounds, tons—every day to feed the nation. They're professionals. They start when they're in their teens and they work until retirement age. They deserve better. The people who feed us should earn enough so that they can nourish their own bodies. Growers live all year from a seasonal harvest. Farmworkers should be able to as well. What I see makes me angry. Anger is important, but you have to use it in a positive way. My anger doesn't make me cynical because we have a solution, a way to change things, a formula—organization.

As I get older, I get more radical. When you're young, you think that somehow things will get better and that injustices will diminish. Now that I'm older, I see that the same injustices are still with us. Now I see the sons and daughters of the exploiters continue the same exploitation. In some cases things are even worse and growers' children are even more racist. That makes me sad, but I still believe that we can overcome—literally—that if we keep working and reaching out and educating people, then we can overcome. I'm an optimist by nature. I've always had a lot faith in people.

My dream is to see a national union of farmworkers run by the workers themselves. Farmworkers need to be politically active in their communities. They need to participate in society. You can't have a democracy

if people don't participate. To me the union means dignity and self-worth. Unionized workers are not afraid to speak out, be themselves, talk, or tell jokes. They have a certain freedom, a certain liberty. When you see working people who belong to a union, you feel their strength.

As agricultural production became more industrialized in the early twentieth century, the need for large numbers of seasonal workers increased. Not surprisingly, farmworker organizing first emerged in California where farmworkers were most highly concentrated and where farm labor first resembled factory work. The first major labor union to organize farmworkers was the International Workers of the World (IWW), popularly known as the Wobblies. The IWW was formed in 1905 in Chicago by a group of socialists and dissident organizers as an alternative to the more conservative American Federation of Labor.

In 1913, the IWW's attempts to improve wages and working conditions among hop workers in California led to the infamous Wheatland riot, in which four people were killed and many workers injured. The riot drew national attention to the low wages and poor working conditions of farm laborers, and resulted in a crackdown on union organizers and a questionable trial in which two key Wobblies were found guilty of murder. The verdict then served as the catalyst for a series of protest strikes along with a general boycott of hop producers. In 1915, the IWW helped establish the first American farmworker union, the Agricultural Workers Organization, whose initial gains were quickly lost after the United States entered the First World War. The IWW lost popular support and was eventually destroyed through government pressure, raids, and the arrest of hundreds of organizers and union members.

In the late 1920s, there was a second wave of farmworker organizing involving Mexican and Filipino immigrants who formed a series of small, ethnically distinct unions. Many of these organizations achieved limited local gains in the form of improved wages and better living and working conditions. Farm labor unrest grew substantially in the early 1930s as the depression reduced workers' wages and substantially increased the number of available laborers. Between 1930 and 1932, there were ten major agricultural strikes in California, several of which involved thousands of farmworkers. The wave of farmworker unrest peaked in 1933, when there were over sixty strikes involving 60,000 workers in seventeen states. Most of these actions occurred in California, where tens of thousands of workers left the fields, including 18,000 cotton pickers participating in a major twenty-four-day strike.

Many of the 1930s strikes were spontaneous, while others were planned by the Cannery and Agricultural Workers Industrial Union (CAWIU). The CAWIU, which was affiliated with the Communist Party, sought wage increases, an eight-hour workday, overtime pay, and the dismantling of the farm labor contractor system. By 1933, the CAWIU had over 20,000 members. As farmworker militancy increased, growers responded with violent tactics, forcibly evicting workers from labor camps, teargassing union meetings, using police to arrest protesters, and forming groups of armed vigilantes who kidnapped, beat, and sometimes killed workers and organizers. In 1934, during a major strike that shut down the San Francisco waterfront, the CAWIU offices were raided and key leaders were arrested, tried, and convicted. Although the organizers were eventually released on appeal, the union dissolved in 1935, torn apart by disputes over ideology and a lack of grassroots leadership.

In 1934, the Southern Tenant Farmers Union (STFU) was formed to organize tenant farmers and sharecroppers in Arkansas, Alabama, and other southern states. The STFU gained initial support by protesting the mismanagement of the Agricultural Adjustment Administration (AAA), which was designed to help farmers and sharecroppers who were severely impacted by the depression economy and plummeting cotton prices. While the AAA's funds were meant to be split evenly between growers and sharecroppers, growers often evicted tenants as a means of keeping all the relief payments themselves. Beginning in 1935, the STFU organized several major strikes that involved thousands of workers and successfully integrated black and white laborers. By 1937, the union had over 30,000 members in seven states.

As the STFU grew, grower opposition became increasingly violent. Union members and organizers were placed under surveillance, sent death threats, arrested on trumped-up charges, and beaten by armed vigilantes. Many STFU leaders fled north for safety after their homes were shot at and their churches burned. Gradually, the STFU fell on hard times, losing all but a few hundred members by the early 1940s. Nevertheless, the union succeeded in placing key issues of rural poverty on the national agenda and drawing attention to the problems of southern farm laborers.

During the 1930s, labor militancy was at its peak throughout the United States. Responding to the economic instability of the depression and a political climate supportive of industrial unions, Congress passed the National Labor Relations Act (NLRA) in 1935. The NLRA established the ground rules for union organizing and collective bargaining, providing American workers with basic protections regarding the rights to organize, strike, and engage in collective bargaining. The law banned employers from interfering with union organizing, refusing to bargain in good faith, forming a company union, or firing or refusing to hire organized workers. The law also established an independent body, the National Labor Relations Board, to mediate disputes between unions and employers. Although farmworkers were included in the original bill, they were specifically excluded from the final version of the NLRA. The congressional record reveals no clear explanation for excluding farmworkers, although their removal was clearly a concession to powerful agricultural interests.

The NLRA, which was passed at a time of significant labor unrest, provided rules for the negotiation of labor disputes and aided the rapid growth of major industrial unions. Nearly half a million American workers were involved in strikes between 1936 and 1937 when industrial giants such as General Motors and U.S. Steel signed their first union contracts. At the same time that industrial unions were rapidly advancing, farmworker organizing continued, but without the protection of the NLRA. The exclusion of agricultural workers from these basic protections dealt a serious blow to emerging farmworker unions.

By the mid-1930s, the number of potential farmworkers had swelled as over 300,000 dust bowl refugees made their way to California. The mass migration of white workers coupled with the forced deportation of Mexican laborers produced a rapid shift in the racial composition of California's agricultural workforce. By the late 1930s, the majority of California's farmworkers were white. Many dust bowl migrants lived in labor camps built by the federal government, where they were fed and housed beyond the control of the powerful growers. The federal labor camps were used for recruiting union members and as strike centers by emerging farmworker organizations such as the United Cannery, Agricultural, Packing and Allied Workers of America (UCAPAWA), which was founded in 1937 with the goal of creating a national farmworker union. UCAPAWA led a number of farmworker strikes in the late 1930s but was unable to develop a successful organizing strategy in part because of the resistance of many dust bowl migrants to the union movement. By 1941, the union had changed its name and turned away from farmworkers, deciding instead to organize laborers covered by the NLRA.

UCAPAWA's work, along with the enormous popularity of John Steinbeck's *Grapes of Wrath* and various journalistic exposés, helped focus public attention on farmworkers' poverty and growers' use of illegal, violent intimidation against union members and organizers. In 1936, Senator Robert La Follette created a special committee to investigate labor rights, free speech, and antiunion practices by employers. Although it had originally been created to document violations of the NLRA, the La Follette Committee expanded its research to consider the situation of farmworkers, eventually recommending that farmworkers be covered by the NLRA. However, no action was ever taken, in part because the report was not issued until 1942, after the United States had entered the Second World War.

During the war years, farmworker unions lost virtually all of their previous gains. Most white farm laborers were drafted into the military or found higher-paying jobs within the war economy. The arrival of tens of thousands of temporary Mexican workers through the bracero program made strikes increasingly difficult, since growers could easily replace striking laborers with guest workers. Organizing the braceros themselves was impossible since they could be repatriated at a moment's notice. Braceros who complained about conditions or agitated for improvements were branded as troublemakers, deported, and later prevented from returning on future contracts.

In 1946, the American Federation of Labor chartered the National Farm Labor Union (NFLU), which operated under the direction of Ernesto Galarza and sought to organize California's largely Latino farm labor force. Although the union had limited success organizing workers, it played an important role in ending the bracero program in 1964. In 1959, the AFL-CIO decided to become involved in farm labor organizing and set up the Agricultural Workers Organizing Committee (AWOC). AWOC waged a number of strikes during the 1960s but failed to achieve significant gains largely because of its reliance on traditional, hierarchical organizing strategies. Another group that challenged the bracero program was the Community Service Organization (CSO), founded in 1952. The CSO, which was dedicated to grassroots organizing within the Mexican American community, formed the Agricultural Workers Association (AWA) in 1958 and provided a new model for farm labor organizing based upon the ideology of the emerging Civil Rights movement.

Harry Steinovic ♦ *Central Valley, California*

Harry Steinovic is a second-generation grape grower. He is now in his seventies and has passed most of the responsibilities for managing the farm on to his sons. His vineyard was among the Delano-area farms targeted by the UFW. For years, Steinovic was on the front lines of grower opposition to the UFW.

The picket lines have long since disappeared, several grape boycotts have come and gone, and it has been over two decades since Steinovic has had any direct dealings with the UFW. Nevertheless, he remains angry at having watched grape growers—himself, his neighbors, associates, and lifelong friends—portrayed as national symbols of abusive agricultural employers.

Farmworker union organizing goes back some years before the advent of the Chavez movement. The farming industry has always been concerned about unions. Basically, our concern involves strikes at harvesttime. Agricultural products are perishable, particularly grapes and tree fruit. If they're not picked on time, they're lost.

Back in the fifties and sixties, most of our workers were Filipinos. Many of them were single and were housed in dormitories on the ranches. In the grape fields there were always negotiations going on with the Filipino crews. Usually the crewleader was the workers' spokesman, delivering their message to the farmer. They'd often ask for higher wages, better bonuses, or improved housing conditions. Those negotiations took place quietly, behind the scenes. They usually weren't very tense. We were dealing with crews that lived in company housing. There was no organized activity, with the growers on one side of the table and the workers on the other.

In the fifties, the word was out that there would be some serious farmworker organizing. We started thinking about what we should do as employers to be prepared. So we formed the South Central Farmers Committee so we'd be ready to handle labor problems. We had a board of directors and access to attorneys and labor relations people in case there was a movement to organize farmworkers. When the organizing started, it was all very sudden. It didn't happen the way we'd anticipated. In the past, problems were resolved with little fanfare. We'd had walkoffs before, but we'd never seen picketing and flag waving.

In September 1965, the strike finally came. That was when we first heard the word *huelga,* which means "strike" in Spanish. They didn't just strike our vineyards, they struck the whole grape industry. It wasn't our employees on the picket lines. The protesters were United Farm Workers' supporters—students, religious people, lots of strangers going up and down the road. They'd park outside the farm with their bullhorns, waving their flags and logo signs. They were making a big hoopla and getting lots of attention. When the strike happened, it was a new day for all of us. The UFW was something different. We were dealing with a new method, a new system of organizing. No one who advised us was aware of their methods or knew how to handle them.

By the end of 1965, it was very big. By then, the UFW had started their boycott. There were clergy and various churches involved, along with some Hollywood entertainers who were enamored with the movement. The UFW also got the attention of major unions. Walter Reuther of the Auto Workers was here. The farmworkers started gaining sympathy from normal, ordinary citizens, and then national political figures got involved. In 1966, Congress started doing hearings.

We turned to our advisers and they said, "Keep your workers on the job. That's the important thing. Don't be concerned about the pickets." Well, that's what we did. We continued to harvest. We had workers who walked off the job, but little by little, they came back. Along with everybody else, we finished the crop. Then we pruned the vines, did another crop, and pruned some more.

Growing grapes was never our problem; our problem was handling the media. We weren't prepared for that. I don't think I'm revealing any deep, dark secrets by saying that farmers are terrible PR people. We're independent, fiercely independent. When somebody asks a farmer something, he'll speak out openly, and if he feels resentment, he'll let you know. Well, that didn't put out too good a public image.

The UFW accused us of paying miserable wages that nobody could live on. That wasn't true. We paid prevailing wages. We were competing with other growers for unskilled labor. Farmworkers are just like any other workers. If they don't like the wage they're being paid, they don't have to work for you. We didn't have the workers tied down. We were just like any other employer, but we were depicted as being selfish, greedy, and disrespectful. Well, most of us are farmworkers ourselves. Hell, I did all the work that these people were doing when I was younger. All of the growers around here had humble beginnings. My father didn't come here with money. He came to America looking for an opportunity, like so many others. We know what hard work is. That's what made me most resentful, being depicted as not caring, as selfish. It was agonizing.

Groups of church people would come in and tell us, "We're willing to pay ten cents a pound more for your grapes if you'd pay your farmworkers more." Well, that's naive. People that shop are going to pay whatever the store charges. If they don't like the price, they won't buy the product, or they'll go someplace else to buy it. You can't just say, "I'm going to pay the farmworkers more and then you'll just pay more for grapes." That's not the way the free market works. We tried to explain to them that we were selling our product at competitive prices, that we were selling the grapes to dealers and chain stores and that we weren't in charge.

Still, we never got in any trouble with the law. We were always very careful during this whole period not to do anything illegal. Now, there were some people killed, but I don't know who you're going to blame for that. We didn't hire thugs. We had security people, but no thugs. We didn't retaliate. You know, a lot of bad things happened here, but that's water under the bridge. Forget it. That happened and it's gone.

We went through five years of growing and selling our crops before we came to the bargaining table with the United Farm Workers. In the last year or two we were under a lot of pressure from the retailers. I remember a chain-store president complaining that not only were they picketing his stores, but they were also picketing his home. As a result of the boycott, because of all the harassment, retailers stopped buying our grapes. They told us that it was a problem we had to solve.

In a situation like that, somebody finally has to say, "This is the end of the line. I've got to sell my product. I'll make a deal with the union." Well, once that happened, it became evident that everybody was going to have to deal with the union. There wasn't anything else to do. We lost. We lost the PR battle, and we paid for it. We learned that we weren't in control of everything, and we acknowledged our loss by signing a union contract with the United Farm Workers. In 1970, we signed the contract at the UFW offices, all of us, in front of the national press. There were probably thirty growers who showed up at the signing.

The contract was terrible. It was a three-year contract in which we gave up a lot of managerial rights. It wasn't difficult making deductions for union dues or paying the welfare and health costs. That was simple. What was hard was dealing with union representatives who were constantly harassing you. It was also difficult employing workers through the union hiring hall. Our workers would have to go to the hiring hall to get a dispatch to come and work for us, but often the union wouldn't send them to our vineyards. That's where the union exposed its real intentions. They wanted to be the ones who decided everything. They wanted to be responsible for the workers' jobs, but it didn't work out because those farmworkers had been with certain ranches for years. They had relationships with particular growers and they didn't like being told to go someplace else to work. That was probably the thing that most bothered farmworkers about the UFW, and that's where they lost a lot of support. They antagonized their own members because they wanted to control them.

In the meantime, the Teamsters started nosing around. Since we couldn't get along with the UFW, we couldn't renegotiate the contract. So the Teamsters became an alternative and we signed contracts with them which were quite favorable, including provisions banning strikes at harvesttime. We had a four-year contract with the Teamsters, but it didn't last because, by then, the Agricultural Labor Relations Act came into effect, banning contracts that were not preceded by worker elections. The Teamsters contract wasn't based on an election, so it was nullified. Later, the Agricultural Labor Relations Board decertified us, so we had no more obligation to any union. The UFW has never come back. They've never tried to organize us again.

The union didn't kill us. We had to fight with them, but our business survived. One of the benefits of the union activity was that for a long time, nobody wanted to get in bed with table-grape growers. We were the bad guys and no one wanted to have anything to do with us. So we were isolated during a time when lots of outside investors were getting involved in agriculture—citrus, almonds, wine growing. Nobody wanted to invest in table grapes, so when the economic turnaround came and there was a demand for grapes, it was all ours. Who owned the grapes? Those of us who had been through all the battles. We didn't have to share our profits with doctors, lawyers, accountants, or anybody else who put money in agriculture to make a fast buck or get a tax write-off. So, there's two sides to every coin.

Farmworkers are no longer enamored of the UFW. They don't trust the union. In fact, as a union, the UFW has failed. What the union has really been working at is spreading the image of Cesar Chavez—his movement, his reputation, his political power. At the UFW everything is still tied to Cesar: "This is the way Cesar would do it. This is what Cesar wanted." They can't give up his image because that's what gets them attention and that's what gets them donations. The UFW has always gone way beyond being a union. Organizing farmworkers was the vehicle, but they're not really union people. They're a social movement. The UFW was always a movement for political power, an attempt to establish farmworkers as a political force. That's what was their undoing as a union. At one time, they had this entire industry under contract, but they couldn't hold it. The UFW failed as a union but not as a social movement.

Farmworkers don't need a union. They've got regulation on top of regulation to protect them. They didn't before, but they do now. We're inspected and reinspected all the time. There's always another agency out there looking out for the farmworkers. The only thing farmworkers really have to worry about is negotiating their wage rate, and that's not that difficult. If there are too many workers, they're not going to be able to demand higher wages. If there aren't enough workers, they can demand higher wages and they'll get what they want. The truth is, there are too many workers.

The most successful farmworker union in American history developed among sugarcane and pineapple workers laboring on Hawaii's large plantations. From the late nineteenth century through the 1930s, the sugar and pineapple industry was controlled by the Big Five plantations, who relied on an ethnically divided workforce imported from Japan and the Philippines. Japanese workers engaged in major strikes in 1909 and 1920, and Filipino workers struck in 1924, leading a violent eight-month struggle in which sixteen strikers and four policemen were killed and sixty organizers were jailed.

In the 1930s, the International Longshoremen's and Warehousemen's Union (ILWU) successfully organized dockworkers in San Francisco, where most of Hawaii's produce was shipped. The union then began organizing dockworkers in Hawaii, gradually expanding their efforts to include all employees of the Big Five plantations, including thousands of farm laborers. While the outbreak of World War II slowed union gains, by 1943, the ILWU had won contracts on all of the major plantations. Union organizers helped register thousands of voters, playing a key role in the election of pro-labor representatives who then helped pass the Employment Relations Act of 1945, providing farmworkers with union-organizing protections. Within a period of eighteen months, the ILWU brought 30,000 new workers into the union.

The plantation owners rejected the union's contract demands, so the ILWU called a strike, which succeeded both because the union controlled the docks and the growers had trouble finding enough strikebreakers on the Hawaiian Islands. Following the ILWU's victory, farmworkers in Hawaii began receiving such benefits as medical insurance, sick leave, paid holidays, pensions, and overtime as well as earning the highest wages of farm laborers anywhere in the United States.

The ILWU's organizing successes led plantation owners to transform their operations; by the 1960s they had mechanized the sugarcane harvest and shifted a significant percentage of their production to plantations in other countries. While the ILWU's success led to a reduction in the both the number of workers hired and the quantity of acres farmed, farmwork in Hawaii became a stable form of manual labor offering reasonable protections and competitive wages. From the late 1940s onward, the working conditions of Hawaiian farm laborers have stood in such stark contrast to the situation of other American farmworkers that they are rarely viewed as members of the same group.

Nelly Pruneda ♦ *Delano, California*

Nelly Pruneda was born in Mexico and crossed into the United States in 1975. Since then, she has always worked in the fields. Pruneda first heard about Cesar Chavez while growing up in Mexico. In 1986, the UFW tried to organize the rose company where she worked. They lost the election.

In 1994, the UFW began a second organizing effort. Pruneda worked as an organizer, secretly visiting workers in their homes and slowly building support for a second attempt at a union election. Through this process she has become a dedicated Chavista—*a follower of Cesar Chavez. Working as an organizer has transformed her life, and Pruneda speaks of the union with deep conviction, unable to contain her enthusiasm.*

Pruneda has a broad, smooth face, a quick smile, and thick shoulder-length hair. She wears a UFW button on her shirt. We talk beside a poster of Cesar Chavez, which is bordered by the curling vines of a potted plant, a ceramic sculpture of the trademark black eagle, and the images of Jesus and Mary.

After what happened in 1986, the company never thought we'd organize. They thought the people had lost heart. What they forgot was that we carried within us the seed of the union, that we were just waiting for the right time to start again. We knew that this time we wouldn't fail. The workers at the company had been there for years. We'd experienced so much mistreatment and indifference.

To hold the election, we had to get a certain percentage of the company's fourteen hundred workers to sign a card with their name and address. If you signed the card, it meant that you supported the union. When we had enough cards, we called the labor board, who certified us and set a day for the elections. By the time the company realized what was happening, it was already too late. There was nothing they could do. They had to give us access to the workers and let us organize. That was something beautiful, a triumph after so much injustice.

We began to organize openly. We made thousands of bulletins and we passed them out to the people. At six-thirty each morning, the organizers were here with their cars and their flyers. The people would come by on their way to work and we'd say, "Here, take this. This information will interest you." Some of the workers were scared to take the flyers, but when they heard their *compañeros* talking, they'd grab a flyer and hide it in their bag. We knew that sometime later, they'd read it.

When I'd speak to the workers, I was always positive, with a smile on my face. I was always aware of Cesar's sacrifices, his principles, the way he suffered. That gave me a lot of courage and I'd tell the workers, "*Compañeros,* we're going to win." We worked day and night, organizing, making up propaganda, teaching the people about the union. Sometimes we didn't sleep.

The company would also hold meetings. They'd stop work in the packinghouse and take us all to the dining room. Sometimes they did this two or three times a day. They'd bring in people who were paid to tell us that the union was no good and that if we won the election, the company would either go bankrupt or move to a different state. That really scared the workers because if the company shut down, everyone would lose their jobs. We had to stand up and tell the workers that they were being lied to, that the company was paying people to scare them.

The election came on a workday. Because the company is so big, they cleaned out a packinghouse, which we used for the election. There were four officials from the company, four officials from the union, election observers who watched over the ballot boxes, and someone from the Department of Labor who came with his official stamp. He handed out papers to all the workers stating that the election was a secret ballot and that everyone was free to vote for whoever they wanted. He explained what a secret ballot meant and that no one should be afraid. The voting went on all day long. We began at seven in the morning and ended the election at nine at night. Then they closed the doors. The president and all the important people from the company entered, along with all of us, the representatives of the UFW.

Two people from the government took the ballots out of the box while representatives from both the company and the union counted the votes. The workers filled four ballot boxes, which were sealed. After we'd counted the votes from one box, they'd hand us another box. The government people would take out each ballot and read the vote—"company" or "union."

In the first five hundred ballots, there were almost three hundred for the company. All I heard was, "Company, company, company, company." I was thinking to myself, "Oh my God, the company's going to beat us." I remember looking at all the company people's faces. They seemed so confident, like they knew they'd win. I saw it in their smiles and I felt sad, deeply sad. I felt that we'd been abandoned. They kept reading, "Company, company, company."

Then a *compañero* who was always at my side said, "Here comes our box. Those votes are ours. The company brought their people in first." They opened another ballot box and the man from the government started to read. I was nervous, but I began to notice that I wasn't hearing "company" very much. I started gaining courage. I heard them read out, "Union, union, union, union."

We won by a margin of over two hundred votes.

We began to cry, not tears of sadness, but tears of joy. When the government agent certified our victory, it was as if we'd received the greatest prize in the world. We have a *compañero* who owns a movie theater and he lent it to us to celebrate. We had a big party, passing a microphone around so everyone could talk about how they felt and how hard we'd all struggled. There was music, and then we had a mass. We stayed out until three in the morning

Since we negotiated the contract, things here have really changed. Before, people were afraid, but now workers can defend themselves. The union gives people courage. The union plants a seed in people's hearts. When you go back home you carry that seed, the way children carry the teachings of their parents. Ever since my children were very young, I've planted a seed in their hearts. I've taken them to church and taught them to respect other people. I know that even if they stray, they'll remember what I've taught them and get back on the right path.

Now, farmworkers are waking up. This is a new time for the union. I see more and more people interested in Cesar Chavez. Before, we had to go out and look for people, and now they're coming to us. Before, when we went to their houses, they'd close the door out of fear. Now it's different. Even the young people come and donate their time. My dream is for all the *campesinos* to be part of the union. That's what we're fighting for.

By far the most famous and influential American farmworker union is the United Farm Workers of America (UFW), founded by Cesar Chavez. The UFW's struggle to improve the lives of farmworkers is known as *La Causa*—"The Cause"—a name linking farmworkers' struggles with the Civil Rights movement and a general questioning of the inequities in American society. Committed to nonviolence, the UFW's vision of social justice extended beyond the goals of traditional union organizing and brought the social demands of Latinos to a national stage. Cesar Chavez is a heroic, near mythic, presence within the farmworker movement and a political icon for the Latino community—the first nationally recognized figure in the struggle for Latino civil rights.

Chavez was raised in California by a family of migrant farmworkers. In order to provide for his family, he left school after the eighth grade to work in the fields. At seventeen, he joined the navy, and when he returned, he married and became an organizer for the

CSO, where he worked for ten years. In 1962, Chavez and Dolores Huerta formed the National Farm Workers Association (NFWA), which used community-based strategies to organize settled farmworkers in California's Central Valley. The NFWA grew to national prominence when they joined forces with the Agricultural Workers Organizing Committee (AWOC), which was leading a strike of Filipino table-grape pickers in the Delano area. Since the NFWA had many more members than AWOC, Chavez became the strike leader. Less than a month after the strike began, several thousand workers on more than thirty farms had left the fields. Growers responded by forcing striking workers out of their labor camps and recruiting replacement crews.

Aware that they were unlikely to win a traditional strike, the NFWA called for a nationwide boycott of products linked to the grape harvest. The boycott originally focused on Schenley, a well-known liquor producer with a recognizable brand name and a unionized nonfarm workforce. The union called for the assistance of university students, urban unions, and church groups and gained favorable national media attention, particularly when growers responded by harassing picketers and threatening violent retaliation. In March 1966, Senator Robert Kennedy expressed support for striking farmworkers at a congressional hearing on the dispute. A day later, the union began a twenty-five-day long, 340-mile march from Delano to Sacramento, an act inspired by the Freedom March held in Alabama two years before. Later that year, the NFWA and AWOC merged to become the United Farm Workers Organizing Committee (UFWOC).

The union also expanded its boycott to other name-brand producers, opening boycott centers in various cities that leafleted and picketed stores. Soon after, Schenley recognized the union and increased wages by 40 percent. By 1968, there were 5,000 members working under union contracts. The union then began a boycott of the entire California table-grape industry, establishing offices in over forty cities. Thousands of consumers stopped purchasing table grapes and several major chains refused to sell boycotted products. Ironically, it was the exclusion of farmworkers from the NLRA that enabled the boycott's success, since many of the union's tactics were illegal under federal labor law.

Grape growers finally agreed to sign three-year contracts with UFWOC in 1970 in a public ceremony at the union's headquarters. By then, the union represented 85 percent of California's grape workers. The contracts gave workers improved wages and formal grievance procedures, prevented growers from using the pesticide

DDT, and required growers to provide workers with drinking water, rest periods, toilets in the fields, and other workplace improvements. Growers had to hire workers through the union and contribute to a union-controlled health plan and a fund for retired and disabled workers. Between 1964 and 1973, from the start of the union's organizing to the expiration of the table-grape contracts, farmworkers' wages in California increased by 120 percent as agricultural wages rose from 45 percent to 62 percent of industrial wages.

The union's extraordinary success in organizing the table-grape industry made California growers nervous. Since it appeared that the unionization of farmworkers was an inevitability, many growers turned to the Teamsters union, who had little popular base and offered grower-friendly contracts. A day before the Delano grape growers signed union contracts, the largest lettuce growers in the Salinas Valley signed on with the Teamsters. Chavez responded with a mass march, but a week later the Teamsters had contracts with an additional sixty growers.

The UFWOC threatened major boycotts of parent corporations and called a strike involving between 7,000 and 10,000 workers, one of the largest farmworker strikes in the nation's history. Picket lines were attacked, shots were fired, a union office was bombed, and Chavez was jailed. Still, the union continued to grow, winning several large contracts in Florida. By 1972, there were over 150 contracts covering more than 50,000 workers. In 1972, the union changed its status to a chartered affiliate of the AFL-CIO, becoming the United Farm Workers of America—the UFW.

In April 1973, just as the UFW contracts were set to expire, almost all of the grape growers signed contracts with the Teamsters. UFW workers responded with a series of strikes. Teamster guards attacked picket lines and thousands of UFW members and supporters were arrested. The growers hired private guards and violence against the UFW escalated, culminating in the death of a farmworker at the hands of a local deputy and the murder of a sixty-year-old worker, who was shot while picketing by someone in a passing truck.

In 1975, following more than a decade of near constant labor unrest, Governor Jerry Brown's government sponsored the California Agricultural Labor Relations Act (ALRA), which provided the legal structure for farm labor organizing. The ALRA set up a system to authorize and monitor secret ballot elections for any union that could obtain signed authorization cards from at least half of a company's workers. A second union could get on the ballot if it received authorization cards signed by an additional 10 percent of the workers. After gaining recognition from the Agricultural Labor Relations Board, union organizers were guaranteed access to the workers and would be protected against intimidation and threats. In order to prevent growers from stalling elections until after the harvest season when many workers were likely to move on to other jobs, the ALRA required elections to be held soon after election petitions were submitted to the state.

With the assistance of the ALRA and an agreement by the Teamsters not to organize field workers, the UFW began to grow again. By the end of the 1970s, the union had won over 250 elections and had over 125 contracts covering 30,000 members. The UFW also expanded its activities to New Mexico, Texas, Arizona, and Washington in an effort to achieve the union's dream of national representation. At its peak in the 1970s, union membership was around 80,000.

The 1980s were a difficult time for the UFW, which was affected by both the election of a conservative state government and the increased influx of large numbers of undocumented immigrants. Though settled farmworkers were often drawn to the UFW's health plan and pension benefits, undocumented migrants were far less interested in union membership and opposed the seniority preferences of union hiring halls. At the same time, the union's continual boycotts lost their novelty and the organization became increasingly plagued with internal problems. By the end of the 1980s, there were fewer than 15,000 UFW members, and by the early 1990s, the union had only a handful of contracts, which covered around 5,000 workers.

Cesar Chavez's death in 1993 marked the end of an era. His commitment to nonviolence and his status as one of the nation's premier civil rights activists brought nationwide attention to the plight of America's farmworkers. Chavez's son-in-law, Arturo Rodriguez, was elected the new UFW president. Since then, the union has engaged in a new wave of organizing efforts that has been remarkably successful. Throughout the 1990s, the UFW has grown steadily, increasing its membership, embarking on successful organizing drives, and signing many new contracts.

Shah Kazemi ♦ *Santa Cruz, California*

Shah Kazemi is the CEO of Monterey Mushroom, the largest mushroom producer in the United States. The company grows, packs, and ships over 100 million pounds of mushrooms each year. In the mid-1970s, the company was purchased by a large conglomerate that owned hundreds of different businesses including a number of food production and processing companies. The conglomerate sent Kazemi to deal with Monterey Mushroom after an especially divisive UFW strike in 1979.

In 1988, Kazemi and several other investors bought Monterey Mushroom. Since then, the company has expanded to include two unionized plants in California as well as nonunionized farms in Tennessee and Texas. In the early 1990s, company workers left the UFW to form their own union. Later they voted the UFW back in. Monterey Mushroom workers have stable year-round jobs. The lowest-paid workers earn nearly seven dollars per hour and pickers average about eleven dollars an hour. Workers receive medical, dental, and vision insurance and are covered by a pension plan.

Kazemi is a smooth, articulate, and charming businessman. He is charismatic, yet controlled.

In the late seventies, when the United Farm Workers organized Monterey Mushroom, there was a bitter confrontation between Cesar Chavez and the former president of the company. Negotiations broke down and in 1979 there was a strike. The president of the company had a personal vendetta against Chavez. He had a redneck attitude and saw the UFW as an anti-American movement. He thought Chavez was a Communist.

Monterey Mushroom was a very small segment of the larger corporation, so when the UFW started picketing the corporate offices in San Francisco, the chairman decided to put an end to the strike. As a condition of settlement, the UFW demanded that the president of Monterey Mushroom be dismissed. The corporation was looking for someone within the company to be the new president. I was working as a vice president of operations in the potato division and they felt I could get along with what they called "the Mexicans." So, in 1980, I came down.

It was a very tense, adversarial situation. Everybody was coming off the strike and there was a lot of mistrust and virtually no communication between workers and management. When I first came down, I asked one of the supervisors where the guys went to drink beer. He told me the workers just bought a six-pack at the corner store and sat in the parking lot because it was cheaper than drinking in a bar. So I said, "Let's go down there." We bought a six-pack, went down to the parking lot, and sat on the curb.

The pickers pointed at me and asked the supervisor, "Who's the new picker?"

"He's not a picker. He's the president."

"He can't be the president. The president wouldn't drink beer in the parking lot." The supervisor couldn't convince the workers that I was the company president. The next day some of those guys came to my office. That was the beginning of the change that took place.

Basically, what was missing here was trust. There was no trust between the management and the workers. I had to come in and create a more trusting relationship. After you have trust, you have mutual respect, and then cooperation comes in. Everything goes from there.

We had to change the culture of the company, to go from an adversarial position to a more collaborative relationship. All the people wanted was to be treated with the respect and dignity they deserved. Before the workers were unionized, the workforce was treated roughly. Obviously, the workers were unhappy with how they were treated. That's why they brought in the union. The contract gave them slightly better wages, more rights, and the collective strength to stand up and say, "No, you can't do that." With the contract, the management couldn't discharge an employee for no reason and get away with it.

We had a lot of meetings with the different crews. We'd bring them in and let them air their grievances. To be honest, many of their grievances were really petty. They complained about everything from the color of tissue paper in the men's room to more significant issues such as favoritism. Since the workforce was not very educated, they had a propensity to get up on a soapbox and reiterate what was just said two minutes earlier. They were all talking about the same things. We'd start at eight o'clock in the morning and continue until ten o'clock at night. The walls were covered with paper that we were writing on, trying to deal with their grievances.

At first, it was hard to negotiate a contract because the company wasn't financially viable. We were paying premium wages and benefits compared to our competitors. I was telling the union, "We're in it together. It's really us against the other guys. We've got to put ourselves in your shoes and you've got to put yourselves in our shoes." That was easier said than done because we were dealing with the ranch committee and they weren't very sophisticated. They were good people, but their level of understanding was not as high as you would have if you were dealing with professional negotiators. So it took a long time to convince people that we had to think about the long term. We involved the workers in the decision-making process, making them responsible for work quality. Gradually, things improved. The company became more successful and we started building and building. Later, we put a package together to buy three other mushroom farms.

The union is not really a big factor to me. My philosophy is to treat workers with respect and dignity and provide decent wages and benefits. With or without a union, I don't change anything from a management point of view. It's obviously easier to deal with a nonunion situation because you have more freedom. Still, we don't allow the managers, supervisors, or foremen in any of our plants to abuse their authority. Even at the nonunion plants, we have grievance procedures. To be honest with you, when things are going well, the union isn't involved. If there are grievances we don't resolve, then the union comes in. In daily business, we don't really see the union.

I've seen a significant change in the living conditions for our workers. I gauge it by the cars they're driving. In the eighties our workers were driving rusty, obsolete, unsafe cars. Now they've got four-wheel-drive vehicles that are three to five years old. The workers are more content. There's more goodwill. I don't know how you can measure that, but we have a turnover rate of less than one percent. When there's an opening, we have six to seven hundred people sign up for the job. In a lot of ways, we're a model company. We treat our people with respect. We're not perfect, but we're more enlightened than the other guys.

A lot of growers think I'm crazy when I talk about the UFW in a positive manner. They think I've sold out the industry. You talk to grape growers or lettuce growers and, to them, there's no way you should celebrate signing a contract with the UFW. To them, the union is the archenemy. They've drawn a line in the sand with the growers on one side and the union on the other. So when we say that we're getting along just fine with the union, it's just not acceptable.

Other growers don't want to face up to their responsibilities. It's easy for them. If you can operate without a union, why should you volunteer? If I were given the choice, I'd also operate without a union. It's not that I'm pushing the union, what I'm saying is, I've accepted the conditions. As far as I'm concerned, I want everybody to be unionized. I'll be honest about it, I want to compete on a level playing field. If the industry in general is not unionized and if the unions continue to demand higher wages, they're going to force the unionized companies out of business. This is a cutthroat, competitive business. We're selling a commodity to buyers and they don't care where that product comes from.

Still, when you really look at it, agricultural employers take advantage of their workers. Farmworkers deserve better. They're human beings just like you and I. They have the right to earn enough to provide decent housing for their families, put food on the table, and pay for their children's education. They're intelligent, hardworking people. As businessmen, we have an obligation to the community at large. We need to provide decent

working conditions, wages, and benefits. Why should farmworkers be excluded from the American dream?

While the UFW is by far the largest and best-known farmworker union, there are a number of other farmworker unions currently operating in the United States. The most visible and successful of these unions is the Farm Labor Organizing Committee (FLOC), based in Ohio. FLOC was founded by Baldemar Velásquez in 1967, when the UFW's boycott was receiving considerable nationwide attention. Workers in the Ohio area were generally Mexican Americans who migrated north each season from Texas to harvest tomatoes, pickle cucumbers, and several other crops.

When growers initially refused to meet with union representatives to improve labor-camp and working conditions, FLOC called for a strike, which led to a series of temporary contracts. Many small farmers in the area grow produce on contract for large food processors such as the Campbell Soup Company or Heinz USA. FLOC soon realized that the food processors were the most powerful economic force in the system, and that small growers could only raise wages in relation to what the processors were willing to pay.

FLOC then developed a strategy of negotiating three-way contracts between unionized workers, small farmers, and large corporate processors. In 1978, FLOC sought union recognition from some of the large processors, who refused. A strike was called, there were several violent incidents, and many growers switched to mechanical harvesting. In 1979, FLOC called for a boycott of Campbell's products. FLOC also sought to pressure Campbell through alliances with church groups and industrial unions. The union drew the public's attention to the impact that Campbell had on farmworkers' lives, citing low wages and child labor, and further pressured Campbell by publicizing its ties to banks, insurance companies, and other businesses eager to avoid bad press.

After years of grassroots organizing, boycotts, and pressure, FLOC signed its first contract with the Campbell Soup Company in 1986. The union later signed contracts with several other major food-processing corporations. By the 1990s, FLOC had over 7,000 members working under union contracts in the Midwest. FLOC contracts provide for higher wages, improved housing, and the elimination of child labor and sharecropping.

In many ways, farmworkers' organizing efforts serve as a reminder of how unions have transformed what it means to be an American worker. Prior to the passage of federal legislation protecting labor organizing in the 1930s and the subsequent rise of major industrial unions, workers in many industries faced conditions not unlike those of farm laborers. As unions gained legitimacy and political power, they established industry norms of living wages, guaranteed health insurance, pensions, paid vacations, grievance procedures, and other modern employment practices. The continued poverty and marginalization of farmworkers stands in stark contrast to the situation of other American workers. Farmworkers' low wages, dangerous workplace conditions, and general disempowered status is directly linked to the fact that so few farmworkers labor under union contracts.

Union membership for American workers peaked in the mid-1950s, when 35 percent of the nation's laborers were covered by union contracts. By the 1990s, the percentage of American workers laboring under union contracts had dropped to less than 17 percent. To the degree that nonunionized workers lack the means to stand up to their employers, their disempowerment may place them in a situation increasingly similar to that of farm laborers. This is especially true in those industries where employers rely on subcontractors and immigrant labor.

Farmworkers have long understood the enormous disparities of power between growers and laborers. They have consistently organized themselves into unions in an effort to improve their lives, engaging in difficult, highly contested struggles that reflect the severe inequities of the farm labor system. Although farmworker unions have achieved meaningful gains, they have been unable to transform the industry anywhere except Hawaii. A very small percentage of farmworkers are unionized, and even fewer labor under union-negotiated contracts that allow them to earn a living wage. Unless social and political conditions change dramatically, it is unlikely that farmworker unions will gain enough political authority to change the farm labor system. Nevertheless, the continued struggles of farmworkers to organize themselves into unions stands as a testament to their courage and willingness to fight against great odds to control their destiny.

Baldemar Velásquez ♦ *Toledo, Ohio*

As a child, Baldemar Velásquez migrated from Texas through various midwestern states. With no financial backing and no formal organizing experience, Velásquez founded FLOC in 1967. He is a charismatic, articulate, and driven leader. In 1989, he won a MacArthur Foundation fellowship.

I remember being out in the fields as a little kid picking cotton in Texas. They kept the Mexicans on one side of the field and the blacks on the other side. We lived in an abandoned schoolhouse. In the winter, my family often got stranded here in Ohio. We wouldn't have enough money to get back to Texas, so we'd borrow from the farmers. In the summer, we had to work off those winter debts.

I was one of the few Mexican students in the rural schools in northwest Ohio. I remember going to grade school with all the white kids. They had everything. They played Little League baseball. They had toys. They got presents every Christmas. As a kid, I remember thinking to myself, "Here I am doing backbreaking work every summer, working ten times harder than any of these other kids, yet we have nothing and they have so much. They don't work as hard as we do, yet they have all those things." I didn't know anything about economics or social structures, but I knew that something just wasn't right.

I wasn't a good student. I went to school because there was nothing else to do and because it was cold at home and warm in the schoolhouse. I liked sports, though, and by the time I was in seventh grade I was a good athlete. I remember that there was one kid—a white, all-American blond—that I was always outdoing in sports. One day, he told me, "You're a pretty good athlete, but you're still a dumb Mexican. Look at your grades." From that point on, I had to prove myself in the classroom. That year and the next year, I was on the honor roll.

Going to school created a lot of confusion for me. I was being raised as a farmworker, and then I'd go to school and they would tell me all about freedom, democracy, equality, and "justice for all." It made me wonder. I also learned math and how to figure things out. In the sugar-beet harvest, we were all paid by the acre. There weren't any Mexicans who knew what an acre was or how to measure an acre. We'd simply ask the farmer how many rows were in an acre and then keep track of what the farmer owed us by the number of rows we worked. We took the farmer's word every time. I found out that even though the farmer told us that thirteen rows of sugar beets made an acre, it was actually eleven rows to an acre. So every time we did thirteen rows and got paid for an acre, we were doing two rows for free. For every five acres, we worked almost an acre free. Our family was often cheated by farmers and labor contractors. It gets to you watching this happen to your family, right in front of your eyes. I kept asking myself, "Why do we put up with this?" Starting when I was about twelve, I began thinking that something had to be done about the way farmworkers were treated.

I graduated high school and went to college and started graduate school. I actually didn't quit doing farmwork until my senior year in college. At first, I thought that what we needed was a civil rights organization for migrant workers, an advocacy group. I thought all we needed to do was to make enough noise to get the proper officials to enforce the laws. One short month of talking to bureaucrats and I discovered they were part of the problem. So I figured we needed a union. I didn't know a lot about unions in those days. I talked to workers about a union, but they wouldn't listen to me because I was too young. I was only twenty and older Mexicans won't listen to young people. So I came up with a plan. I started publishing a newspaper called *El Campesino.* I put in stories and photographs of farmworkers. I editorialized. I passed the papers out in the migrant camps and in the community, using the newspaper as my mouthpiece.

Then I set up a confrontation at one of the big labor camps. It had guards and a ten-foot fence topped with barbed wire. It looked like a prison camp. I wanted to dramatize the problems of gaining access to the labor camp. I brought a reporter, a bunch of college students, and about twenty workers. Sure enough, the police were there. I waited until people started coming out from their cabins to see what the commotion was all about. As soon as I had a big audience, I got in an argument with the policeman there. I told him that I was going to go into the camp to distribute the newspaper. I told the workers, "You have the right to have visitors. You're not prisoners." I got arrested. From that day on, the word spread like wildfire. There was a Mexican willing to get arrested for people's rights.

One day, I organized a debate with some farmers. By this time, I was in college. I had a fairly good vocabulary, and I was able to shoot down all the farmers. The people liked that. They'd never heard a Mexican talk to white people like that. I won a bunch of converts with that demonstration and that meeting. I had a core of people that could help me organize, and that's how we started FLOC.

Basically, what we wanted was to cut out all the cheating and abuses by farm labor contractors. We wanted a contract that said, "The workers have these rights. The farmers have these rights. We are going to make sure everyone is held accountable." We had our first strike at the peak of the harvest. We stayed out of the fields for three or four days until the tomatoes started rotting. The farmers wanted to salvage their investment. They wanted to get us back into the field. We signed the first contract in 1969. We got a couple of cents more per basket, legal recognition, and a guarantee to be hired back the next year.

That's when my real education began. I started to understand that it's the food processors and not the farmers who have economic control of the industry. The farmer contracts to grow a crop for a big company like the Campbell Soup Company or Heinz and it's the company that sets the price. Out of whatever the company pays, the farmer has to cover his overhead and pay his labor. So, we were negotiating with a party that didn't actually determine the price. That's when I understood that we had to get a collective bargaining agreement with the food processors rather than the farmers.

In 1970, we started organizing things on a company-wide basis. We concentrated on all the farmers that were contracted through a particular company. It took us from 1971 to 1978 to organize that base. When we couldn't get meetings with the companies, we finally held a strike against Campbell with about twenty-five hundred workers. Then we started a national boycott of Campbell's products. For seven years, we picketed those fields each summer and ran the boycott year-round. I don't think we ever hurt the company economically, but we raised some doubt in the consumer's mind about the legitimacy of their products.

We kept getting stronger each year, and we weren't going away. They acknowledged that the boycott was bad for business and in 1986 they did what they said they'd never do—Campbell signed a three-party agreement between the company, the workers, and the farmers. Over these last six years of collective bargaining, we've been able to create a relationship with both the farmers and the food processors. We're winning them over to our side. We'll never agree on everything, but now we have mechanisms for the dialogue to continue. Now they acknowledge that we have a right to have a say in this whole business.

I was never sure if Campbell would ever sign the contract, but then that's the difference between our struggle and the other unions' struggles. Most unions only fight when they think they're going to win something. We were willing to fight indefinitely. We were struggling because it was the right thing to do, not simply because we wanted to win. That's what Campbell didn't realize. The struggle was never really about money. It was always a question of justice, of being treated with respect, of being looked at as human beings. Some hearts are being changed in the process. Now the growers and the food processors have to deal with us as people, whereas before they refused to deal with us. Now they're experiencing a different side of the workers. Now they have to address the fact that we have brains, feelings, and real concerns.

We're not advocates, we're organizers. Advocates are social service agencies, federally funded programs, lawyer's groups, and others. They acquiesce to double standards. They perceive the solution to farmworkers' problems as stronger federal laws or increased funding for farmworker support programs—whether it's Head Start, food stamps, or emergency assistance. There's nothing wrong with helping someone in need, especially if it's done out of compassion for people who are poor and need a hand. But that's separate from the solution.

In fact, the assistance that federal programs offer is a double-edged sword. Sure, they help the workers, but they also institutionalize the exploitative relationship between the worker and the industry. Through these programs, workers are getting from the government what they should be earning as a reward for their labor. Establishing a union allows workers to have a forum to participate in the decision making that affects their lives. If we had all the agriculture workers in this country organized, there would be ways to sort out farmworkers' problems.

10. Migrant Children
Tell Me What a Childhood Is

THE EARLIEST MEMORIES of migrant children are often woven out of images of hard work and constant movement, the seemingly endless expanse of row crops and orchards, the cold of early morning, the heat of a midday sun, miles of highways and curving dirt roads linking one temporary home to another. Farmworker children grow up in a world defined by continual uncertainty in which they are forced to internalize the pressures of poverty and the instability of seasonal labor. Too much rain might delay a harvest; a sudden freeze might ruin the crop; too many workers might arrive in the fields. A good job could last two months or two weeks. Children learn to accept that their family's daily existence is structured by forces beyond their control.

Migrant farmwork blurs the separation between work and home life. Many of the most basic elements of daily living—where a family stays and for how long, what school the children attend and when—are determined by the shifting demands of agricultural labor. In the most extreme cases, farmworker children have no real homes. Their families crisscross the nation in a constant, often random, search for work. These children grow up shuttling back and forth from one labor camp to another, sleeping in cars parked at highway rest stops, camping in the orchards where they work.

Jose Martinez ♦ *Lawrence, Michigan*
Jose Martinez is the fourth of eight children. For years, his family has migrated back and forth from Texas's Rio Grande Valley to southeastern Michigan, where they pick asparagus, strawberries, cherries, blueberries, grapes, and apples. His family of ten earns about $15,000 a year.

Although neither of his parents finished elementary school, Martinez has just completed his first year of university. This summer Martinez is working with a federally funded home-study program that provides migrant children with reading and math workbooks and school supplies. Every two weeks, Martinez and the other program staff visit students at their temporary homes in labor camps and local rental housing to see how they're progressing. They tutor students, talk with them, and encourage them to stay in school. "I try to push them. I always tell them to do the work and get smart. The little ones will do it, but sometimes the older kids just don't care about school. They work all day. They've been through it for so long. They're tired."

I was in second grade the first time I stepped into a field to work. The first crop I picked was blueberries. I remember that I was kind of lazy. I was young and didn't really understand why we were out there. As I got older, I learned that it was my responsibility to work.

Until we were old enough to work legally, we'd get paid under the names of older family members. We needed the money and me and all my brothers were an essential part of our family's economy. We all contributed. It wasn't something we thought about. We just did it. Working was what we did to survive. It didn't matter that it was illegal.

Did I lose out on having a childhood? Tell me what a childhood is. If a childhood means coming home from school and playing ball and staying home every Saturday and Sunday to watch cartoons, then I missed out on a childhood. If a childhood means growing up and experiencing what it is to be a child, then I didn't miss out. Migrant kids have a different type of childhood. We see childhood through totally different eyes.

The migrant experience was hard for me. It was difficult to work and go to school at the same time. Since we'd come up to Michigan before the end of the regular school year, I had to complete two months of extra schoolwork before we left Texas. Then, when school started again, we'd enroll here in Michigan, stay until early November, and then go back to Texas. Sometimes the school in Texas wouldn't accept Michigan's courses, or vice versa. Then, we'd have to do makeup work. Every year, we had to make adjustments. It was a lot harder then being a regular student.

A lot of migrant kids drop out of school. Why? Well, let's say you're a sophomore in high school. You've had a real hard time getting to be a sophomore because you've been traveling back and forth every year. You're tired of working and taking classes at the same time, and by sophomore year you're not really interested in school. Outside of school there's a lot going on. You're working. You've made a lot of friends. You go to parties and dances. You don't see a big need for school. You're thinking, "What's wrong with what I'm doing now? I'm working. I'm bringing in money." You can drop out now and work, even if it's in the fields. If you work real hard, you can buy a nice truck, get married, and then you're off to a good start. You're thinking about what's going to happen today, tomorrow, and the next day. You're not thinking about two or three years down the road.

Migrants only think about today. They don't think about what tomorrow might bring. That's why there's lots of migrant parents that don't take education seriously. They can't justify an education over having their kids be providers for the family. They don't see that as a fair trade. They're not bad parents. They're just not used to making long-term investments.

On my father's side, I'd say that about ninety percent of my family is in the migrant stream. The other ten percent live in Mexico. We're the first of the Martinez kids to get an education. I think we're a unique family. Our parents have always pushed us to get out of the migrant stream, to break out of this cycle that so many people are stuck in. My parents always told me that I had to go to school. I remember my mother saying, "Go to school, son, so you won't have to be mules like us." That really stuck with me.

I felt comfortable going to school in Michigan, but I felt different. I didn't have many friends here. People were friendly, but they distanced themselves from me. I guess I did the same to them. In school, I was never friends with the growers' kids. I knew them, but they didn't make an effort to be friends with me. They tried not to treat me differently, but it was unavoidable. I was the only brown face there. Any time that something Spanish came up, they'd point at me, "Speak some Spanish for us."

In high school, you want to be accepted, to be a part of a crowd. For some reason, I didn't think that any of them were part of my crowd, or even close. I could talk to them fine. I could speak their language. I just didn't think that I fit in. It's not that I was envious, they were just totally different from me. Also, I always knew that I'd be leaving. I didn't want to make friends and then leave in a month or two.

When I went back to Texas, I had no problems making friends. In Texas it's like ninety percent raw Mexicans and Mexican Americans. I formed my group of kids and we were the stuff. If they weren't migrant kids, then they'd been migrants. They'd all worked in the fields. Michigan and Texas were two totally different worlds. Every time I went back to Texas, I felt like I was going home.

It's hard for me to say whether or not migrant life was good. Good in what sense? I didn't really like it. I don't think anybody in third grade wants to go out and work every day during the summer. Still, being a migrant benefited me in a lot of ways. I know what it means to work hard to earn a dollar. I think my family became stronger because we worked as a group. Being a migrant is a big reason why I'm in college because I know that with a degree I won't have to be a part of that cycle anymore.

A lot of growers view migrants as disposable labor. When they want workers, they bring them up, and when they don't want them anymore, they send them back to Texas or wherever they're from. The growers know that there are always lots of people willing to work—"If you don't want to do it, we'll get someone else." There's one grower we've worked with for about six years. My father developed a kind of friendship with him. He feels grateful because the farmer's allowed us to work for him for so long. Maybe I should be thankful, too, but I don't feel that way. In fact, I think he's the one who should be grateful. He'll tell us, "I'm lucky to have you guys because you're excellent pickers. You do the job right." Well, if we've been doing such a good job, why doesn't he pay us more? In the six years we've worked for him, he raised the price of a flat of strawberries—that's eight pints—from a dollar and eight-five cents to a dollar ninety. In six years, the price he pays has gone up five cents.

We've been used. The growers have used us. They've overworked and underpaid us for a long time. I take that for a given, I accept it, and that's part of being a migrant. Don't get me wrong. I don't accept the situation in the sense that I think it's right, I accept it because I know what's going on. I've always been mad at the growers, but it's part of being a migrant to understand that no matter how upset you get, your anger won't change a thing. That's just how it is.

When I first arrived at the university, I was upset that other students didn't know anything about migrant farmworkers. I was angry. What do you mean you don't know what a farmworker is? How do you think you get all those apples you eat? I was also upset that they didn't know a thing about Cesar Chavez, who he was, and what he stood for. I'm not surprised anymore. Now I understand that they really don't know. Whose fault is it that people don't know anything about farmworkers? Is it the migrants' fault? Is it society's fault? I think that if more people knew about farmworkers, maybe things would be different.

The responsibility I have, first and foremost, is to my family. One of the main reasons I'm going to university is to give something back, not only to my parents, but to my younger brothers, to get them out of this cycle. I want to get ahead so that when I finish university and have a good job, it will be time for my parents to stop working. I wish I had enough money right now to say to my mother and father, "You've worked hard enough. That's it. You don't need to work anymore."

I see myself finding a stable job and achieving financial security. I see myself being successful in the sense that I'll be out of the migrant cycle. Then I won't have to put up with working in the fields and getting underpaid. Still, I don't think I'll ever stop being a migrant. Once you're a migrant, you're a migrant for the rest of your life, whether or not you travel from place to place, working the fields. Even when I have a degree, I'll still be a migrant, on the inside anyway.

How would I like to see migrant work change? I'd like to see the migrant stream stop. Undo it. Tear it up. Even as we speak, my little brothers are out there picking blueberries.

The poverty, uncertainty, and instability of farmworkers' lives weighs heavily upon their children. There are currently over 2 million farmworker children in the United States, 300,000 of whom migrate. Eighty percent of migrant children live below the poverty line.

Working and traveling together, migrant family members grow deeply dependent upon each other. The family provides an organizing principle for daily life, a much needed sense of stability and order. While one temporary home shifts to another and today's classroom fades into tomorrow's, the family remains constant, the center of daily life. Beginning at a very young age, many farmworker children take on key family responsibilities. They watch over babies in the shade of an orchard and feed younger siblings playing by the side of a field. Older children labor in the fields or stay at home, cooking, cleaning, and caring for their younger brothers and sisters.

Farmworker children often work alongside their parents, both because many families rely on their children's earnings and because child care is expensive. Forty percent of migrant children over seven work in the fields. Farmworker children typically grow up with the idea that working is an essential part of childhood. As children grow older, their role as productive workers gains increasing importance. Migrant children in their teenage years are sometimes key contributors to their family's economic well-being.

Since most farmworker families are foreign-born, and 80 percent of migrant parents do not speak English, children also help their parents make sense of the life in the United States. They often act as translators, helping their families communicate with everyone from the telephone company to the court system to teachers at the local

school. Farmworker children translate letters, read instructions, pay bills, and sometimes negotiate with growers.

Troy Lambert ♦ *McFarland, California*

While still a small child, Troy Lambert's father traveled from Arkansas to Oklahoma in a horse-drawn covered wagon. Lambert's father met his mother in Oklahoma, where her parents were share-croppers. Like many small farmers, they went broke in the early 1940s and moved out to California, following the path traveled by so many dust bowl migrants. Lambert's grandparents on his father's side remained in Oklahoma, where they continued to live without electric-ity, running water, and other basic conveniences until the late 1950s.

Lambert is the second oldest of five children. When he was a teenager, his father was discharged from the military and the family began working as migrant farmworkers. Lambert's father was a Pentecostal preacher who gave sermons in different churches as the family traveled from place to place.

Lambert is now in his mid-fifties. He has a gentle, unassuming manner, bifocals, and a thick mustache. Although he claims to have been painfully shy as a young man, you would never guess this today. We sit in his modest home, drinking coffee at the kitchen table. Half in jest, Lambert reminds his wife of his long-standing offer to take her to an Oregon bean camp for a second honeymoon. "She never did migrant work. I'd like her to see how we used to live. She'd enjoy it. It's sort of like camping. You live out in the country in a little cabin."

While I was growing up we followed the crops from one place to an-other. Back then, ninety percent of the workers were white. We were con-sidered Okies. Nobody around here really looked down on us because this whole area was filled with what they called Okie towns. I've always thought of myself as an Okie.

For ten years, we never lived in one place for more than four months at a time. We'd start here in McFarland picking potatoes and chopping cotton. Chopping cotton was the most miserable job. All day long you'd just walk and chop, thinning the cotton, leaving two or three stalks. For a while, we went to pick prunes. That area didn't have any housing, so we'd live along the river, camping out, cooking over a fire. Then we'd go to Oregon to pick beans. Everything we owned for seven people fit in our car. The trunk would always be full—clothing, sheets, blankets, cooking utensils. My mother got to where she could really pack the trunk of a car.

It seemed like we were always trying to find a better crop, something that would last longer. A lot of times the crops didn't come off in time, so if we didn't watch out, we'd be broke before we got to our next job. We were always trying to figure out ways to have less time off between jobs. We were poor, but we didn't know it. Back then, everybody was poor. I think that's where the difference lies. It seems like nowadays if you say that someone is poor, that means they're supposed to be miserable.

The labor camps weren't a bad place to live because there were always lots of kids there. The same people usually came back each year. They were a fairly good group, so you were glad to see everybody. It was like a neighborhood. We worked with everybody who lived there and sometimes we'd write letters to each other. We had a good time. I've lost touch with most of those people, but one man called me about a month ago and there was a girl I used to know who came by to visit one time.

I enjoyed the way I grew up. I liked moving around. Sometimes I think that if we had something like a mobile home to live in, then it would have been great to follow the crops. Also, since we never had any money, we never stopped to see things. We'd drive within a hundred miles of the Grand Canyon but never stop to see it. I can't blame my parents for the way they raised me. They did what they thought was right. We could have worked harder than we did, but they didn't push us. I saw parents that took out belts and whipped their kids to make them work. My parents didn't do us that way. They treated us good.

I have no regrets, except that sometimes I wish that we'd stayed in one place so we could have finished school. We missed a lot of schooling. Back then, the schools didn't work with you like they do now. Then, they didn't have Migrant Education programs. Now the kids get more help. They have special classes, one-on-one tutors. In our day, migrant kids didn't get nothing. Sometimes the schools wouldn't even let us into the classrooms. They'd say, "You're migrants. You're just going to leave in a few weeks." Since technically the younger kids had to be in school, they'd set up a place in the labor camp, like a day-care center, for the migrant kids. There were also times when they'd actually close the public schools so kids could go harvest beans.

I started high school six weeks late and quit when I was fifteen. I was a lousy student, but my younger brother was always an A student. He went to high school for three years, but since we were moving around so much, he eventually failed out. It really hurt my brother not to finish school. My brother could have been more than what he is today if we'd stayed in one place until he graduated. I made up my mind that when I had children, they would start and finish at the same school.

So, when we got married, we settled down—right here in McFarland. I knew that more than anything else, I wanted my kids to have stable schooling. I also knew that financially we were better off staying in one place. I started doing seasonal farmwork. I worked in the potato shed and from there I'd go and make grape boxes. Those jobs lasted about nine months out of the year. The other three months, I'd have to get out there and hustle. Sometimes I'd go out and chop cotton. About that time, I realized that I was getting older. I started wondering if I could keep doing the same work, running and sweating, when I was sixty years old. That's when I decided to leave farmwork. I went to work at the school as a custodian.

You know my parents wanted to be migrants. They could have stopped anytime. There was nothing stopping them. There were plenty of steady jobs back then, but they preferred to do what they were doing. It just fit them. Even after we'd all moved away, my parents kept traveling up to Oregon. They continued migrating until they were in their sixties. They even tried to pick apples in their seventies.

Migrating becomes a habit. Sometimes you just want to move on. To this day, when it starts getting hot here, I want to head north, up to Oregon like we used to do. I don't know how to explain it. Sometimes I just have a desire to move, to leave, to travel, like a gypsy. It's taken me a long time to get over wanting to leave, wanting to go on down the road to try someplace else.

Migrant work is a good life. I'd like to have a job where I could control my hours, where I could decide that if I didn't want to work that day then I didn't have to—even if I might have to work double tomorrow to make up for it. I'd like to be able to schedule my time. With migrant work, you could usually do that. You could get up in the morning and be out in the fields at daybreak, or you could sleep in until ten o'clock. No one bugged you about stuff like that. Other jobs aren't good in that way. As a migrant, you're more in control of your life. Of course, the trouble with migrant work is that if you can't find work, or if it rains too much, then there's no money coming in. If you were able to make enough money as a migrant to have a normal life, not to get rich, but to support yourself when you got older, then I think it would be a good lifestyle. What it comes down to is migrant work would be good work if it paid better.

Before the mid-1960s, children working in the fields were completely exempt from coverage by the minimum-wage law and other protective labor legislation. Although farmworker children are now covered by federal child labor laws, they are subject to a number of special exemptions. While the minimum age for working in the United States is sixteen, children as young as fourteen can work in the fields with virtually no restrictions and children twelve and thirteen years old can do farm labor with their parents' approval. Those same children would have to wait years before they could sweep floors, sell shoes, flip burgers, or accept virtually any nonagricultural job. Children working on small farms, whether farmers' children or hired laborers, remain completely excluded from any protective legislation.

Perhaps what is most surprising about the special exemptions for farmworker children is that farm labor is one of the most dangerous occupations in the nation. Each year, 24,000 children are injured on farms and 300 die as a result of work-related accidents. In other dangerous occupations, such as logging and mining, the minimum age for workers is eighteen.

Hattie Wilson ♦ *Fort Pierce, Florida*

Hattie Wilson's parents separated before she can remember. Her earliest memories are of Belle Glade, an agricultural town located on the southern shore of Lake Okeechobee. For many, Belle Glade represents the classic Florida migrant town. The community inspired Zora Neale Hurston's descriptions of farmworker towns in her novel, Their Eyes Were Watching God. *Belle Glade also plays a central role in Edward R. Murrow's classic documentary "Harvest of Shame," which begins with images of workers piling into trucks at the downtown loading dock, on their way out to the fields.*

Belle Glade remains a farmworker town, although Haitian, Latino, and West Indian immigrants have changed the ethnic composition of the towns' traditionally African American workforce. Belle Glade also remains one of the poorest communities in the nation. Workers still go out to the same loading dock each morning looking for work and still pay exorbitant weekly rents to live in old wooden shacks and crumbling concrete-block housing. Entering Belle Glade, one passes a sign that welcomes visitors with the town's motto, "Her Soil Is Her Fortune."

As far back as I can remember is 1954. What makes that so outstanding in my mind is that it was very cold. I didn't have any shoes, so my mother put three pairs of socks on my feet.

I remember that we couldn't find a place to stay because my mother had us kids and was a single woman. None of the contractors wanted a single woman with children on any of the labor camps. I remember walking all over town looking for a place to stay. I was stepping on things and I could feel them, which reminded me that I wasn't wearing shoes.

It was getting late and we still hadn't found anywhere to sleep. We passed a house that was raised up on stilts. My mother crawled up under the house, cleared a space, and dug a little hole in the ground. She put me and my brother in the hole and told us to stay very quiet.

When she came back, she took us out from under the house and told us she'd found a place to stay. It was a little room. I remember the room had kerosene lighting. It was always smoky and we coughed a lot. There was only one bed and so my mother put my brother and me on a pallet on the floor. Every day, she'd go out to the fields to pick string beans. I can remember her bringing beans home. Oh God, we ate so many beans. I was sick to death of string beans. We lived there for a couple of years.

Then my mother met a man, Mr. LaMar. He had the most evil eyes I've ever seen on a human being. They were like glass. There was nothing behind them, no warmth, no compassion, no nothing. They were just clear, see-through eyes. Oh, but that man could sing. He had the most beautiful voice. You couldn't imagine how such a voice could come from that man. When you looked at him, they didn't match. He sang like an angel, but the man was a demon.

Mr. LaMar came to live with us. He and my mother would work in the fields and my brother and I would play around the house. We were only allowed to play outside so long as we could see Mama. Whenever she got out of sight, we were to go inside and lock the door. I was about six years old at the time. We weren't in school and there was no preschool or day care. We just kept to ourselves and did exactly like she told us.

Then Mr. LaMar started coming home during the day, leaving my mama in the fields. He would make my brother sit in the corner facing the wall, with his back to us. Then he would force himself on me. I can remember seeing him spit in his hand to lubricate himself. He had no idea I was only six years old. My brother would hear me crying, but he'd be afraid to turn around and watch. I can remember hearing my brother beg with Mr. LaMar to leave me alone. Then Mr. LaMar would throw something—a cup, a bottle, a glass—and tell him to shut up.

I don't remember how many times he did that to me because for a long time I tried to forget that it ever really happened. My moods and eating habits changed. I wasn't as playful as I'd been. My mother noticed these changes. She'd ask me about it, but Mr. LaMar warned me that if

I ever told my mother, he'd kill my little brother. When I started to cry after my mother questioned me, she knew something was wrong.

One day, Mr. LaMar came home early again. My mother must have been watching. I'd been hemorrhaging and he took my panties and threw them in a fifty-five-gallon barrel that we used to burn trash in. When my mother came in, she had my panties in her hand. Her fingers were bloody from the panties, which were still wet.

"Who did this to you?"

I didn't answer. I just knew Mr. LaMar was going to kill my brother.

When I started to cry, she didn't ask me anymore. She just went into the kitchen and started cooking up something very hot. It made my eyes water. There was a mist in the house that made me cough and sneeze. My mother told us to go outside. I didn't know what it was then, but I know now. It was a mixture of Red Devil lye, honey, Clorox, and a few other chemicals. She put in the honey so the mixture would adhere to whatever she threw it on. When she finished cooking it up, she set it aside to cool. She used to chew snuff which came in a big tall can, Navy snuff. She poured some of the mixture into one of the cans, put the top on it, wrapped it up, and put it in her blouse.

Then she let her hair down. That was the first time in my life that I ever saw my mother let down her hair. It fell just below her hips. Then she dipped her fingers into the kerosene lampshade and painted her eyelids using the soot like mascara. She made up her face, put on a pretty dress, high heels, the whole works. She got all dressed up. She didn't have any stockings, but I sat and watched her lotion her legs so they looked real nice.

Then Mr. LaMar came home and she told him, "I want you to get dressed up and we'll go down to the juke."

He said, "OK," and they went out.

When they came back, Mr. LaMar was drunk, but my mother was walking tall and straight as usual, like she hadn't had a drop of alcohol. She sat on the side of the bed. Mr. LaMar was so drunk that he fell over while he was trying to undress. Then my mother helped him up and put him into bed. She didn't even bother to take his shoes off. In a few minutes, he was snoring.

While he slept, my mother took all of our little clothes and put them in a paper bag and stood us by the door. Then she took this can from her bra, pulled the top off it, and poured the mixture into Mr. LaMar's ear.

He started screaming.

Oh, it was the worst screaming I've ever heard. With every scream, you knew that he was in absolute agony. He tried to claw at his ear and whenever he did that, pieces of meat would be slinging all over the wall. They stuck to the wall. It was burning him. She poured the stuff all over the man's ear, and it was burning.

I was crying and looking away, but my mother stood behind me and held my face towards Mr. LaMar. She said, "Do you see that? I got him! I got him! Look at that! I got him!"

Then she grabbed me and my brother and we left Belle Glade that night.

Almost without exception, migrant parents dream of better lives for their children—stable jobs, higher wages, the promise of a more secure and ordered life. Most farmworker parents also understand that the best opportunities for their children lie in education—learning English, gaining basic skills, and finishing high school. The majority of farmworker parents have limited formal education and 70 percent of migrant parents are functionally illiterate, making it difficult for farmworker families to help their children succeed in school.

Migrant children have always had serious problems completing high school. In the past, local school systems in rural areas were often overwhelmed by the sudden influx of farmworker children, who would appear and disappear with the harvest. Students had no way of transferring records from one school to another and no way of ensuring any coherence between what they learned in a series of different, disconnected schools.

In 1966, the federal government responded to these problems by creating the Migrant Education program, which helps state education departments serve the special needs of migrant children. The program currently costs around $350 million a year, roughly half the federal budget targeted for migrant workers. States use Migrant Education funding in a variety of ways, including hiring counselors and special tutors, forming drop-out prevention programs, providing medical and dental services, arranging for transportation, and working to integrate parents in their children's education. A significant amount of money is directed toward summer-school programs for workers' children, particularly in northern states, where many farmworker families reside from the late spring through the early fall.

In order to help students transfer records from one school to another, the government created a centralized system known as the Migrant Student Record Transfer System. Three regional program coordination centers have been established to ensure that educational programs are more or less consistent and to facilitate communication

between different state providers. These centers provide workshops and training seminars for educators, share Migrant Education curricula, and generally work to improve the communication between different school systems serving migrant students. Around 620,000 children currently participate in Migrant Education programs.

The federal government also provides special funding for Migrant Head Start programs, which help prepare migrant children for entering school. Most Migrant Head Start programs are operated by local schools or nonprofit organizations that apply for federal grants. Over 30,000 children are served by Migrant Head Start programs each year. The Office of Migrant Education also sponsors programs to assist farmworker children in completing high school equivalency degrees and in paying for their first year in college.

While these programs have improved the educational possibilities for farmworker children, migrant students remain, on average, two years below their grade level in reading and math skills. Almost half of all migrant students never graduate from high school.

Connie Smith ♦ *Visalia, California*

Connie Smith is one of ten children. Her parents were farm laborers who emigrated from Mexico. Her husband's parents were dust bowl migrants who left Oklahoma to work the fields of California's San Joaquin Valley. She grew up on a ranch not far from where she now teaches. Although she worked in the fields as a child, her father did not migrate and made education a priority. All of her brothers and sisters graduated from high school.

For many years, Smith was a classroom teacher with a certificate in bilingual education. She taught both migrant and nonmigrant students in the local public school system. Now, Smith works full-time in the Migrant Education program, providing one-on-one counseling and coordinating a variety of services for migrant children.

I was a teacher for quite a few years before I started working in Migrant Education. I was a good teacher, but I wasn't the best teacher I could have been. I didn't realize what an impact teachers can have on their students. Now I'm real intense, real aggressive. For me, it's almost become a crusade to keep my kids in school.

A lot of times, migrant kids are not in one school long enough to really get grounded. They go from one school to another and teachers make the assumption that they got what they needed in the last school. A couple of years of missing lots of time in school adds up, and kids fall behind. Often, by the third grade migrant kids have missed so much school that they're way behind the other kids. We now know that by the third grade we can usually determine where a kid is going to be when and if he graduates from high school. If he's low in the third grade, he's probably going to be low when he gets into high school. If by the third grade, a kid is way behind, they usually won't catch up unless real efforts are made.

A lot of migrant kids lose so much school and fall so far behind that they accept the idea that they're not going to succeed in school. Then they decide not to try and become nonstudents. I have one kid like that now who's in eighth grade. Like a lot of migrant kids, he's got a reputation. He was sent to my office several times last month for not doing his work.

"What are you doing here?"

"I didn't do my work."

"How come?"

"I don't know."

You have to understand that when he says, "I don't know," it means that the assignment was beyond him. Then you have to hook him up with someone who can help him. A lot of teachers hear "I don't know," and it just stops there. They think the kid has a bad attitude or that he doesn't want to work. In his own way, he's asking for help. He may shrug his shoulders, he may not say anything, but that's his way. A lot of teachers don't understand migrant students. They'll just stop with the shrug.

You have to be willing to go that one extra step, to see the kid as a person, not just a student who isn't trying. That's why I make it a goal to be real positive with kids. Years later, students will come back to see you and they'll thank you. It's amazing. I was at Fresno State the other day, walking along the campus when I hear this voice, "Mrs. Smith!" I turn around and I'm looking at this kid who was one of my students.

"Mrs. Smith, this is my last semester. I'm going to be a teacher!"

Then she started thanking me for being a good influence on her life. That's not a once-in-a-lifetime thing. That happens all the time. I'll be walking in Wal-Mart, and kids will call out, "Mrs. Smith," and tell me what they're doing. I think that one of the really great things about being a teacher is knowing that you've had an impact. It makes you feel really great.

On the other hand, you also run into kids that are wasting their lives. Then you have to ask yourself, "What more could I have done?"

In Migrant Education, we have to work on many different levels and become involved with the whole family. We help families get housing and food and have their health needs met. That's part of our job. If kids come to school hungry, they can't learn. If they come to school in pain because their teeth hurt, they can't learn. So we reach out to both the students and their families. That's one of the things that makes Migrant Education unique. Families look to us as a real resource. They see a teacher as someone who not only knows about education, but someone who knows about the world in general, about how the system works. Migrant parents will ask you how to set up a phone in their home or how to turn on their gas. They'll ask you about problems with their children or about how to get assistance.

Our migrant parents are loving, caring people. They want their children to have really good lives. They give their kids what they think is best. There are very few parents who want their children to work in the fields. Still, they often don't realize the kind of commitment it takes to support a child through school. Every parent that I talk to wants to help their children, but a lot of times they don't know how. Many don't have enough education. There are a lot of migrant parents who are illiterate or have very limited skills.

Sometimes parents don't get home until really late, so there's no chance for the older kids to do their homework because they're busy watching their siblings. In some homes, there's no quiet place to do their work. I always tell parents that even if you can't help your children with their schoolwork, at least let them know that you really care about them and that you want the best for them. Sometimes migrant parents can only see concrete things as a sign of their love—like buying their kids good shoes or a bicycle. It's a very frustrating experience for some of these parents because even though they want the best for their children, they often don't know how to get it.

School is the way out for migrant kids. As educators, we need to be really aggressive in what we do to help these kids catch up. As a classroom teacher, you try not to make distinctions between migrant and nonmigrant students, but a lot of times you can't help it. Migrant kids come in and out of different schools, enter late, leave early, and often fall behind. It's too bad that these people are categorized a certain way, but migrant kids need extra help. If we don't educate them when they're young, as early as possible, they're just going to fall farther and farther behind. If we don't educate these students, they're not going to get educated. It would be a really wonderful world if we didn't need Migrant Education, but we do.

Farmworker families are often large and overwhelmed by the problems they face. Many families struggle with alcohol and drug abuse and live in a social world of violence and despair. Farmworker children are often the victims of neglect and abuse. They grow accustomed to tragedy, living through broken families, teenage pregnancies, debilitating accidents, and the everyday stress of poverty. There are husbands who beat their wives, parents who hit their children, crewleaders who threaten and humiliate workers. Children watch as other young people drop out of school and find themselves working in the fields, struggling in much the same way as their parents. As farmworkers' children grow older, they often reproduce the violence they've lived through, caught in a repeating cycle of poverty and abuse.

Some families collapse under the weight of their struggles. Husbands disappear, children run away, often desperate for a different way of life. In many cases, migrant children are forced to take on the burdens of adult responsibilities, providing for their families, raising their siblings, and running the household. Some families disintegrate, while others are brought closer together by the problems they share. Many farmworker families exhibit extraordinary strength and unity, working together, supporting each other, and struggling against the threats and challenges of the outside world.

Dora Medina ♦ *Faison, North Carolina*

Dora Medina is the oldest daughter and the second-oldest child in a family of twelve children. Each of her brothers and sisters were born about a year apart. Medina grew up migrating with her family, traveling back and forth between Texas and Ohio in a large truck. Her father never went to school and her mother only studied up to the third grade. Neither of her parents spoke much English, so the children had to act as translators in all the family's dealings with the non-Latino world. Beginning at a very young age, Medina took on the responsibility of caring for her younger brothers and sisters. In addition to working in the fields, she cooked, cleaned, washed, and helped raise her siblings. Her parents were stern, disciplined, and traditional.

I was six years old when I first remember helping out in the fields.

We'd go out early in the morning while it was still cool. Sometimes there would be a fog, and you could only see the rows a couple of feet away from you. We had a little stretch of field that we worked. When it started getting hot, we'd quit for a little while, and in the afternoons we'd go back for another round. There were times that we needed to get the field picked and so at night Mom would park the car at the end of the field and turn on the headlights so we could see the cucumbers we were picking. It's not like we were good workers, but we helped. That's the way we grew up. We were all in it together.

As far back as I can remember, I always had a little baby in my arms. I was like the second little mother. While I worked, the babies would be at the end of the field inside a car or a truck. They'd be crying and they'd be dirty. They were always hungry and always thirsty. Once in a while, the little children would come out to where we were in the fields and we'd have to carry them back. Sometimes they'd get so cranky that Dad would say, "I'll take your row. You go out there and just stay with them for a while."

Some days we'd tie a bedsheet to a tree and make a little tent. We'd lay the baby in the middle and cover it up so it could breathe and the mosquitoes wouldn't get to it. Then we'd work for a few minutes and go back to check if the baby was fine and then run back to the field. Other times, we'd have the other little children take care of the smallest ones.

As a child, all I knew was field work. In school, I would think, "I don't know how to count, multiply, or do division. All I know is that I can fill up a hamper with tomatoes and cucumbers." There were times we didn't even go to school. Mom would say, "Let's not even send them to school, we're only here for a couple of weeks." Then we'd see the school bus passing by. Being in the hot sun, we'd think how good it would feel to be on that bus, in a cool place.

We were always leaving one place and going off to another where a farmer promised us more. There was always a different farmer, always a different house. If we had a bad day today, we'd hope that tomorrow would be better. In the migrant stream, tomorrow is as far as you look ahead. Tomorrow . . . tomorrow.

Christmas in a migrant camp is the saddest type of Christmas. I remember one time we were stranded on a labor camp in late December. We asked our parents what we were going to do for Christmas. Mom said, "We don't have nothing." We were really torn up about that. Then one of my sisters went outside and found a small tree. She pulled that little tree inside our room and wrapped a ribbon around it.

Another Christmas we were in a big migrant camp in Ohio. Some people took pity on us. They made little sandwiches for us and had someone dress up like Santa Claus and carry in a box of toys.

Mama always raised us to be polite, but when they said we'd get toys, it was hard to be patient. We ran for the boxes. Everybody was going, going, reaching for something. I saw a doll. I saw that face, that little hair, and I remember grabbing it and knowing that it was going to be mine. I remember telling everybody, "This is mine. My doll. Nobody's going to touch it." The doll had long blond hair, which was what attracted me to it. She had red, rosy cheeks. Her little face had an innocence to it. I fell in love with that doll.

The doll was plastic and it was missing a leg. Some of the other toys were also broken and I felt a little disappointed that we were getting hand-me-downs. At the same time, I think it made us feel close to those toys. I remember how my brothers and sisters took pity on a little teddy bear that was torn. "Poor little thing."

We all sort of grasped for something.

I chose a light purple dress for my doll, lilac color. The dress belonged to the littlest in the family. I remember that it covered the doll's defects, so then she was fine as fine. At that time, I was fighting for my privacy, fighting to be an individual. In a family with twelve kids, everybody wants to have their own stuff, and that doll was mine. My doll. I put a little cord around her neck and that held her up there on the wall high enough so that nobody would touch her. Nobody could get her down from up there but me. I didn't play with the doll, but she was mine.

Having that little doll made me wonder about the way we were living. We worked hard all the time and we had nothing. I was getting frustrated and I remember thinking, "Is this all there is to life?" I didn't want to work in the fields any more. I wanted something better. I wanted stability. I wanted out. From that moment on, I thought about getting married and having children. I wanted someone who would understand me, someone who would take me out of the fields. I thought to myself, "I want to belong to somebody."

All children growing up in poverty are forced to bear the burdens of their parents' difficult lives. In this sense, farmworker children represent an extreme example of a larger problem in American society, where one out of every five children lives below the poverty line.

What is perhaps most striking about the situation of farmworker children is the harsh manner in which the labor needs of a particular industry—producers of fresh fruits and vegetables—directly impacts their experience of childhood. With all their belongings sealed in boxes, bags, and suitcases entire families travel across our nation from one field to another. The coherence of the world of migrant children is stitched together out of disparate experiences, memories bound by the endless expanse of the highway, the pressure to keep moving, and the hope that things will be better a bit farther down the road. Although few Americans are aware of the mass movement of farmworker families across the nation, we are each of us dependent upon this system, our lives linked to the struggles of farmworker children.

Veronica Zacharias ♦ *Woodlake, California*

Veronica Zacharias was born in the Central Valley. Her father emigrated from Mexico, but disappeared when she was quite young. Her mother's family were farmworkers who traveled up from Texas to settle in California. When Zacharias was about four years old, her mother remarried and moved to Oregon. One of the main reasons her mother left the Central Valley was to keep her children from growing up in a farmworker community mired in repeating cycles of seasonal employment and poverty.

While growing up in Oregon, Zacharias only worked in the fields once, picking pears for three weeks with an uncle who had traveled north from California. She grew up speaking broken Spanish and knowing little about the world of migrant laborers. When she was sixteen, she moved back to the Central Valley to live with her aunt and grandmother where she finished high school and started college.

I met my husband during my last year of high school. He was a farmworker from Mexico without any papers. I fell in love with him. I figured that I wanted to spend the rest of my life with him. We decided to get married when I was in college.

Once we were married, he didn't want me to go to school anymore. He was jealous and insecure. He didn't want me to be around other people. He wanted me to help him work in the fields. My family stopped talking to me when I married him. My grandmother was especially disappointed. She wanted me to go to school and become a teacher and I ended up marrying a farmworker from Mexico. When I left the house she told me to never return.

So, I left college and got pregnant with Letty, my first child. About a month after she was born, I went to help my husband in the fields. I started picking olives, then oranges, and then tomatoes. At first, I would leave my daughter with a baby-sitter, but then I started taking her with me to work. I would sit her by my set on a blanket next to the ladder. As I was picking, I would watch her and talk to her. I gave her toys to play with and sometimes my husband would sing to her. There were lots of families there and they'd all come by to talk to her. It was kind of fun.

When she was two, she said that she wanted to help me. We were working on tray grapes, where you dry grapes to become raisins. So I gave her some trays and she rolled them up. She always stayed right next to me and when it got hot she'd fall asleep under the grape vines.

When I got pregnant with Angelica, I kept on working in the fields. I stopped picking when I was about six-months pregnant. The following year, I had Ramon, so then I had two small children a year apart. I'd leave the little ones with a baby-sitter and take Letty with me to pick. A few years later, when I was pregnant with David, I worked until my eighth month. I always liked working, but once I got to a certain month, I couldn't climb the ladders, so I'd pick from the bottom of the trees.

By then, my husband and I were drifting apart. My husband's brother told us that you could make good money working in the cherries, picking as a family. At first my husband didn't want to take us, but I wanted us all to go. I wanted to keep us together. I felt that if we traveled together as a family, maybe we could stay close.

That's when we started really migrating.

The first year we went north, our car broke down in Oregon and we had to push it through the pouring rain. When we finally got to Washington, we couldn't find work. Eventually, we found a grower who gave us a job and let us sleep in the orchard. There was no bathroom and no showers, only an irrigation pipe with cold water. All six of us slept in the station wagon, my kids in the back and my husband and I sitting up front. We'd set the stove outside and cook. I felt bad for my kids because it was cold and we were all so uncomfortable. Later, a labor camp opened up and we went there to set up our tent. There were some type of insects biting us at night and we all got sick. We were miserable.

We tried this for three years, but every year it got worse. Eventually, we split up, and later got divorced. Once my husband left, my son Ramon started working really hard. At that time he was twelve years old. We were so deep in debt that most of the money he earned I used for bills. By then, Ramon was already making good money. Everywhere we went, he was always there with us. He was the man of the house. Although he was only twelve, we depended on him, emotionally and economically.

It was a lot of pressure for him. So, when Ramon was a freshman in high school, I felt that he needed a break from picking. I wanted him to put all his energy in schoolwork, so I told him he didn't have to pick oranges on the weekends. Then, I noticed Ramon's mood changed. He no longer cared about his grades. He had always been an A student and he started getting Ds and Fs. On the weekends, when we all went to church, he'd say that he didn't feel like going. His friends were getting him into trouble. I ignored it for a while, but then I felt that I had to do something. So I grounded him from his friends and took him back to work in the

fields. I told him he was either going to work hard in school and get a good education, or else he was going to end up doing farmwork. That straightened him up.

I don't think it's wrong to take the children to the fields. I've always had my kids with me while I've been working. I like having them with me, even if they just sit there under the tree in the shade. I like the closeness of having my family together and watching them. I think it's good for children to be with us in the fields, even if when they're young it's against the law. Working is good for kids because it teaches them how to be responsible and helps them understand where the family's money comes from. I spend more time with my children when we pick together as a family. It's not just that it helps economically. I feel that we're closer, working together and helping each other.

My responsibility is to raise my children, keep them safe, keep them together, and keep them from getting into trouble. That's why we work together. I'm protecting them. I want my children to continue their education so that they won't fall back to working in the fields like I did. I'm very proud of my kids. I see how close we are, how hardworking they are, and how well they're doing in school. I figure that in a way it was my destiny to be a farmworker, to teach my children this way of life so that they could do better, so that they won't have to struggle like we do now, from day to day.

Ramon Zacharias ♦ *Woodlake, California*

Ramon is the third of Veronica Zacharias's four children. He is sixteen years old and a junior in high school. He is the fastest and most productive worker in the family. For several years, his earnings have supported the family.

It is Christmastime and the living room is filled with small, bright lights. Strands of tinsel are wound around the window frames. There is a pile of wrapped presents in one corner and an orange-picking sack crumpled beside the sofa. Ramon talks quickly, bursting with energy, shifting from one topic to another, excited. He has close-cropped hair, an oversize white T-shirt, and baggy black pants. He is immediately likable, open to questions, and confident.

When we first migrated to Stockton, my parents tried to put me in school. I wasn't used to being in different classes with different people. I was used to having my friends around me. The classroom was divided, half the room was Hispanic, the other half was white. There were two sides and we never mixed. The whites looked at you with disgust. They never tried socializing with you. I tried to get along with everybody, but they didn't like people who worked in the fields.

Still, I wasn't going to complain. I knew I'd only be there for a month. So I decided to skip school. My sister and I would go out to wait for the school bus in front of the labor camp. After the bus passed, we'd climb back into the apartment through the window. We'd stay in the house all day. We'd sweep and wash, so when my parents came home from work everything was clean. Then my mom and dad figured, "Why make him go to school? Why not just take him out to work?"

I was nine years old when I started picking cherries. I remember my first day. Everybody was getting their sets and I just got up there and started picking. Later, the crew boss came over and he tells my dad, "Look at your son, he's picking really fast." Before I knew it, I was getting faster and faster. My dad didn't make anything of it, but my mom was really surprised. The same day after work, she said, "Ramon, you picked really fast. How do you do it?"

It was really easy for me to pick. It has a lot to do with hand-eye coordination. I think what helped me was playing video games when I was little. To pick well, you just stay focused on what you're doing and keep a positive mind. You can't go to the fields, start picking, and let yourself get frustrated. When I'm in the fields, I just keep laying 'em on. I stay in a rhythm. I don't stop. I stay focused and positive. I don't like to talk when I pick because talking slows you down. Sometimes I race the people on either side of me because I like the competition. I always try to be fastest. When I'm really ahead, I might stop and take a little rest. Then, when I see that someone is about to catch up to me, I start going again. That's how I pick.

I've always felt like I had to show everybody that I can do as good a job as anyone else. If I'm not giving it my best, then why should I even go out there and pick? When we go to the fields, I always work my hardest, and when we come home, I always study. I've always wanted to prove that I could work and keep my grades up.

My parents got divorced when I was twelve years old. After that, I knew I was going to have to be more responsible. I knew that I'd have to work more and stay at home. My mother told me, "Ramon, remember, you're the man of the house now." She said she'd have to depend on me more than anybody else. After the divorce, I would go to work whenever I could. I was supporting our family. We always worked together, but I was earning at least half the money. They called me the moneymaker. I thought that because I was supporting the family, I'd get more respect from my sisters and brother, but they treated me just the same. They still yelled at me, told me what to do, and bossed me around.

At the beginning of the school year, we go to Fresno to pick grapes. We come back in late September or early October. I miss about a month of school, so I have to catch up on all my studying. Then we go to school, and every weekend and during vacations, we pick oranges. In May, during the last quarter of school, we go to Stockton to pick cherries. Then we're on independent study which is where they just give you work to do and when you come back, you turn in your work and get it signed by your teacher. After school ends, we go to Washington to pick more cherries. In one camp in Washington, we live in tents. We live in the woods, just like camping. So, to me, it's like a vacation. The only thing that makes it different from a vacation is the work. After work, we go to the movies or to the mall. We go hiking every chance we get. We do everything together, as a family. Then we come back to California.

My friends always ask me how come I don't join sports teams. I like playing football and basketball, but I've never had the time for teams. Usually I just work, study, and watch over my little brother, David. They ask me how come I don't go to parties on the weekends, and I tell them, "I have to work the next day. I can't stay up until midnight and then expect to work in the morning. I got to get my rest." I'd rather spend time at home with my mom and my family than go out with my friends. It's just something you feel after you've worked with your family over the years. You get used to having them always around. We're very close. We have our differences, but we're always there for each other.

It's been a good experience for me to work. Like my mom says, "This is a taste of what will happen if you don't get an education." Farmwork is hard. I'm used to it, but I can't imagine myself still working in the fields ten or twenty years from now. I really admire the people who get up every single day and work in the fields. They don't complain, they just get up and work, knowing that they're going to be doing that for the rest of their lives. They're out there working every day and no one acknowledges the pain they go through. They're the people who make this state what it is. If they were to stop working, then everything in this area would come to a halt. So, I admire farmworkers.

Even though we're poor, I feel middle class. I'm out there working and everything, but I'm not unhappy. I've got whatever I need. I have a roof over my head, nice clothes, a future to look forward to. I basically have everything planned out. I'm going go to into the Marines and then go to a four-year college and see if I can get a degree.

To me, being a migrant means following work wherever it calls. If the job is in another state, then we go to another state. Being a migrant means I have less free time than other kids. It isn't bad to be a migrant. It just means more work.

11. Back Home
Mexican *Ranchos*

THERE ARE THOUSANDS of communities throughout rural Mexico so deeply dependent on migration that virtually every man of working age leaves home to cross the border and seek employment in the United States. Over the last thirty years, the migration of Mexican workers has grown so substantially that there are now significant regions of the country that are completely dependent on the dollars migrants send home to their families. Currently, about two-thirds of our nation's migrant farmworkers—an estimated 600,000 mostly male laborers—travel to and from Mexico each year. The majority of these workers leave their families back home in Mexico, generally in rural *ranchos*.

Rural Mexican society has traditionally been highly insular. The tens of thousands of *ranchos* that dot the Mexican countryside were generally poor, isolated, and dependent on small-scale agriculture, sharecropping, and intermittent day labor. Families worked adjoining fields, planting, tending, and harvesting the same basic crops, their lives structured by the repeating rhythms of the seasons. Young people usually married within their own or neighboring communities and rarely settled far from where they were born. Daily life was premised on the comfort and predictability of membership within a close-knit community.

From the 1970s to the present, rural communities have grown increasingly dependent on migration. In many *ranchos* the entire male population travels north each year, appearing and disappearing in a constant cycle, leaving behind towns filled with women, children, and the elderly. Residents of *ranchos* who once spent their whole lives within the same small circle of relatives, friends, and neighbors must now cope with divided families and the extended absence of men.

Communities long accustomed to a relatively insular existence are now being integrated into a larger world, forced to balance the benefits of improved earnings with the uncertainties and stress of migration.

Maria Gutierrez ♦ *Pajacuaran, Michoacán*

Maria Gutierrez is forty-five years old and has five children. For the last fifteen years, Gutierrez's husband has gone north to work in the fields of California's San Joaquin Valley. He leaves each January and returns in early October.

We sit in the living room of Gutierrez's home. There are crosses set against the pale blue walls, a photograph of the pope, and a framed image of Jesus with an exposed, luminous heart. The door opens onto the street, where trucks and buses crawl noisily up a hill. From the back of the house come the muffled sounds of rock music played behind the closed door of her eldest son's room.

Gutierrez speaks in a steady, measured fashion, open yet resigned. Her face is smooth, her eyes steady. She has a soft, delicate, sad smile.

In his youth, my husband was never interested in going to the United States. He lived alone, working his land and taking care of himself as best he could. When we got married, he decided to go to the United States. He was forty-four. He crossed the border without papers along with two of his nephews. Ever since then, he has left and returned, left and returned.

My husband works the grapes in Delano, California. When he first arrives, he weeds with a hoe from six in the morning until three each afternoon, picking the ground so the soil is soft. Then he strips the leaves and prunes the plants, cutting off extra branches so the ones that remain will grow large. Later he picks grapes, clipping them off the vine and placing them in boxes. He has to bend over and walk around on his knees. The heat is intense. His clothes become soaked with sweat. The farmers use lots of chemicals and sprays, which irritate my husband's eyes, nose, and throat. Sometimes he gets sick. His nose bleeds. He coughs up blood. My husband leaves work each day beaten and exhausted. He's now fifty-eight years old.

Things here began to change around fifteen or twenty years ago when lots of men began to go to the United States. Now, everyone dreams about the north. The men return with money, cars, and clothes. Then a friend or a neighbor says, "Next year, I'm going over there, too." Soon "next year" becomes three years and then six years and then nine years. It just keeps growing.

Although economically things are better in town than before, morally things are worse. You never know how a man will react to the north. There are so many men who go over there and then forget about their families. I know men who have gone north with my husband and never returned. Marriages fall apart and many women and children are left alone. Now all the young people want to go to the United States to work in the fields. It makes me very sad because even boys of fifteen and sixteen are going north. Without papers, how will they find work? Many turn to the easiest jobs, like selling drugs or robbing people.

When your husband is away, you worry a lot. You think about so many things. You worry that he might be caught by Immigration or have an accident, as happens to so many people. You worry that an animal might bite him as he crosses over the hills in the desert, or that he might drown in the river. The men don't go over there to enjoy themselves. They go there to suffer.

Economically our lives have improved. We don't have much—just some conveniences, a television, a stereo—but we eat much better than before. Now there's lots of fruit, canned foods, and imported things. We have five children in school, with the oldest at the university. Now we can pay for their schooling. It wasn't always like that. Although we have more money, we don't live a normal life. I stay here alone with our children, without the support of my husband, without his help. The separation is difficult.

My oldest son is now seventeen and he also wants to go north. His father doesn't want him to go, but he's curious. He wants to see what it's like over there. My other son is ten and even he talks about the north. He watches television and dreams about Disneyland. My daughters, too. They all want to go north to see what it's like. All my children are thinking about getting ahead. They have new dreams, new ideas. Maybe it's for the best, but I don't like it. I'm afraid. I don't want to think like they do. My husband says that in the United States the young people are free and won't obey their parents. They call attention to themselves. They wear whatever they want, go to dances when they feel like it, and come home at all hours of the night. They become aggressive because there's so much immorality and no control. We don't want to take our family north. I wouldn't want my children to become like that.

Without your husband, you feel empty and sad. When my husband is away, I look at photographs and read letters. I talk to my children. I say: "If your father were here, he'd really enjoy this meal." "If your father were here, we'd go out to the country." "If your father were here, the older kids wouldn't hit the little ones." "If your father were here, everything would

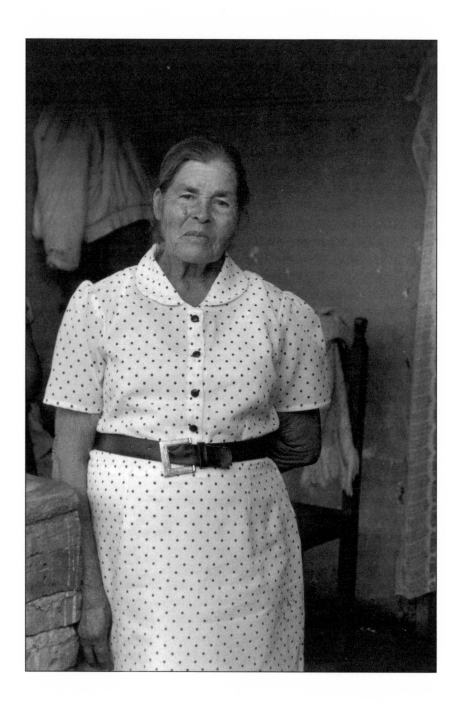

be different." That's what we say: "If your father were here . . ." But, of course, he's not here.

I write to my husband about our lives, our daily routines, and how the children are behaving. The children miss their father a lot. They understand the situation, but they don't accept it. I'm very much in love with my husband. When he leaves, I cry. My children also cry, although we won't cry in front of him. You can't really accept the situation. The five months while he's here pass so quickly, and when he's gone, time passes so slow. We have a calendar and we count each day with an *x*. We make it, from year to year, but it's difficult.

Towards the end of September, I tell the children, "Soon your father will be back." We never know exactly when he'll return. He doesn't like to tell us. He arrives as a surprise. Before he returns, we're tense and nervous. We wait for the knock on the door. The children are always so happy when he finally arrives. When my husband is here, I feel protected. Then, everything is different.

What more can I say? I am like so many women. The men go to the United States. That's what they have to do, and the women are left behind. We suffer—cousins, nieces, neighbors. Here, there is sadness. Above all, there is a lot of sadness. Sometimes in order to lessen the pain, I put on music—classical music, instrumental music, *rancheras*. There's one song I really like:

> *I went away and wandered,*
> *always dreaming of returning to your arms,*
> *returning, returning, returning to your arms.*

I like that song very much. So does my husband.

While Mexican immigrants generally take jobs wherever they find them, working as gardeners, construction workers, dishwashers, janitors, and mechanics, farm labor plays a key role in the culture of migration that is restructuring family relations and reconfiguring social life throughout rural Mexico. The temporary, seasonal nature of farmwork ensures that there is always a steady turnover of workers and new jobs. Farm labor's informal structure makes agriculture particularly accessible to undocumented immigrants, since workers are hired without contracts and often paid in cash. Migrants from rural areas are drawn to farm labor because they are accustomed to, and often enjoy, working in the fields. The seasonal nature of farm labor is especially important for immigrants who return to their *ranchos* on the off-season—to visit their families, tend their fields, and care for their children.

Rodolfo Gutierrez ♦ *Pajacuaran, Michoacán*

Rodolfo is Maria Gutierrez's eldest child. He is seventeen. After graduating high school, he entered a local university where he's studying to be an accountant. Rodolfo is polite, calm, and thoughtful. He wears a baseball hat and an Oakland Raiders T-shirt. A thin chain hangs around his neck, the small golden cross resting just above the team's insignia. Maria retires to the kitchen as we speak. Occasionally, the younger children wander into the living room.

My father left for the first time when I was two years old. Since then he's gone north every year.

I remember what it was like when I was a child. I wouldn't see my father in the house and I'd ask, "Where is my father?" I had nightmares. I don't know if I felt lonely, or if I dreamed bad things were happening to me or that I was wandering alone, but I often woke up crying. It was especially difficult when I was very young. Later, when I was about seven or eight, I began to understand. Then, I didn't miss my father as much because I knew that he had to go away each year to work.

Still, you never really stop missing him. It's different when my father is here. I don't know how to describe it. When he's here, we aren't afraid of anything. We feel secure. It's as they say, the father is like the foundation of a house. The father is what makes a house strong so it doesn't collapse in on itself. If the father leaves, it's as if you removed the foundation and then the house seems false and insecure.

My father's leaving has always been very hard for my mother. She's had so much work taking care of us, so many responsibilities. She's had to do everything, to be both a mother and a father. My father has always left me in charge. He says, "I'm leaving. You're the oldest. You're the one who has to be an example. When I'm not here, you have to take my place." When I was around twelve, I began to feel truly responsible. I worked whenever there was a chance. I went out to the fields to earn money planting, fertilizing, harvesting.

Young people here go north when they're about eighteen. When they return, they say the work is very hard. Over there, they're truly alone, far from their families. Still, the majority return here with the idea of going back north. They come back in November and December with nice clothes—baggy pants and loose shirts. They wear jewelry. When they return the town is full of cars and trucks from up north. Here, even with a good job, you could never afford a car, but they say that over there it's easy to buy a car. People see the cars they bring back, and then they also want to go work in the United States.

I know a lot of guys from here who've gone north and returned really different, really *cholo*. They change—their personalities, their ideas, their clothes—their whole way of being. When they come back, they don't show their parents the same respect. They think that because they've earned money they can run their own lives. A lot of young people who go north want to stay there. There are some students who go north to spend their school vacations working. They say that when they come back they'll continue studying, but once they go to the United States, they leave school and just keep traveling north to work.

Until I was fifteen, I never wanted to go north. I still don't have a strong desire to go, but over the last year, I've grown more interested. My father says it's better to study. He doesn't want me to go through what he's suffered. My mother also wants me to stay here. I know it's difficult over there, but I want to see it firsthand. I want to know if it's really as hard as they say. I wonder if going north will harm me, if I'll return changed like so many others. Still, if I go north, I won't stop studying. I just want to open my eyes, to see what life is really like in the United States.

Many Mexican communities that are now dependent upon migration to the United States first began sending large numbers of workers north through the bracero program. In large regions of central and western Mexico, it is actually the U.S. government's labor policies that first exposed rural communities to the benefits of earning dollars working in America's fields. Braceros returned to their *ranchos* with stories about life on the other side and fancy clothes, radios, and dollars. Those who saved money often invested in small plots of land, purchased animals, or built homes for their families. Mexican braceros established close contacts with American employers and grew accustomed to earning dollars and traveling north on seasonal contracts. After the program ended, many braceros settled in the United States, while others continued traveling north, crossing the border to work the same fields, and then returning home to their families at the end of each season.

Augustin Magaña ♦ *La Yerbabuena, Michoacán*
Augustin Magaña is the mayor of La Yerbabuena, a rancho with a long history of migration to the United States. La Yerbabuena stands out among the ranchos of western Mexico and is well known for its commitment to community works. The streets are paved and well cared for. The park in the center of town is immaculate, its gar-

den filled with flowers and surrounded by benches bearing the names of families who contributed to the construction costs. Facing the park is a large modern church with stained-glass windows.

Everywhere one looks in La Yerbabuena there are signs of prosperity. The houses are two and sometimes three stories tall, with intricate detailing and balconies. There are satellite dishes on nearly every roof, and new pickup trucks with Florida or California plates are parked along the well-swept streets. Settled into steep hills where fields of corn once grew, there are concrete foundations of houses under construction. Each year, the owners return from the United States with money to continue building.

Magaña is supervising the installation of streetlights. He wears a white cowboy hat and a crisp white shirt with a pen clipped to the pocket. He is a slight man with a deeply lined face, thin lips, and an air of certainty about him. Every year since 1956, Magaña has traveled to the United States to work in the fields. When his term as mayor ends, he plans to return to Florida to pick oranges.

La Yerbabuena used to be really poor. The houses were made of stone. The streets were unpaved, pure dirt. When it rained, you couldn't go out in clean clothes because there was so much mud, water, and sewage. There were also animals in the streets—pigs, burros, horses, dogs. It was a disaster, and not just here, but in all the *ranchos*. There were no gas stoves and no electricity. In the hills, you sowed by hand. If you had a piece of flat land, you plowed with a pair of oxen, but most of us used hoes. It was hard work. Life was tough.

Then things began to change. People began to go to the United States as braceros. We were on contracts, some for forty-five days, others for six months. We couldn't all go, but working in the United States was the only way to buy clothes or get something for your family to eat. Everyone that went to the United States tried to save their money to come back home and build a house for their family.

In the old days we suffered just to grow old. We ran around without shirts and pants. Now, we have nice houses filled with conveniences—clean water, electricity, televisions, satellite dishes. Everyone now has radios, tape decks, stoves, refrigerators, electric irons, and freezers. We talk to our children about what things were like so they'll appreciate what we've done. Some remember when we first paved the streets, put in electricity, and installed clean water. Even those who never saw what our lives were like, even those who weren't born into the same world as us, know that back then everybody was poor. Life is better these days, thanks to God and the chance to go to the United States. If there was no way to get into the United States, La Yerbabuena wouldn't be the way it is.

We're a very unified community. If the community needs something, we call an assembly. We discuss the good and the bad sides of an issue and then we reach an agreement. The people here think a lot about improving things. We all work together because without unity there's no strength, no community. For example, each neighbor is responsible for paying part of the cost of paving the streets. We measure the width of the street and homeowners must pay the cost of the pavement from the center to their side of the street. All the homeowners share the costs; those with bigger plots of land pay more than those who have less. Whoever doesn't have money to pay his quota can pay with work by helping the engineers or the masons. Everyone has to do his part.

We still lack lots of things in La Yerbabuena, like telephones. There's a phone booth in the center of the plaza, but we can't make calls directly from our homes. That's being planned for later this year. We're also thinking about building a bridge, which we really need.

To be the mayor is a big responsibility. You have to visit people who don't want to pay their water bill or those who make a scene, getting drunk in the street, breaking bottles, or fighting. You have to attend to everyone. You have to deal with gossip. You have to try and solve people's problems, to fix things with kind words and not be aggressive. Being the mayor is one of the obligations of being a member of our community. I don't really like being mayor, but if you refuse the job, it looks bad. We're all the children of our town, so we have to do what the community asks of us.

Over there, you never feel really happy because you miss your *rancho.* When you're in the United States, you're always thinking about the family you've left behind. You're always dreaming of returning to your *pueblito,* to your beautiful Mexico. Here, if you get tired of being in the house, you can walk over to the plaza, wander through the streets, or go out into the countryside. In the United States, you need to ask permission from the landowners to walk through the country. There, the laws are strict. Even if you're just out walking, the police can stop and investigate you. There's more freedom here.

Everybody knows about La Yerbabuena. They're all impressed with how we've fixed up our *pueblito.* La Yerbabuena is an example for all the communities in the area. You know, there are some towns that don't fix themselves up. They aren't interested, or they're unable to. Or, they don't go to the United States.

From the 1970s on, migration continued to expand in a largely informal manner. Workers returned from the United States each year with cars, clothes, and money. Like the braceros before them, they bought land and built houses, often appearing to grow rich virtually overnight. The comparative wealth of migrants was significant by the economic standards of isolated *ranchos*, many of which were accustomed to a subsistence economy where wages were low and salaried jobs hard to come by. Migrants' material success led others to leave their homes and travel north, producing a steady increase in the number of men who sought to improve their lives by working in our nation's fields.

Santiago Lopez ♦ *Tinaja de Coyote, Guanajuato*

Tinaja de Coyote is the last rancho at the end of a steep dirt road, high in the hills of southern Guanajuato. Burros wander slowly through the streets, which are paved with stones. Thick clumps of butterflies rest on the ground, fluttering up into the air as you walk past and then settling again into a colored mass. From behind tall stone walls, you can see thick, green stalks of corn and hear the sounds of radios playing and women working. There is electricity in Tinaja de Coyote, but still no satellite dishes.

Santiago Lopez is thirty-one. He has worked in the United States every year since he was eighteen. We sit in the shade at a wooden table at Lopez's brother's house. His brother, Manuel, is in Michigan picking apples. As we talk, Manuel's wife cooks us beans and tortillas and opens up bottles of sweet orange soda.

I remember what the *rancho* was like in my childhood. Twenty years ago, all the houses were built out of stone and the roofs were made of woven grass. We used cow manure to cover the holes between the stones and the women would mix ash with water to paint the insides of our homes so they'd be nice and white.

We lived year to year from the corn and beans we harvested. If we needed money, we'd sell some beans. If there was a bad harvest, that year we wouldn't buy anything. Back then, nobody had new clothes and we often wore shirts my mother sewed out of empty sacks of flour. Hardly anyone owned shoes. We wore huaraches made out of old car tires. There was no electricity, no radios, and no television. We didn't even know about those things. Our plates and jugs were made out of clay. We hardly ever saw anything plastic. Every few months men would come by with burros carrying things to sell, but we were so poor we could hardly afford a plastic bucket.

Childhood was sad. There were no toys. We used sardine cans or batteries as toy cars. I started working when I was five years old. Back then, there was no school here. I went to school for only two years, starting when I was twelve.

Lots of children used to die. My mother's first child died when she was a year and a half old. If someone got sick, you would sell an animal to pay for the treatment. Many people died because they had no money and no animals to sell. In those days, there was no road. You had to walk fourteen kilometers to the nearest town. People would leave the *rancho* with someone who was sick and return with a corpse.

Most of the land here is owned by wealthy people who own lots of animals—cows, bulls, horses. The landowners always dressed well, ate well, and lived much better than the rest of us. If we saw one of the landowners from far away, we'd say, "Look, it's the boss." He'd come over with his nice hat and fine clothes while we were wearing torn clothing covered in patches. Everyone worked for the landowners. They'd lend us land and oxen to help plant. At harvesttime we'd make two piles of whatever we'd planted—corn, beans, garbanzos. One pile was for us and the other pile was for the landowner. If a landowner had twenty people working for him, he'd get twenty piles, while the families that worked the fields got one pile each. Often the harvest wouldn't provide enough to last all year and we'd have to borrow from the landowners. They'd lend us corn and beans, but we'd have to pay them back the next year which meant we had to plant more land and work even harder. We were always in debt.

Men from the *rancho* started to go to the United States in the late seventies and early eighties. The men who went north came back to the *rancho* with new clothes, cowboy boots, and Texas hats. They built brick houses and brought back radios and tape decks. My brother Manuel first went north in 1979. After spending a few months there, he came home and built a house. When I saw that, I wanted to go north, too, and my brother said he'd help me.

In 1982, my father sold some corn to pay for my trip. At the border, I paid a *coyote*. He took five people across, all cousins or friends from the *rancho*. We ran through the desert and then they took us to a house near Fresno where other people from our *rancho* were living. When I arrived at the house, they turned on the hot-water faucet and made me a cup of instant coffee. That was the first thing which surprised me about the United States. I had never seen a water faucet before. I thought, "Look how easy life is here." I looked at all the lights, the wide streets, and the big houses. Everything surprised me. It was all so nice.

In California, I lived with people from our *rancho*. I shared a house with a group of men. We each paid fifteen dollars a week for rent and fifteen dollars for food. We had guys sleeping on the carpet, the sofa, and on folding mattresses. We took turns at the stove and bathroom, but it was fine because we all knew each other.

Lots of people offered us jobs and the work seemed easy. We were used to working all day, from sunrise to sunset, ten or twelve hours without resting. After my first three days of work, I received a check for eighty dollars. Eighty dollars in three days? Here in the *rancho,* we never earned anything until the harvest ended, and if there was a bad harvest, all your work was in vain. I sent the money back to my father. I had lots of jobs with different *mayordomos.* Grapes with one boss, olives with another, pruning trees in the winter, picking peaches, plums, nectarines. When you finished with one boss, you'd just go off with another.

Before, we never went north because we didn't know anyone there. Now, everyone goes to the United States and we've all got relatives there who can help us find work. If you lose your job, there's always someone who can lend you money until you find another job. It's good that the men from the *rancho* are over there working. Even though we suffer, living far from our families, we suffered more before.

These days, all the men from our *rancho* go to the United States. The landowners are still around, but nobody wants to work for them anymore. You see the land over there, full of weeds, grass, and trees? That whole hill used to be covered with corn. The landowners used to get a lot of work out of us, but not anymore. Those times have passed. These days, we dress just as well as they do.

The *rancho* has improved. We now have electricity, a road, bridges, a primary school. Everything we have comes from the money we earned working in the United States. In a few years, we'll have a high school, and maybe a sewage system. Things will keep improving.

Water is a big problem in our community. Now that it's raining things are fine because when it rains, we store the water. Still, for six months each year, there's no rain and then there's no water to wash clothes, bathe the children, or give to the animals. During the dry season, all the water we drink comes from a small spring about two kilometers from here. The women have to bring water back in containers which they carry on their shoulders, climbing all the way home. The stream from the spring is only about a quarter of an inch wide. There are two *ranchos* that drink from that spring, so it isn't enough. This year we began taking up a collection to drill a well. Right now, we're collecting a hundred dollars from each man who works in the United States. There's a guy in Illinois, my brother in Michigan, and two men in California with notebooks and pens who gather the money and mark down what each person has given them. Everyone cooperates and when we have enough money, we'll dig the well.

I'd like it if the Americans would work with us in the fields, even if it was only for a day. It would be a good experience for the *gabachos* to pick with us, carry a ladder, and listen to us talk. It would help them understand our lives. Then, when they saw workers in the fields, covered with mud, they'd know that we've come to the United States from the *ranchos* of a poor country in order to work. Then, they might understand that we're just trying to get ahead.

At first glance, the *ranchos* where there are no men seem simply quiet. Old people sit in the sun. Children attend school and play in the streets. Women care for their homes and work the fields. Still, there is an uncomfortable stillness to the silence. The *ranchos* exude an emptiness, a weighty sense of absence. Even the most casual conversations reveal the fact that these communities exist in a state of constant waiting. The women and children who remain at home speak longingly of the several months each year when the men return, when husbands come back to their wives and fathers see their children again. When migrants come home, people say that the *ranchos* feel alive again.

Families learn to bear a steady burden of insecurity, born of the cyclical absence of men and the enormous space that separates the *ranchos* from the distant land where the men work. Families wait nervously for news. Have the men arrived safely? Have they found jobs? Are they doing well? Letters pass back and forth across the border. There are occasional phone calls. The distance breeds uncertainty.

Traveling to the United States can be dangerous, particularly for those without papers. Sometimes accidents occur or workers fall sick. Some migrants get in trouble with the law or lose themselves in drugs or alcohol. Others take up with women they meet up north and abandon their families. Some migrants never return. Many families eventually leave their communities, preferring to live together in the United States rather than suffer the dislocation of seasonal migration and the stress of a divided household. Interestingly, even those families who rarely return to Mexico typically build large homes in their *ranchos,* many of which remain empty for months and even years at a time.

Enrique Perez ♦ *Francisco J. Mujica, Michoacán*
Enrique Perez lives in an adobe house near the entrance to his rancho. *The community lies in the middle of a wide valley at the end*

of a rutted two-lane road, several miles off the main highway. It's the rainy season. The fields shine bright green under the afternoon sun, as dark, bluish clouds hover menacingly in the eastern sky. There are stands of broad leafy trees and open pastures covered with purple flowers. In the distance, high upon a hill, there is a white cross.

In the 1950s, Perez traveled to the United States. For several years, he worked in the fields, eventually returning to his rancho to plant corn and care for his animals. Since then, his community has gradually become so completely dependent on migration that there are now few people who actually live there. Most families have moved north together and now labor in the strawberry farms of northern California.

Perez, his wife, brother, and a few young children sit beside a tree outside their house, watching the road, the fields, and the distant hills. A dog sleeps nearby. Chickens wander in and out of the yard, pecking at the earth; a cluster of small chicks loses its way in the tall grass. Perez offers to give me a tour of the rancho. *We talk as we drive slowly through the community along crumbling paved roads that fade into mud tracks dotted with pools of water. Except for a goat tied to a tree and a lone cyclist, the* rancho *appears abandoned.*

In a *rancho* like this, you could die of old age, having worked all your life to support a family and never built a house like the ones you see here now. Forget it. In our *rancho,* workers always built adobe houses. Many homes weren't even covered with mud and they were never painted. Now the *rancho* is filled with modern houses. Look at them! These are the houses of the emigrants.

There's a big difference between the old days and now. Before people started migrating to the United States, we didn't own many things, not even radios. The first radios in our *rancho* were brought here by braceros. Now, you see satellite dishes, televisions, video recorders, computers. All of those things come from the north.

Still, most of the houses here are empty. Very few people live here now, only some old people and small children.

A family of five owns that house over there. They've been in the United States for three years now. Since the children are in school, they don't come back anymore. Last year, only the wife returned. There are a few single girls who take care of the house. The family sends them about forty dollars a month.

An old widow lives in that house. It's been several years since her husband died. She has five children. They're all in the United States. They send her money.

Over there, there used to be an old house that was falling down. Then a young man who'd saved a few pennies bought it. Look at it now. Look at that satellite dish. And he doesn't even live there. He's off in the United States with all his children. He works in the strawberries with a lot of the other families. Each year, he comes back to the *rancho,* alone.

It's the same with that beautiful house over there. They also live in California and pick strawberries. They were just down here for about two months.

Watch out, the road here is bad and the car might get stuck.

You know, the Americans don't really like us. They only want us to go there to work, like animals. The Mexicans go there to suffer doing hard work, while the Americans stay out of the fields. In the time I worked in the United States, I never saw an American in the fields. They prefer to work as secretaries, machinists, pilots, drivers. You never see them out picking. They hire Mexican supervisors to work their own countrymen to death. They're real tyrants. They want to look good for the American boss, so they work the Mexicans really hard. You can't even stop to light a cigarette because they're always yelling, "Faster, faster. You're getting paid to work, not stand around."

Here there's another house, a big house. It's empty, too. The owner is up north. He comes back two weeks a year and then you won't see him again until the next year.

Look, here you've got another house owned by a young guy. The people who build these houses are the ones who take care of their money and know how to save. The ones who go over there to drink and go out with women never save a thing. They spend every penny they earn.

Nobody lives in any of the houses from here to that post. That's seven empty houses. They're all in the United States with their families. Sometimes the owners come here, but they always go back north, sometimes for six months, sometimes for a year. The only person who really lives there is a guy who watches the houses and plants a little corn.

Here in our *rancho,* there are a lot of empty houses.

Look, here are some children. They must be coming home from the school over there where they teach English. You see, there used to be a lot of people here. Then, after the amnesty, whole families left. More and more people keep going north. Just a few weeks ago, four more men left the *rancho* with their families.

Those cars are also from the United States. All the cars in the *rancho* come from over there. In Mexico, you could never buy a car working the fields. For an ordinary worker, it's hard to buy a mule.

Look, here are some more empty houses. Look at them. They left a few months ago. The owner just put the roof on that house, but it still doesn't have any doors. He's over there struggling to make some money to finish the construction. Still, that boy's in good shape. He's over there with his family. He doesn't drink or waste money.

It makes me happy to see these changes. I'm proud of all these people. These days, the *rancho* looks better than before. Look at all these beautiful houses. The only thing they're missing is someone to live in them.

Experienced migrants help others travel north, lending relatives money to cover smugglers' fees and helping friends and family find work and establish themselves in the distant United States. As migrants share information, job contacts, and housing, social networks develop. As these networks expand and become increasingly complex, the risk and uncertainty of migration is greatly reduced. A young man going north for the first time can borrow money from a family member already earning dollars, cross the border with a trusted *coyote*, and arrive in the United States where friends and family are waiting. Often, within a matter of days, the new arrival will have a job working alongside people he's known all his life.

After a few seasons' experience, a recent immigrant usually knows enough to help someone else—a brother, a cousin, a friend— leave his *rancho* to travel north, providing the new migrant with the same assistance he received. It is now common to find entire labor camps, whole blocks of rental housing, and even entire neighborhoods populated by men from the same or neighboring *ranchos*. Many contractors depend on familial connections to fill their crews, and there are growers whose entire workforce travels north each year from a cluster of small Mexican towns. As ever-greater numbers of migrants travel north, working in the United States has become a virtual obligation for many young men.

Alberto Mosquera ♦ *Purépero, Michoacán*

Alberto Mosquera is training to be a priest among the Missionaries of San Carlos, a Roman Catholic congregation dedicated to serving the pastoral needs of migrants and refugees. Mosquera's order was founded in 1887 by Monsignor Juan Batista Scalabrini, an Italian bishop, who was moved by the difficult struggles of Italian emi-

grants who left Europe in search of better lives, generally settling in the United States.

The Missionaries of San Carlos serve migrants' needs in twenty-six countries throughout the world and in fifty-one cities in the United States and Canada. Their "Prayer for the Migrant" begins:

> *Oh, Jesus, I pray to you for all those who wander far from their homes and suffer the migrant's life. They are our brothers in search of a better world, refugees fleeing violence, exiles of poverty.*

Mosquera was born in Colombia where he studied sociology before being drawn to a religious life. For several years, he worked in Colombia with families displaced by guerrilla-, army-, and drug-related violence. After completing his training in Mexico, there is a strong possibility that Mosquera will be sent to work with a community of migrants somewhere in the United States.

The story of these towns is very sad. Right now, if you went to one of the *ranchos* around here, you wouldn't find any young men. They're all working in the fields in the United States. For most of the year, the *ranchos* here are filled with women, children, and old men.

Young men here dream of going to California, making money, coming home to get married, and building a house. They think this is what a man must do. They build American-style houses, extravagant two-story brick homes with satellite dishes, big garages, and electrical appliances—televisions, video recorders, tape decks, washing machines, microwave ovens. These large houses filled with things have enormous symbolic power. They draw attention to themselves, showing everyone in town that the man is a migrant who's returned with lots of money.

In the United States, the men work very hard. They rarely talk about all the bad things they experience, how they're mistreated, underpaid, cheated, and even beaten. They buy things to show that they can control something in the world. The houses, appliances, and things migrants buy are acts of protest, reactions to the poverty and suffering they endure. Some houses are so big, they look like temples.

You see, the problem here is one of social injustice. The men migrate because they have no opportunities here. They see emigration as the only solution. They have no alternatives, no goals, no plans. They never say, "I want to study," or "I want to be a doctor, a professional." They don't stay in school and they won't even talk about careers.

Traditionally, in *ranchos* like these you find a popular religiosity which involves a great deal of discipline and respect. Children internalize strong moral values regarding life and family. When the men emigrate, they lose these values. They change. They return with aggressive attitudes. Some come back with drug and alcohol problems or different ideas about sex that clash with this environment, which remains very traditional. Migrants often lose their sense of community obligation. Their goals become individualistic and their attitudes become characteristic of North American culture. The men invest in their homes, but not in their community. The houses are new, but the streets in most of these *ranchos* look the same as they have for years.

We celebrate a Eucharist for the migrants when they return each December. We welcome them home and pray for them. We offer objects which symbolize the life of the community, such as a suitcase. We'll hold up a suitcase and say, "Lord, we offer you this suitcase as a symbol of those who have to migrate to other places to find work." We also offer huaraches as a symbol of the true path or a map of the world as a symbol for those who cross borders searching for work. The goal of the Eucharist is to keep migrants from losing their cultural identity or their faith. At the end of the Eucharist, the migrants give testimonies of what it's like to live in the United States, to work, suffer, and return. We do this so the migrants understand that they're a part of the community. When migrants lose their faith, they become very individualistic. Their marriages fall apart. Sometimes they never return.

Christ was a migrant and each migrant wears the face of Christ. The migrant's suffering is the spiritual embodiment of our world's problems. We need to understand that migrants are not machines. They are the children of God. We never speak about "illegals" because, for us, no human being is illegal. A person may not possess the required papers to cross a border, but he can never be illegal. We need to look beyond borders because, in the end, we are all brothers. The Christian community in particular should remember that Christ himself was a migrant. Christ was a wanderer who said, "Because I was a stranger and you gave me shelter."

Ranchos often exhibit an economic prosperity that is striking, revealing both the transformative power of dollars and the complex effects of a culture of migration. One often finds a strange combination of cultures in these communities, where newfound wealth exists side by side with the signs of traditional rural life. Large multistory houses stand beside rutted roads and cobblestone streets. Rows of satellite dishes line the rooftops of newly constructed houses as chickens peck in the yards. Burros graze calmly, their dull eyes reflected by walls of smoked glass. Thick stalks of corn rise up beside freshly painted two-car garages.

Since the economic prosperity of migrants has more to do with the success of particular families rather than the overall condition of the *rancho*, there are now marked discrepancies in wealth within communities. Before workers migrated, most residents were poor farmers with nearly identical economic situations. Now, one finds beautiful homes filled with modern conveniences set beside adobe houses that lack indoor plumbing. In general, migrants invest in their own family's well-being rather than seeking benefits for the community at large. Even in *ranchos* where there are many successful migrant families, streets remain unpaved and public squares lie in a state of disrepair—benches upturned, statues crumbling. Many *ranchos* struggle with an uncertain identity, unsure of how to balance their dependence on foreign earnings with what remains of a commitment to the community.

Rocío Arriola ♦ *Dos Estrellas, Michoacán*

Dos Estrellas lies on one side of a small mountain. La Yerbabuena is located on the other side. The two ranchos are linked by the same river and young men from one community often marry young women from the other. Since Dos Estrellas has only recently grown economically dependent on migration to the United States, the community still looks more or less like a traditional rancho. The streets are made of packed earth or cobblestone and most houses are built of adobe. The community stands in stark contrast to its neighbor.

Rocío Arriola's father has migrated for a number of years, but their family has yet to achieve financial stability. In part this is because he is an older man who has trouble earning as much as other workers. Arriola is twenty years old. She is polite, articulate, and pretty. We sit by the town basketball court as the sun sets over the hills and children ride by on bicycles, laughing. A car pulls up and a man steps out with a suitcase and a cardboard box wrapped in twine.

"Look," she says, "he's just come back from the north."

These days, all the men from town go to the United States and almost none of them have papers. The men only study up until sixth grade. They don't go to high school. "Why study," they say, "when you can go to the United States, earn money, come back with a car, and build a house?" Two weeks ago, my brother left with some of his friends and two older men. He's seventeen. It was his first time. He's already in California, working in the grapes.

In November and December, it's very nice here. There's a good feeling in the streets. We have dances in the soccer field and boys without *novias* come from all over to look for girls. They come back from the United States in cars and trucks, with elegant clothes, nice jeans, and silk shirts. That's when couples form. The girls and boys go out into the streets. A boy will walk over to a girl and start talking. They'll get to know each other and the boy will ask the girl if she wants to be his *novia.* Sometimes the girl will say yes right away and other times she'll say that they should wait. Here, we're very reserved. Couples walk hand in hand, but they don't kiss in public. The boys always want to leave a *novia* behind so they'll have someone waiting for them. When they go to the United States, they leave with promises. They say that they'll write. They say, "Wait for me, I'll be back." "I want you to be good."

When the boy returns, the couple talks and they'll decide to get married. Then, an agreement has to be made between the girl's parents and the boy's parents. It's the custom here for the couple to go to the girl's house and to bring the girl's family a basket of fruit—bananas, oranges, apples, watermelon—along with a bottle of tequila. Then the family prepares a meal. The boy needs to have money to take care of all the groom's responsibilities—the wedding dress, the reception, the mariachi band, the wine, and the food. When the boys return, there's often a competition to see who has the biggest parties, the best mariachi bands, or the best food.

The boys over there always know what we do here. I don't know how they know, but if you dance with some boy, they'll hear about it in the United States. From their point of view, a girl with a *novio* shouldn't walk in the plaza with another boy or let him invite her for an ice cream. If a girl dances two or three songs with a boy, they say that she shouldn't stay and talk to him. Sometimes there are arguments and the boys get mad and end the engagement.

The boys are always very careful. They watch out for each other. They'll return to their families, calm as anything, thinking that their wives don't know about what they do. Still, there are rumors. News doesn't arrive here all at once, but little by little. There's always someone who's a bit indiscreet and opens his mouth. A boy might tell his girlfriend something and then she'll tell her friends and then those girls will tell others. Or, sometimes when the boys come back and they're standing at the corner talking, you might walk by and hear things. That way, word gets out and the women hear about boys who are misbehaving. We hear

about other women and about the boys who go out into the street and spend all their money.

The women here are afraid, really afraid. Over there, it's all men. We know that the men have little adventures over there. There are even some who have second families. With all the freedom that the men have over there and with all the things they do, the wives are afraid that their husbands might come back with some kind of illness. The women who are most afraid are the ones whose men stay in the United States for a long time. That's when they worry that they'll lose their husbands. The men always say that they'll be back, but there are some who leave and never return.

Here, the women generally stay at home. We work in the fields, preparing the land, weeding, harvesting the corn. As time passes, things are changing. We're moving forward. Our ways of thinking are changing. The men are going off to the United States to get ahead and we also want to move forward by going into town and working.

A friend and I were the first girls from the *rancho* to go work in town. I began when I was fifteen, working in the house of a family who had gone to the United States. I went without my father's permission. I told him that we needed the money. People here criticized us behind our backs. They said that what we were doing was wrong. Still, they saw that we were helping our families, earning money to buy clothes and shoes. Things are changing. Now even those who were most opposed to us—the ones who said all kinds of bad things about us—are allowing their daughters to work.

Still, my girlfriends only think about having fun, going out to dances, and getting married. They dream of finding a boy, marrying, and then staying here while their husbands are over there working, far away. I'm the only girl in town who thinks about studying. Right now, I'm studying high school at home. I want to enter a preparatory school to study to be an accountant, but here in these small towns there are no jobs for people with careers. I want to get ahead.

Like my friends, I also want to get married, but I don't want to end up like the women here, always complaining because their men spend more time in the United States than at home. Perhaps it would be better to stay here and be poor, eating just a little, but living together—two people together. That's my way of thinking, but I imagine that in the end my future will be just like that of all the other young women here—get married, start a family, and live torn apart by migration. It's not what I want, but I suppose that will be my future.

The massive ebb and flow of farmworkers back and forth across our southern border is restructuring life in Mexican *ranchos*. This process is also transforming American society. Migration involves interdependence, even when the connections are hidden and the long-term consequences remain shifting and uncertain. The care and harvest of our nation's fruits and vegetables is now dependent upon a transnational workforce. The migration of male workers that enables our country's agricultural system is redefining the significance of our borders and binding us, as consumers and citizens, ever more closely to the struggles of distant families and their changing lives.

Manuel Lopez ♦ *Hartford, Michigan*
Manuel Lopez is Santiago Lopez's older brother, the first member of the Lopez family to cross into the United States to work in the fields. He first left his rancho, *Tinaja de Coyote, when he was seventeen to harvest beans in the coastal state of Nayarit. There, he earned enough money to pay for a trip to Tijuana, crossing the border into the United States.*

Lopez returned home, built a house, married, and spent the next several years as an undocumented worker. In 1986, he received working papers through the amnesty provisions of IRCA. Lopez now works as a foreman for an apple grower. The labor camp where he lives is filled with men from several adjoining ranchos—*cousins, brothers, friends, old acquaintances.*

It's Sunday at the camp, toward the beginning of the season. Groups of men come and go in a collection of old cars. Men cluster in small groups drinking beer and telling stories. Lopez is clearly a leader, respected and trusted by all. He carries himself with pride and grace.

All of us on this camp are from the Guanajuato. In our *rancho,* there are seventy or eighty houses and in each house there is a mother and several children who live off what we earn. Dollars support our families. Checks from the United States arrive everywhere in Mexico. In order to survive back home, you need to have someone—a father, a brother, a friend—working here.

We migrate to survive, not to get rich. I first came to the United States almost twenty years ago and I have nothing more than a house for my family. Eight people live off my earnings—myself, my wife, four daughters, a son, and an uncle. I earn around nine thousand dollars a year. Life in Mexico has become more expensive, and here, the wages have gone down. Each year we have to work even harder for what we earn.

I've had opportunities to work in factories because I have a brother in Chicago. Still, if I left the fields for a more stable job, I wouldn't be able to return each year to Mexico. The first year they might give me a week's vacation, the second year maybe two weeks. Then, I'd have spent almost two years without seeing my family, and my children would only know me from the photographs I send home. I want my children to know me. I want to show them how to do things, to give them advice, to scold them and teach them to be good. That's why so many of us work in the fields and spend our lives traveling back and forth across the border.

There is no life sadder than that of a migrant. Sometimes you feel so screwed you can't even dream, living here, far from home, far from your family. Every year, I tell my wife what it's like here. She asks me questions, but it's rare that a woman can understand our lives and our suffering. In some ways, it's our fault. When our families ask us to send them pictures, we put on our best clothes and stand somewhere nice, surrounded by flowers. We'll send them a picture of a big, beautiful house that a rich *gabacho* owns, with two brand-new cars out front. Back home, they'll say, "Look at my husband. That's the house he lives in. Look at those cars. He's living so well up there." We never take pictures of ourselves on top of a ladder, the way we really are, covered in dirt. We should take photos of ourselves working in the orchards, coming home each day tired, cooking up beans, washing our clothes.

I know everyone on this labor camp and they've known me since I was a child. On Sundays, we gather together to talk, eat, drink beer, and spend time together. Sometimes we gather as many as a hundred people from back home. The *mayordomo* here is related to many of the workers. He gives all of us jobs when we arrive each year. That's how people get here from Mexico.

Immigration isn't going to stop. As long as Mexico has no good jobs, people will keep coming. These days, so many men are coming to the United States that there are even little *ranchos* that are disappearing. All of Mexico is coming north. Since I'm here, I can help bring someone else. I'll find work for them and then, later, they'll help someone else. If a young man in Mexico asked me whether he should come to the United States to work, I'd say "Come north. I'll give you a hand. We crossed over, saved a little money, and built a house."

The Space between These Hands

HANDS SERVE as the unifying image of this book, linking farmworkers to other Americans in a direct, immediate, and visceral manner. Hands touch, feel, caress, and labor, reminding us that, in the
end, production is always linked to people—to their lives, struggles,
and stories. From the generations of African Americans working
under the threat of violence, to the Chinese and Japanese immigrants
of the late nineteenth and early twentieth century, to the dust bowl
migrants of the 1930s, to the millions of braceros who crossed into the
United States from the 1940s through the 1960s, to the hundreds of
thousands of transnational migrants who currently labor in our nation's fields—the history of America's farmworkers is the tale of an
entire class of laborers who have been repeatedly denied access to
our nation's promise that hard work will be justly rewarded.

Farmworkers have long been the poorest of America's workers,
recruited from among the most powerless among us, historically denied equal protections, and still, after repeated exposés, campaigns,
and legislative acts, their poverty and marginalization continues.
While the fresh fruit and vegetable industry faces special challenges—
perishable products, changing weather conditions, market fluctuations—there is no inherent reason why farmworkers should be our
nation's poorest laborers. The fact that they work in a seasonal industry, that they travel from one place to another, or that they work for
multiple employers does not mean that farmworkers must live in
poverty. Furthermore, farmworkers' troubling situation is not the result of a few bad growers or a handful of unscrupulous contractors.
Instead, the abuses farmworkers suffer, their low wages and marginalization, can only be understood as the product of our nation's farm

labor system—a social and economic structure whose defining logic has remained remarkably consistent for years.

The key components of the farm labor system have been a steady oversupply of workers and the use of a series of techniques to consistently disempower farmworkers. The agricultural industry has relied on successive waves of vulnerable immigrants and poor domestic workers, repeatedly using its influence to loosen immigration restrictions, create guest worker programs, and otherwise ensure that there are always more than enough workers available to labor in the fields. Growers have continually sought to define farmworkers as a special group of laborers who do not merit the same workplace protections or rights to organize as other American workers. The farm labor system has combined these features with a reliance on layers of contractors and subcontractors, allowing large companies to distance themselves from the workers they rely upon and forcing farmworkers to struggle within an informal world that is difficult to regulate.

In a sense, farmworkers represent an alternate history of American society, an image of what life could have been like for countless other laborers. When other workers were provided with basic labor protections in the 1930s—minimum wage, Social Security, unemployment insurance, the right to organize—farmworkers were specifically excluded. When other employers were forced to compete for domestic workers, growers used their political influence to negotiate guest worker programs allowing only agricultural employers access to imported foreign labor. In this way, farmworkers have been historically defined as second-class workers.

In the 1960s, farmworkers were provided with many basic protections, as well as special protective laws and a series of health, education, and social service programs. While these interventions improved the lives of many workers and their families, they failed to transform farm labor into a job that could provide a living wage. Even unions, which made significant gains and probably hold the greatest possibility of helping farmworkers address the disparity in power between farmworkers and their employers, have been unable to significantly improve the overall conditions of our nation's farm laborers. Farmworkers' special status has become institutionalized to such a degree that the only way to significantly improve the lives of migrant farmworkers is by challenging the structure of our nation's farm labor system.

There was a moment in the late 1960s and early 1970s, as unionization was sweeping California and various protective laws were being instituted, when it seemed that farmworkers would soon become more or less like other American workers—laborers who earned a living wage and were integrated into general society. In fact, just the opposite has occurred. Farmworkers' real wages have dropped steadily along with the wages of all low-wage workers. Increasingly, many American workers are starting to look more like farm laborers. American workers providing basic services and manual labor are increasingly employed under conditions that strongly resemble the farm labor system—working in uncertain, shifting, temporary jobs that provide no benefits and often do not pay enough to keep workers and their families above the poverty line. Industries of all types are now turning to contractors and subcontractors, allowing even the largest and wealthiest of companies to treat nonprofessional workers differently than their own employees and creating a world of structurally disempowered nonunionized workers who earn low wages and receive no benefits.

This trend reflects a growing divide in American society between those who control wealth and those who do not. Increasingly, the better educated and more fortunate of Americans enjoy the benefits of modern employment relations—good wages, health insurance, safe working conditions, vacation pay, and reasonable contracts. At the same time, those laboring at the bottom of the employment ladder must struggle to satisfy their most basic needs in low-wage, temporary jobs. As the more fortunate isolate themselves from those less fortunate, living in different neighborhoods and sending their children to different schools, they know little about the lives of the low-wage laborers their world depends upon.

The growing divide between the rich and the poor is marked by a separation between producers and consumers and the increasing invisibility of production. Our nation is characterized by enormous material wealth and the almost magical availability of a diverse array of commodities whose production seems automatic and effortless. Yet all the things in our world are made—put together out of materials taken from the earth, assembled by people and machines, shipped from one place to another, distributed, catalogued, marketed, and sold. The invisibility of production is partly the result of a shifting global economy where a significant percentage of labor-intensive production is conducted in foreign countries. Farm laborers are an exception to this trend, since as long as there are farms in the country, there will be farmworkers. Even as agriculture becomes increasingly technological, the industry cannot do without hand labor, people willing to stoop in the fields; climb ladders in orchards; and fill buckets, baskets, bins, and tubs with fruits and vegetables.

Thinking about farmworkers, considering the space between farm laborers' hands and the hands of each consumer, connect ordinary Americans to agricultural production in a direct manner. Listening to workers, their employers, union organizers, *coyotes*, migrant children, *riteros*, and other voices from the world of farm labor reveals how the simplest act of purchasing fruits and vegetables links every American to a complex web of interconnected lives, revealing the human dimension of an enormous productive system.

The apparent invisibility of production is a form of social forgetting, a politics of glossing over the real social and economic relations that allow for our high standard of living. Considering the world of farm laborers presents a powerful corrective to a society easily enamored of its own self-serving myths. Still, it is Americans' deeprooted desire to believe in equality and the march of progress that makes farmworkers' situation so poignant, creating a discomfort born of our country's failure to live up to its own ideals.

Farmworkers' stories need to be heard, their world revealed, and their lives recognized. Farmworkers' poverty needs to be understood as the product of a system that has developed over many years. The only way to meaningfully improve the lives of our nation's farm laborers is to transform the structure of this system, a process which must begin with an understanding of the direct connection between farmworkers and all Americans.

Photographs

Sources

WITH THESE HANDS presents statistics and historical information gathered from a variety of sources including academic studies, journalistic exposés, government reports and Congressional hearings. This section is designed to help direct interested readers to a number of useful and important sources regarding America's farmworkers, many of which were central to the research conducted for this book.

There are several classic works on migrant farmworkers, the most famous of which is John Steinbeck's *The Grapes of Wrath* (New York: The Viking Press. 1939), which describes the struggles of dust bowl migrants in California. Another important work is Zora Neale Hurston's novel, *Their Eyes Were Watching God.* (Urbana: University of Illinois Press. 1965) which deals with the lives of African American farm laborers in Florida. Also worth reading is Carey McWilliam's important and powerful study, *Factories in the Field* (1939; reissued, Berkeley: University of California Press. 1999) which is notable in part because many of the conditions documented are similar to the situation faced by today's farmworkers. Another classic work is Edward R. Murrow's television documentary, "Harvest of Shame," which deserves special mention because of its significant societal impact after it was first aired on Thanksgiving over thirty-five years ago.

There are a number of different works concerning the current conditions of migrant farmworkers in the United States. For general statistics on farmworkers, the best source is the National Agricultural Workers Survey (NAWS) conducted by United States Department of Labor. Statistics from the NAWS studies are available in a series of continually revised government publications.

For a general overview of current conditions, one may consult David Griffith, Ed Kissam and Jeronimo Campaseco's *Working Poor: Farmworkers in the United States* (Philadelphia: Temple University Press. 1995). Another good general source for information on farmworkers is the *Report of the Commission on Agricultural Workers* (Washington, DC: U.S. Government Printing Office. 1993), an investigative body created through the Immigration Reform and Control Act of 1986. For an excellent review of current government programs for migrant workers, one should consult Philip L. Martin and David A. Martin's *The Endless Quest: Helping America's Farm Workers* (Boulder: Westview Press. 1994). For a general discussion of issues related to Mexican migration to the United States, a very good reference is Douglas Massey, Rafael Alarcón, Jorge Durand, Humberto González's, *Return to Aztlan: The Social Process of International Migration from Western Mexico* (Berkeley: University of California Press. 1987).

There are several good books on farm labor history, many of which are regionally focused. To gain a better understanding of farm labor in California, a good resource is Cletus E. Daniel's, *Bitter Harvest. A History of California's Farmworkers 1870–1941* (Berkeley: University of California Press. 1981). For an excellent study of farmworkers in the eastern United States, one may turn to Cindy Hahamovitch's, *The Fruits of Their Labor: Atlantic Coast Farmworkers and the Making of Migrant Poverty, 1870–1945* (Chapel Hill: University of North Carolina Press. 1997), which may be read alongside William Friedland and Dorothy Nelkin's book on the East Coast migrant stream in the 1960s and 1970s, *Migrant: Agricultural Workers in America's Northeast* (New York: Holt, Rinehart and Winston. 1971). A first-rate study of debt peonage in the South is Pete Daniel's *In the Shadow of Slavery: Debt Peonage in the South* (Urbana: University of Illinois Press. 1990), which ties in well with *Where Mules Outrate Men*, a report prepared by the North Carolina Advisory Committee to the United States Commission on Civil Rights (Washington, DC: U.S. Government Printing Office. 1979). For information on migrant workers in the Midwest, one may turn to Dennis Nodin Valdes' *Al Norte: Agricultural Workers in the Great Lakes Region, 1917–1970* (Austin: University of Texas Press. 1991). Also worth mentioning is Jacqueline Jones' discussion of farmworkers in her fine book, *The Dispossessed: America's Underclasses from the Civil War to the Present* (New York: Basic Books. 1992).

Over the past forty years, there have been a number of important books on farmworkers and, while some do not adequately reflect current conditions, these sources provide important insights to the continuity of farmworkers' social exclusion. Several books worth reading are Truman Moore's *The Slaves We Rent* (New York: Random House. 1965), Ronald B. Taylor's *Sweatshops in the Sun: Child Labor on the Farm* (New York: Beacon. 1973), and Ronald L. Goldfarb's *Migrant Farmworkers: A Caste of Despair* (Ames: Iowa State University Press. 1981). Of special merit are Robert Coles' compelling books on migrant children, *Migrants, Sharecroppers, Mountaineers* (New York: Atlantic Monthly Press. 1967) and *Uprooted Children: The Early Life of Migrant Farm Workers* (New York: Harper & Row. 1971).

To learn more about the bracero program, one should consult Ernesto Galarza's classic work, *Merchants of Labor* (Santa Barbara, CA: McNaly & Loftin. 1964) which played an important role in creating political pressure for dismantling the program. An excellent and more recent study is Kitty Calavita's *Inside the State: The Bracero Program, Immigration and the I.N.S.* (New York: Routledge. 1992). For information on the H-2A program and sugar cane harvesters, one should read Alec Wilkinson's extremely well-written book, *Big Sugar: Seasons in the Cane Fields of Florida.* (New York: Knopf. 1989) and view Stephanie Black's powerful documentary film, "H-2 Worker" (New York: First Run/Icarus Films 1992).

There are a number of very good books on farm labor organizing including: J. Craig Jenkins' *The Politics of Insurgency: The Farm Worker Movement of the 1960s* (New York: Columbia University Press. 1985), Dick Meister and Anne Loftis' *A Long Time Coming: The Struggle to Unionize America's Farm Workers* (New York: Macmillan. 1977), Linda C. and Theo J. Majka's *Farmworkers, Agribusiness and the State* (Philadelphia: Temple University Press. 1982), and Patrick H. Mooney and Theo J. Majka's *Farmers' and Farmworkers' Movements* (New York: Twayne Publishers. 1995). There are many works which focus on Cesar Chavez and the UFW, including Susan Ferriss and Ricardo Sandoval's *The Fight in the Fields: Cesar Chavez and the Farmworkers Movement* (New York: Harcourt Brace & Company. 1997), Jacques Levy's *Cesar Chavez: Autobiography of La Causa* (New York: Norton. 1975), and Peter Matthiessen's *Sal Si Puedes: Cesar Chavez and the New American Revolution* (1969; reissued Berkeley: University of California Press. 2000).

There are also several important government reports on farm

labor that are worth reading, including the classic LaFollette Committee report, *Violations of Free Speech and the Rights of Labor* (Washington, DC: U.S. Congressional Report 1150. 1941) and the United States Congress Senate Committee on Labor and Public Welfare, Subcommittee on Migrant Labor's *Migrant and Seasonal Farmworkers Powerlessness Hearings* (Washington, DC: U.S. Government Printing Office. 1970–71). More recent hearings worth looking at include the United States Congress House Select Committee on Aging's *After 30 Years, America's Continuing Harvest of Shame* (Washington, DC: U.S. Government Printing Office. 1990).

There are many sources for information on farmworker programs and farmworker social statistics. For a consideration of migrant education issues, it is useful to consult the National Commission on Migrant Education's report, *Invisible Children: A Portrait of Migrant Education in the United States.* (Washington, D.C.: U.S. Government Printing Office 1992). For information on farmworker health, one should read the National Advisory Committee on Migrant Health's *1993 Recommendations* (Rockville: National Advisory Council on Migrant Health. 1993) as well as Valerie Wilk's *The Occupational Health of Migrant and Seasonal Farmworkers in the United States.* (Washington, DC: Farmworker Justice Fund. 1986). In addition, there are numerous informative GAO Reports concerning the H-2A Program, Migrant Legal Services and other issues related to farm labor issues.

Those interested in farmworker memoirs should read Elva Trevino Hart's *Barefoot Heart: Stories of a Migrant Child* (Tempe: Bilingual Review Press. 1999) or Frances Esquibel Tywoniak's *Migrant Daughter: Coming of Age as a Mexican American Woman* (Berkeley: University of California Press. 2000) For an accessible and compelling portrait of the world of undocumented immigrants, one should consult Ted Conover's *Coyotes: A Journey Through the Secret World of America's Aliens* (New York: Vintage Press. 1987). There are also several moving books of photographs (some with text) including Herman Leroy Emmet's *Fruit Tramps: A Family of Migrant Workers* (Albuquerque: University of New Mexico Press. 1989) as well as the excellent photography of Ken Light and Alan Pogue, whose work appears in this book.

Acknowledgments

WRITING AND RESEARCHING *With These Hands* was only possible with the assistance and cooperation of many individuals and organizations and the support of various professional contacts, acquaintances, friends, and family.

In order to gather the stories presented in the book, I traveled across the country by car, conducting interviews in fifteen states in the eastern, southern, midwestern and western regions of the United States and in three states in west-central Mexico. I used many strategies to find people to interview for this book. In some cases, I would simply show up at labor camps, homeless shelters, or job pick-up points to speak with workers. In other cases, I would set up meetings in advance identifying interview subjects with the assistance of advocacy groups, growers' organizations, unions, social service providers, journalists, and others. For helping me gather information and meet interview subjects I am grateful to the following people: in Florida, Ernesto Gonzalez, David Thomas, Kristin McGregor of the Dade County Farm Bureau, Walter Kates of the Florida Fruit and Vegetable Association, Debbie Singer, Jack Scarola, Laura Germino, Greg Asbed, Marshall Berry, the Coalition for the Homeless, the Orlando Rescue Mission, Lou Lippman, Steve and Juanita Mainester, Father Frank O'Laughlin, the Sugar Cane Growers Cooperative, the United States Sugar Corporation; in West Virginia, Hannah and Garry Geffert; in Ohio, Berna Romero and Fernando Cuevas of FLOC; in Washington, D.C., Valerie Wilk, Bruce Goldstein and Mike Hancock of the Farmworker Justice Fund, Roger Rosenthal, Shelly Davis, Cindy Schneider and Bea Bobotek of the Migrant Legal Action Program, Rick Mines and Ruth Samardick of the United States Department of Labor, the American Farm Bureau, Peter Daniel at the National Museum of American History, and Mike Amitay; in New Jersey, Keith Talbot; in Maryland, Delores Street of the Governor's Commission on Migratory and Seasonal Farm Labor; in Virginia, Ruth Brown of the Delmarva Rural Ministries and Eloise Wilder of the Virginia Agricultural Growers Association; in North Carolina Carolyn Corrie of Student Action with Farmworkers, the Dixon family, Christine Alvarado of St. Martin's East Coast Migrant Head Start Center, Chris Harlan, Jennie McLaurin, MD of the Tri-County Community Health Center, Mary Lee

Hall of Farmworker Legal Services, and especially Asencion Faulkner; in Texas, Bill Beardall, David Hall and the staff of Texas Rural Legal Assistance; in Michigan, John Dominguez of the Van Buren Intermediary School District and Gary Gershawn of the Michigan Migrant Legal Assistance Project; in Mexico, Prof. Gustavo López Castro of the Colegio de Michoacan, Alberto Vázquez Cholico, Guillermo Fernandez, and Padre Giovanni Bizzotto and others at the Misioneros de San Carlos; in California Ralph Abescal, Gloria Hernández, Claudia Smith, Efraim Camacho, Jesus López, and Sergio Mendez of California Rural Legal Assistance, Milly Trevino-Sauceda, Michael Wagner of *The Sacramento Bee,* Trinidad Castro for taking me to the olive fields, Mike McGarvin at Poverello House, Russell Williams of Agricultural Producers, Barbara Tisler and the Shafter Senior Center, Ron García, Betsy Schwartz, Anna Rubalcava, Silvia Alba and Dr. Paul Nava, all of whom work in Migrant Education, Roberto and Juanita Ramirez, Roy Gabriel of the California Farm Bureau, Brian Haddock of the California Grape and Tree Fruit League, the Monterey County and Fresno Farm Bureaus, Arturo Rodriguez, Jocelyn Sherman and Marc Grossman of the United Farm Workers union. I also appreciate the assistance provided by Rod Parker of the National Council of Agricultural Employers, Sister Noreen Dennehy of Catholic Social Services, Vic Rivera, Al Wright, Dr. Karen Mountain of the National Migrant Resource Program, Deron Johnson of *The Packer* and Steve Buckner of *The Grower.* I owe very special thanks to the following dedicated farmworker advocates who have profoundly influenced my life: Greg Schell, Robert Williams, Mary Ellen Beaver, Sauveur Pierre, and Jim Boon.

During most of my travels, I relied on very limited finances. This meant that I often stayed with friends, acquaintances, and people I met along the way. While travelling with very little money has many disadvantages, there is a certain beauty to having to rely on the kindness of others. I was fortunate to have come into contact with many generous and trusting people while researching this book. Many thanks to the following people who allowed me to stay with them during my travels: in Michigan, Sondro Cinti and Billie Ochberg; in Pennsylvania, my very dear friends Tim and Basia Kerner; in North Carolina, John and Ann Harvey, a cousin I'd never previously met, Bob Landau, and Luis and Lupe Reyes; in Washington, D.C., a committed activist and good travelling companion, John Bonifaz; an old friend from my hometown, John Siegal and his partner Ellen Tynan, special thanks to Nancy Carmichael, a woman of great generosity and an open heart; in Georgia, Sister Noreen, Sister Theresa, Sister Janet, Sister Bernadette, and Sister Elise of the Immaculate Conception Convent; in Florida, a true friend and superb lawyer Jim Green, as well as Mark and Denise Finnegan and Sister Maureen Kelleher; in Alabama, my buddy Marcus McCrory; in Texas the famous David Hall and Marinda Van Dalen; in California Saul and Sylvia Shaefer, Chriss and Eva Zouboulakis, my rediscovered cousin Steven Schneck, Don Mancini, and special thanks to Cary Berger for being such a good guy; in Illinois, Ira Bashkow, Josh and Carolyn Shapiro, and *un fuerte abrazo* to Marco and Lisa Reategui, who have proved to be wonderful and supportive friends time and again. I am especially grateful to my cousins Barry, Ellen, Jennifer, and Rebecca Massie for letting me stay in their home, rest, write, and drive their car up and down the Central Valley.

All of the interviews used in this book, and many of those that never made it into the final text, were transcribed from recorded tapes, a process involving hundreds of hours of hard work. I transcribed many of the tapes myself, but I also relied on the skill and patience of a number of excellent transcribers including: Amy Borrell, Bob Jackson, Alice Li, Matt Sherwin, Bietriz Riefkohl-Muñiz, and Alex Stern. I had the very good fortune to work with three especially talented transcribers who deserve special mention: Paul Adams, the first person to deal with this material other than myself; Heather Cantwell, who displayed enormous maturity and perseverance; and Julia Guzmán López in Michoacán, Mexico, a woman of great strength, patience, and talent.

Several people read through the book during various stages of its development, providing me with helpful comments and suggestions. I am particularly indebted to David Griffith, Philip Martin, and Julia Lieblich for their comments. Thanks also to Gabe Lyon for help with the photographs and to Neda Ulaby for being an invaluable editor and friend in the final stages of the project. I am also especially grateful for the support of Margaret Hennessy in Florida and Julie Rigby in Chicago.

Some portions of the research of this book were partially funded through grants. I very much appreciate the assistance I received from the Division of Social Sciences at The University of Chicago and the MacArthur Foundation by way of the Council for Advanced Studies in Peace and International Cooperation. I am grateful also to Mary Watson for always being upbeat, charming, and helpful, and Anne Ch'ien for making sure that everything always worked out. I would also like to thank Terry Karl for allowing me to work as a Visiting Scholar at Stanford and to the staff at the Center for Latin American Studies at the University of Chicago. I owe a special debt to my advisors at the University of Chicago: Terry Turner, Marshall Sahlins, and especially John Comaroff, for his continued belief in my varied projects.

I am very much indebted to my agent Tony Gardner who has been instrumental in making this book a reality. It has been a pleasure to work with the excellent folks at Harcourt Brace, and I feel particularly grateful to my professional and patient editor, Walt Bode.

It is impossible for me to imagine this project without the support, careful editing, advice and joyful presence of Victoria Sanford.

I owe special thanks to my great aunt and uncle Florence and Elliot Westin and to my parents who have displayed considerable patience with my wandering and shifting projects. My brother, David, continues, as always, to be a great inspiration. For this reason and others, the book is dedicated to him.

Above all, I extend my gratitude to all the people I interviewed for this project. *With These Hands* would have been impossible without the cooperation, enthusiasm, and honesty of the many people who spoke with me about their lives. I hope that this book serves to honor their sincerity, openness, and profound desire to have their stories heard and their lives recognized.

Index